香港日瀚国际文化传播有限公司 编
華中科技大学出版社
http://www.hustpas.com

PREFACE

X是未知数。近年来许多艺术活动都喜欢冠以"X"，以未知来吸引人的注意。

日瀚公司编辑的系列丛书也取名《X建筑》，邀我写序，实不敢当。推辞不过，只好提起笔来试着琢磨一下这个"X"。

首先，"X"之于建筑倒是有几分贴切：每个建筑从策划到设计，从建造到使用的过程都充满着"X"。一个务实的定位或一个虚夸的妄想将决定建筑的不同命运。一个认真的设计或一个粗糙的设计，一个有创新的设计或一个保守平庸的设计将决定建筑的不同品位。一个精心的建造或一个低劣的施工，一个负责任的长久的质量的保证或急功近利的低价策略将决定建筑质量的天壤之别。还有建成之后的使用，有的精心维护，不断完善，有的随意拆改，疏于管理，建筑之寿命难以预期。如此看来，编入本书的建筑作品都是历经风险，从无数X中有幸求解而得，实在不易！

再则，"X"之于建筑师也有几分关系：相对二十多年前计划经济时代国营设计院一统天下的局面，而今设计行业百花齐放，既有国营大院，又有民营小院，既有合资公司，又有独资外企，既有合伙人事务所，也有个人工作室。而在不同机构中工作的建筑师亦个个不同。年龄不同，教育背景不同，国内、国外眼界不同，观念有别。从业时间长短，经验积累不同，职业素养各异。企业目标是设计产值还是作品价值？个人追求是经济效益还是职业责任，或是艺术成就？有人说主要是吃饭但也想立碑，有人顺心就要作品，烦心就出产品，有时也出些次品，但绝口不提。如此看来，入选这本书的作品不同，风格迥异和设计机构尤其是主创建筑师的价值取向和个人立场息息相关。

其三，"X"之于建筑思潮更为恰当。当下信息时代，媒体强大，各种建筑理论思潮传播神速，几乎没有时间差。各种流派作品也令人目眩。可学的，可仿的，可试的，可做的有太多的选择。你想学习先锋的，还是主流的？你想追求时尚的还是经典的？你想走国际化还是本土化的路？你是面向当下的还是探索未来的？对大多数人来说，答案可能很难确定，徘徊踌躇在所难免。如此看来，即使入选这本书的作品也不一定能反映建筑师的一贯立场，即使是这些建筑师也很难断定他们的方向肯定不变。

其四，"X"之于建筑的评价更是有趣。同一座建筑，不同的人有不同的解读。看的人和用的人不见得观点一致，专业的人和非专业的人认识的深浅会有差别，还有不同的文化背景，不同的语境，不同的心态，甚至不同的心情都会使人对建筑的评价大相径庭，最通俗的评价就是起外号了，"大裤衩""水煮蛋"之类的绰号让多少宏大的作品变成笑谈，这还真是咱们国人的长项呢！如此看来，即使入选这本书的优秀作品在不同人的眼里都会被不同地解读，这些建筑师们也会给人们留下不同的印象，这是我们自己完全无法也无需控制的。

这许多作品，这许多建筑师，这许多建筑背后的故事，这许多建筑人的心声，这许多思潮的影响和创作的方向，被不知多少读者、观者、用者品读评判，于是信息量被无限地放大、扩张，于是就可称为"X建筑"了。

二〇一〇年六月十八日

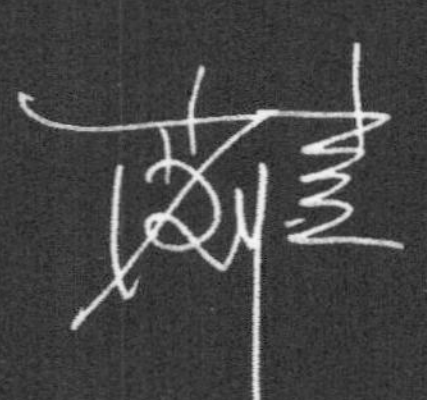

"X" is unknown. Recently, many art activities like to be named with the letter "X", which seems to be more attractive by using it.

RIHAN Company names this series as "X architecture" and invites me to write preface. I couldn't decline and try to ponder the meaning of "X".

Firstly, "X" is rather proper if used for architecture. Buildings are filled with many conditions like "X" from planning to design, from constructing to the process of using. The building's destiny would be determined by practical orientation or egregious mirage. The different taste of building is decided by serious design or rough design, creative design or conservative and mediocre design. The quality of the building will be determined by an elaborate construction or a low-grade construction, a responsible assurance for quality or a low-price strategy just for quick achievement. After completion, some of the buildings are gotten elaborate maintenance and constantly improvement, but some others are changed randomly or neglected. So, the lives of the buildings are difficult to forecast. The buildings edited in this book are all gone through risks, out of the countless "X" to be built finally, which are really difficult!

Moreover, "X" also has relationship with architects. By contrast to the planned economy over 20 years ago, when state-run design institutions are the whole, not like today, there exist many kinds of institutions including both big state-run institutions and private companies, both joint ventures and wholly owned foreign enterprises, both partners offices and private studios in the design industry. The architects working in different agencies are also different. There exist gaps between people with different ages. The concepts are different because of different education backgrounds of home or abroad, which cause diverse sights. Different time length and accumulated experience cause different professional accomplishment. Is Enterprise target to design for production value or work's value? Is personal pursuit economic benefit or professional liability or artistic accomplishment? Someone says that design is mainly for surviving, but also for building one's style. If happy, to produce better works, but when boring, to get just results, even sometimes, inferior ones. Thus, the works with different styles and design institutions in this book are related to the value orientations and personal positions of the architects.

Thirdly, "X" is more appropriately used for architectural thoughts. Currently, there exists powerful media in this information age, so all kinds of architectural theories spread quickly, almost no time difference. Works with various genres also make us dizzy. What should we choose to learn, to imitate or to try? Do you want to learn the pioneer or the mainstream? Do you want to pursue fashion or classical style? Do you want to choose international or localized ways? Do you like facing current markets or future exploration? For most people, the answer may be difficult to determine, which could be unavoidable to hesitate. Thus, the selected works of this book do not seem to reflect the architects' consistent positions, and even these architects also are difficult to determine that their directions must remain unchanged.

Finally, the comments to the building by using "x" are more interesting. Different people have different interpretations to the same building. The men with just looking not likely have the same viewpoints with the people in using. Professionals have distance in the knowing depth with those non-professionals. Different cultural background, different contexts, different attitudes, and even different moods will make different evaluations to building. The most popular evaluations are to give them nicknames like "big short pants (da ku cha)", "a boiled egg", which make many grand works into drolleries, which are our Chinese adepts! Thus, even the outstanding works chosen in this book will be different to interpret in different people's eyes. These architects will give people different impressions, which are not be completely controlled and also needn't to care.

So, these works, architects, the stories hidden behind buildings, the aspirations of these professionals, the influences and directions of these different thoughts, which all will be interpreted by so many different readers, audiences and people in using. The quantity of the information is enlarged and expanded infinitely, then these buildings could be called "X architecture".

Cui Kai

June 18, 2010

CONTENTS

以设计师的姓氏笔画为序

CONTENTS

以设计师的姓氏笔画为序

Superstar: A Mobile China Town

超级明星：移动中国城

设计单位：MAD建筑设计事务所
主持设计师：马岩松、党群
设计团队：陈淑瑜、傅昌瑞、郑涛、黎紫翎、David William Nightingale、Matthias Werner Helmreich、Bryan Alan Oknyansky、Zach Hines、Tom James
设计时间：2008年

Design firm: MAD
Director in charge: Ma Yansong, Dang Qun
Design team: Chen Shuyu, Fu Changrui, Zheng Tao, Li Ziling, David William Nightingale, Matthias Werner Helmreich, Bryan Alan Oknyansky, Zach Hines, Tom James
Design date: 2008

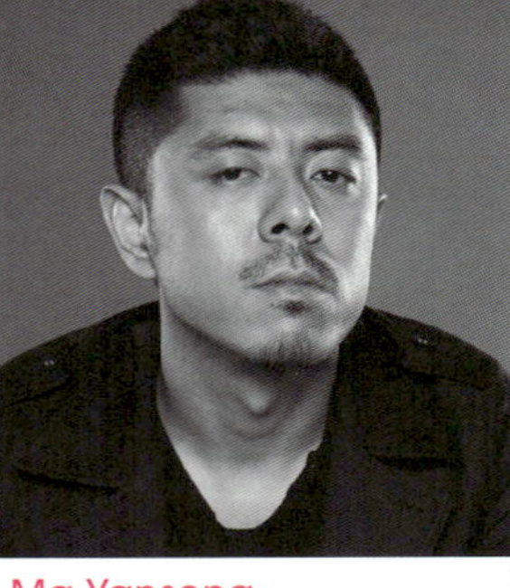

Ma Yansong
Copartner and Founder of MAD

马岩松
MAD建筑设计事务所 合伙人 创立人

1975年出生于北京，毕业于美国耶鲁大学（Yale University），获建筑学硕士以及Samuel J. Fogelson优秀设计毕业生奖。曾经在伦敦的扎哈·哈迪德建筑事务所和纽约埃森曼建筑事务所工作。马岩松2004年回到中国并成立了北京MAD建筑事务所，同时任教于中央美术学院。他先后在魏玛包豪斯大学、英国AA建筑学院、哥伦比亚大学、第23届世界建筑师大会、南加州建筑学院、南加州大学、丹麦建筑中心、哈佛大学和麻省理工学院等地做过演讲。

马岩松获2001年美国建筑师学会（AIA）建筑研究奖金，2006年度纽约建筑联盟青年建筑师奖。他的建成作品红螺会所和胡同泡泡32号被英国伦敦设计博物馆分别提名为2009年度以及2010年度设计奖。2008年，马岩松被ICON杂志评选为全世界20位最具影响力的青年设计师之一。

马岩松领导的MAD建筑事务所多次在国际竞赛中胜出，其中包括2006年在加拿大多伦多Absolute超高层国际竞赛里中标的“梦露大厦”设计（2011年建成）。他也由此成为历史上首位在国外赢得重大标志性建筑项目的中国建筑师。MAD目前在世界范围内有各种规模和类型的建筑项目，其中包括正在施工中的、位于天津滨海新区的358米超高层——中钢国际广场、鄂尔多斯博物馆、北京嘉德艺术中心、台中会展中心、重庆森林等大型公共建筑和住宅项目。

马岩松的作品包括曾在2002年引起国内外建筑界广泛关注和讨论的”浮游之岛“——重建纽约世界贸易中心方案，这件作品后来被中国国家美术馆馆藏。他的艺术装置作品”鱼缸“”墨冰“曾分别在中国国家美术馆和中华世纪坛展出。2006年MAD在意大利威尼斯举办了个展”MAD in China“，与威尼斯双年展同步展出。同年在北京东京画廊举办了名为“MAD under Construction”（建设中）的建筑设计个展。2007年MAD在丹麦哥本哈根的丹麦建筑中心展出一个名为”MAD in China“的漂浮城市系列个展。2008年8月，受第11届威尼斯双年展邀请，MAD在主展馆展出”超级明星：移

动中国城 ˇ。2009年MAD以瞩目的位置出现在比利时欧罗巴中国艺术节的建筑单元《中国当代建筑的前沿——心造展》中。2010年4月马岩松与奥拉维尔・埃利亚松(Olafur Eliasson)在UCCA举办联合展览。

Ma Yansong, Who Comes from Beijing, received his Master of Architecture from Yale University in 2002. Prior to founding MAD in 2004, Mr. Ma worked as a project designer in Zaha Hadid Architects in London and Eisenman Architects in New York. He has taught architecture at the Central Academy of Fine Arts in Beijing. He also lectured in Bauhaus, Architectural Association (AA), Columbia University, XXII UIA World Congress of Architecture, Southern California Institute of Architecture (Sci-Arch), University of South California, Danish Architecture Center, Harvard University, and Massachusetts Institute of Technology (MIT).

Ma was the winner of 2006 Architecture League Young Architects Award. He also received the American Institute of Architects Scholarship for Advanced Architecture Research in 2001 as well as the 2002 Samuel J. Fogelson Memorial Award of Design Excellence. His works, Hongluo Clubhouse was nominated for the Brit Insurance Designs of the Year 2009 and Hutong Bubble 32 was shortlisted for Designs of the Year 2010 by Design Museum in London. In 2008, Ma was selected as one of the 20 most influential young architects today by ICON.

His works have won numerous international design competitions, including: the 2006 Absolute Tower Competition in Toronto which is under construction and scheduled to complete in 2011. On-going projects include the Sinosteel International Plaza, a 358 m high rise tower in Tianjin Binghai New District, Erdos Museum in Inner Mongolia, Poly Art Center in Beijing, Taichung Convention Center in Taiwan, Chongqing Urban Forest.

“非永恒城市”第11届威尼斯建筑双年展

类型：城市概念

MAD的“超级明星：移动中国城”在第十一届威尼斯建筑双年展的主题馆“非永恒城市”展出。该单元邀请了来自全世界包括MAD、BIG、WEST8在内的十二位青年建筑师，针对日益丧失活力和特征的罗马郊区，为它的未来提供新的城市肌体组织。本届策展人为Aaron Betsky，主题是“ARCHITECTURE BEYOND BUILDINGS”（超越房屋的建筑），展览时间为2008年9月14日至11月23日。“超级明星：移动中国城”是MAD构想的一个新型中国城。

散布在全世界各个角落的中国城，和那里的商场、加油站、麦当劳一样，如同毒素，使得每个城市变得千篇一律，无聊透顶。而中国城里没完没了的餐厅，一成不变的仿古建筑，附会着西方世界对中国的僵化想象。这里没有真实的生活，如同这个国家遗留在异乡的一座座陈旧的主题公园，毒害着城市空间和人们的理解力。我们要想复活就必须以毒攻毒！

“超级明星：移动中国城”是MAD对这种过时并过剩的中国城所做出的回应。“超级明星”是一个整体、和谐、不断更新的未来中国城模型。它是一颗存在着丰富真实生活的行星，人们可以在这里享受中国食品，享受有品质的生活，进行各种文化、教育、体育活动。这是一颗创造和生产的行星，人们可以在这里的工作室学习，想象并实现他们的想法。

同时，这是一个由它所包含内容驱动整个系统运转的新型社会。“超级明星：移动中国城”在不妥协地改变与固守原则的保守中爆发出未知的能量。它可以停留在世界任何一个角落，与它所处的环境交换全新的激情和能量。它是一颗自给自足的行星：这里的农业中心提供所有的天然食物，不需要从地面环境中提取能源，并且可以回收利用所有的废物。它是一个空中居所，有真正的湖泊、雪山和梯田等自然景观，有养身中心，全行星的体育活动场所，以及饮用水源。这里的奥林匹克中心可以每四年降落在主办城市，不需要再重复建设昂贵的体育设施。这里还有一个电子墓场来纪念在这颗行星中逝去的世界公民。“超级明星：移动中国城”是一个梦想家园，这里没有等级制度，没有上下关系，而是一个技术与自然，未来与人文的混合物。

“超级明星：移动中国城”的第一站是罗马的郊区。它将带给这个永恒的过去一个无法预知、永远变化的未来。之后它将降落在纽约、迪拜、洛杉矶或某个不知名的岛屿、丛林和草原。

欢迎来到“超级行星”，今天的中国城。

"Uneternal City" 11th Venice Architecture Biennale

Type: Urban Concept

Along with shopping malls, petrol stations and branches of McDonalds, the old Chinatown renders all cities boring and alike. It is nothing more than restaurant streets and fake traditional buildings, representing a kitsch image of contemporary China with no real life inside. It is a historical theme park that poisons the urban space. There must be a shock therapy to remedy this situation.

Superstar: A Mobile China Town is MAD's response to the redundant and increasingly out-of-date nature of the contemporary Chinatown. Rather than a sloppy patchwork of poor construction and nostalgia, the Superstar is a fully integrated, coherent, and above all modern upgrade of the 20th century Chinatown model. It's a place to enjoy Chinese food, quality goods and cultural events; a place to create and produce, where citizens can use workshops to study, imagine and realize their ideas.

Equally important to what this neo-community contains is how it operates. Superstar: A Mobile China Town is a benevolent virus that releases unknown energy in between unprincipled changes and principled steadiness. It can land at every corner of the world, exchanging the new Chinese energy with the environment where it stays. It's self-sustaining: it grows its own food, requires no resources from the host city, and recycles all of its waste. It's a living place, with authentic Chinese nature and health resorts, sports facilities and drinkable reservoirs, even a digital cemetery to remember the deceased. It's a travelling Olympic party that can journey to the host city every four years. The Superstar is a dream that's home to 15 000 people. No hierarchy, no hyponymy, only a fusion of technology and nature, future and humanity.

The Superstar's first destination will be the periphery of Rome. The Superstar will provide an unexpected, ever-changing future embedded in the Eternal past.

Welcome to the Superstar, the Chinatown of today.

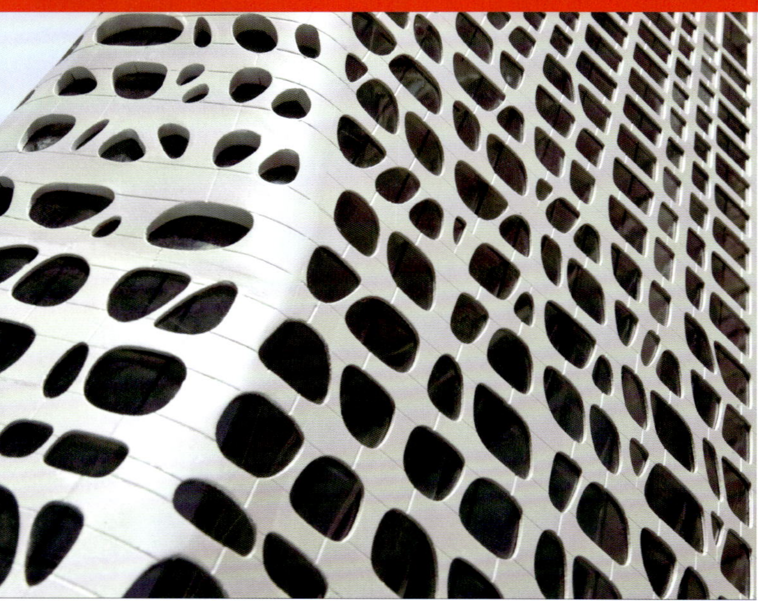

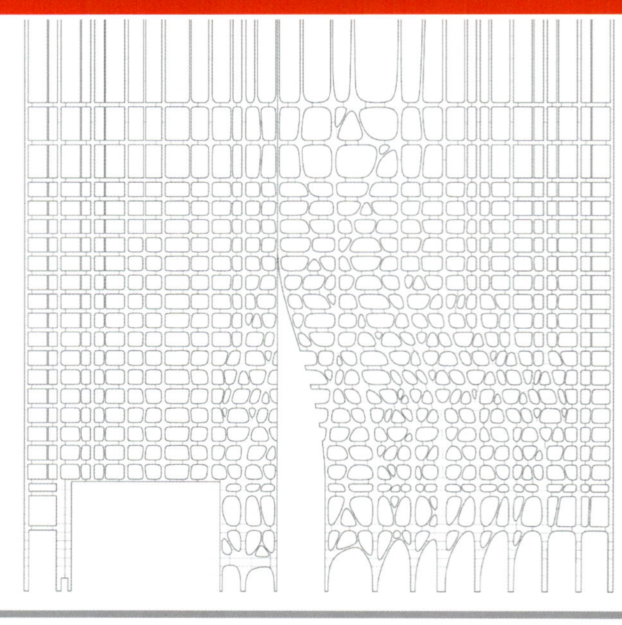

Conrad Hotel

港丽酒店

设计单位：MAD建筑设计事务所
主持设计师：马岩松、党群
设计团队：Flora Lee、刘亦昕、Yuteki Dozono、谢怡邦、Gabrielle Marcoux、Uli Queisser、唐柳、Art Terry、Rasmus Palmqvist、Diego Perez、Alan Kwan、Helen Li、Albert Schrurs、Simon Lee、Dustin Harris、Bryan Oknyansky、Andy Chang、Matthias Helmreich、黄伟、Howard Kim
基地面积：7 779 m²
建筑面积：56 994 m²
建筑高度：106 m
酒店建筑师：美达麦斯国际建筑咨询
结构工程师：北京建筑设计研究院
电气工程师：北京建筑设计研究院
幕墙顾问：华纳工程咨询（北京）有限公司
室内设计师：Lim.Teo + Wilkes Design Works Pte Ltd
景观设计师：泛亚国际

Design firm: MAD
Director in charge: Ma Yansong, Dang Qun
Design team: Flora Lee, Liu Yixin, Yuteki Dozono, Xie Bangyi, Gabrielle Marcoux, Uli Queisser, Tang Liu, Art Terry, Rasmus Palmqvist, Diego Perez, Alan Kwan, Helen Li, Albert Schrurs, Simon Lee, Dustin Harris, Bryan Oknyansky, Andy Chang, Matthias Helmreich, Huang Wei, Howard Kim
Site area: 7 779 m²
Building area: 56 994 m²
Building height: 106 m
Hotel architect: Metamax
Structural engineers: Beijing Institute of Architectural Design (BIAD)
Mechanical engineers: Beijing Institute of Architectural Design (BIAD)
Facade/cladding consultants: King General Engineering, SuP Ingenieure GmbH
Interior designers: Lim.Teo + Wilkes Design Works Pte Ltd.
Landscape designer: Earthasia Design Group

北京的CBD是依照20世纪初现代主义工业革命前后的西方标准建造的。这里的建筑成为资本和地位的表达，但本质的不同是，它完全没有一百年前西方人建造摩天楼时挑战技术和未来的野心，而成为一片在大规模的复制中生产出的钢筋混凝土机器，它们追求效益，缺乏灵魂。

在这样的建筑群落中，北京港丽酒店是一次“慢速度”设计。类似神经组织的立面单元被植入到一个方形的建筑体量中，引起了形体的轻微变化，并生长成为一张有机的建筑表皮。整个建筑如同一个融化中的方盒子，成为城市网格体系中一个转变的开始——液态的意念入侵到固态的效率之中，工业流水线生产的标准构件被具有差异性的工艺制造所取代。

在建筑风格的演化中，不同历史时期的人们都曾以手工艺打造出富于生命力的建筑物，他们表达出人的意念冲动以及对自然力量的虔诚，突破了建筑的沉重，以上升的精神成为那个时代的城市文化标志。北京港丽酒店所要表达的是中国当代城市发展中的“慢速度”——建筑的产生与人的生存过程一样，是一种聚集能量、形成特征的演进过程。他们不再是大规模的工业复制品，新的城市效率是在现代工业的精确控制下所产生的差异性，以及人们在城市生活中不断有新的发现的可能性。

The CBD of Beijing was built according to the west standard set up around the industrial revolution of the early 20th century. The high-rise building is the symbol of the capitalism, but far from the ambition of more than one hundred years ago, when people tried to challenge themselves with modern technology and future dreams, The contemporary CBD buildings are the concrete machines, the copies copy in mass production. They are meaningless, crowded and soulless.

Situated among those buildings, Conrad hotel is the outcome of the slow-design. The facade element, which looks like the nervous tissue, is planted into a simple cubic. It is the toxin that destroys and transforms the surface into an organic envelop. The whole building is turned into a melting box, a starting point for the urban grid to change from the solid efficiency into the liquid idea. The standard product of the production line is therefore replaced by the digital craft of difference.

During the architecture evolution, people of different historical times tried to create organic buildings by their hand-made crafts. Their works are the representation of the worship of nature, the courage to break the heaviness of building and the passion of life. It is the spirit of sublime that became the culture icon of the era and the city. Conrad hotel is the design that appreciates the slowness in the fast urban development in China, the product of architecture is like the growing process of urban dwellers in the city, it is the evolution of energy and identity. The new urban efficiency is the difference produced by the precise control of high-tech modern industry, and it creates the new possibility for people living in the city to discover their own new experience.

Taichung Convention Center

台中会展中心

设计单位：MAD建筑设计事务所
主持设计师：马岩松、党群
设计团队：Jordan Kanter、Jtravis Russett、Irmi Reiter、Diego Perez、戴璞、Rasmus Palmquist、Art Terry、Chie Fuyuki
设计时间：2009年
基地面积：70 318 m^2
建筑面积：216 161 m^2
建筑高度：39 m～85 m

Design firm: MAD
Director in charge: Ma Yansong, Dang Qun
Design Team: Jordan Kanter, Jtravis Russett, Irmi Reiter, Diego Perez, Dai Pu, Rasmus Palmquist, Art Terry, Chie Fuyuki
Design date: 2009
Site area: 70 318 m^2
Building area: 216 161 m^2
Building feight: 39 m～85 m

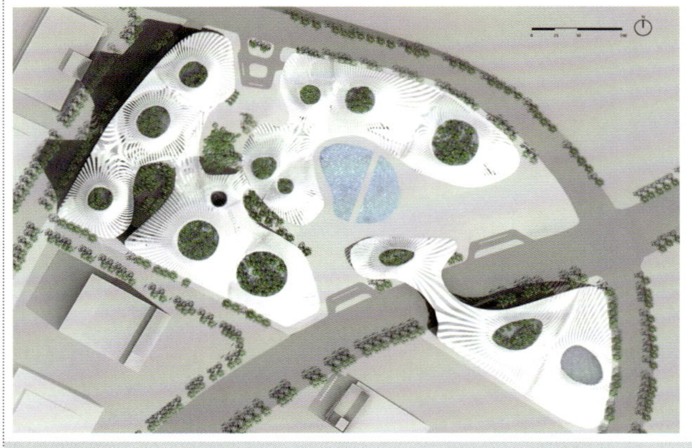

受台中市政府和台湾土地开发公司委托，北京MAD事务所最近完成了他们在台湾的第一个项目——台中会展中心的方案设计。

这是一组连绵起伏的建筑群落，褶皱状的“山体”模糊了建筑、景观和城市公共空间的界限，构成一幅展现东方自然精神的未来世界。方案传承了中国对建筑群体和空间序列追求的传统，并把东方文化中与自然和谐相处的精神气质贯穿其中。在这个规模庞大的建筑群中，重要的不再是某个建筑单体本身，建筑物的形象是统一化的，而他们所围合的空间则成为主体，那是一种在空气、风、光线之间形成的自然秩序，以及由此建立起来的人与自然之间的情感共鸣。

台中所需要的是一件超越地域，重新定义城市文化景观和社会生活的大型都市艺术品，以独特的建筑观和全新的建筑宣言，使台中跃升成为世界文化先锋。

当今地标式建筑的特征已经由对高度的原始追求转为面向未来和自然的文化诉求。地标不仅仅是视觉上的冲击，更应该是一个聚集城市活力，激发交流和想象力的戏剧性生活场景。

这块基地本身就有着它丰富的生命力——平静的表皮下蕴藏的能量渴望被表现出来，地形本身就是一件具有潜力的自然艺术品。建筑物好像当地的“环形山”，相互之间牵动，围合，转化为连绵起伏，具有中心汇聚点的建筑形体，形成建筑与自然地景的对话。

包裹“群山”的建筑表皮是由一系列的绿色技术构成的复合生态皮肤。褶皱状的连续外表皮为建筑提供自然的空气流动，收集太阳能并维持最低的能耗。

由“群山”围成的院落相互连接，构成了室外空间的自然序列。正如传统的紫禁城和中国园林中对于人与自然和谐共生的追求一样，这个建筑群落的意义更多地表现在其非物质的属性，即围合空间极其自然的精神——一棵树、一片竹林、一潭池水成为了空间的主体。这是基于传统哲学和美学的可持续发展观，而不是基于技术的。

Beijing based MAD Architects has recently completed the design for the Taichung Convention Center, its first project in Taiwan commissioned by the Taichung city government.

The design is conceived as a continuous weave of architecture and landscape that blurs the boundary between architecture, public space and urban landscape, proposing a futuristic vision based on the East's naturalistic philosophy. This project inherits Chinese architecture's long-standing attitude towards holistic integration and the order of space. It employs Eastern philosophy of a harmonized synthesis between human and nature. In the face of the project's enormous scale, the architecture no longer exists as a series of individual blocks, but instead is unified as a collective form. The resultant space enclosed within comes into focus, in a natural order emerging from air, wind and light, fostering a resonance between human and nature.

The city of Taichung requires a metropolitan landmark that goes beyond the local to renew urban life and redefine the cultural landscape of the city, which, through unique architectural concepts and proposing a new kind of architectural philosophy, launches Taichung into the arena of world class cultural cites. Today's landmark buildings are no longer characterized by mere considerations for height, but have turned to cultural inquiries of future and nature. More than making visual impacts, landmark buildings should foster public recreation, and inspire communication and imagination.

The site for this project is inherently characterized by an energy-rich landscape. Under its calm surface, topological potentials await to be discovered and expressed as urban landmarks. On the one hand, the architecture's crater-shaped formation and resulting rotundas are the outcome of found site conditions. On the other hand, it simultaneously shapes and influences the surrounding environment, opening up a dialogue between architecture and landscape. The surface of the "mountains" is a high-tech, eco-friendly pleated skin system. The smocking-like envelope provides air flow to the building while keeping energy consumption at a minimum by utilizing solar energy.

The open courtyards enclosed by individual "mountains" are integrated into a natural sequence of outdoor spaces. Like the quest for a harmonic coexistence between people and nature exemplified by Forbidden City and ancient Chinese gardens, this project seeks greater meaning in its non-material qualities, spaces encircled with the upmost naturalistic spirit. A single tree, a patch of bamboo, or a pond becomes central figures of the space. This approach to sustainable development is based not on technology, but on traditional philosophy and aesthetics.

Photographer：Fang Zhenning

Photographer：Fang Zhenning

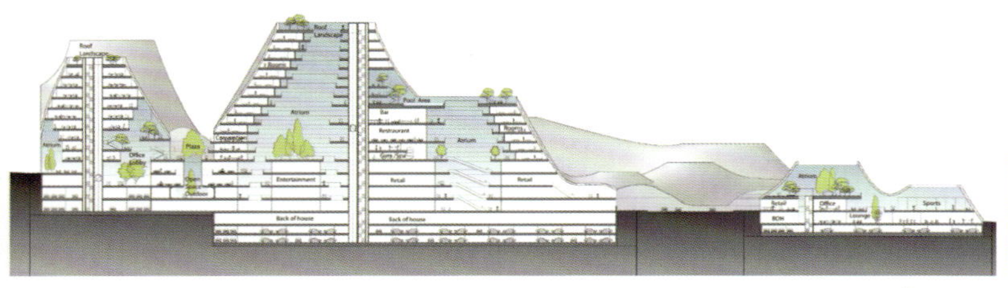

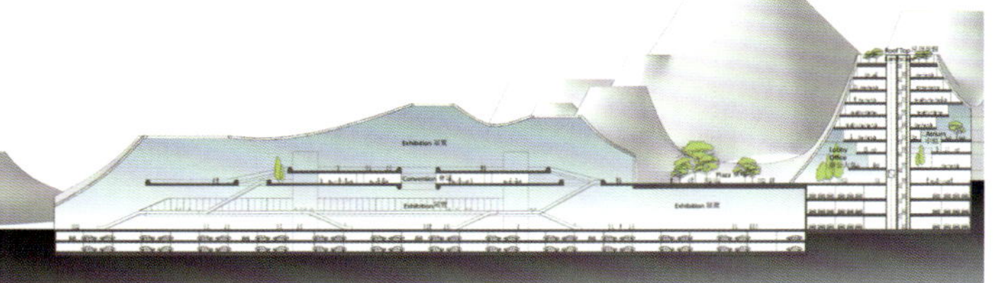

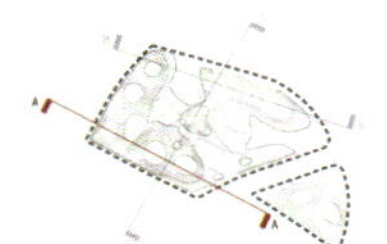

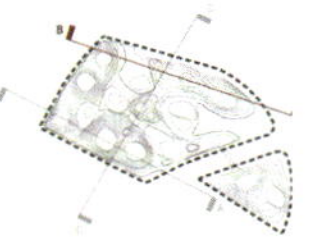

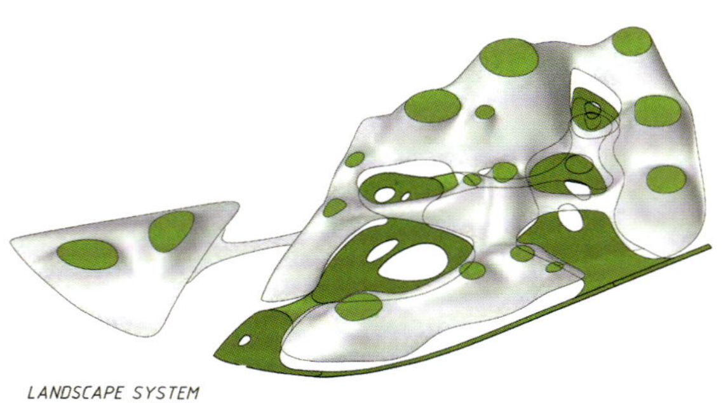

LANDSCAPE SYSTEM
景观系统

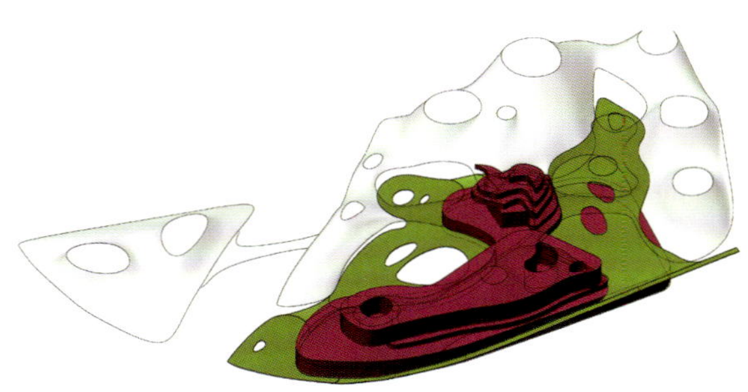

CONVENTION & LANDSCAPE RELATIONSHIP
会议&景观关系

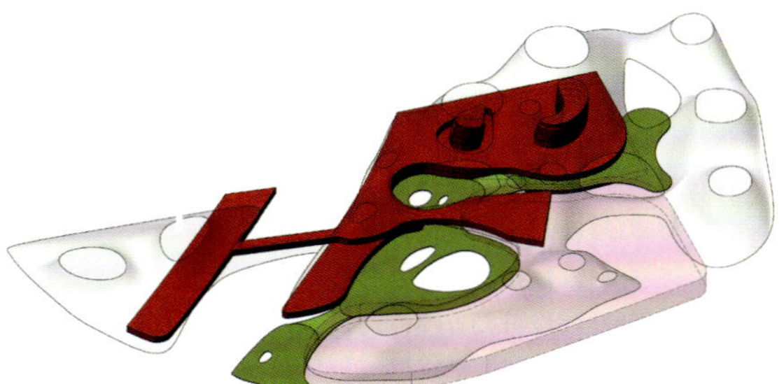

RETAIL CORRIDOR
商业连廊

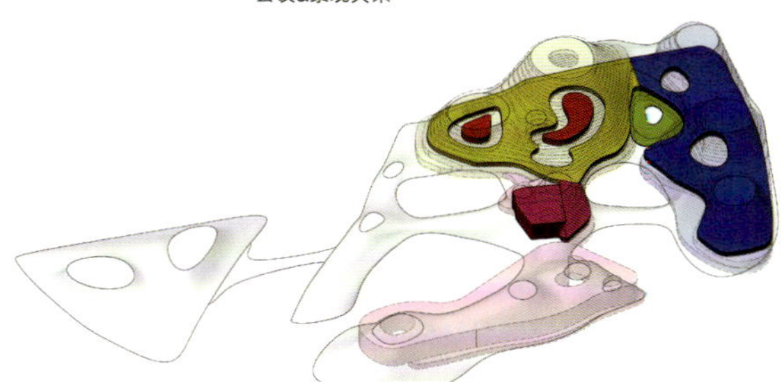

PROGRAMME CONNECTIVITY BAND
功能联系图

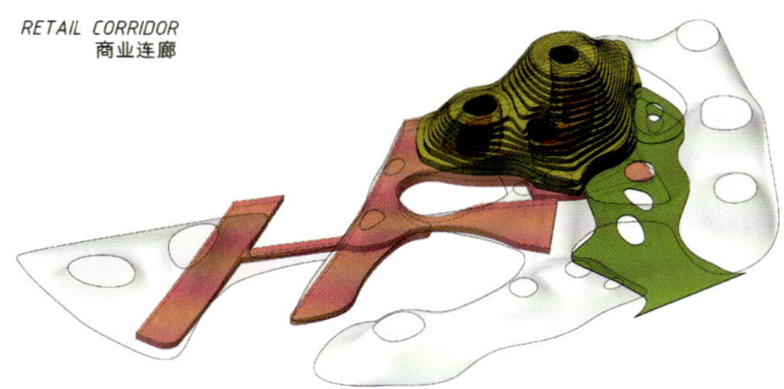

HOTEL & RETAIL RELATIONSHIP
酒店&商业关系

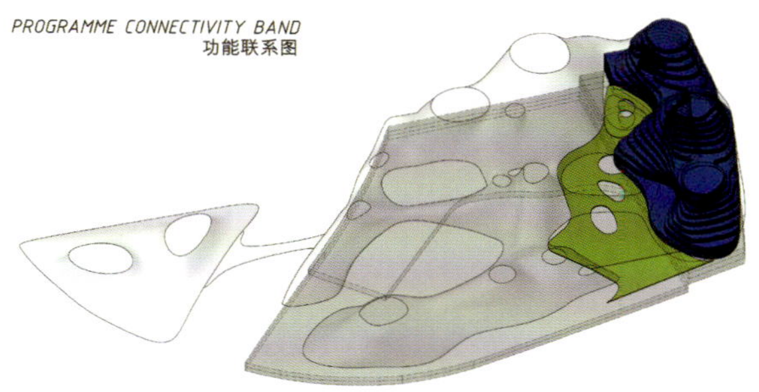

OFFICE & PARKING RELATIONSHIPS
办公&停车关系

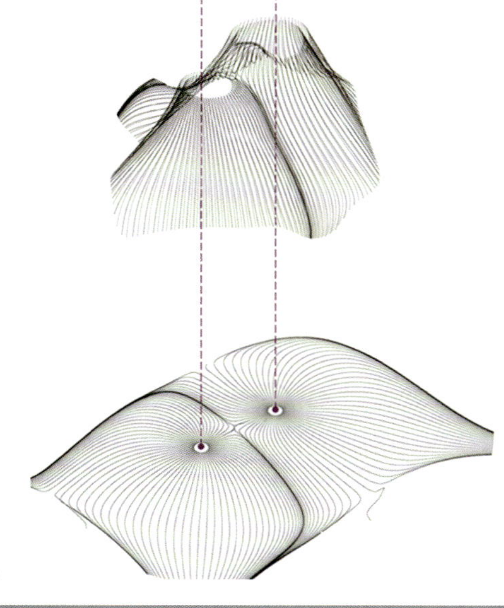

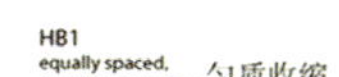

HB1
equally spaced, shrinking members 匀质收缩

HC1
equally spaced, growing members 匀质扩散

HD1
variably spaced, uniform members, gaped 多样性空间 开口

HB2
equally spaced, shrinking members, justified 匀质收缩 对齐

HC2
equally spaced, growing members, justified 匀质扩散 对齐

HD2
variably spaced, uniform members, split and justified 多样性空间 切割+对齐

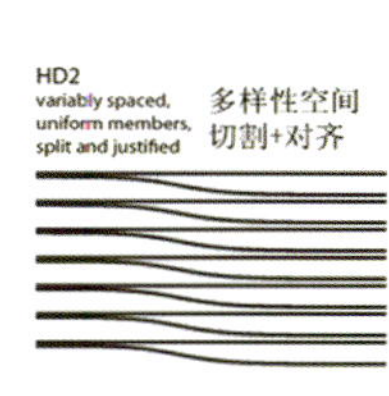

HB3
equally spaced, shrinking members, justified and symmetrical 匀质收缩 对齐+对称

HC3
equally spaced, growing members, justified and symmetrical 匀质扩散 对齐+对称

HD3
variably spaced, uniform members, split and symmetrical 多样性空间 切割+对称

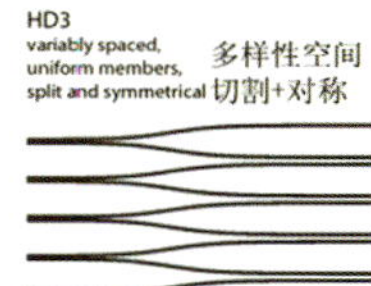

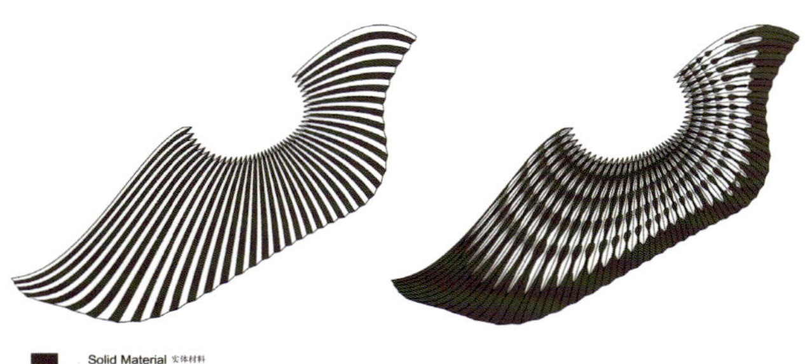

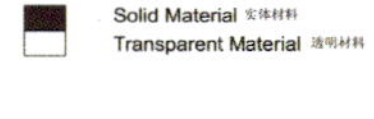

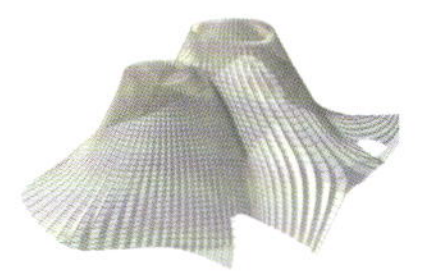

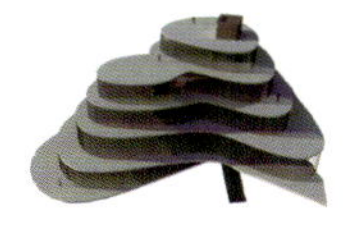

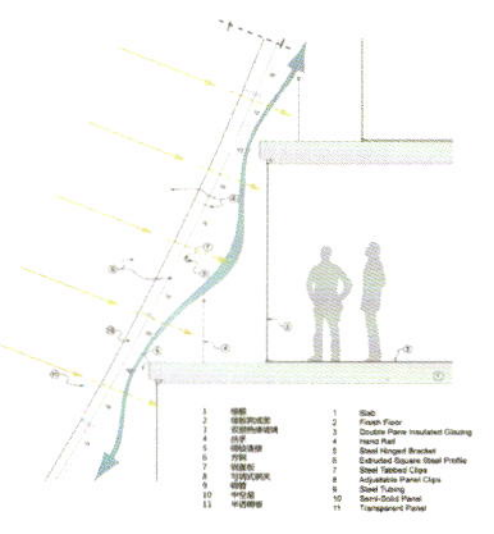

Ma Qingyun
MADA s.p.a.m.

马清运
美国建筑师协会会员
黛拉及哈利·麦荣誉教席
美国南加州大学建筑学院院长
马达思班创始合伙人/主席/设计总监

马清运1965年生于西安，获得清华大学建筑系建筑工程学士学位及美国宾夕法尼亚大学建筑学硕士学位。1996年在费城创立美国马达建筑设计事务所，1999年在中国与陈展辉创立马达思班建筑设计事务所，并在过去十年带领设计团队以大量设计研究成果与建成项目，使马达思班成为世界瞩目的代表中国当代建筑设计思考及实践能力的事务所。其作品曾在世界各地展出并相继在俄罗斯ICIP国际竞赛、越南国际建筑设计、法国戛纳国际商业房地产展览会、美国《建筑实录》《商业周刊》联合颁发的中国最佳住宅等国际性大赛、奖项上获得殊荣，他个人也曾被评为"建筑先锋""欧亚建筑新趋势代表人"，2010年更被《商业周刊》评为全球"最具影响力的27位设计师之一"。马清运带领马达思班的实践跨越艺术、教育、商贸、时尚、展览及公益等多个领域。

马清运不但精于实践，并且勤于教育和研究。他曾经在多所中外大学和学术机构执教及演讲，包括同济大学、南京大学、深圳大学、美国哈佛大学、康奈尔大学、柏林工大、哥伦比亚大学、荷兰贝尔拉格学院、法国建筑专业学校、瑞士苏黎士高工等。2007年开始，担任美国南加州大学建筑学院院长。他还积极参与公益及市政咨询的工作，曾担任北京申办2008年奥运会的建筑陈述专家，青浦区城市发展建筑顾问，海口市城市发展建筑顾问，洛杉矶城市公共空间策略顾问委员会成员。近年更为四川灾区免费设计中小学校，在甘肃、陕西的落后地区参与"绿色澡堂"公益项目。

为推动中国当代建筑与世界的交流与融合，马清运还致力于出版、展览与宣传活动。2006年协助组织国际著名建筑师雷姆·库哈斯在哈佛大学举行的珠江三角洲城市状态的研究，并担任库哈斯先生《大跃进》一书的评论员。2003年马清运参与了法国蓬皮杜艺术中心的"Alors, la Chine?(Then, China)"展览策划工作并撰写策展文字，2004年独立组织策划了"马达现场"系列欧洲巡展，2007年担任深圳·香港城市\建筑双城双年展总策展人，2008年策划美国纽约Cooper-Hewitt国家设计美术馆的"中国制造"展，2010年在故乡蓝田策划了巴黎艺术家为期4个多月的"上山下乡"驻地计划。

photographer:Chen Zhanhui

Guang Hua Lu SOHO

北京光华路SOHO

设计单位：马达思班
其他合作单位：北京市建筑设计研究院
建筑类型：商业、办公
占地面积：10 189 m²
建筑面积：75 438 m²
甲方：SOHO中国

Design firm: MADA s.p.a.m.
Other consultants: Beijin Institute PF Architecture Pesian
Use of the building: Commerce \ Office
Site area: 10 189 m²
Building area: 75 438 m²
Client: SOHO China

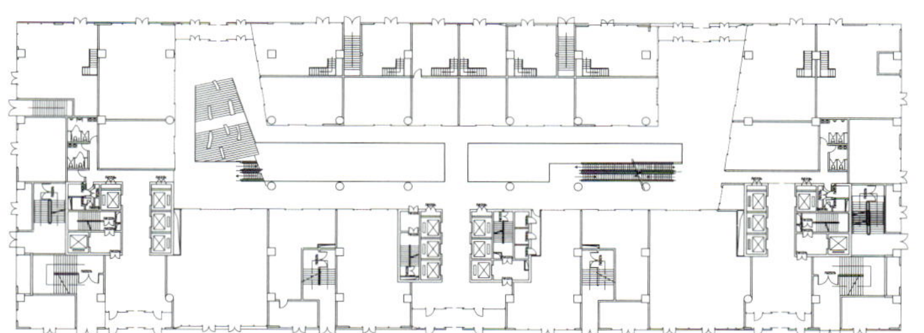

photographer:Chen Zhanhui

photographer:Jin Zhan

Ma Qingyun was born in 1965, obtained his bachelor degree from Tsinghua University and master degree from University of Pennsylvania, returning to China in the year of 1999, and has become one of the most influential architects in China. In the past 10 years, he led the design team to yield substantial design results and complete many projects, making MADA s.p.a.m. a globally focused architecture company representing Chinese contemporary architecture design and practical ability. The company's works were also successively exhibited in Russia ICIP International Contest, Vietnam International Architecture Design Contest, and Cannes International Business Real Estate Exhibition. Ma was also named one (of 27) of the World's Most Influential Designers and awarded with the titles of Architecture Pioneer, the Representative of new tendency of Eurasia jointly awarded by *Architecture Record* and *Business Week*. Now, Ma Qingyun is leading MADA to a company which crosses culture and education, fashion, exhibition and Visual Strategy, etc.

Apart from his dedication to his private practice, Ma Qingyun is also wildly involved in academic activities. He has served as a visiting professor and critic at notable institutions such as Harvard University, Columbia University in the US, and ETH, Berlage and Berlin Technical University in Europe. In 2007, Ma Qingyun was appointed dean of the School of Architecture at the University of Southern California.

Ma's active engagement and unique position in the discourse of urbanism and architecture has made him one of the most frequent participants in exhibitions and publications, either as an exhibitor or a curator. In 1996, he coordinated Rem Koolhaas' first Harvard Project on Cities which resulted into the book *The Great Leap Forward*. In 2003, he wrote the main curatorial text for the most important exhibition on Chinese contemporary art and architecture in Pompidou Center, Paris. Furthermore, in 2004, Ma Qingyun curated a series of "MADA on site" exhibition traveling through European cities to "collide" Chinese urbanism with European cities. In 2007, Ma Qingyun was the chief curator of the 2007 Shenzhen and Hong Kong Bi-city Biennale on Urbanism\Architecture. In 2008, the "Made in China" China construction exhibitior at the Coopper-Hewitt National Design Museum in New York, Ma Qingyun brought up urban issues to worldwide discussion. In June of 2008, he participated in the Map Games exhibition in Beijing: Dynamics of Change, a visual art and architecture project covering 2005 through 2008.

photographer:Chen Zhanhui

photographer:Chen Zhanhui

SOHO中国命名已成为一种潮流。它代表一个印章或是一个品牌？在我们的提案中，我们对SOHO的称谓分外敏感，并试图延长其命名的生命力。我们提出了两个设计方案：这山和那石。山是人们选择居住和工作的场所，在农业社会，山是智慧和贵族的象征；石则象征了耐力和毅力，它也是代表文明和进步的工具。

方案由三个部分组成。低层部分是零售业，它提供了最大的可用零售面积。第二部分是中部集合了众多小公司的办公空间，它提供了一个巨大的充满活力的新兴社区。褶皱和漏洞部分则形成了各种公用设施，如大厅、花园和会议空间。第三部分是顶部的两个屋棚的组合。他们为大企业提供了威望和隔离。

光华路SOHO自成一个微观都市片断的核心，丰富的商业形态和不同的人群汇集于此，提供完整的日常生活、吃喝玩乐、工作消费。2007年6月2日 光华路SOHO开盘当天就创下了13.4亿元的巨额销售额，它势将成为北京CBD的时尚地标。

SOHO China has become a name with tradition, i.e. will last into future. But it is a name stamp or name brand? In our proposals, we are over sensitive of the name soho, and trying to elongate its power of naming, we propose two design schemes named So-hill and So-Rock, in Chinese they are NaShanZheShi Hill is where people choose to live and work. In agrarian society, hill is a symbol for intelligent and nobility and becomes a prime address postfix in contemporary city. Rock in Chinese symbolizes endurance and persistence. It represents instrument for civilization and advancement.

The hill is made of three portions. The lowest portion is the retail portion which is the fullest and offers the maximum usable retail areas which is lit from the "caves" taking places at the middle portion. The second middle portion is office for congregation of small companies. It offers a great sense of energetic startup community. The holes and folds offer possibilities of communal facilities such as lounge, garden, and conferences. The third portion at the hill top is made of two penthouses like cluster. They offer large companies great sense of prestige and seclusion.

photographer:Chen Zhanhui

photographer:Chen Zhanhui

photographer:Jin Zhan

photographer:Chen Zhanhui

photographer:Jin Zhan

photographer:Chen Zhanhui

photographer:Chen Zhanhui

photographer: Jin Zhan

photographer: Zhanhui Chen

Xi'an Television Broadcasting Center

西安广播电视中心

设计单位：马达思班
占地面积：62 854 m²
建筑面积：81 117 m²
甲方：西安广播电视局
其他合作单位：深圳大学建筑设计研究院/中广电广播电影电视设计研究院/西安建筑科技大学

Design firm: MADA s.p.a.m.
Site area: 62 854 m²
Building area: 81 117 m²
Client: Xi'an Television Broadcasting Bureau
Other consultants: The Institute of Architectural Design & Research, Shenzhen University/CMG Radio, Film and Television Design and Research Institute/Xi'an University of Architecture and Technology

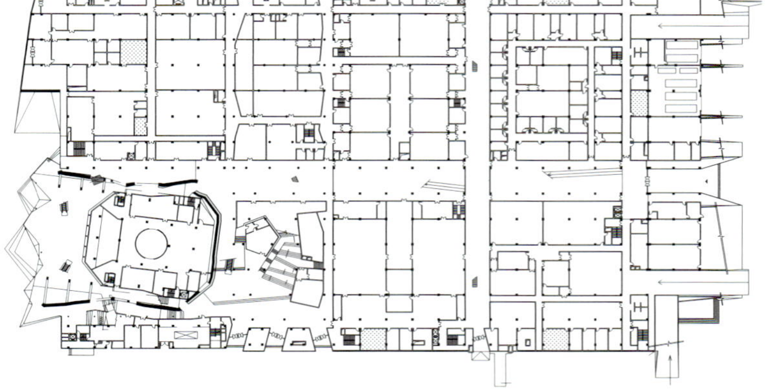

photographer:Chen Zhanhui

photographer:Zhanhui Chen

photographer:Chen Zhanhui

本项目设计承袭了西安汉唐文化中表现出的舒展大度、简洁雄浑的特征，使建筑群尽量整合布置，整体处理，突出并夸张了给定的建筑面积条件下的尺度概念。整体建筑中的诸多功能由一道有象征意义的“墙”围合在一起，暗示了西安城墙大地艺术的气质，又合理地统一解决了四周场地标高不同的问题，同时，还表达了西安广电“媒体城”的寓意。

场地的设计中顺应了曲江仿唐公园景观的地势、地貌特征，建筑群中组织了一道非常明确的南北轴线，回应了汉唐以来大型建筑群依轴线组织的建筑方式。这道建筑的轴线还同北面的曲江轴线系统形成了一个轴线的贯通体系，延长了曲江公园业已形成的南北轴线。此轴线在竖向上则顺应场地大的标高变化，在穿越建筑群内部时由北向南逐渐跌落，将场地的标高变化引入室内，既展示了曲江自然的地脉地貌，又加强了大型公共空间的纪念性。

This project inherits the generosity, concise and stately chcracteristic of Han Tang culture of Xi'an, which expressed by integrated as a whole and enhances the scale perception under determined site area condition. Diversified programs are enclosed by a symbolic "wall" not only to suggest the Land Art temperament of Xi'an Wall, but also solved the problem of contour difference on the site around, At the same time it metaphors Xi'an TV is a "Media City".

The site planning continues the typology and landscape of the imitated Tang Dynasty Park of Qu Jiang to reverberate the traditional Han Tang large-scale construction, which always respects the organization of axis system. The architectural axis follows the alignment to the Qu Jiang Axis on the North, also extending the existing North-South axis of Qu Jiang Park. This axis also trails the major height variations of site and falls down from north to west. When passing thru the inner space of the building complex, the height variation also brings to the interior to not only demonstrate the natural landscape typology of Qu Jiang, but also emphasize the monumentality of the grand public space.

photographer: Jin Zhan

photographer: Chen Zhanhui

photographer: Chen Zhanhui

photographer: Chen Zhanhui

photographer: Jin Zhan

Winery

Jade Valley Planning

蓝田玉山村规划

设计单位：马达思班
主设计师：马清运、陈展辉
摄影师：陈展辉

Design firm: MADA s.p.a.m
Lead designer: Ma Qingyun, Chen Zhanhui
Photographer: Chen Zhanhui

Winery

Winery

Winery

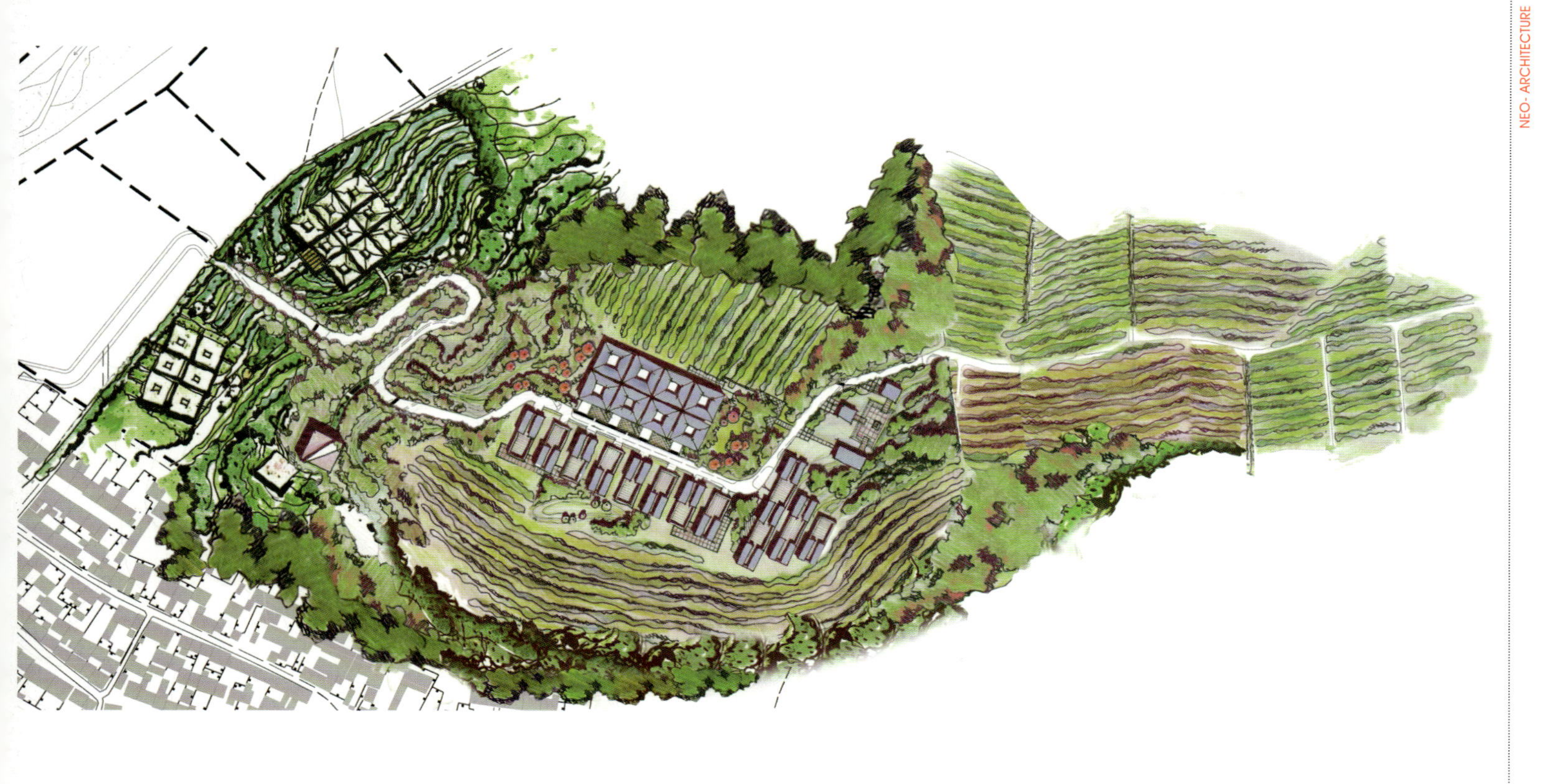

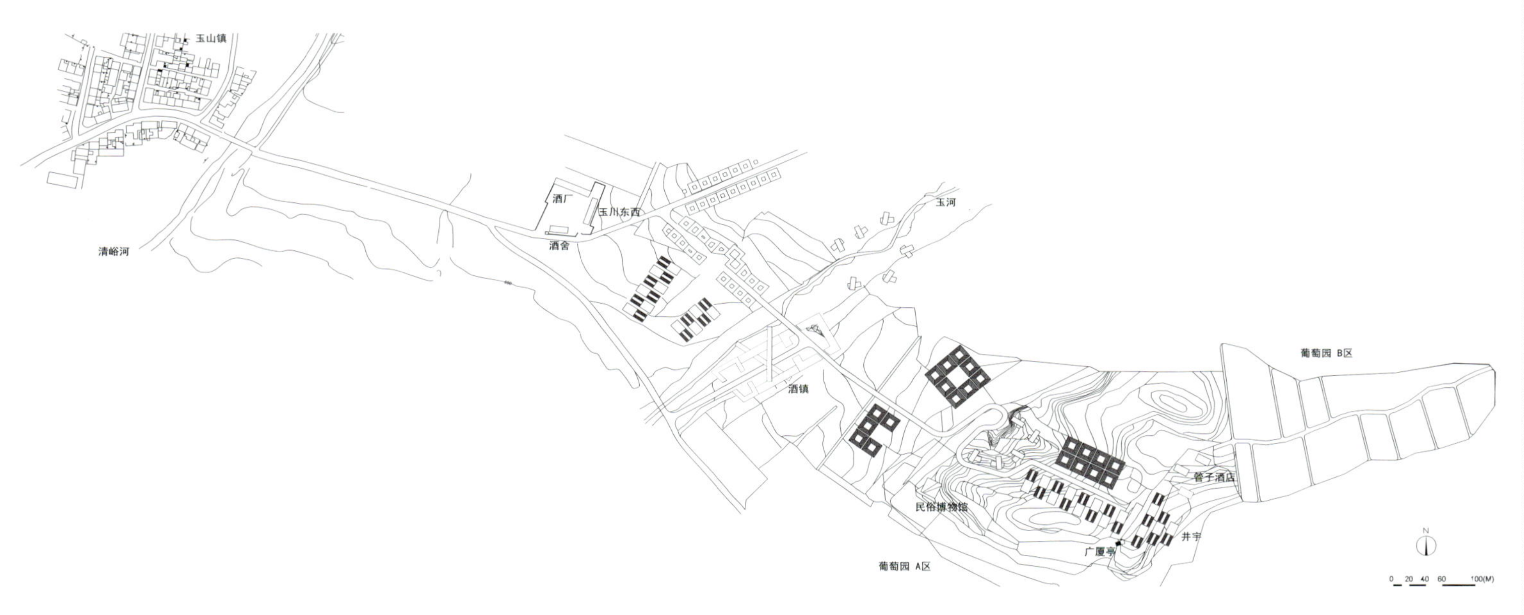

玉山村位于中国陕西省蓝田县，俯瞰灞河、清峪河冲积平原，背靠秦岭山脉，周围是大片的葡萄园，玉山村计划既是一个商业计划，也是集艺术博物馆和世外桃源于一身的建筑实践项目。

蓝田是一个能够激发中国人家园意识、文化认同感和乡愁的地方。这一系列实践涉及特色旅游、建筑、红酒文化、艺术、教育的研究，同时探讨了本土与全球化的关系。这片土地所积累的人文历史、自然生态、社会营造章法都将被作为经络脉线重新耕耘和编织。

该计划结合当地自然的土原坡地地形，依山势规划建筑和种植用地，将人工建筑和雕塑适当地涉入自然景观；建筑形态上吸收当地民居特色，以关中民居的半坡庭院组织，采用当地传统建筑材料和当地手工建造模式，结合现代建筑工艺，形成了独特的现代本土特色建筑，完成了本土地域主义与全球化的对话。

Jade Village is located in Lantian County, Shaanxi Province, China. It overlooks the river plain formed by Bahe River and Qingyuhe River, backs on Qinling Range and is surrended by large expanses of vineyards. Jade Village Planning is not only a commercial plan, but also a construstion practice project intergrating artistic museum and Shangri-la.

Lantian is a place that can inspire Chinese people's homeland consciousness, culture identity and homesickness. Such practices involve studies about tourism, construction, red wine culture, art, eduction as well as the relationship between localization and globalization. All art history, nature and ecology, and social rules accumulated in this land will be reorganized.

This plan plans construction and cultivated land in line with the local geography and intergrates artificial construction and statues into natural landscape. The construction absorbs local features, adopting the framework of Banpo courtyards of Guanzhong residents, the local traditional construction material and the mode of handbuild. Combining modern construction techniques, it is a unique construction featured by modern and local characteristics and is a dialogue between localization and globaliation.

Red Wine Manor

Winery

Red Wine Manor

Jade Valley

Jade Valley

Jade Valley

Jade Valley

Jade Valley

Public Art

Public Art

Public Art

Zhongshan Qinghuafang Villa

中山清华坊

设计单位：东方华太建筑设计公司
合作设计：广州集美组室内设计工程有限公司
规划用地面积：130 327.3 m²
总建筑面积：51 136.5 m²
建筑密度 20.2%
容积率 0.39（按地上面积计）
绿化率 50.9%

Design firm: Sino-Sun Architects & Engineers Company
Cooperation firm: Guangzhou Newsdays Interior Design & Construction Co. Ltd.
Building area: 51 136.5 m²

华太设计
SINO–SUN

东方华太建筑设计工程有限责任公司

Sino-Sun Architects & Engineers Company

东方华太是由一批海外留学人员主持的国家甲级建筑设计单位，经过十几年的辛勤耕耘，已发展成具有良好品牌的优秀设计团队，也是国内建筑设计界有一定影响的设计公司。公司以建筑设计为主，同时涉及规划、景观及室内设计。

东方华太追求：创新+质量+服务

设计理念

东方华太坚持艺术与技术相结合的创作设计理念，尊重环境、技术和经济等客观条件，追求建立在理性基础上的个性和创新。

东方华太遵循质量第一、服务至上的原则，强调质量是设计工作的灵魂，服务是设计工作的保证。通过有效的管理体系、创新的设计手法来实现项目品质和价值的最大化。

设计作品

东方华太以北京为中心，辐射中国其他城市，设计作品以公建、住宅、文教为主，公建类如中国国际科技会展中心、宏源国际大厦、上海中欣大厦、延庆商业街、北京机电产品交易市场、南京欧风街等，住宅类如北京建外SOHO、上海云间水庄、迁安怡景、呼和浩特新希望家园、银川民生城市等，文教类如北京师范大学珠海校区、中央音乐学院珠海校区、北京科技大学、中央财经大学、中国矿业大学等，设计作品遍及全国。

学术交流

公司在进行技术创新的同时，也注重学术研究与交流，鼓励员工在建筑学术杂志上发表专业论文，对设计实践及时总结，用新的设计理念来指导自身的实际工作。公司积极参与各种建筑

Sino-Sun Architecture Engineering Company

Sino-Sun is a design institution entitled with national top level and presided by some personnels who study abroad. This company has been one excellent design group with good brand and a certain kind of influence in China after thriving for more than ten years. Our company focuses on architecture design, involving planning, landscape and interior design at the same time.

Our pursuing object: innovation + quality + service

Design concept

Sino-Sun abides by the conjoint design concept of art and technology, respecting environment, technology and cost objectively, pursuing personality and innovation on the basis of logic.

Sino-Sun keeps the regulation that "quality is the first and serve is the best", emphasizing that quality is the soul and serve is the guarantee of design works. According to the efficient management system, innovative design techniques will realize the best qualities and values of the projects.

Design works

Sino-Sun takes Beijing as center, radiating other cities in China. The projects give priority to public buildings, houses and cultural and educational buildings. Public buildings include China International Science and Technology Exhibition Center, Hongyuan International Building, Shanghai Zhongxin Building, Yanqing Shopping Street, Beijing Machine and Electrics Products Trade Market, Nanjing European Style Streets, etc. House projects include Beijing Jianwai SOHO, Shanghai Yunjian Water Village, Qian'an Yijing residential district, Huhehaote new hope houses, Yinchuan Minsheng towns, etc. Cultural and educational buildings include Zhuhai campus of Beijing Normal University, Zhuhai campus of Central Musical College, Beijing Science and Technology University, Central Financial University, China Mining University, and so on. So our projects spread all over China.

Academic exchange

Sino-Sun pays attention to the academic research and exchange during the course of technology innovation and positively encourages employees to release professional articles. Experiences are summarized to improve the design practices. New concepts are applied to guide our practical works. The company positively takes part in every kind of architectural forum and exhibition, enforcing academic exchange with craft

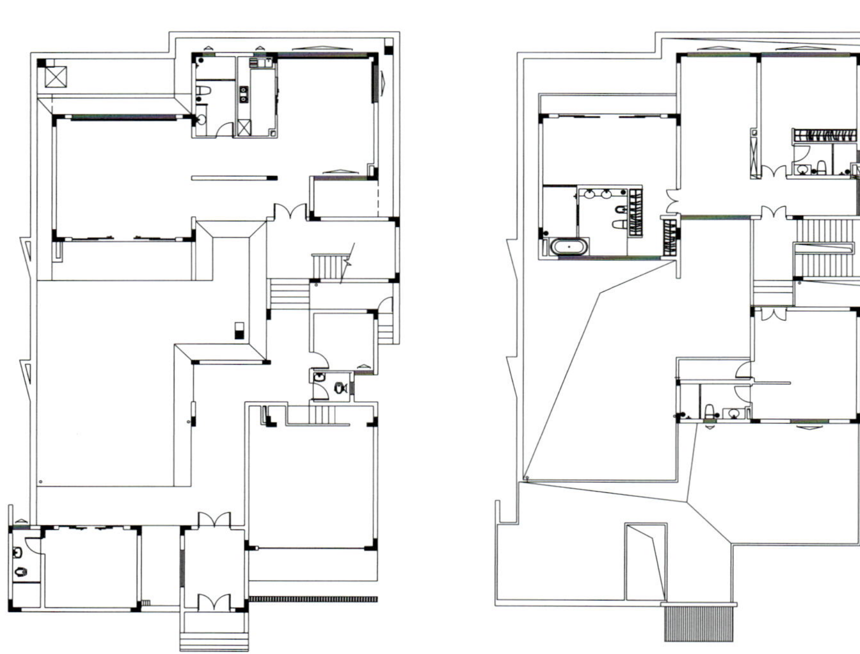

首层、二层平面图

论坛和展览，加强业界的学术交流，推动国内建筑设计界水平的共同提高。公司员工在各专业杂志上发表的学术文章有《建筑形体与设计创意》、《北师大珠海校区设计》、《“过渡”建筑》、《船与海的联想》、《空间•色彩和质感的艺术》、《与城市共生》、《再现童话故事》、《简约建筑的人性化》、《走中国特色的建筑设计之路》等。

国际合作

东方华太开展广泛的国际设计合作。在合作过程中，学习国际先进设计理念和手法，不断提高自身的设计水平和质量。在与日本山本理显设计工场合作设计建外SOHO的过程中，感受到简约建筑的人性化；通过与法国AP3设计公司合作设计的中国银行金融研修院项目，了解了建筑的“过渡”性理念；与加拿大ABCP设计公司合作设计的南昌浙大科技园区，共同创造了科技园建筑的亲自然品质。合作的境外设计公司还包括澳大利亚DEM设计公司等。

获奖作品

上海云间水庄获建设部人居经典综合大奖

“板楼”方案获北京市住宅设计竞赛优秀设计奖

北京华展国际公寓获北京市优秀工程设计二等奖

中央财经大学计算机教学楼获北京市优秀工程设计佳作奖

迁安怡景获2005住宅建筑风格创作设计优秀奖

银川民生城市花园获2005年度精瑞住宅住区规划设计优秀奖

CIHAF2005中国二十大规划建筑设计事务所之一

作为中国馆的代表之一参加第六届巴西圣保罗建筑与设计双年展

建外SOHO Ⅰ～Ⅲ获北京市第十二届优秀工程设计二等奖

中国国际科技会展中心获北京市第十二届优秀工程设计三等奖

呼和浩特新希望家园获2006年度精瑞住宅住区规划设计优秀奖

用地概况

清华坊位于中山市老虎臀，规划分为A区、B区、C区地块，一期为A区的平缓地带，联排低层住宅部分为一期工程。北为山景，建筑物退缩用地红线6 m以上；南面为规划道路，绿化退缩4 m以上；西面为天然湖泊；东面相邻为厂房，退缩红线10 m以上。一期总规划用地面积为130 327.3 m^2，地理环境优美，道路及市政设施较为完善，地块平整，利于建设开发。

平面布局

1.整个小区的地理位置显赫，风景优美，根据这个特点，营造一个园中有园、宁静致远、优雅恬淡的的优美环境。高低错落的建筑隐藏在万绿丛中，整个小区绿意盎然，传统民居与现代建筑风格相结合，创造出一个低层低密度生态居住小区。生态、人性化、独特的文化氛围构成本清华坊独有的气质。

2.根据不同的方位和朝向，提供多样化的户型，通过合理的布置，使每户的客厅、主房朝向好的或较好的景观，每户均配置独立的后花园，充分结合周围的优良环境，提高本小区的生活品位，增强其市场吸引力和竞争力。

3.通过合理的布局，提供新型、有特色、人性化的社区服务和物业管理空间，为住户提供高雅、方便、舒适、优美的生活环境。

4.通过小区对外出入口的合理配置，进行封闭式的管理，提高小区的生活安全。

绿化设计

本地块处于清幽的青山绿水中，依山傍水，绿树成荫，鸟语花香，具有得天独厚的自然环境。

1.本规划设计是一低层低密度的高尚住宅区，均为联排式，在每户的底层均设有独立的车库和私家花园，户主可以根据个人的喜好对私家花园进行个性化设计，私家花园与整个小区的绿化景观和中心湖泊相呼应，使人感到犹如住在公园中，充分体现了“以人为本”的设计理念。在单体设计中充分考虑住户的品位及要求，各个功能房间的布置及相互关系都经过精心设计，确保其达到居住的舒适性，并使其富于生活情趣。在建筑的后花园处理上，我们设计了一种高墙深院的传统民居庭院的效果。在立面屋顶造型处理上，借鉴传统民居与园林亭阁的特点，与现代风格相结合。立面的处理采用了极具传统民居特色的屋顶，在立面上通过不同颜色的处理，使建筑融入整个大的自然环境中，使之成为一个有机的整体。

2.中心湖泊区为小区主入口，也是整个小区的中心景观，与山景遥相呼应，形成和谐整体的效果，结合自然的景观和各私家花园的小型园景，形成层次丰富的、有生气的景观空间环境。

3.在小区的环境道路两边，在适当的位置设置有特色的园林绿化小品和雕塑，增加小区的文化气氛，形成小区内部的景观轴线，具有很强的秩序感和丰富的个性空间，使住户更加亲近自然，与自然融为一体，并使邻里之间的交往更加亲切，富有情趣。

4.主题商业铺位部分为二层联通式建筑，风格上以现代为主，力求反映地方文化精神和个性，利用绿化广场、铺地、绿化、灯具、广告牌、遮阳设施等创造出浓厚的商业气氛，在内部设计上尽量采用人性化设计，以满足现代人购物、休闲的生活需要。

5.中心会所位于B区的半山腰，可俯视整个中心景观，与重重叠叠的山峦相影成戏。

呼和浩特新希望家园获2006年度C&US.China展览会的中国建筑文化传承奖之金斗拱奖

集美岸上篮山小区获2006年度百年建筑优秀作品奖

在2006–2007年度北京地产年度风云榜上被评为北京地产十佳建筑设计机构

呼和浩特新世界家园获2007年度精瑞住宅住区规划设计优秀奖

中山清华坊获2009年度百年建筑住宅类综合大奖

空港企业园获2009年度百年建筑公建类规划设计优秀奖

brothers to push the design level upward. The main articles include:*Architectural Form and Design Creation,the Design of the Zhuhai Campus of Beijing Normal University,"Transition"architecture,the Association of Ship and Sea,Arts of Space · Colors and Character,Accretion with city,reproduce fairy tale,the Humane of Simple Architecture,the Way to Design owning Chinese Special Character*, etc.

International cooperation

Sino-Sun puts up international design cooperation broadly, during which we learn international advanced concepts and tact, so as to improve the design level and quality. When we cooperate with Riken Yamamoto, we feel the humanity within the simple building; according to the cooperation with French design company AP3, we design the financial research college of Bank of China and understand the concept of "transition" in architecture; in the project of Zheda Science and Technology Park in Nanchang, we create close-natural quality with APCP design company of Canada. Other abroad design companies include DEM of Australia, etc.

The site situation

Qinghua fang Villa locates in the tiger area in Zhongshan. The site is divided into three districts of A, B and C. The first developed area is the flat area of A, which is low row-houses. On the north of A, the buildings move back from the red line of the site for more than 6 m; on the south of A, green land moves back for more than 4 m; the western site is natural lakes and the eastern is factory. they are back away from the red line for more than 10 m. The first phase of construction is 130 327.3 square meters, around which surroundings are very beautiful, and the roads and infrastructures are prefect and favorable for construction.

The site layout

1. The location of the residential district is very eminent with beautiful scenery. According to this character, we construct the elegant environment with silent gardens. Buildings of different heights locate and sink in green surroundings. The combination of traditional houses and modern style buildings create residential district with low rise and density. Ecology, humanity and unique cultural environment construct the unique spirit of Qinghuafang.

2. Based on the different locations and directions, this project supplies divers house types. According to the suitable plan, we make every guestroom and main room own good landscape. Every house is collocated unique rear garden. Sufficiently integrating with beautiful environment, we improve the quality of life and enhance its attraction and competitiveness in the market.

Landscape design

This site locates in the green hill and on the side of water. Green trees and beautiful flowers make it a unique natural environment.

1. This project belongs to top grade residential district, all of the houses are row-houses. There are special garages and private gardens in the ground floor of every house. According to their personal preferences, the owners may put up individual design to their own private gardens. It makes people feel live in the park to echo with green landscape and central lake, which sufficiently embodies the design concept of "people as core".

In the design of single house, we consider the owners' tastes and demands, delicately designing every functional house and their interrelationship to insure the owners' comfort and make it full of life sentiment. In the design of rear garden, we get effect of the yard in high walls to make people feel like living in the traditional building. As for the roof, we

take the traditional house and garden for reference, correlating their techniques with modern style. In the facade, we use the traditional roof and different colors to make the building merge into nature to be a whole.

2. In the district of the central lake, we layout the main entrance and form the central landscape of the whole residential district, echoing to the hill landscape. These kinds of integrated effect combine with the natural landscape and the small garden of different private gardens to form spatial landscape with abundant levels and lively environment.

3. In the two sides of the landscape roads, we set up the special garden decorations and sculptures in suitable places to enhance the cultural atmosphere, which also form the landscape axis and embody strong orders and abundant individual space. These methods make owners more close to nature, making neighborhood more friendly and full of interesting things.

4. The main biz area is the joint building of 2 levels, whose style reflects the localized cultural spirits and personalities. We create the rich biz atmosphere according to green square, grounds, lamps, billboards and the instruments for keeping out sunlight. In the interior design, we adopt human-oriented design to satisfy people's demands for shopping and leisure.

5. The central chamber is located on the moutainside where we can overlook the whole central landscape, which is merged into surrounding hills.

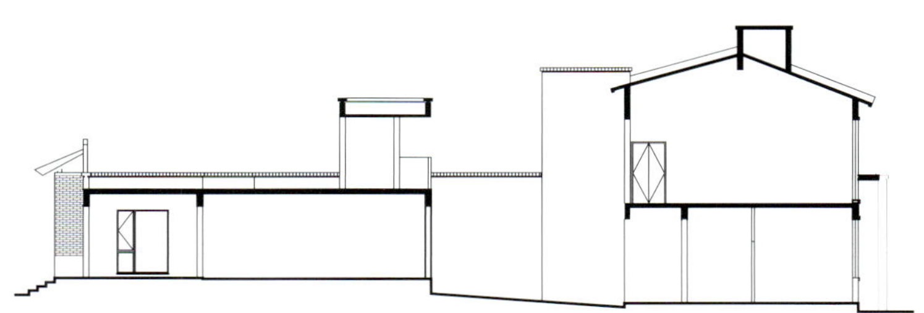

Beijing Konggang MAX Enterprise Park

北京空港MAX企业园

设计单位：东方华太建筑设计工程有限责任公司/美国Perking Well
建筑面积：196 806.19 m²
建筑密度：27.9%
容积率：1.242
绿地率：15%
绿化面积：16 891.35 m²

Design firm: Sino-Sun Architects & Engineers Company/America Perking Well
Building area: 196 806.19 m²

创造一个有生气、可变化的社区：随着现代工业与科技的不断发展，工业社区的发展与变化是不可避免的。所以，在本社区中，通过精心设计一个可以不断叠加的“企业独栋”母体，使其可以随着企业需求的变化而发展。在总图设计上，亦为未来的生长与变化预留了空间。充分利用自然风雨阳光，营造一个绿色社区：为了使每个员工都有良好的朝向与自然光，每个独栋都采用了倾斜30°角的总图布局。同时，在冬季风入园的西北边采用较为密集的布置，可遮挡寒冷的冬季风。而在夏季入园的东南边，采用疏朗的布局，可导入凉爽的夏季风。通过精心布置的道路系统，使各个“企业独栋”都有自己的“地址”、“可识别性”和独立的入口；园区内环路的选位照顾到了内、外两区各“独栋”的入口需要，也使各企业独栋有了自己的“X路XX号”的独栋地址。环路使初次来访者在错失了某企业入口后，可以方便地“环”回来。同时，环路还创造了一个不受干扰的内部绿园。提供一个方便、有效、便于识别的地下停车系统：地下停车“环”地上环路而建，沿道路停车，从而使各企业独栋都有“自己”的、近便的停车区。几个有韵律下沉的绿化庭院，为其提供了自然光和绿色，提高了可识别性。各企业独栋的立面设计采用模数化、母度化的合成面板与玻璃幕墙系统，通过其质感（纹理、光色）、色彩与透明度使不同企业具有不同的个性。各企业独栋的入口则可根据其性质（IT\化工……）进行个性化设计。用适当的建筑语言为园区创造视觉形象：工业化、简洁、高效的外墙模板系统符合空港工业区的个性。体块化的配套用房与独栋反映其高效的内部功能。通过不同的组合，营造出园区高效率、生机勃勃的氛围。采用集中与分散相结合的原则，在各企业独栋周边形成绿园，而中心集中绿化系统则通过贯穿东西的集中绿化与组团间的铺地相穿插，达到使用与观赏相结合的效果。

为了改变以往企业园区呆板、机械的形象，本项目选用新型的Terracoda挂背防水系统。由于瓷板为传统手工建材之一，具有可能性与亲人感，而机制的长条型陶板又具有机械加工、大规模生产的现代工业感，从而使园区的建筑达到亲切、生动的人文感与欣欣向荣的现代工业感。U玻具有传统手工玻璃的质感，而机械制造的长形U玻在重复使用后，又产生了现代工业化的集成感，再加上U玻的丰通透，如传统商航的采光性，为室内提供一种温和的企业环境，亦为建筑营造出一种全新的建筑形象。

To create a lively and changeable community: because of the continuous development of industry, science and technology, the development and change of industrial community are inevitable. So in this community, we design one matrix of "detached building of corporation" that could be added continuously and change with the corporation's development. In the layout of master plan, we set up the space for company's future growth.

We create one green community by using natural wind, rain and sunlight: in order to provide every worker with good direction and natural light, every single matrix adopts the layout of inclining 30 degree. At the same time, we adopt the dense layout in the northwest where the winter wind enters, so the winter wind could be kept out. In the southeast, we adopt the open plan for introducing the cool summer wind.

According to the efficient and elaborate road system, every detached building has their own "location", "ID"and single entrance: the location of the circle road in the park considers the entrance demands of the single buildings in the district bath inside and outside, making every building own the location of "number xx, x road". The circle road makes visitors come back conveniently to find the company again after leaving it. Simultaneously, the circle road creates one inner green garden which couldn't be disturbed easily.

We supply one underground parking system which is convenient, efficient and could be discriminated easily: the parking area is followed by the circle road of the ground; the cars are parked along the roads, so every company has their own close parking area. Several sunken green yards with rhythm, supply natural light and green landscape for the parking area, so as to enhance the identification. According to texture, colors and transparency, the facades of buildings adopt the compound panels and glass curtain wall system with module and matrix, showing different personalities.

The entrance of every company has individual design along their different characters (IT/chemistry). We create the vision form by using suitable architectural languages: industrial, simple and high efficient module systems of exterior walls correspondent with the personalities of the airport industrial districts. The box buildings and single houses reflect the interior functions with high efficiency. According to different combination, we create the lively and efficient atmosphere. We adopt the correlated regulation of centralization and dispersion to form the green gardens around detached building. The central green system gets the effect of correlation of usage and landscape with the centralized green land from east to west and the intercrossing ground in the clusters.

In order to change the stiff and mechanical appearance, this project chooses

Terracoda —a new system of waterproof. There are two main materials in this building: china panel and pottery panel. As one of the traditional craft materials, china panel has the character of kindness. The long pottery produced by machine shows the feeling of modern industry. Decorated by these two different materials, the buildings express two different feelings. U-Profile-Glass shows the character of hand-made glass, and the repetition of the long U-Profile-Glass of mass production produces the feeling of modern industry. In addition, the transparency character of U-Profile-Glass supplies a warm interior atmosphere creates one new architectural form.

Haikexing Returned Overseas Students Industrial Park. Shenzhen

深圳市海科兴留学生产业园

设计单位：深圳市同济人建筑设计有限公司
设计师：叶宇同、张凌飞、吴诗杰、樊晓文
投标时间：2009年06月

Design firm: Tongji Architects Co.,ltd. Shenzhen
Designer: Ye Yutong, Zhang Lingfei, Wu Sijie, Fan Xiaowen
Design date: 2009.6

场地概述

深圳市海科兴留学生产业园，由深圳市海科兴留学生产业基地投资有限公司开发建设。项目总用地面积为10.6万平方米，位于龙港区坪山街道六联社区。南临宝龙工业城，北临宝山第三工业区，西临宝山路（规划），东临创业路（规划），呈不规则的7字形，由相连但产权独立的6.4万平方米和4.2万平方米两块地构成。本设计为一期用地范围，面积为6.4万平方米。基地西临宝山路（规划），东临创业路（规划），车行、人行及市政管线主要从宝山路引入。场地地形相对平坦，自然标高在41.67–56.80之间，南高北低，除西南和东南角局部高差较大外，大部分场地高差有2米。

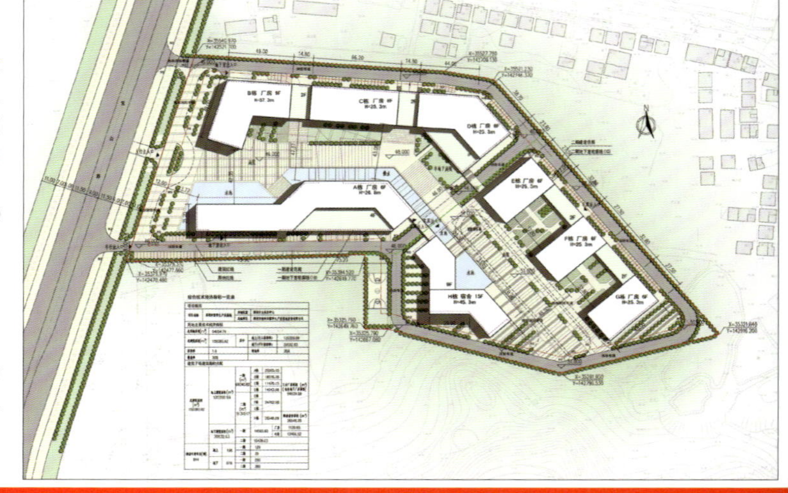

规划设计

1．设计构思

本设计力图营造在城市喧嚣背景下创造一个相对安静独立的学术、产业、文化交流场所，倡导人文传统的合作与交流，打造开放的人性化交流空间，营造高品质的厂房生活园区。

Ye Yutong, Zhang Lingfei, Tan Hui, Wu Shijie, Li Renda, Fan Xiaowen
Tongji Architects Co.,ltd. Shenzhen

叶宇同、张凌飞、谭辉、吴诗杰、李任达、樊晓文
深圳市同济人建筑设计有限公司

叶宇同 国家一级注册建筑工程师、同济大学建筑系建筑学、工学硕士、香港建筑师学会会员、深圳市同济人建筑设计有限公司总经理、总建筑师。

近年主要作品：深圳香榭里花园、福建石狮服装城、武汉后官湖泛地产规划、东莞华尔登国际大酒店、淘金山湖景花园、南京罗托鲁拉小镇、茵悦之生花园一期、深圳国有免税大厦、重庆华立天地豪园、武汉新地东方花都（原为武汉东方恒星园）、东莞星汇中心等。

张凌飞 国家一级注册建筑工程师、深圳市同济人建筑设计有限公司助理总经理、创作研发部主任。

近年主要作品：深圳香榭丽花园、福建石狮服装城、武汉梁子湖半岛俱乐部、东莞丽江豪园、武汉新地、东方花都（C区）、东莞华尔登国际大酒店、东莞星汇中心、东莞愉景东方威尼斯、深圳可园6–7期、深圳淘金山湖景花园、深圳国有免税大厦等。

谭辉 深圳市同济人建筑设计有限公司 主创设计师

近年主要作品：中航格澜郡二期、东莞茶山镇时代商业中心、成都茂业中心 、成都蜀都城市广场、山西太原茂业中心、深圳市怡化大厦 、惠州东湖路旧改项目等。

吴诗杰　深圳市同济人建筑设计有限公司　建筑师

近年主要作品：江西鹰潭天恒大厦、深圳香蜜湖高尔夫练习场 、海南石梅湾餐饮中心改造项目、深圳虚拟大学园平台大厦等。

李任达　深圳市同济人建筑设计有限公司　建筑师

近年主要作品：东莞茶山美丽湾畔花园、时代商业中心、成都茂业中心、梅林天然气调度大厦、东莞石碣新行政办公大楼。

樊晓文　深圳市同济人建筑设计有限公司　建筑师

近年主要作品：成都蜀都城市广场、深圳梅林天然气生产调度大厦、深圳留学生产业化基地、深圳市龙岗外国语学校、深圳市怡化大厦等。

Ye Yutong, is a first class registered architect with national level, Master of Architectonics and Engineering of Tongji University, member of the Hong Kong Institute of Architects, director and chief architect of Shenzhen Tongji Architecture and Design Limited Company.

In recent years, his major works include:

Shenzhen Xiangxieli Park Residence Community, Fujian Shishi Clothing Business Center, Wuhan Hougong Lake District Planning, Dongguan Wellton International Hotel, Taojin Hill Lake-landscape Park, Nanjing Luolula Village,Yinyue Park (the 1st phase), Chongqing Huali Tiandi Park, Wuhan Xindi East Park, Dongguan Xinghui Center, etc.

Zhang Lingfei, is a first class registered architect, assistant director of Shenzhen TongJi Architecture and Design Limited Company.

In recent years, his major works include:

Shenzhen Xiangxieli Park Residence Community, Wuhan Liangzi Lake Island Club, Wuhan Xindi East Park, Dongguan Wellton International Hotel, Dongguan Xinghui Center, 2nd prize of engineering survey and design of quality in Dongguan, Dongguan Yujing East Venice, Taojin Hill Lake-landscape Park, Shenzhen Dutyfree Building, etc.

2. 规划结构设计

园区主要功能为工业厂房和配套宿舍。是一个功能齐全、品质高尚的现代化高新技术园区。设计在分析了项目特质的基础上，把握以人为本，以入驻企业为本，创造合理功能布局的前提条件，对规划结构进行合理分区，并通过对未来项目操作的研究得出将地块进行分期开发的规划策略。园区道路沿红线布置，地块转折处一条道路将园区分成两个主要部分，靠近宝山路的地块主要为生产厂房片区，第二个地块为厂房及配套宿舍区。园区功能分区明确，结构清晰，力图创造一个功能设施一体化的高档型科技生活园区。

3. 场地景观设计

场地设计中充分考虑基地现状条件，结合南面山体，布置丰富的景观空间。园区内室外场地基本平整。建筑沿用地红线两边布置，中间形成纵深式景观广场。广场由宝山路园区入口延伸至南面山体，将人流自然地引入其中，并沿着广场向园区内部前进。广场中心布置条状与点状式相结合的景观水系，结合部分景观绿化，形成供人们休息纳凉的绿轴，并自然地将广场分成两个部分，丰富了广场空间，个性化园区景观氛围，使自然景观与人造景观交相辉映，相得益彰。

4. 规划空间设计

在对园区空间感受的营造中，我们除了对场地设计精心研究以外，还充分探索了不同建筑组团的围合形成的空间形态对人们行为活动的影响。在初始的规划设计中，建筑物基本沿红线两侧平行布置，于是形成了内部线状的广场空间，将人们从宝山路顺引到南面山体。入口处精密的厂房是整个园区的形象中心，其周边保留相对开放和独立的小广场，形成人流聚集和引导性的场所。进入园区，中心绿轴式的广场空间开阔舒适，人们通过其中可方便地到达各栋建筑，形成交通休闲一体化空间。在建筑高度的设计上，考虑到宝山路为城市主干道，又是整个园区的主要出入口，沿宝山路的建筑高度相应较高，形成整个园区的形象展示面。进入园区，建筑高度相应降低，退让山势，保留大量的自然景观可视面，并结合广场景观设计将南面山体的自然风光引入园区。二期宿舍周边布置大量的绿化和广场，为生活在园区的人们提供丰富的休闲和活动平台。

5. 规划流线设计

设计中充分考虑人车分流。车行流线沿基地外环绕整个园区，车辆可方便停靠在路边的停车位上，并可方便通过道路旁的地下室出入口进入地下停车场。人行流线在建筑围合的线性空间内引导。人们即可选择拥有丰富景观的中间庭院露天穿行，体会高尚的环境品质，也可在建筑架空骑楼下休闲散步，享受建筑下的阴凉。

建筑设计

设计原则：简洁大方的形态空间，流畅稳重的立面造型，开放舒适的交流场所，建筑形体设计力求打造一种学院化，活泼律动的建筑意向；庭院化布局，为各种产业项目提供交流平台，实现功能的开放性和技术上的共享性；设计为岭南建筑风格，适应深圳亚热带气候。各建筑单体底层局部架空，树立开放的入口形象，给予来往行人明确的入口引导。架空层相互联系，成为人们步行的绝佳场所。建筑形体力求简洁，内部交通组织流畅，建筑立面采用小开窗设计，墙面贴深灰色面砖，局部设置遮阳百叶，色彩搭配庄重，高雅，使建筑充满了文化与科技的信息。

Tanhui is the chief designer of Shenzhen Tongjiren Archirecture and Design Limited Company. In recent years, his major works include:
Zhonghang Gelanjun (2nd phase)
Dongguan Chashan Times Commercial Center
Chengdu Trade Center
Chengdu City Square
Shanxi Taiyuan Trade Center
Shenzhen Yihua Mansion
Huizhou East Lake Road Renovation Program

Wu Shijie is an architect of Shenzhen Tongjiren Archirecture and Design Limited Company. In recent years, his major works include:
Jiangxi Yingtan Tianheng Mansion
Shenzhen Xiangmihu Golf Court
Hainan Shimeiwan Catering Center Renovation Program
Shenzhen Virtual College Park Terrace Mansion

Li Renda is an architect of Shenzhen Tongjiren Archirecture and Design Limited Company. In recent years, his major works include:
Dongguan Chashan Beautiful Bayside Garden
Dongguan Chashan Times Commercial Center
Chengdu Trade Center
Meilin Gas Deployment Mansion
Dongguan Shijie New Administration Office Building

Fan Xiaowen is an architect of Shenzhen Tongjiren Archirecture and Design Limited Company. In recent years, his major works include:
Chengdu City Square
Shenzhen Meilin Gas Production Deployment Mansion
Shenzhen Oversea Students' Industrial Base
Shenzhen Longgang Foreign School
Shenzhen Yihua Mansion

(Site Outlines)

Returned students industrail park of Shenzhen Haikexing is developed and constructed by Shenzhen Haikexing based investment Co.,Ltd. The project located in six joint community of Pingshan street in Longgang county. it is south to Baolong Industrial City, north to the third Baoshan Industrial Zone, west of Baoshan Road (Planning), east to business Road (Planning) and shaped as 7 irregular, comprising the connected, but independent of 64,000 square meters of property rights and 4.2 million square meters of two cases. This design is a land area of 64,000 square metres. It faces Baoshan Road (planning) in the west and Chuangye Road in the east (planning). Roadway, footway and municipal pipelines are mainly led from Baoshan Road. The terrain is relatively plain, with an elevation between 41.67 to 56.80 m. The south side is higher than the north. The altitude difference in most area is about 2 m, but in some places in the southwest and southeast it is bigger. .

(Planning And Design)

1) Design Concept

The design seeks to under the noisy city background create a relatively quite and independent academic, industrial and cultural place where we can promote the cooperation and exchange of humanities, create open and human-oriented communication space and form high-quality life in plants.

2) Planning Structure Design

The main function of the park is for industrial plant and supporting dormitory. It's a fully functional, high quality, modern high-tech park. On the basis of the characteristics of the project, the design divides the preconditions of people first, assigned companies first and proper function layout. And it draws up the planning strategy of development by stages after it studies the operation of future projects. The roads in the turning point of the lots divides it into two main parts: one near to the Baoshan Road is mainly the production area, while the other plants and mating dormitories. With definite function division and clear structure, the park seeks to create a first-class high-tech park and facility.

3) Landscape Design Site

The site planning creates profound landscape after the full consideration of the current base conditions and southern mountains. The park area is basically level both inside and outside. The construction land, with red lines on both sides, forms deep landscape square in the middle. Extending from the entrance in the Baoshan Road to the southern mountains, the square natually leads people to flow forward into the inner parts along the square. With the striped and punctiform waterscape in the center, the square becomes the green axis for people's rest. At the same time, it natually divides the square into two parts, enriching the square space, individualizing the atmosphere in the park, and enhancing both the beauty of natural scape and artificial scape.

4) Planning Space Design

Experience in the building of the park space, in addition to careful study of the site design, it also fully explored different architectural tour of the enclosed form of spatial form on people's behavior activities. In the initial planning and design of buildings on both sides of the basic parallel arrangement along the red line, then formed a square within the linear space, which will lead people to the south from the Baoshan along the mountain. Precision factory park entrance is the image of the entire center whose surrounding area to retain a relatively open and independent small square to form a crowd gathered and the leading place. Entering into the park, the center axis of the square formed a comfortable green open space where people can easily reach each architecture, forming of integrated transport recreational space. In the height of the building design, taking into account the Baoshan urban trunk road is the park's main entrance along the building height of the corresponding higher Baoshan Road, forming the image of the entire display surface park. Into the park, the building height lower accordinglyand yield of the mountain, retaining a large number of natural landscape visual surface, and landscape design to combine Square south mountain scenery into park. Two quarters arranged around a lot of green and square, for the people living in the park provides a wealth of leisure and activities of the platform.

5) Streamline Design Planning

Take full account of people and vehicles 'shunting in the design. Dealers flow line along the base of the outer ring around the entire park, the vehicle can be easily parked on the roadside parking spaces, and can facilitate the passage of the road next to the basement entrance into the underground car park. Pedestrian flow line enclosed in the building tour guide linear space. People can not only choose to have a rich open-air courtyard in the middle of walking through the landscape and understand the noble quality of the environment, but also can take a walk on the elevated balcony and enjoy the shade under construction.

Architectural Design

Design principles: Simple form of generous space, smooth facades and prudent style, open communication and comfortable place.

Strive to create a kind of architectural form College of Design and the lively rhythm of construction intentions; courtyard of the layout of projects for various industries provide a platform to achieve functional openness and the sharing of technology; It's a Lingnan architectural style in order to adapt to the Shenzhen sub-tropical climate. The single floor building local overhead and the Opening of the entrance of the image, to give a clear entrance from the pedestrian guidance. Elevated levels interrelated, which become an excellent place to walk. Building physical concise, smooth internal traffic organization, building facade design with small windows, dark gray brick wall stickers, and set the shutter of local color with solemn, elegant, all of these make the aichitecture full of culture and technology information.

Chengdu Maoye Centre

成都茂业中心

设计单位：深圳市同济人建筑设计有限公司
设计师：张凌飞、谭辉、李任达
基地面积：273 000 m²
建筑面积：339 000 m²

Design firm: Tongji Architects Co.,ltd. Shenzhen
Designer: Zhang Lingfei, Tan Hui, Li Renda
Site area: 273 000 m²
Building area: 339 000 m²

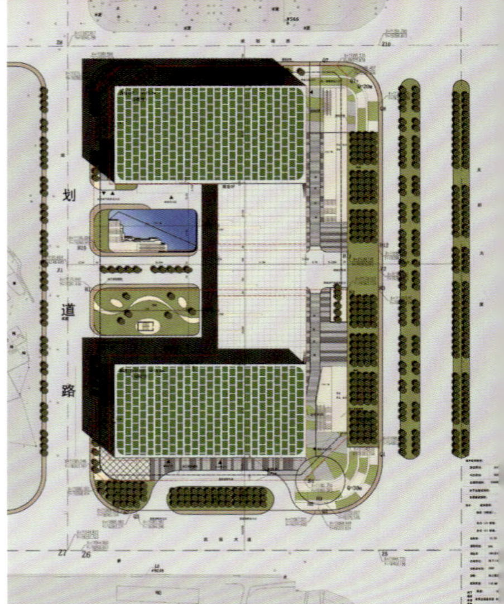

项目位于成都市高新区，天府大道与武侯大道的交汇处，地理位置十分优越。总用地面积273 000平方米，总建筑面积339 000平方米。

由于用地分南北两部分，两者之间是消防路，因此形成了两塔一裙房的规划概念。

成都茂业中心包括地下3层，地上35层，总高度119.8米，包括4层商业裙房，AB塔楼（公寓、办公），C塔楼（高级办公）。

成都茂业中心采用现代简约风格，整栋大楼分南北两塔，利用灯带围绕整栋大楼，使两塔楼形成一个有机的整体，而不是单纯的几何图形，并且裙房紧接塔楼采用全幕墙形式，不仅体现出内部缤纷的商业世界，更给人拔地而起的气势。塔楼南北立面高宽比例约为2米，形体方正，因此在塔楼的南北立面上采用凹凸窗上下错位的形式，并配以不同质感的玻璃，形成棋格的效果，寓意"棋"开得胜。

Project is located in Chengdu,on the fluence of tianfu road and wuhou road. The geographical position is quite exceptional. Area of ground is 273 000 square meters, and area of building 339 000 square metres.

Because the fire protection road departs the site into two parts, so we use the planning concepts of two towers into a skirt.

Chengdu Maoye Centre includes 3 floors underground and 35 floors, with height of 119.8 meters. It includes business for 4 floors, the tower AB(condominiums, offices) and the tower C (office).

Chengdu Maoye Centre uses the modern economical style. The whole building includes south tower and north tower. With light belts circling around the whole building, it makes the two towers an organic whole instead of simple geometrical figure. Annex close to the tower uses full curtain wall, displaying colouful commercial world and up-going vigour.

The physique of the tower looks upright and foursquare, with its South and North elevations' height-width ratio to be around 2. Therefore, the south and north elevations will be decorated with concave-convex windows and different kinds of glass to create the visual effect like a chequered plate, which symbolizes sweeping victories in Chinese.

Shenzhen Literature & Art Center

深圳文学艺术中心

设计单位：朱锫建筑设计事务所
主设计师：朱锫
建筑用地面积：9 999.65 m^2
总建筑面积：62 200 m^2
建筑密度：52.1%
容积率：4.3
绿地率：40%

Design firm: Studio Pei-Zhu
Lead designer: Zhu Pei
Site area: 9 999.65 m^2
Building area: 62 200 m^2
Volume fraction: 4.3

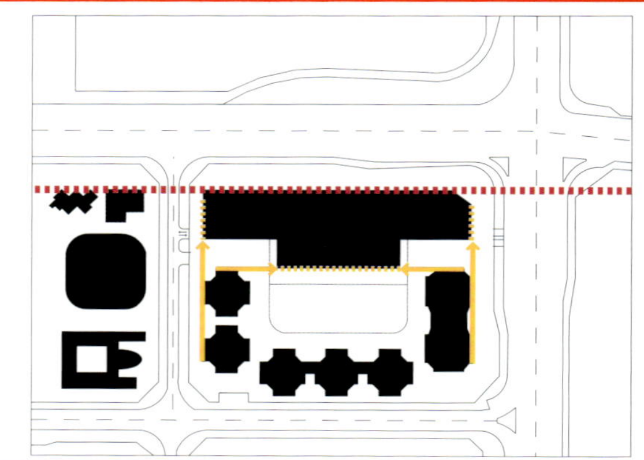

Zhu Pei
Studio Pei-Zhu

朱锫
朱锫建筑设计事务所

学历
1988 清华大学建筑学硕士
1995 美国伯克利大学建筑与城市设计硕士

获奖
2007 “全球设计先锋”，美国
2006 “中国建筑奖”，美国
2005 “WA中国建筑奖”，中国
2004 “中国建筑艺术奖”，中国

展览
2008 德国德累斯顿，活着的中国园林—幻象到现实
2008 巴黎，中国建筑展
2008 巴塞罗那，中国建筑展
2008 英国维多利亚博物馆，创意中国展
2007 奥地利，中国制造展
2006 第一届西班牙加纳利艺术·景观·建筑双年展（与雷姆·库哈斯、MVRDV共同参与）
2006 荷兰中国当代建筑展
2006 中国建筑艺术双年展
2005 巴西圣保罗双年展
2003 法国蓬皮杜中国建筑艺术展

项目与竞赛
2007 被古根海姆基金会选为北京古根海姆博物馆设计师
2007 被古根海姆基金会选为阿布扎比古根海姆艺术馆设计师
2007 艺术家蔡国强的工作室及住所
2007 艺术家岳敏君的美术馆
2004 数字北京大厦（奥运项目） 获国际设计竞赛一等奖

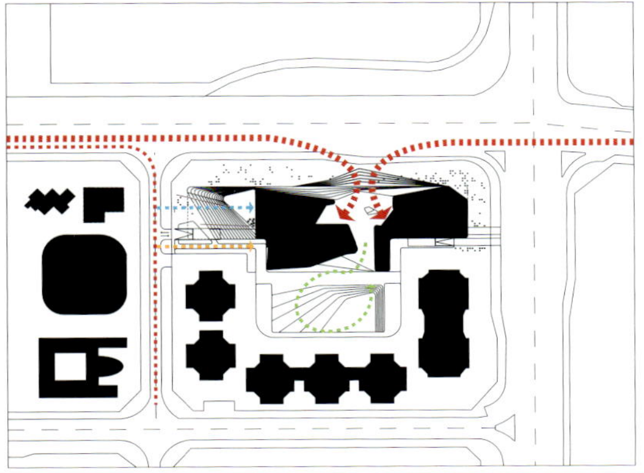

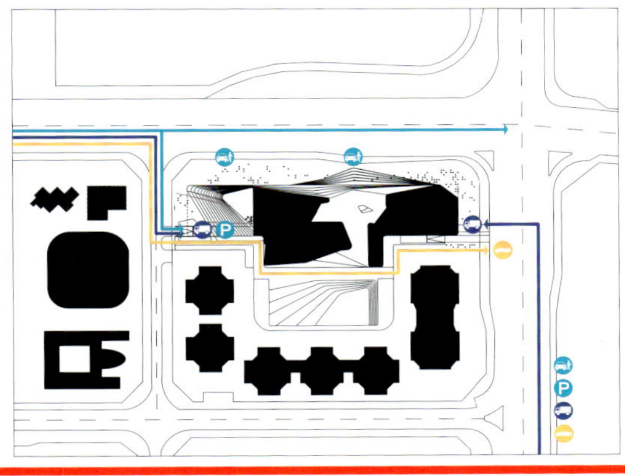

Education

Master of Architecture, Tsinghua University

Master of Architecture & Urban design, UC Berkeley

Awards

2007 Design Vanguard, Architectural Record

2006 China Award, Architectural Record

2004 WA China Architectural Prize

2003 China Architectural Arts Award

1989 Award of Special Merit from UNESCO

Exhibition

2008 Chinese Gardens for Living - illusion into reality, Dresden, Germany

2008 Solo exhibition RISD, University of Rhode Island, N.Y.

2008 China Construction, Cooper-Hewitt National Design Museum, N.Y.

2008 Exhibition of Chinese Contempory Architecture, Paris

2008 Exhibition of Chinese Contempory Architecture, Barcelona

2008 China Design Now, Victoria and Albert Museum, UK

2007 China Production, Austria

2007 Xisi Bei International Invitation Exhibition, China

2006 1st Biennale of the Architecture and Art of the Canary Islands, Spain (participated together with Rem Koolhaas and MVRDV)

2006 Chinese contemporary architecture, Rotterdam

2006 Biennial Beijing, Beijing

2005 Biennial Sao Paulo , Sao Paulo

2005 U space Art exhibition, Beijing

2004 8 Chinese Young Architects, Beijing

2003 Alors, la Chine?, Centre Pompidou, Paris

Projects & competitions

2007 Guggenheim museum Beijing, for Guggenheim Foundation

2007 Guggenheim Art Pavilion Abu Dhabi, for Guggenheim Foundation

2007 Courtyard House Renovation for artist Cai Guoqiang

2007 Art Museum for artist Yue Minjun

2004 Digital Beijing, an Olympic project for 2008, Beijing, won the first prize in national design competition

城市

深圳文学艺术中心位于深圳中心区东侧，莲花山城市公园南侧。由于基地周边区域的特殊性，我们认为建筑的主要城市特征应取决于北边和西边城市界面的影响。因此我们在建筑的北侧立面构思了一个贯穿南北的多层城市空间，即“城市舞台”。它是建筑功能的核心，有效地将各个功能区连贯为一体。建筑西端塑造了向城市中心开启的“城市之窗”和半下沉的广场艺术空间，以寻求和城市中心区及莲花山城市公园的呼应关系。

地段南侧三面高达百米的深色塔楼为建筑基地构筑了一幅复杂沉重的城市背景。我们反其道而行之，构思了一个简洁的、近乎于白色的具有很强的雕塑感的建筑，它简约、明确、肯定的水平向体量横贯地段东西，好似中国传统绘画中写意的一笔，在繁乱复杂的城市背景中脱颖而出。

沿城市主干道的步行人流借助建筑北面略微内凹的阶梯缓缓进入。城市人流定义了建筑西翼的悬挑，以强调其对城市中心的指向性。视觉景观的通透将莲花山、文学艺术中心与中银花园南北串连，为室外休憩空间提供指引。同样的通透又使城市舞台向更高更远处伸展，将人们引向高处楼层和地下空间。

贯通建筑南北的穿越式空间 ——“城市舞台”为该建筑的中心，与正常建筑思考不同，这个空间不是正，而是负，不是实，而是空，“空”是一切，而不是无，是无穷大。一切城市活动均可能发生在这个无限的空间之中。这个“城市舞台”是一种城市态度，一个宣言，它向人们宣告了城市文化应该是透明的、大众的、充满诗意的、艺术精神的文化。

这个“空”又是城市空间的延伸，因为有了这个空间，中银花园不再是私家绿地，它成为城市公共空间的一部分。一个可供人们休闲、欣赏艺术的内院、广场。公众可以自由穿越这个“城市舞台”而步入北侧和西侧的街道、广场、绿地、公园。公众不仅是观看者，同时又是被观看者、城市舞台的表演者。从而实现城市、建筑、艺术、公众之间的交流融合。文学艺术中心是一个充斥着目光、感受和交流分享经验的场所。城市肌理、建筑、艺术和公众在这里融合，建筑的力量和感染力也由此产生。

功能联系和城市舞台

功能排布的设计目标是构筑一种诗意的空间氛围，为艺术和想法间的沟通提供可能。

“城市舞台”空间既是整个建筑人流的汇聚中心，又是公众进入该建筑的起点和终点。该空间的形式灵感来源于自然山岩洞体，人类文明中最早的绘画和文字却诞生于岩洞之中。这种自然、流动的空间概念语言被贯穿在所有内部空间之中。

深圳文学艺术中心的功能概括来讲是将多种艺术形式融合在一个功能整体内。“市民的参与”是将此复杂的功能综合体联系在一起的设计纽带和原则，也是文学艺术制造者和文学艺术消费者沟通与交流的先决条件。

建筑学强调了多种层面上的沟通。沟通的首要条件是中心流线的布置，它为使用者提供了联系建筑纵向横向多层功能的可能。第二个条件是在同一功能分区的不同使用空间内，它们在排布和空间形态上的不同可能。通过将不同艺术种类型式归统到单个功能体内，在不同功能分区间就形成了多方面的积极的联系。这些联系有内容层面上的，也有形态上的。在功能的实际布置过程中，人的活动跨越了其所属功能分区——“越界”，并实现了最大限度的沟通、互补、加强、激活等。建筑在组织和设计上尊重了各个分区的独立性，但也通过智能感应系统和布局的临近性，实现了它们之间所需的便捷高效的“邻里关系”。

功能技术

目标是为不同的艺术和文学组织提供选择的多样性和多向性。艺术家们在制作艺术作品的同时，也创造了艺术空间。故此，建筑应适应创作活动的需要而灵活设计。

展览功能是文学艺术中心连接各功能分区的纽带，它与交通功能紧密联系，空间形式灵活多变。综合成果展示空间和视觉艺术空间以不同的展览空间形式穿插于建筑内部，它们分别位于建筑首层、二层及地下一层。空间布置从向公共开放到供内部展示，从自然采光到人工照明，从表现主义的空间形式到经典的展览流线，体现了能动的、多样的、适应力强的系列陈列区。他们在设计上力求适应不同文学艺术创作门类和组织的需求。其中，中心展览厅与一部分室外露台相连，为艺术研讨会提供了场所，又可供贵宾使用。

黑匣子剧场位于地下一层，通过门厅与外界相连，门厅与观演空间之间设有检票控制的附属门厅或开敞露台，这样既丰富了观众在这一系列连续功能区间内的空间体验，又满足了安全和控制的建筑要求。

黑匣子剧场是一个内空间相对高以容纳技术设备和灯光设备且布局简单的建筑组件。为了让摄影机等器材不至于被建筑空间所限制，影视工作室也同样具有层高高室内容量大的空间要求。这两种用房的建筑形式有一定的相似性，加之从影剧院技术角度来讲，两者空间设计概

Site Response - Urban Landmark

Shenzhen Literature and Art Center is located directly east of Central Shenzhen and south of the Lotus Mountain Park. Given these site proximities, we believe the major character of the architecture is indicated by the north and west influences of the site. The northern facade is emphasized with the creation of a north-south oriented multi-tiered public space – the Urban Stage. The Urban Stage is the central program element that binds the various roles together into a cohesive Art and Literature Center. The western edge of the site features an elevated cantilever and Urban Window that reaches toward the city center. Beneath the Urban Window is a sunken outdoor space that will be used to exhibit art work while allowing the building to directly respond to the adjacencies of new city center, the Lotus Mountain and the Guanshanyue Art Gallery.

The site is directly north of a dark and heavy cluster of towers which provide a complex and imposing urban backdrop. Our strategy is to contrast the negative context with a simple and tranquil white entity. The serene object has a strong sculptural feature which is at once both precise and eloquent. The building's dominant horizontal formal language extends from west to east across the site, reminiscent of a strip of traditional Chinese ink painting.

The urban flow of pedestrians along the street level pushes the north facade in towards the site for a gentle approach. The urban flow also lifts the cantilever to gesture towards the city center. The nature flow from the Lotus Mountain Park through the Literature and Art Center to the Zhongyin Park connects people with the outdoors and relaxation. The nature flow expands the urban stage outward from the center and connects people to the earth and the sky.

The north-south oriented Urban Stage is the focus for the entire Literature and Art Center. Departing from conventional architectural thinking, the Urban Stage is not a positive space but is in essence a negative one. It is a 'solid' emptiness; it doesn't refer to nothing or absence, but refers to all things and the presence of endless possibilities. Simply stated, the 'emptiness' is an endless infinity, a vast opportunity. The many possibilities of urban activities are "on stage" in this infinite space. The Urban Stage is the reflection of Shenzhen's urban attitude and a declaration for it! It proclaims that the culture of the city should be open, transparent, and democratic. The Urban Stage belongs to the public, It is a place filled with the atmosphere of poetic and artistic culture.

The atmosphere of the Urban Stage becomes an extension of the urban environment. Zhongyin Garden which before was a private green space is transformed into an essential part of the city due to the spatial link with the Urban Stage. People have many opportunities to relax and appreciate art at the Literature and Art Center. The open spaces and the Urban Stage provide easy access for visitors to the building functions as well as maintaining clear links to the streets, squares, gardens, and parks to the north and west. The Literature and Art Center is a place to observe and be observed, to perceive and share experiences. The urban context, architecture, art and public blend

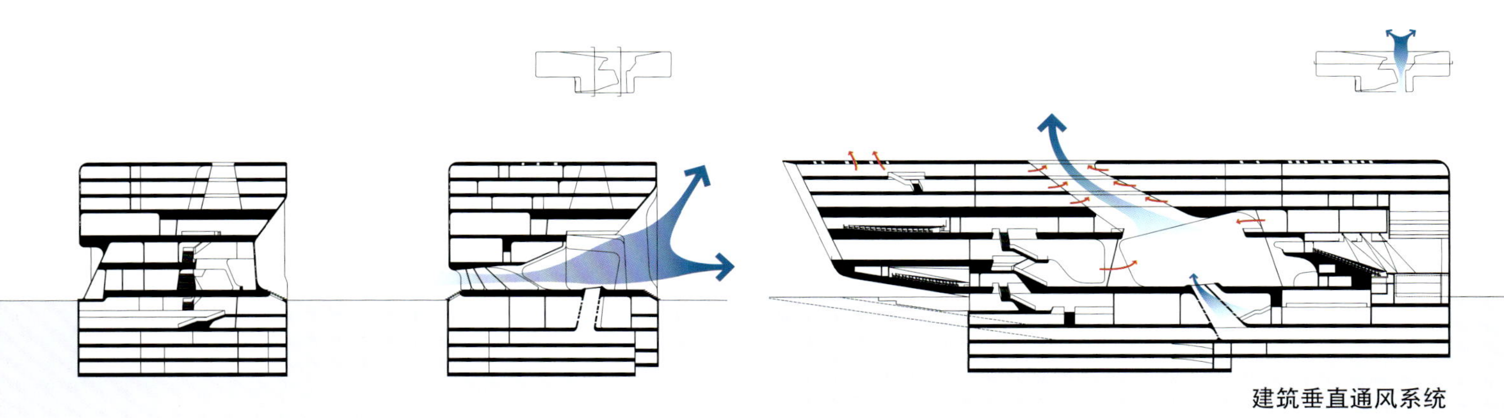

建筑垂直通风系统

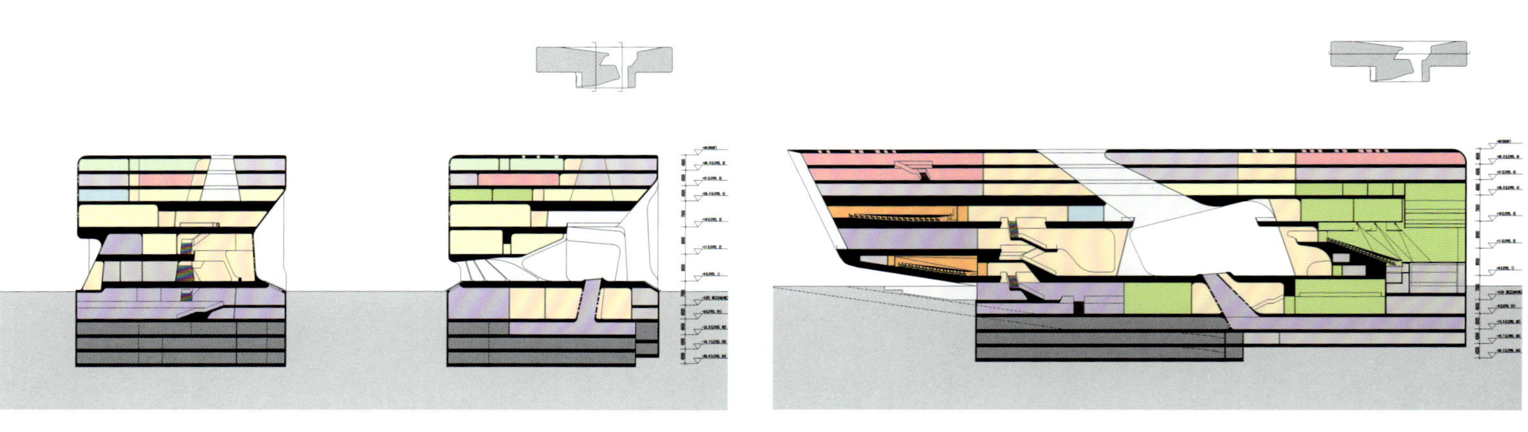

念上的共性也要求他们在空间基本形态上有很大共通性。紧邻的视觉艺术展览空间为空间的灵活利用增添了可能。视觉艺术空间与下沉广场连接。为此，在这个项目中，相邻功能空间的布置使技术流线的性质变得十分关键和高效。

创意剧场是当代建筑设计观念内的视觉艺术剧院，同时也是一个可变的、灵活性强的视觉艺术创意工厂。我们的设计考虑利用前台区域的开敞性，使其具备向观众席延伸并融入观众席的可能，并将前台的体积感降到最低。台口被简洁的幕布和板件所定义，这种台口组成形式在当代演艺空间里被广泛采用，具有一定的趣味和灵活性。此空间能为观众和演出者的视觉和言语交流提供良好的沟通渠道和场所，观众不再是被动地接收和接受艺术信息，而是积极地参与到演艺活动中。

舞台设有侧台可供更换布景之用。部分舞台和左侧台可连通室外装卸载平台，以实现为表演服务的卡车/集装箱的直接快捷抵达。这种做法避免了在建筑内部为观演货运专设一个竖向交通核而造成的室内使用面积的浪费。

另外一个邻近性体现在影视和摄影的后期制作区间和录音及音乐制作工作室的布置。它们两者均要求相似的音效技术及特殊的音效处理机制；其使用者具有相似或相同的技术背景。它们的邻近性是顺应功能需求的体现：在影视和媒体制作中，后期制作和录音室都是必须的环节。

综合多功能厅、排练厅等功能厅位于建筑三层，与贵宾接待区连接。设有观景阳台，从阳台上可以俯观“城市舞台”；这个区域位于建筑中心，是理想的举办会议和小型舞会的场所。

市民文化大讲堂、国际会议中心和会议室与主要艺术展览区域的相邻布置，为来访者提供多种选择和兴趣交流的机会。

图书馆、文学和艺术典藏位于建筑的顶层。这寓意了对知识渴求的无止境和图书馆作为凝聚智慧的场所的“崇高”地位。图书馆的阅览区最大限度地采用天光并借助“城市窗口”联通天际。

艺术创作空间中的作家公寓和艺术家工作室与图书馆相邻布置，以实现入住学者艺术家与其他来访者间的交流和研究。艺术工作室还开有天窗以保证日间充足的自然采光。

为避免大规模的装载和卸载货梯占用过大过高空间，部分地面层空间层高相对较高，特设的地面装卸载区在建筑较低楼层，方便卸货卡车驶入。这样也增加了上层空间的利用率。中心装卸载区服务建筑中部展览区域，视觉艺术空间和影视艺术空间/黑匣子剧场分设单独的装卸载区以适应其独立的功能要求。创意剧场侧台设置直接连通室外的保障高效的货物运输。

绿色建筑

深圳文学艺术中心设计提倡健康与自然和谐统一的艺术创作、学术研究和生活态度。向天空开启的贯穿多层的中庭为营造建筑内部小气候创造了纵向及横向自然通风的条件。中部的公共广场是建筑实现南北通风的场所；而进入“城市舞台”的自然气流被中庭竖向空间自下而上地导向天空，带走建筑多余热量。

整个建筑除了西侧面向城市中心及南侧面向雕塑公园的界面为玻璃幕墙外，其余界面均为实墙。实墙上星星点点的开窗密度和面积与室内空间功能对应，形成的星罗棋布的纹理又恰恰

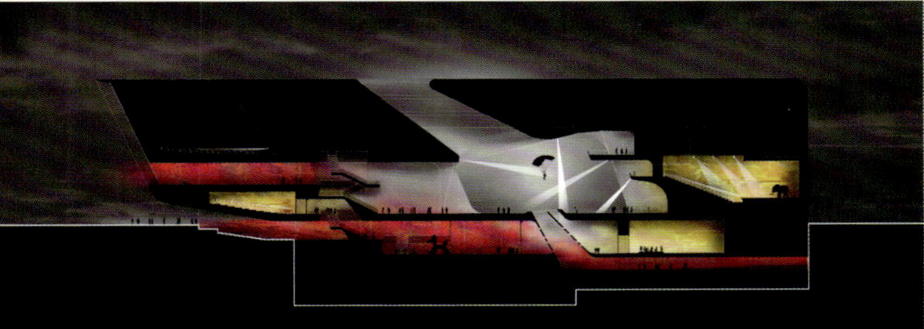

together to create the positive energy of the building. The center has a resemblance to a forward moving boat; the building is a flagship boat on an adventurous expedition towards the impressive future of Shenzhen's literature and art.

Program Connections and Urban Stage

The goal is to form poetic space and architecture for the communication of ideas and art.

The Urban Stage is the central space for people to gather together as well as the starting and ending destination for the public touring through the building. The space's formal language is inspired by the naturally formed caves in the mountainous areas of China that were the origins of the earliest known Chinese drawings and writings. This natural and flexible spatial typology is consistent through the main interior spaces to provide a stimulating and responsive environment for the appreciation of art and literature.

The program of the Shenzhen Literature and Art Center combines several art forms in a single building. The program's intention shows a desire for this building to nature participation – a conscious exchange between producers and consumers of literature and art.

The architecture of the building promotes participation on several levels. The first part of this is the central public circulation (urban stage) that allows people to come in contact with all of the exciting roles of the building. The second part involves the great potential for positive synergies between the various roles. This synergy does not occur only on the level of content, but also in form. There are many programmatic and pragmatic moments in which activities can connect, complement, reinforce, excite, and inform each other beyond the normal limits of their traditional roles. The organization and design of the building respects the autonomy of the various functions but makes it possible, through intelligent sensitivity of natural adjacencies, for each of the pieces to seek and form connections in convenient and flexible methods. The Urban Stage is the central program element that binds the various roles together into a cohesive Art and Literature Center.

Program Technical

The goal is to provide the different art and literature organizations with a range of flexibility and scales. It is expected that the creative groups can reinvent and innovate their space and their use of space. The architecture will be flexible for the creative exploration.

There are various exhibition spaces throughout the building. The range of exhibition spaces ranges from highly public to private, from daylight to darkrooms, and from expressive forms to traditional settings. The design provides a very dynamic grouping of spaces that each can be interpreted and used for different types of expositions as desired by the different literature and art groups. The main exhibition space has an

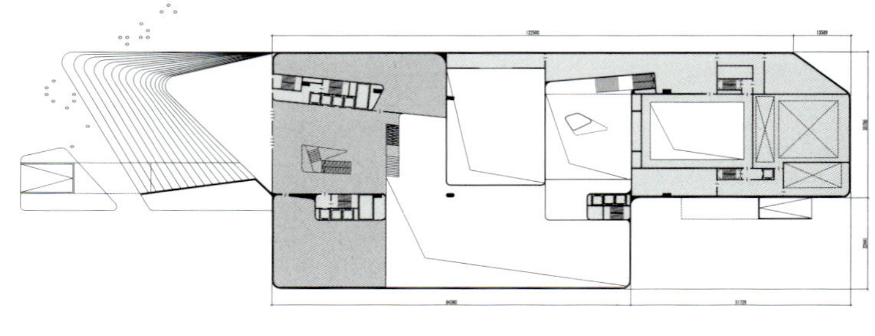

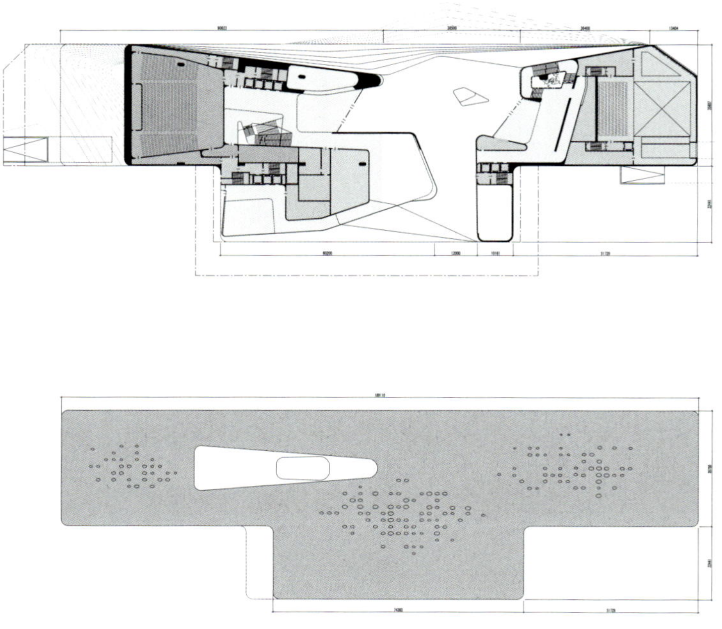

呼应了中国传统文化中的琴棋书画。在建筑立面构成的图案既抽象于水平的书法文字，又酷似进行中的一盘棋。当然，这种窗的图案也同时寓意计算机数字语言，体现了尖端科技在文学艺术创作管理中不可或缺的作用。

概念剖面

深圳文学艺术中心为我们提供了这样一种独特的聚会与交流场所……

周五晚上的艺术沙龙在中心展览厅里照常进行，专业电影工作者和电影爱好者们齐聚于市民文化大讲堂欣赏精彩的影视讲座，创意剧场内粤剧名伶刚刚开唱，与观众高度互动的多媒体展览在视觉艺术画廊和电影制作工厂同时上演，人们流连于设计师命名的商店，一个本土摇滚预演正在黑匣子剧场进行。城市舞台将这些精彩点滴汇聚一齐，人们在这里分享交换各自对生活对艺术对创作的激情和理想。

周日的午后，深圳文学艺术中心成为了家庭和来访者休闲和聚会的去处。一个为孩子安排的即兴演出激活了下沉庭院的气氛，视觉艺术未画廊和中心展览厅内聚集了艺术发烧友，市民文化大讲堂呈现着关于中国书法历史溯源的讲座，到访者在图书馆里遨游于典籍的海洋，一个实验式舞蹈组合在黑匣子剧场上演他们的第一次演出，人们在设计店铺里购买心仪的艺术作品，可别忘了钢琴演奏会正在创意剧场里进行！城市舞台将这些精彩点滴汇聚一齐，人们在这里分享交换各自对生活、对艺术、对创作的激情和理想。

深圳文学艺术中心即使在工作日也是散发艺术光热的能量体，研究工作者在图书馆里交流，艺术家和作家们在他们的工作室和沙龙内里进行创作，国际会议厅举办了一场关于艺术教育的国际研讨会，深圳本土文学运动的学术交流会在市民文化大讲堂里进行，视觉艺术画廊和中心展览厅合作举办中国雕塑的回顾展，员工们在紧锣密鼓的筹备下一届文学和艺术双年展。城市舞台将这些精彩点滴汇聚一齐，人们在这分享交换各自对生活对艺术对创作的激情和理想。

小结

深圳文学艺术中心将成为深圳城市文化的标志。它是深圳独特的文化交流空间及艺术思想的传播平台。我们的创作目标是营造一个文学艺术交流殿堂，它同时也是市民共享深厚文化盛宴的场所。它也像是一艘航空母舰，载着深圳人对文化艺术的梦想与渴望，远航！

attached outdoor balcony convenient for art openings and VIP use.

Access to the Black Box Theater and Main Theater is gained by moving from the public performing arts lobby and into a ticket-controlled secondary lobby or balcony. This maintains the sequential experience of moving through the dynamic space while also preserving security and control.

At level B1, The black box theater is a large, tall, and flexible space. The film studio is also large, tall, and flexible in essence. The rooms have an adjacency making technical circulation very practical and efficient. The close proximity also enables the arts organizations to flexibly use either or both rooms for highly adaptable events and exhibitions. The possible program potentials increase greatly with the main Visual Art exhibition spaces directly adjacent to the film studio and black box. The Visual Art space has an independent entry from the Sunken Courtyard.

The Main Theater features a contemporary design without a proscenium. This gives the artistic direction flexibility to extend the stage into the audience for active participation. The proscenium can be added with simple means such as curtains and panels. In addition, the orchestra pit can be set in three positions: stage level for increased performance space, audience level for increased seating capacity, and pit level for musical productions. This flexibility provides interesting opportunities for avant-garde theater and dance.

Functionally, the stage has side stages for the convenient changing of sets. A strip of the stage-left side stage is a large platform that connects to the loading zone lower in the building for quick and convenient loading of trucks. This solution avoids putting in a separate elevator core in the building that would potentially take valuable area away from the backstage zone.

The positioning of the post-production suites for Film and Photography close to the music/recording studios and also demonstrates a instance for collaboration. Both programs make use of similar technologies, both need special acoustical considerations, both use staff with similar backgrounds. Their adjacency is more than natural.

The Multifunctional Hall is located on level 3 with direct access to private prefunction space, vip areas, and balconies overlooking the Urban Stage. The location is ideal for private meetings or banquets within the heart of the building.

The Citizen's auditorium, Congress Center and meeting rooms are concentrated with close proximity to the main art exhibition space to provide opportunities for cross-interest between visitors.

The library, literature and art archives are located at the top of the building. As a metaphor to the quest for knowledge, the library is a beacon of wisdom from the top of the center. The library and reading rooms are located to provide maximum natural lighting from skylights and access to the Urban Window.

The residential apartments, literature creation spaces, and art studios are located adjacent to the library for ease of research and intellectual discussion between the in-house residents and visitors. The art studios have direct access to daylighting though skylights.

To avoid massive loading elevators throughout the building, some of the spaces needing relatively tall ceilings and specialized loading are placed at the lower levels, where the trucks arrive. This way, it is easier to optimize the space in the upper levels. There is a central loading dock for the main building. There are separate loading docks for both the Visual Arts program and the Film Studio/Black Box Theater program. This allows for secure loading for these programmatically independent spaces. The main theater has direct street level access to the side stage for secure and efficient transport.

Green Strategy, Pattern

The Shenzhen Literature and Art center also contributes to a healthy and natural lifestyle by using green technologies and an effective energy use scheme. Rainwater and gray water collection is integrated into the building as a valuable water recycling and management method. High-efficiency LED lighting and occupancy sensors will minimize energy waste in the building. The building construction will emphasize recycled content and high-quality materials. The central sky opening utilizes natural stack ventilation. In conjunction with solar fans on the roof, the opening will pull fresh air from the Urban Stage up and through the entire building. This ventilation and natural light penetrates deep into the building and connects the people with a healthy green lifestyle.

While there are portions along the western and southern facades which are partially glass curtain walls, the rest of the building envelope is a solid wall with windows placed in a programmatically responsive pattern. Photovoltaic panels are integrated into the façade pattern and on the roof at locations to optimize functionality. The inspiration for the formal/graphic language of the varied size openings originates in specific Chinese traditions and cultural activities. In Chinese philosophy art is not the final goal; art is a process to personal refinement and growth. Ancient music instruments, chess playing, calligraphy and ink painting are all methods of artistic refinement of character. The window openings and window densities are placed according to the needs of the program with no excess, but the logic of the patterns is informed not only by the abstract form of horizontally written Chinese characters, but also as an ongoing intellectually refining game of chess. The Literature and Art Center is a hub for communication and sharing of ideas, the window patterns can also be interpreted as representations of modern digital language.

Concept Sections

The building is alive with activities 24 hours a day, 7 days a week!

A typical Friday evening could have an art opening in the main exhibition gallery, a film lecture in the Citizen's Auditorium, a Peking Opera production in the Main Theater, an interactive media exhibition in the Visual Art Gallery and Film Studio, shopping in the design store, and a rock concert in the black box theater! The urban stage is the central connection that ties all the activities together. It is where people gather and share their experiences.

On a Sunday afternoon, the Shenzhen Literature and Art Center becomes the destination for families and casual visitors. There is an impromptu performance for children in the sunken courtyard, the Visual Art and Main Exhibition Galleries are full of art enthusiasts, the Citizen's Auditorium presents a lecture about the art origins of Chinese calligraphy, visitors expand their knowledge in the library, an experimental dance group performs in the black box theater, people are buying art in the design store, and a piano recital is occurring in the main theater! The urban stage is the central connection that ties all the activities together. It is where people gather and share their experiences.

Summary

The Shenzhen Literature and Art Center will be a cultural and urban landmark for Shenzhen. The center will be Shenzhen's platform for allowing communication and collaborations between different cultural activities and ideologies. The center has a resemblance to a forward moving boat; the building is a flagship boat on an adventurous expedition towards the impressive future of Shenzhen's literature and art.

Tea Room, Jinhua Architecture Park 5

金华建筑艺术公园5＃茶室

设计单位：成都市家琨建筑设计事务所
设计团队：刘家琨、申捷、汪维
地址：浙江省金华市金东新区
总占地面积：0.88 m²
总建筑面积：96.2 m²
材料：公共市政材料、常用耐用材料、电线杆、抱箍、型钢、钢绞线、钢隔栅、水管、阳光板、铝合金型材

Design firm: Jiakun Architect&Associates
Design team: Liu Jiakun, Shen Jie, Wang Wei
Location: Jinhua, Zhejiang, China
Site area: 0.88 m²
Scale: 96.2 m²

Liu Jiakun
Jiakun Architects &Associates

刘家琨
成都市家琨建筑设计师事务所
主持设计师

刘家琨，成都市家琨建筑设计事务所主持建筑师。主持设计的作品被选送参加德中文化年、法中文化年、荷兰NAI中国当代建筑展、俄中文化年及威尼斯建筑双年展等多个国际展览。曾获得亚洲建协荣誉奖、2003年中国建筑艺术奖、建筑实录中国奖、远东建筑奖、中国建筑学会建筑创作大奖，作品被《a+u》《AV》《area》《MADE IN CHINA》《AR》等出版，并应邀在麻省理工学院、英国皇家艺术学院、巴黎夏佑宫及中国多所大学开办讲座。

主要建筑作品

1. 艺术家工作室系列
2. 红色年代娱乐中心
3. 鹿野苑石刻博物馆
4. 摩托罗拉成都软件中心
5. 四川美术学院雕塑系
6. 上海青浦建设展示中心
7. 四川安仁建川博物馆聚落
8. 中国国际建筑艺术实践展客房中心
9. 广州时代玫瑰园公共空间及景观设计
10. 四川美术学院新校区设计艺术馆
11. 中国当代美术馆群 张晓刚馆
12. 再生砖计划
13. 胡慧姗纪念馆

荣誉

2010年 建筑实录中国奖——最佳公共建筑奖
2010年 建筑实录中国奖——最佳历史保护建筑奖
2009年 中国建筑学会建筑创作大奖
2007年 远东建筑奖
2006年 建筑实录中国奖——最佳公共建筑奖
……

Liu Jiakun works as chief architect of Jiakun Architects Studio. The projects led by him were selected by Chinese Young Architects' Work Exhibition in Germany, Chinese Contemporary Architecture Exhibition in France, NAI China Contemporary, International Architecture Exhibition in Russia, and International Architecture Exhibition in Venice Biennale: Architecture, and many other international exhibitions. He also won the Honor Prize of the 7th ARCASIA, Chinese Architecture Art Prize 2003, China Architectural Record Awards, Far East Awards and Architectural Design Award from Architectural Society of China. The projects have been covered by Publications: A+U, AV, area, MADE IN CHINA, AR, etc. He was invited to give lectures at MIT, Royal Academy of Arts, Palais de Chaillot in Paris and many universities in China.

Major Works

1. Artist Studios Series
2. "The Red Era" Entertainment Center
3. Luyeyuan Stone Sculpture Art Museum
4. Chengdu Motorola Software Center
5. Department of Sculpture of Sichuan Art Institute
6. Shanghai Qingpu Construction Exhibition Center
7. Jianchuan Museum Aggregation in Anren, Sichuan
8. Reception and Dining Center of China International Practical Exhibition of Architecture
9. Guangzhou Time Rose Garden Landscape and Culture Space Design in residential community
10. Design Department on new campus, Sichuan School of Fine Arts
11. The Institutions of Chinart, Zhang Xiaogang Art Gallery
12. "REBIRTH BRICK" PROPOSAL
13. Hu Huishan Memerial House

Honor

Architectural Record China Award, 2010, Best Public Project
Architectural Record China Award, 2010, Best Preservation Project
Far East Award, 2007
Architectural Record China Award, 2006, Best Public Project
...

基地位于大坝之下的低地，大坝之外为广阔的河景。茶室升离地面以获得视野和风，成为休憩饮茶时的基本愿望。以轻盈对应体量厚重的大坝，相互衬托，相得益彰。升起、风、视野、轻盈构成方案的基本意向。
化整为零，减小体量——以集群为形象特征，以独立性为使用特征。
电线杆用作柱子；电杆配件组装钢平台；槽钢用作吐水槽——公共市政材料构成材料主题。
窗扇机械制动，自由开合；门利用重力，自动关闭；上水管兼栏杆扶手；推拉台/门隐藏便器——可动性和意外性激发体验乐趣。
这些小型结构体可以延展和渗透到——任何电线杆可以到达的地方。

The site is a piece of lowland behind the dam, in front of which is the broad view of river; Rising from the site to get the view and wind meets with the basic desire when having tea, making it small and light to be the contrast and supplement to the big dam. Rising, wind, view and lightness are the major intentions of the design.
Entirety converting into scattered ones makes small volumes – group image and independent function.
Electric pole is used as column; steel platform is composed of electric pole fittings; steel channel is used as rainwater gutter – having normal municipal material as material topic.
The windows can be freely opened and closed by a set of mechanism; the door will be closed voluntarily by gravity; water supply pipe is used as handrail simultaneously; sliding box/door can cover toilet pan – mobility and surprises stimulating joyful experiences.
Electric poles can reach anywhere , so do these mini-structures.

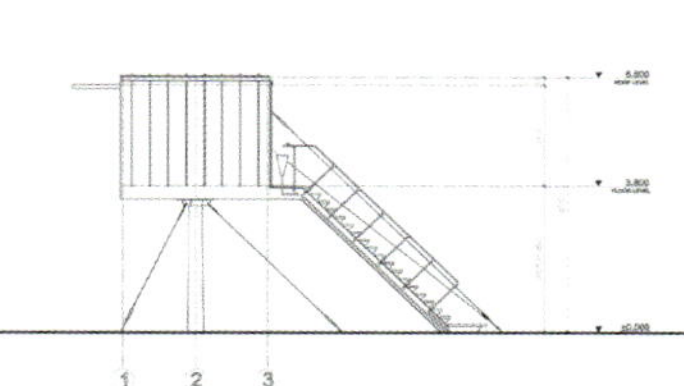

南立面图
SOUTH ELEVATION

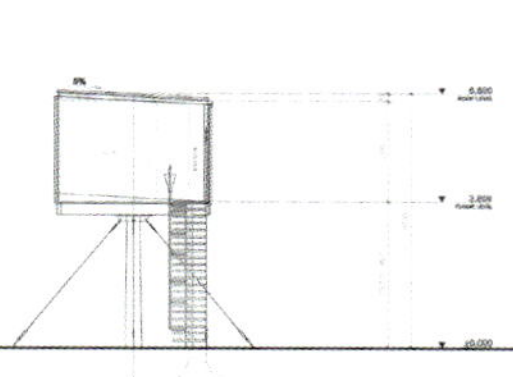

东立面图
EAST ELEVATION

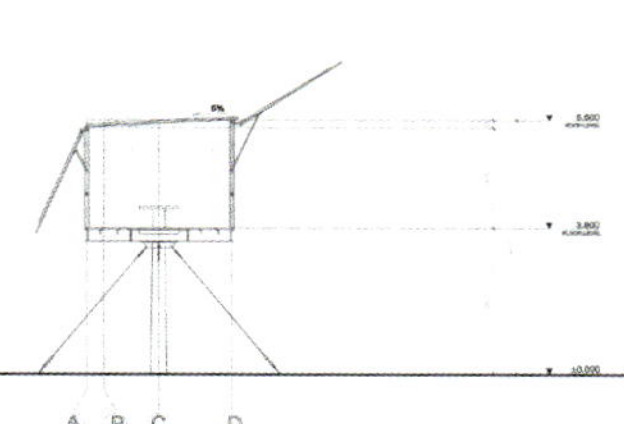

b – b剖面图
b—b SECTION

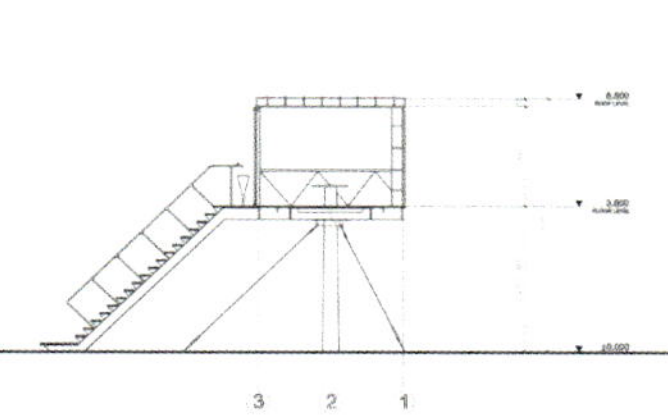

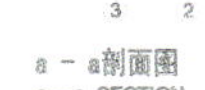

a – a剖面图
a—a SECTION

铝合金型材肋
aluminum alloy section as ribs

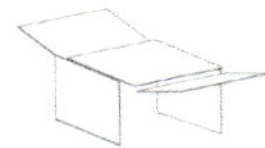

阳光板围护
sunlight plates for enclosure construction

型钢骨架
section steel skeleton

钢隔栅楼面
steel grilled floor

电线杆配件组装平台
platform composed of electric pole fittings

电线杆以拉索稳定
electric pole stablized by cable

钢隔栅踏板
steel grilled stair tread

上水管兼栏杆扶手
water supply pipe as well as handrail

保护钢索
steel cable for protection

整体
the entirety

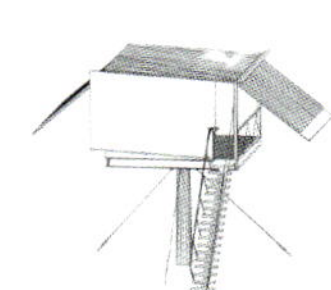

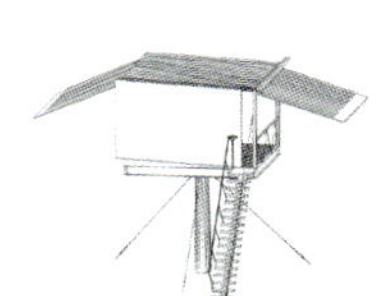

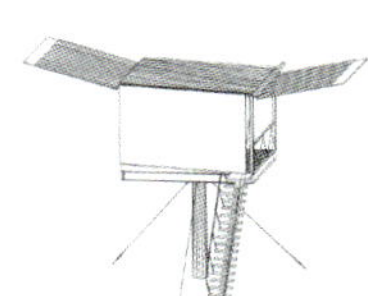

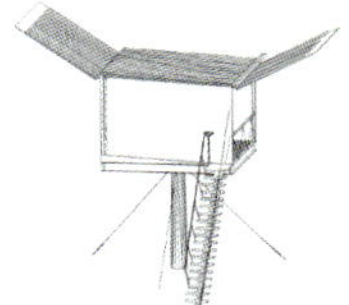

机械制动，窗扇自由开合；利用重力，门自动关闭一。
The window can be freely opened and closed by a set of mechanism;The door will be closed voluntarily by gravity.

Shanghai Xiang-dong Buddha Statue Museum

上海相东佛像艺术馆

设计单位：成都市家琨建筑设计事务所
设计团队：刘家琨、杨鹰、罗明、张曈、李静
项目地址：上海嘉定菊园新区沪宜路4352
业主：上海菊园资产管理有限公司
总建筑面积：4 947 m²

Design firm: Jiakun Architect & Associates
Design team: Liu Jiakun, Yang Ying, Luo Ming, Zhang Tong, Li Jing
Project location: Shanghai Jiading Juyuan New District
The client: Shanghai Juyuan Asset Management Co., Ltd.
Scale: 4 947 m²

上海相东佛像艺术馆设计理念——内心丛林（刘家琨）

内心：指在大都市的喧嚣浮躁中为现代人创造一处获得精神休憩的静谧场所。

内心：也指废弃的厂房大空间中的一个独特世界。

丛林：指传播和传承佛教精神的寺庙经院。

丛林：也指在室内空间中采用质朴野逸的形式语言，营造拾阶登高，低回路转、穿林过涧的山林景观的设计手法。

在具体设计中，考虑到此馆由旧厂房改建而成，故保留厂房内原屋顶珩架体系和重要墙面肌理，在大空间中局部加建一层作为办公空间和夹层展厅等，保留的大空间作为入口展厅用层层递升的方式与夹层展厅联系，让参观流线循环一体。建筑语言上以佛教精神为指引，借鉴了佛教文化遗址的造型语言，同时用当代材料来加以颠覆，力图用恰当的材料、构造、空间和色彩来传达当代语境下的蕴涵历史意韵的佛像博物馆。

参观流线：由大厅进入到展区后，利用原大厂房的高空间，作平台及台阶曲折上升，在此放置大件展品，引导参观人流经此上至二楼夹层；在二楼参观完杂件展品后，进入木佛展示空间；出来后由楼梯再次回到一层，参观夹层下石刻展品；参观结束后通过一长甬道回到入口大厅及休息区。

The Design Concept of Shanghai Xiang-dong Buddha Statue Museum – Jungle of Inner-self (Liu Jiakun)

Inner-self: means to create a quiet place for the people in the modern society to have a spiritual rest in a setting of loud and impetuous metropolitan culture.
Inner-self: also means an unique world inside a massive space from an abandoned factory.
Jungle: means an institution of Buddhist temple which both transmits and inherits the spirit of Buddhism.
Jungle: also means to use unadorned and rough formal language in order to create a kind of space that you can see steps leading up, paths winding away and back, and mountain and jungle landscape which is designed where men are passing through jungles or jumping across streams.
During the design, considering this museum was originally renovated from an old factory building, so we have kept intact original roof truss system and those important wall textures left from old time, added an additional level as office space and mezzanine exhibit space within the massive space that was conserved in the factory, and made a circulation of visiting as a whole cycling system. Architecture language is guided by the spirit of Buddhism and borrowing some formal language referred to Buddhism cultural relics, meanwhile overturning it with new materials which are used in contemporary time. As a result, our goal is to create a museum which expresses an inherent spirit contained throughout history in a way of using appropriate material, construction, space and color in a more contemporary setting.
Circulation for visitors: after entering into the exhibition area from main lobby, there is a high ceilinged space from original factory building, a set of stairs winds up and leads to a platform which is to hold a display for a large piece of item, and from here visitors can walk up to the upper mezzanine level before they reach the main wooden Buddha exhibition area; Then after viewing this area, people exit out and walk down back to the first level through the set of stair, where they can visit some stone carved displaying items; Finally, after the main tour, visitors walk through a long corridor and find themselves back into the entry lobby and a lounge.

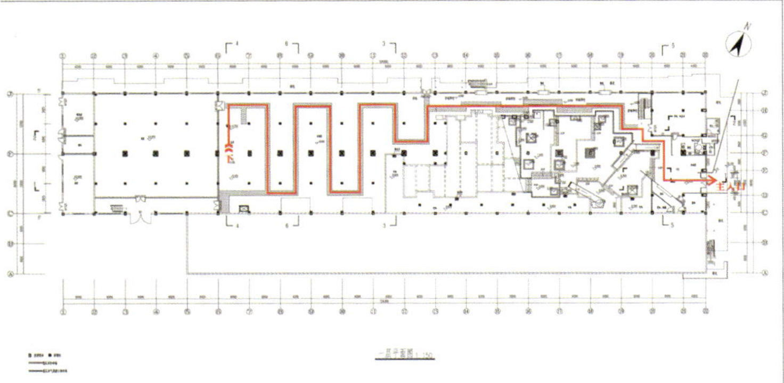

主要参观流线：
The main flow line to visit

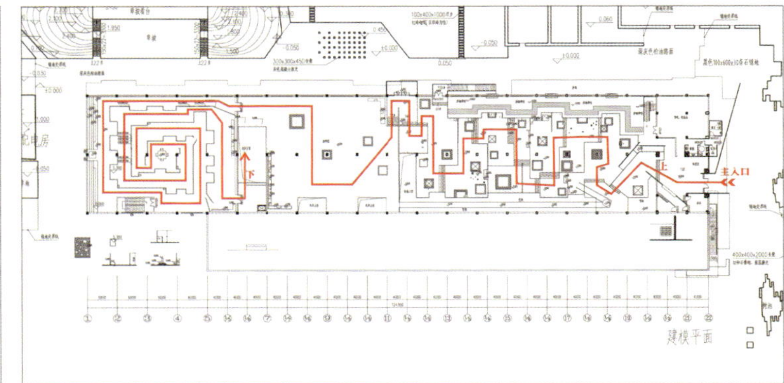

主要参观流线：
The main flow line to visit

OCT Art & Design Gallery

华·美术馆

设计单位：URBANUS都市实践
地点：深圳
设计：2006年–2008年
建成：2008年
规模：2 620 m²
设计团队：孟岩、刘晓都、邓丹、姚晓薇、Cedric Yu、程昀、郭东海、王彦峰
建设方：深圳华侨城房地产有限公司

Design firm: Urbanus Architecture & Design Inc.
Location: Shenzhen
Project: 2006–2008
Construction: 2008
Size: 2 620 m²
Design team: Meng Yan, Liu Xiaodu, Dengdan, Yao Xiaowei, Cedric Yu, Cheng Yun, Guo Donghai, Wang Yanfeng
Client: Shenzhen OCT Real Estate Co.Ltd

Liu xiaodu, Meng Yan, Wang Hui
Urbanus Architecture & Design Inc.

刘晓都 孟岩 王辉
URBANUS都市实践建筑事务所

URBANUS都市实践建筑事务所是由刘晓都、孟岩和王辉主持的建筑创作团体，创建于1999年，目前有深圳公司和北京公司。建成作品包括土楼公舍、大芬美术馆、华侨城创意园规划改造、唐山城市展览馆、华·美术馆、大连海中国·美术馆、招商海运大厦、深圳规划大厦、地铁大厦等数十项。事务所多次应邀参加国际知名建筑展览及交流活动，受到包括《纽约时报》等重要媒体的广泛关注。多项设计作品发表在《时代建筑》、《世界建筑》、意大利Domus、Abitare、荷兰Mark、美国《Architecture Record》、英国Blueprint、a+d、日本a+u、西班牙a+t、德国Bauwelt等权威设计杂志上。入选美国建筑师协会会刊《建筑实录》年度全球10个最具影响力的先锋设计事务所，并多次获得重要的设计奖项。目前正在进行的项目有中广核电总部大厦、深圳前海湾地铁上盖物业、白云观珍宝花园、天津余家堡、华强北中电大厦综合体、上海嘉定复华科技园、雅昌艺术馆、深圳水晶岛规划设计（与OMA合作）等。

展览

2010上海世博会深圳案例馆总策展人及展览设计师

Solo：

2008–2009 "土楼公舍–中国廉租住宅"个展，
库珀·休伊特国家设计博物馆，纽约

Group：

2010 "东西南北中"——十年的三个民间叙事

2010 "设计的立场—8种态度，中荷跨界设计展"，上海

2009 "深圳·香港城市/建筑双城双年展"，深圳，香港

建设中的华侨城洲际大酒店展馆原是建于20世纪80年代早期的深圳湾大酒店的洗衣房。在高速发展的城市中，虽一同并列于深南大道南侧，这座存在于华侨城西班牙风情主题酒店和典雅的何香凝美术馆夹缝中的旧厂房，因其单调的建筑形式早已成为不为人留意的都市残留物。厂房的所属方考虑到其优越的地理位置，决定将其保留并改造为附属于酒店的艺术展馆。 它虽是邻近的国家级美术馆为展览空间的延伸，但酒店展馆的特殊定位，决定了改造后展馆的独特性：其设计既要突显个性，与两边建筑风格形成差异性对比，同时也要体现与两端建筑的关系及整体性。改造策略完整地保留了原建筑立面的窗墙体系，加建的立面通过包裹的手法，将单一的原始六边形通过复杂有机的组合形成由实至虚，由小到大，多层次渐变的三维视觉效果。从而，在车辆由西至东快速通过的瞬间，形成强烈的视觉冲击力，通过立面结构的缩小放大，逐层递减，如同面纱般轻轻揭开，最终透出原建筑立面的戏剧性变化过程。

展馆的室内设计再次运用立面所含有的六边形元素作为基本平面形态，在竖向上作90°的拉伸，形成一系列折叠平面互相交叉，互相切入构成的复杂但带着明确功能元素的公共空间。这种表达形式改变了原本单调的立面几何图案，用三维方式生成新的室内空间，这种"突变"形式使设计产生了不可预料的惊喜结果。

The site has had a rather unremarkable history. Originally made for a laundry facility for Shenzhen Bay Hotel in the early 1980s, it is situated along the main road, between a Spanish-style OCT Hotel and the Hexiangning Gallery. Over many years, the warehouse itself remained unaltered while the city around it rapidly transformed. Considering the significance of its location, the owner decides to remodel the warehouse in a meaningful way. For Urbanus, the remodelling of the site poses difficult questions as how to address the existing urban condition, and how new interventions would relate to it. The main architectural gesture is to wrap the entire warehouse with a hexagonal glass curtain wall. The pattern is created from 4 different sizes of hexagons. As a result, the new wall becomes a lively theatrical screen.

The geometric pattern is more than just surface deep. It is actually a three-dimensional matrix of intersecting elements that project into the gallery spaces, structuring the building's interior design. The result is the creation of delightful and unexpected spatial experiences.

Under the leadership of partners Liu Xiaodu, Meng Yan and Wang Hui, URBANUS is a think tank providing strategies for urbanism and architecture in the new millennium. Founded in 1999, URBANUS is now based in Beijing and Shenzhen. The completed works in clude Urban Tulou, Dafen Art Museum, OCT Loft Renovation, Tangshan Urban Planning Museum, OCT Art & Design Gallery, Maritime Museum of Art ,Tower of China Merchants Maritime & Logistics Ltd, Shenzhen Planning Building, Metro Tower etc. URBANUS has been exhibited internationally in prestigious shows and presented in prestigious newspapers and magazines, including New York Times, T+A, W+A, Domus, Abitare, Mark, Architecture Record,Blueprint, a+u, a+t, Bauwelt. It was featured as one of the ten global "Design Vanguards" by Architectural Record in December, 2005, and has been awarded with many prestigious architecture prizes. The further projects include Baiyunguan Shopping Complex, Tianjing Yujiapu Tower, Jiading Fuhua Science Park, Yachang Art Gallery and Shenzhen Bay Metro Plaza, Shenzhen Crystal Island (in collaboration with OMA) and CGN Headquarter Building etc.

EXHIBITIONS

2010 Expo Shanghai Chief Curator and Exhibition Designer

Solo:

2008-2009 "Tulou: Affordable Housing for China", Cooper Hewitt National Design Museum, New York

Group:

2010 "Compass"–Three Narratives about the Past Ten Years

2010 "Taking a stance – 8 positions", Dutch culture centre, Shanghai

2009 "The Shenzhen & Hongkong Bi-City Biennale of Urbanism \ Architecture", Shenzhen

2009-2010 "Chinese Gardens for Living, Europalia 2009", The Square, Belgium

2009-2010 "Building from Heart, Europalia 2009", The Square, Belgium

2008 "City\Village Research", Parsons Design School, New York

2008 "Building China", Architecture Center, New York

2008 " Exhibition of Chinese Contemporary Archi ecture", Paris\Barcelona

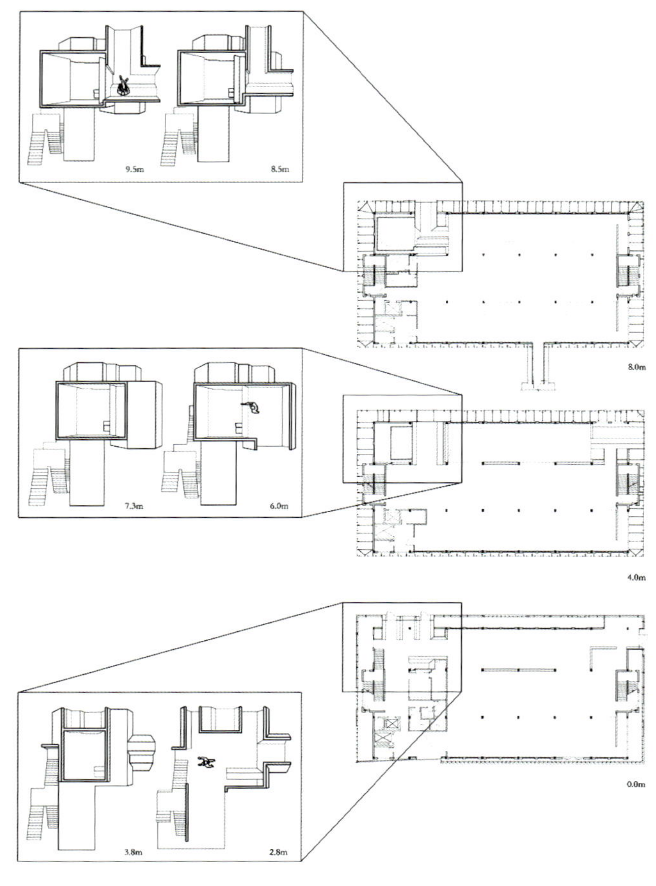

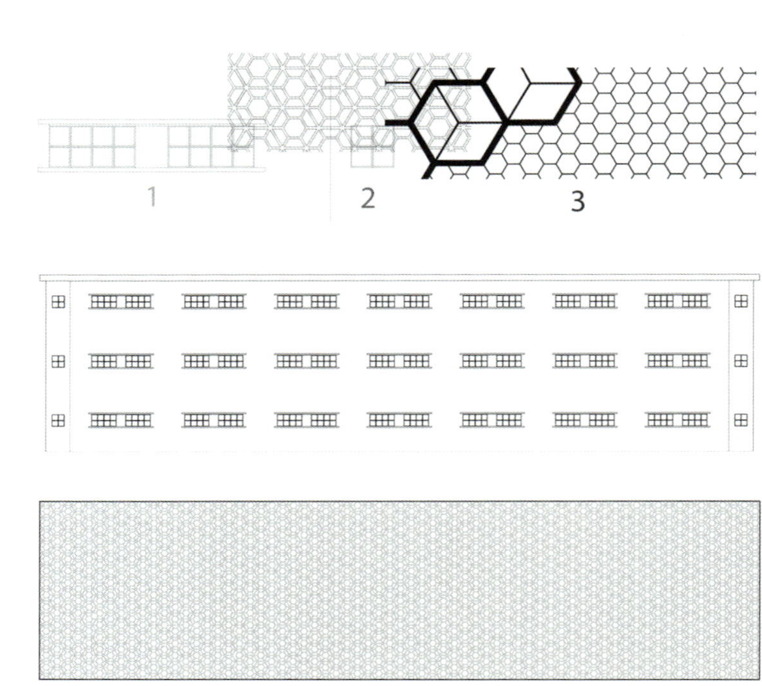

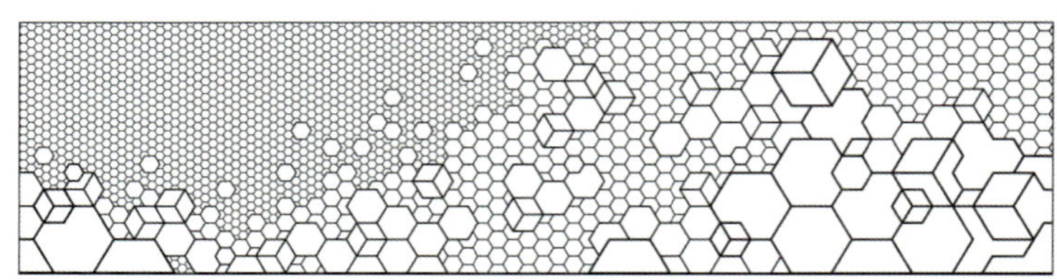

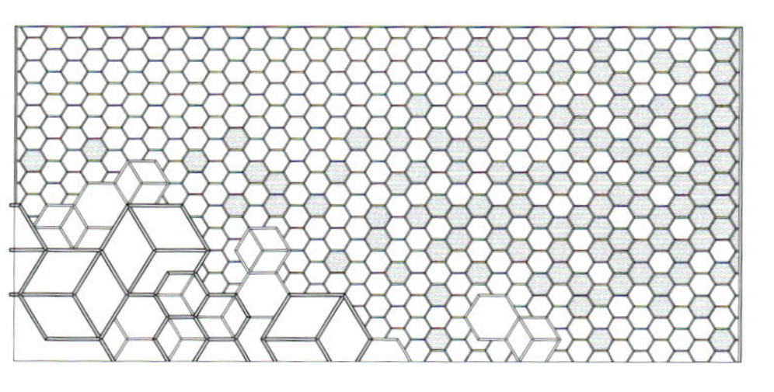

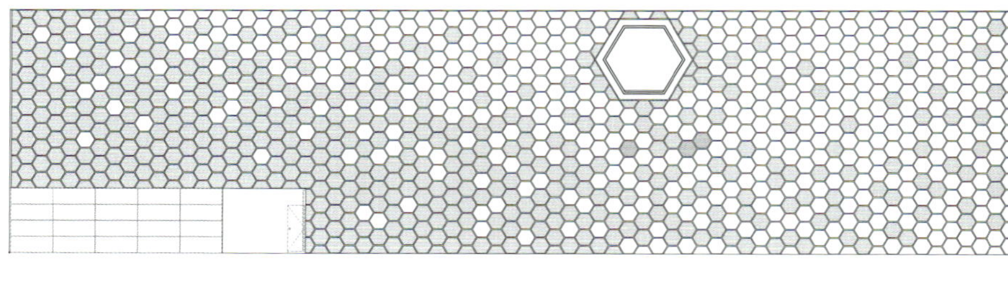

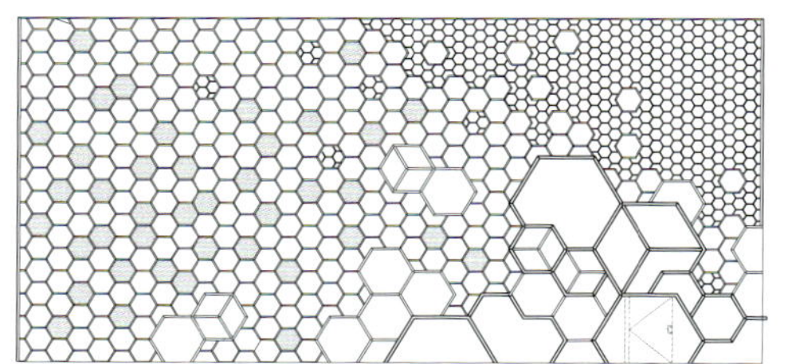

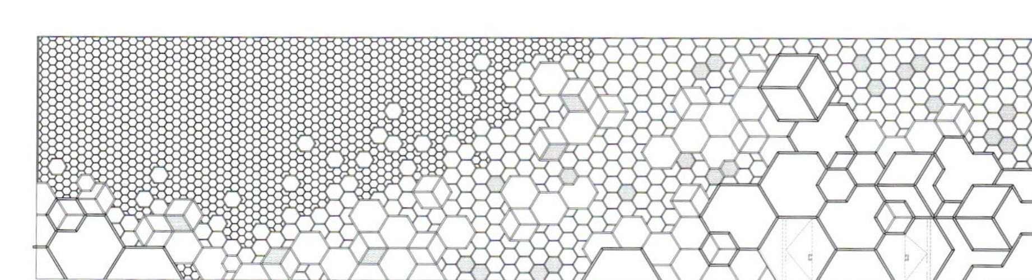

2009–2010 "活的中国园林展" 欧罗巴利亚中国文化年，布鲁塞尔

2009–2010 "心造－中国当代建筑前沿展"，欧罗巴利亚中国文化年，布鲁塞尔

2008 "城中村研究" 展览PARSONS 设计学院，纽约

2008 "中国建筑五人展" 纽约建筑中心

2008 "当代中国建筑展" 法国建筑师学会，巴黎、巴塞罗那

2007 "里斯本国际建筑与设计三年展" 葡萄牙建筑师协会、葡萄牙世博馆，里斯本

2007 "深圳·香港城市/建筑双城双年展"，深圳、香港

2006 "鹿特丹 '当代中国' 建筑、艺术与视觉文化大展" 荷兰建筑师协会（NAI），鹿特丹

2005 "圣保罗国际建筑与设计双年展"，巴西建筑师协会，圣保罗

2005 "第二届广州当代艺术三年展"，广州

获奖

2010 第三届美国《建筑实录》最佳公共建筑奖（2项目获奖）及年度建筑奖

2008 中国建筑传媒奖之 "居住建筑特别奖"

2008 第四届WA奖优胜奖和佳作奖

2008 第二届美国《商业周刊/建筑实录》中国奖 "最佳室内设计奖" 和 "最佳公共建筑奖"

2008 T+A 2007 建筑中国 "年度建筑设计机构奖"

2007 07深圳·香港城市\建筑双城双年展 "最佳公众奖"

2006 首届美国《商业周刊/建筑实录》中国奖 "最佳公共建筑奖"

2005 入选美国《建筑实录》年度全球十大设计先锋

2004 第二届WA佳作奖和鼓励奖

2007 "Lisbon Architecture Triennale", Portugal Pavilion, Lisbon
2007 "The Shenzhen & Hongkong Bi-City Biennale of Urbanism \ Architecture", Shenzhen/ Hongkong
2006 "China Contemporary "Architecture, Art, Visual Culture, Rotterdam, Netherlands
2005 "The 26th Sao Paulo BBiennale", Sao Paulo
2005 "The 2nd Guangzhou Contemporary Art Triennale", Guangzhou

AWARDS
2010 Best Public Project, Architectural Record China Awards 2010 and Project of the Year
2008 China Architecture Media Award, Residential Architecture Special Prize
2008 WA Chinese Architecture Award 'Winning Prize' & 'Honorable Mention'
2008 Best Public Project / Best Interior Project, Business Week/ Architectural Record China Awards
2007 T+A Annual Prize of Architectural Design Organization
2007 Shenzhen & Hong Kong Bi-City Biennale of Urbanism/ Architecture- Best Public Prize
2006 Business Week / Architectural Record China Awards- Best Public Project,
2004 WA Chinese Architecture Award 'Honorable Mention' & 'Merit Award'

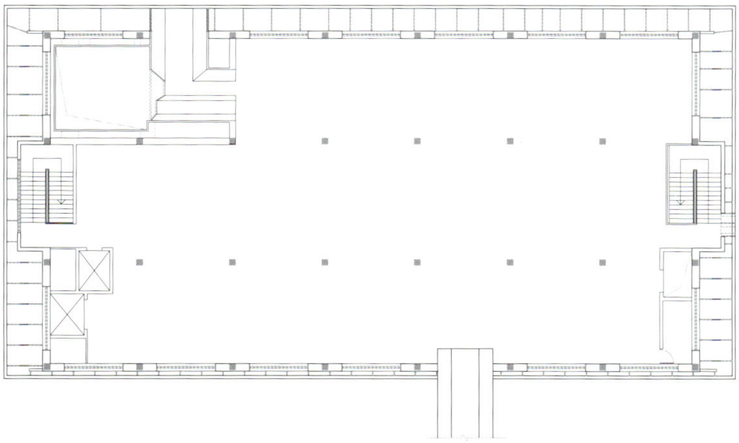

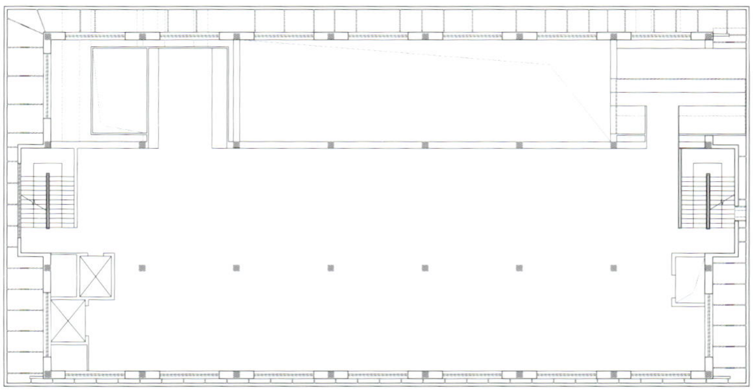

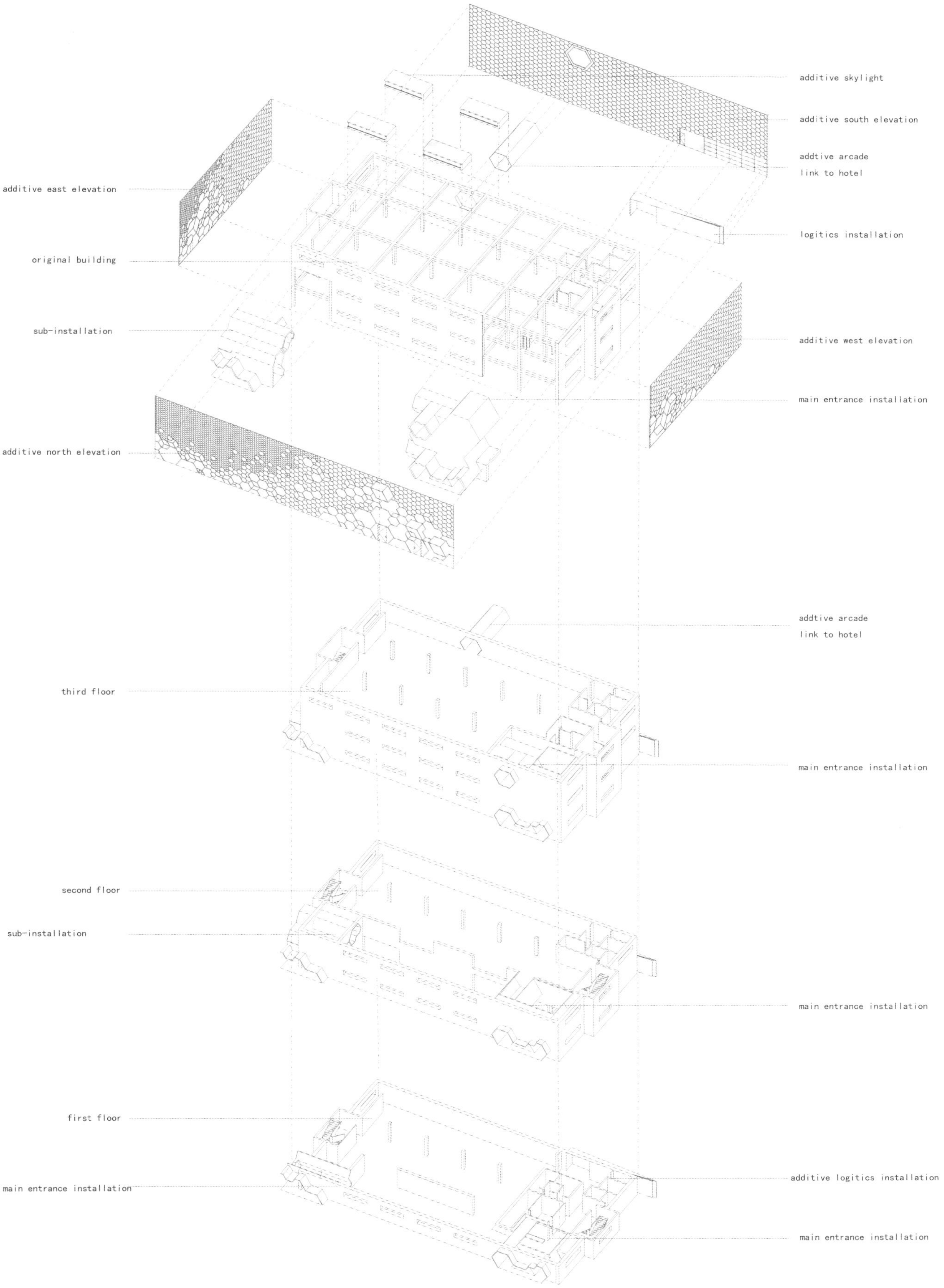

additive skylight

additive south elevation

addtive arcade
link to hotel

additive east elevation

logitics installation

original building

sub-installation

additive west elevation

main entrance installation

additive north elevation

addtive arcade
link to hotel

third floor

main entrance installation

second floor

sub-installation

main entrance installation

first floor

additive logitics installation

main entrance installation

main entrance installation

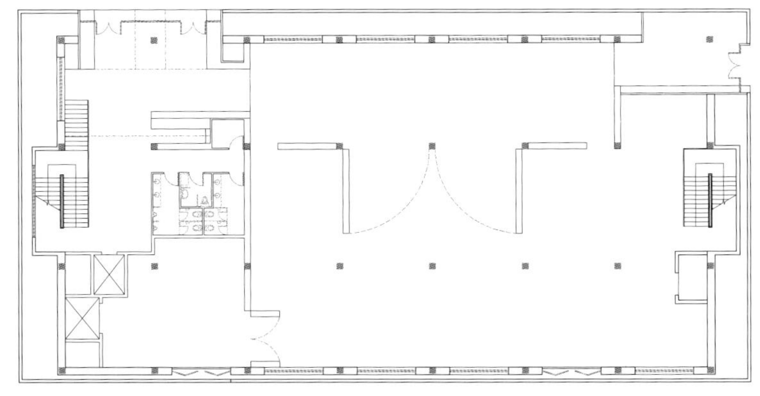

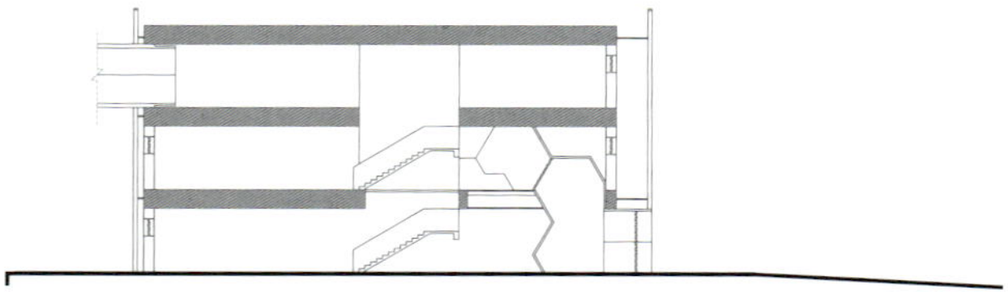

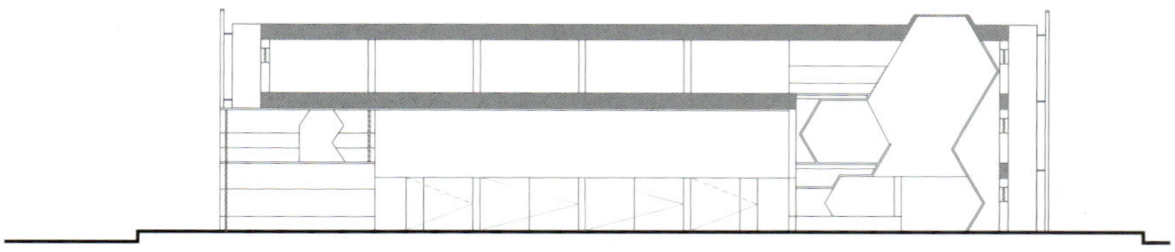

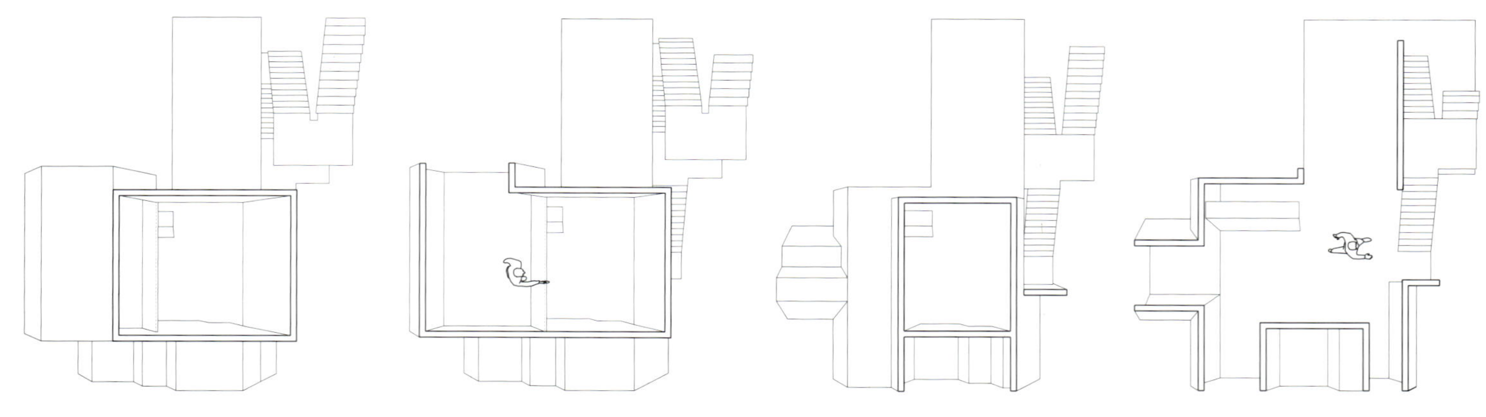

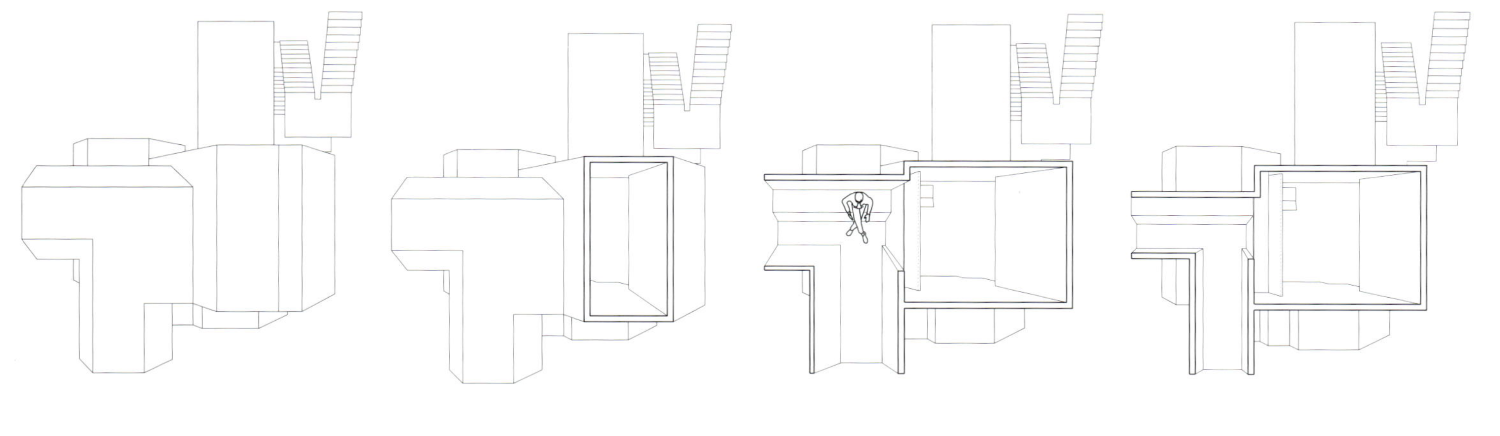

Tangshan Urban Planning Museum
唐山城市展览馆

设计单位：URBANUS都市实践
地点：河北省唐山市
设计：2005年—2006年
建成：2008年
用地面积：22 850 m²
建筑面积：5 900 m²
项目组：王辉、刘旭、张柳娟、陈春、王鹏、刘爽、段云龙、赵利卫、王玮
建设方：唐山市规划局

Design firm: Urbanus Architecture & Design Inc.
Location: Tang Shan City
Project: 2005–2006
Construction: 2008
Buliding area: 5 900 m²
Design team: Wang Hui, Liu Xu, Zhang Liujuan, Chen Chun, Wang Peng, Liu Shuang, Duan Yunlong, Zhao Liwei, Wang Wei
Client: Tangshan Urban Planning Bureau

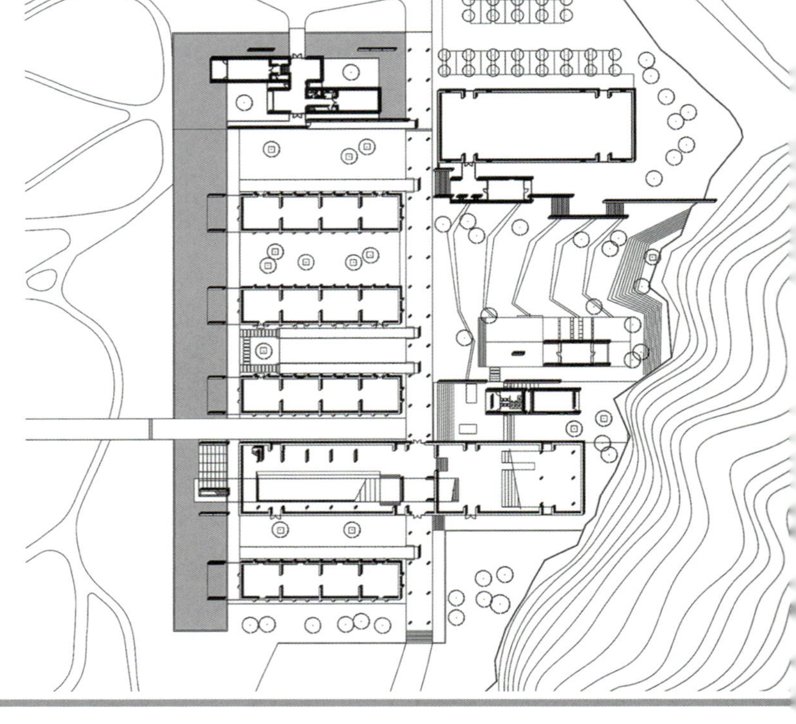

不同于一般城市定位在新、奇、异标准之上的规划展示馆，唐山城市展览馆的主体是由几座朴素得几乎没有任何审美价值的旧建筑构成。它的前身是位于市中心大城山西麓的原唐山面粉厂，其封闭的围墙隔阂了山与城市。因此，工厂在新的都市条件下搬迁后，市里动议将数十座规模庞大、结构完好的单层厂房和仓库彻底拆除，用开阔的绿地公园来连接山体与城市主干道。作为一个容积率很低、人均绿化率很高的城市，这种城市美化运动只是给城市增加了绿地，却没带来生机。唐山市规划局的领导意识到了这个问题。在评估基地上厂房的价值时，发现几幢仓库是日伪时期建的，如果采用"公共空间＋公共建筑"建设模式来保留，会使这个公园成为城市的亮点。在这个理念的指导下，URBANUS都市实践完成了博物馆公园的构想，用保留下来的四栋日伪时期的仓库和两栋地震后建的仓库作为展示唐山近代工业、民俗和城市的平台，使公园成为一个城市记忆的场所。

保留下的六栋平行的建筑恰巧垂直于山体，构成了一种有意味的韵律。改造设计通过非常少的加建，更强化了这种韵律，使山有节奏地从建筑间的空隙中溢到城市，形成了大城山—山脚后花园—厂房间小院—大公园—城市主干道一系列有层次和有序的城市开放空间体系。这个序列与邻近的铁路公园何凤凰山连接，又构成了宏大的城市公共空间网络。人们在这个连续的整体中漫游，不仅仅在享受物质性的绿地和园林，也在享受历史和文化。材料使用上也很节制，只用通透的金属格栅和防腐木板，来强化场所固有的工业化精神和自然的面貌。在这些另类、却也朴素的材料映衬下，原封保留的旧仓库的墙面透出了内在的美。沿公园一面，每个仓库增添出一个钢结构门廊，让封闭的仓库具用一种开放性。这些门廊落在反射水池上，使旧建筑的美进一步放大。"人"字形仓库的屋面用"X"形钢结构来代替，形成的侧高窗使原先封闭的室内变成明亮的、非常完美和标准的展示厅。

对于已经厌烦了平庸的生活环境的普通市民而言，通过享受宜人的公共空间，再来品味熟视无睹的建筑，是重新认识自己城市价值的绝好途径。

加建部分的笔墨不多。通过新旧部分的材料对比，对老仓库的屋顶和门廊夸张重构，用水池和连廊统一离散的个体等等处理手法，精心地呵护和放大厂房和山体间构图上的天作之美，在新的环境下彰显毫无美学价值的原有建筑群的内在美。

博物馆群原本计划有多元化内容，但最终只作为单一的城市史和城市规划的展示，一定程度上略有遗憾。但是，这也帮助这个改造项目成为正朔，有助于启发人们去思考、去热爱、去保护、去利用那些平庸的城市建筑。虽然它们于建筑史几乎毫无价

If the 1976 earthquake was an accidental demolition to Tangshan, the current urbanization movement is intentionally to erase less appealing urban structures. The city's former grain depot is one of such victims. Located on the foot of Da Cheng Hill, the cradle land of Tangshan, this gated depot blocked the connection between the hill and the city. The government thus has decided to clean it out to create an open green land to reconnect the city with the hill. Under the efforts of both Tangshan City Planning Bureau and the architect, this action has changed from merely beautifying the city as its primary goal to renovating part of the existing buildings into a museum park. Four granaries built during the Japanese-occupying era, and two warehouses built after the earthquake are saved to serve as the base structures for new museum programs.

Since the six existing structures are perpendicular to the hill with such a beauful rythem, the new additions are carefully designed in order not to interfere this original layout. Therfore, newly built programs, such as the VIP reception, museum store, and café, are shaped paralle to the existing buildings to provide visual corridors to the hill. Materials for the new are also restricted to metal grating and wood in order to make a contrast to the well preserved exisiting stucco wall, and to generate a harmonial materiality in line with the park. The original roof is replaced by an "X" shape structure to introduce skylight to the interior. A patio is added to each old structure to give a sense of connection and openness. The reflection pool helps to amplify the unique beauty of the museum group. The new layout of the whole building group also forms a spatial sequence to introduce the hill to the city through a series of gardens, courtyards and the park. This sequence makes the promenade of the museum a wonderful experience, and facilitates the park with cozy venues for outdoor urban acitivities and events. In addition, it becomes the most favorite community common place for the surrounding old workers' housing that lacks public amenities.

The museum will exhibit both the history and new plan of the city and its affliated counties. In daily life, even such an exuberant collection of city history and culture can hardly attract normal city residents. Therefore, a more lively antique trade market is planned at the entry area to bring more people's awareness of the park's programs. The museum park's historical theme gives the residents an opportunity to understand the city's past that has very few physical traces left, and a place where they renew affections to the city. It also serves as a reminder to the city officials of their root when they plan the urban future. Unlike most of arrogant urban planning museums that are aloof to the public, this modest facility is friendly for the public access, and thus promotes the public participation in the urban policy making.

The recycling of exisiting urban structure is meaningful to the civic life. Aside from

值，但它们毕竟记录了城市的一段历史。这点于唐山更有意义。这个与深圳同时建设的城市，有着与被城市化烟熏火燎的深圳迥然不同的性格。这种性格就是平常心。但随着城市化飓风扫荡进二线城市，新的审美价值观已不容许城市再继续平庸。今天的城市化运动和当年的地震一样，都在抹杀唐山平凡的现当代建筑史。但对于这个毫无花拳绣腿、震后重建的城市，平凡是一种朴实的城市精神和恬静的城市生活方式，是一种一般市民可承受的体面环境。它不逊于一线城市火热的生活。当人们走进展览馆去畅想城市未来后，走出展馆又能体会城市的历史。这种平衡有助于去思索今天的城市化行动所应有的策略、立场和价值观。这个建筑提醒着城市建设的执行者，城市化不是地震。

carrying on the city memory, it helps to reinforce the urban confidence which is losing in this city. Nowadays, the fenetic urbanization illustrated by crazy designs in the frontier cities, such as Beijing, Shanghai and Shenzhen, has driven the secondary tier cities to copy the development models neither suitable to their economic reality, nor appropriate to their urban characteristics. It is necessary and urgent in today's practice to set a model for less developed cities to demonstrate how to install decent urbanity from a banal setting. As one of the examples of such efforts, this museum park design, which has been well applauded by both city officials and citizens, has proved that good renovation work not only preserves urban structure, but also preserves urban spirit.

3M 层高办公
3M High Office
6M 层高门厅
6M Level Lobby
使用锁扣金属屋面
Metal Cladding
增加天窗
Additional Skylight
改造内部空间
Interior Renovation
保留原有外墙
Exterior Wall Reservation
门廊
Arcade
水池
Pond

保留部分原有结构
Partial Structure Reservation
并置换屋面
Roof Renovation
玻璃
Glazing
混凝土
Concrete
混凝土结合其他材料
Concrete Mixed with Other Material
木质
Timber

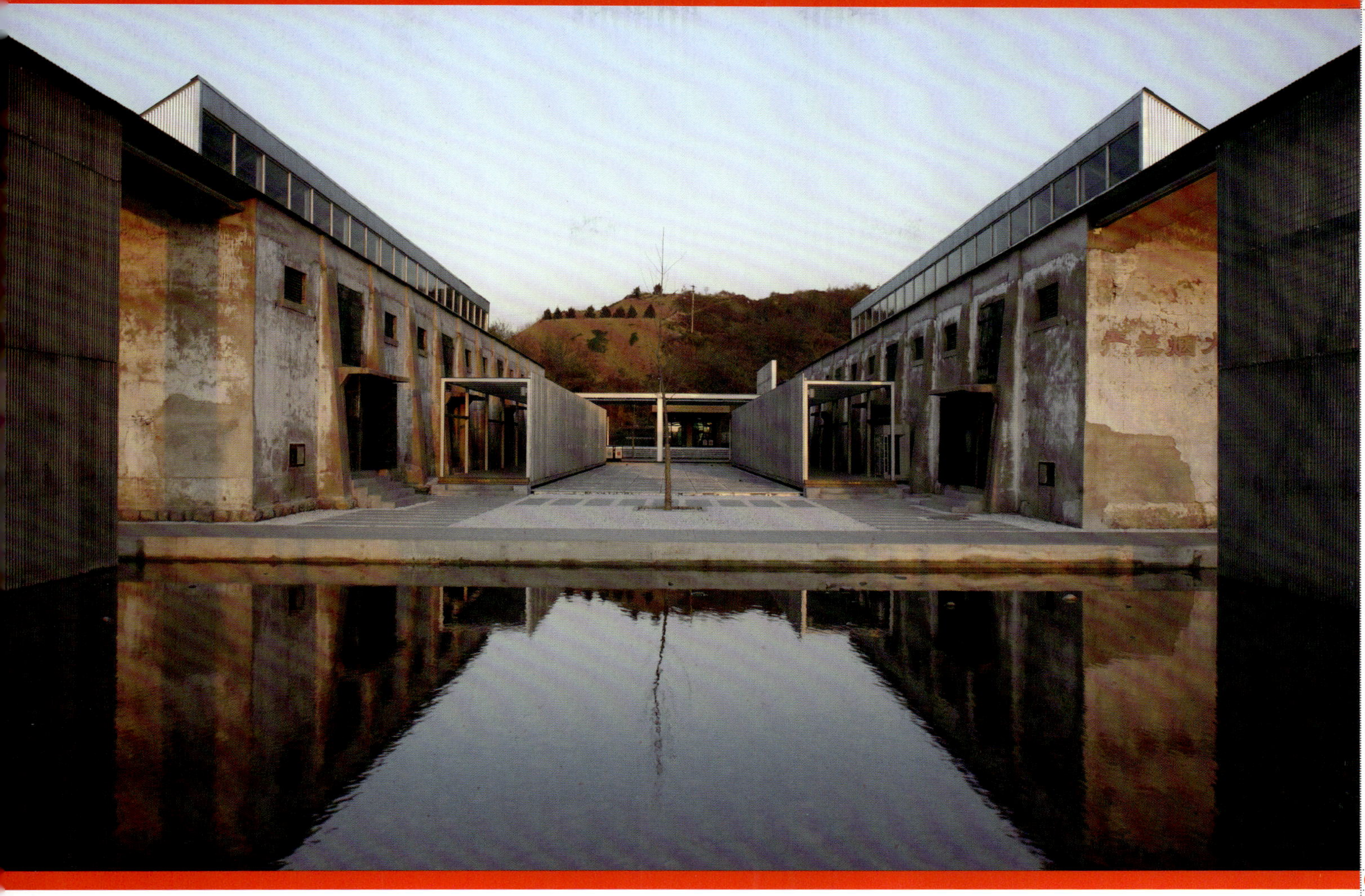

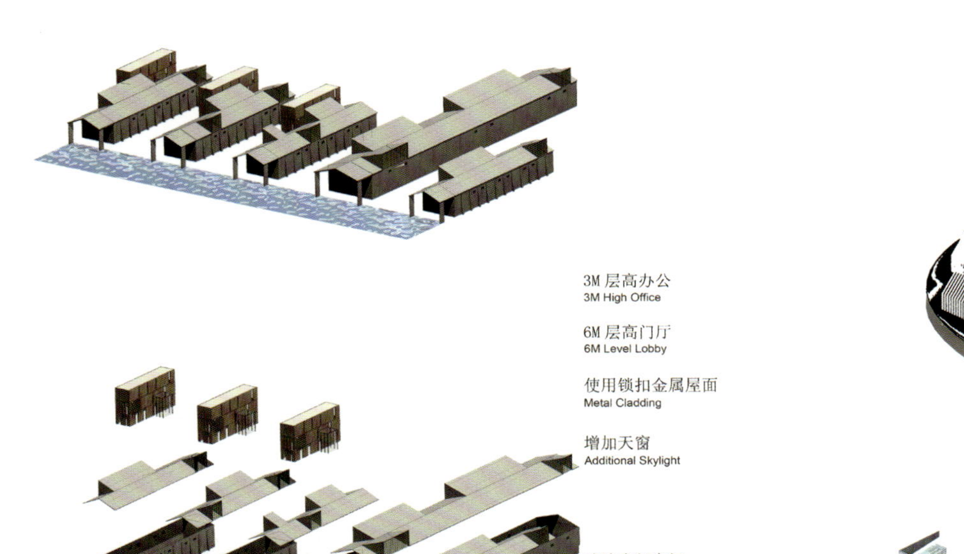

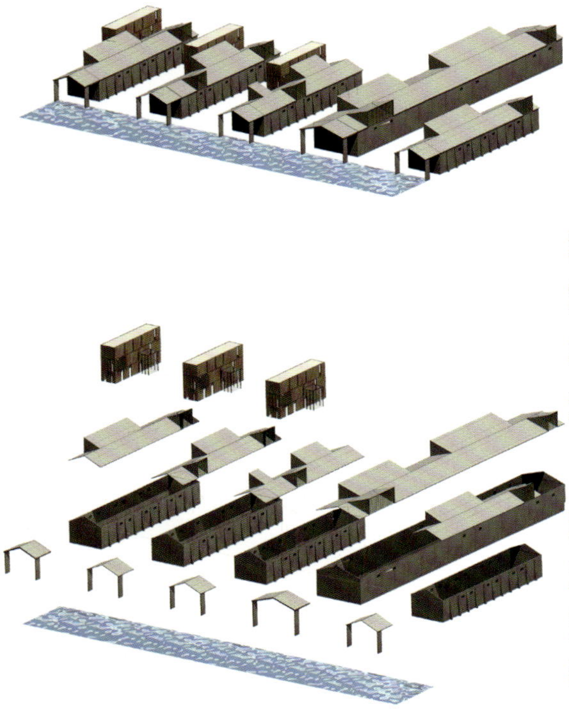

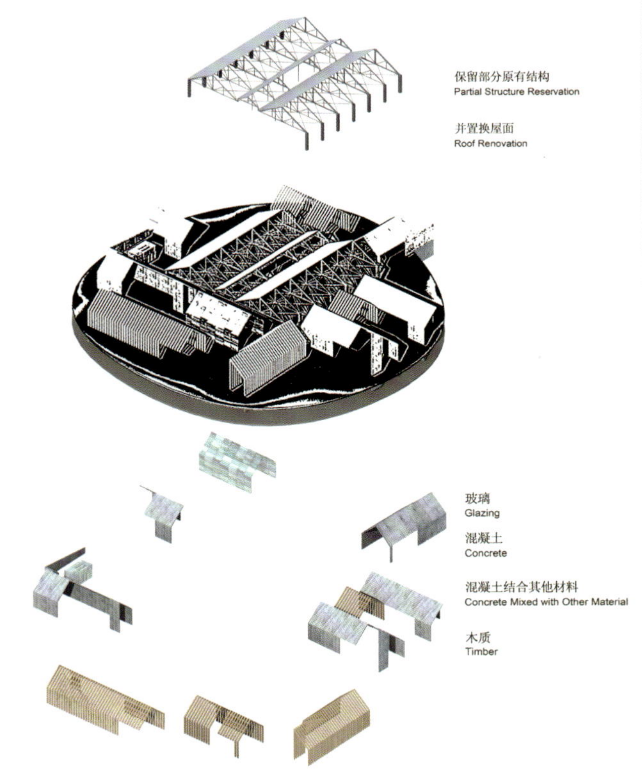

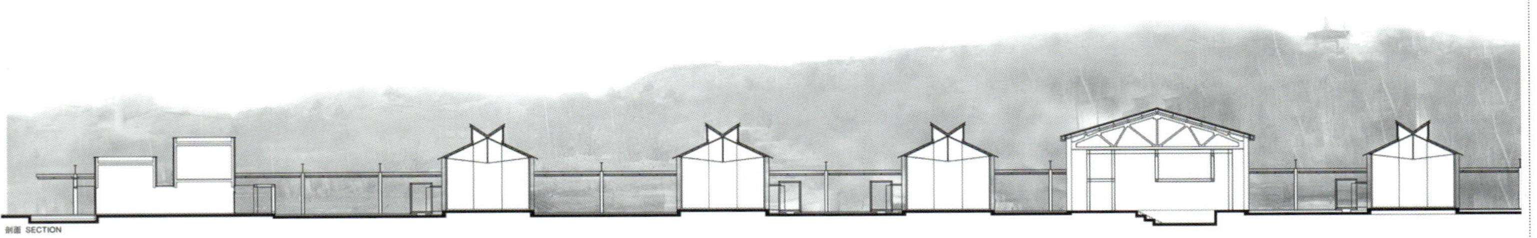

剖面 SECTION

Pleasant
scenery
中国·唐海
唐山

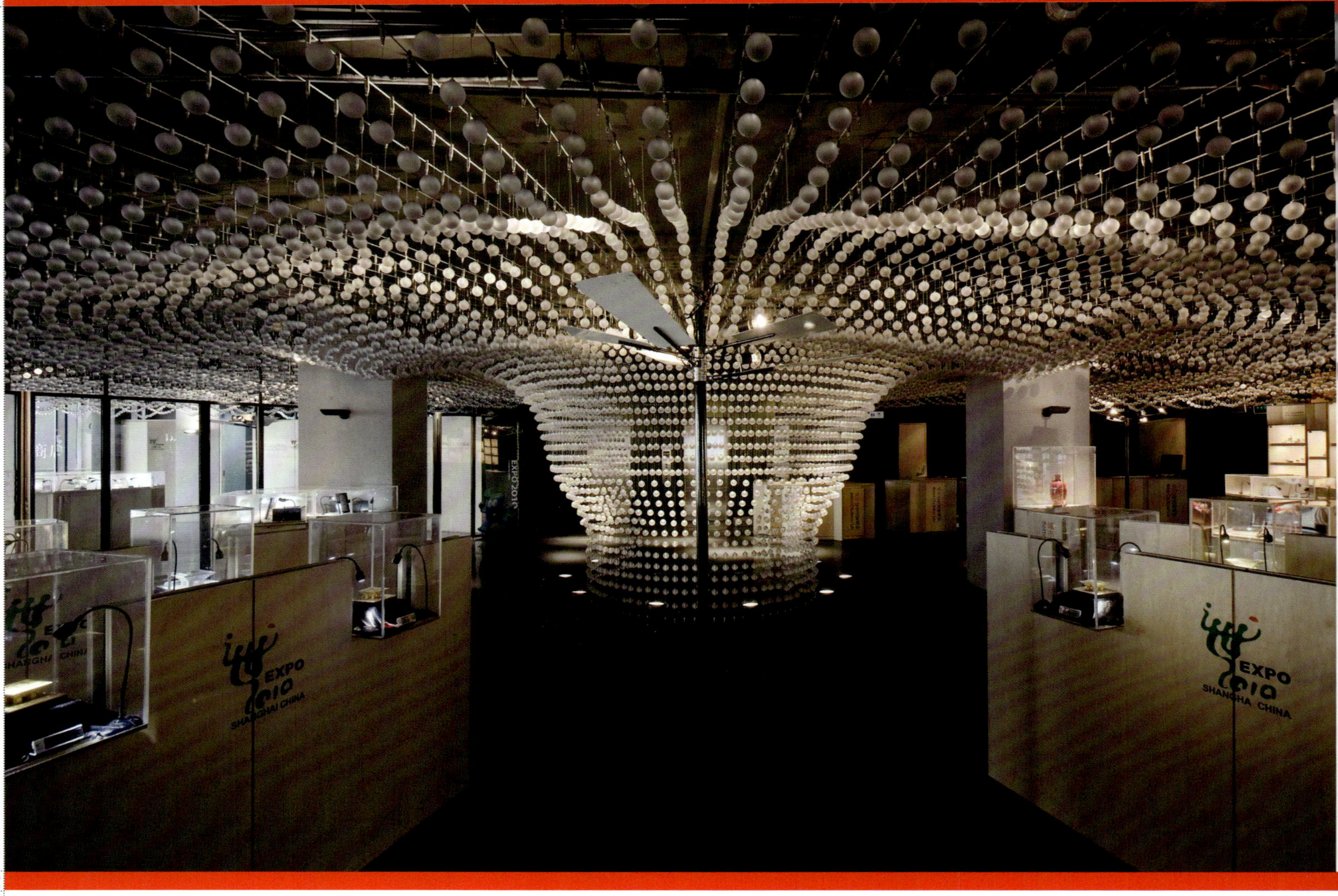

EXPO Future Store
世博未来商店

设计单位：刘宇扬建筑事务所
项目地点：上海南京路步行街
项目类型：商业／室内
建筑规模：800 m^2
设计／建成：2009年 ／ 2009年
RFID技术：上海交通大学
灯光设计：Uno Lai
摄影师：Jeremy San

Design firm: Atelier Liu Yuyang Architects
Location: Shanghai Nanjing Rd. Huangpu District, Shanghai
Form: commerce / interior
Scale: 800 m^2
Design/Built: 2009/2009
RFID technology: Shanghai Jiaotong University
Lighting design: Uno Lai
Photography: Jeremy San

世博未来商店的设计灵感来自于一滴水。通过参数化设计，一万八千个半透明的水晶玻璃球形成渐变的水波天花，从商店的中心呈放射状弥漫开来。而天花的形象也隐喻了世博所带来的影响会如同水波一般向全国乃至世界不断传播。商品陈列及其他空间组成部分放弃了传统的笛卡儿网格，采取了新的极坐标网格。灯光设计在整个场内布置了十二组 “灯树”，以折射光的方式表现出有别于传统商业空间的视觉体验。此外，RFID技术被结合在所有的产品展示之中，真正体现属于未来的购物模式。

The design concept comes from a drop of water. Through digital parametric modeling, a sea of acrylic spheres were created to form an intricate ceiling installation. The overall layout abandoned the Cartesian grid and took on a polar grid, permeating radially from the entrance of the shop. Twelve sets of "tree lights" were installed to give reflective lighting to the acrylic spheres, creating a new visual language seldom seen in commercial interiors. RFID technology was adopted in all of the merchandise display shelves to offer a new model of shopping that truly belongs to the future.

Liu Yuyang
Atelier Liu Yuyang Architects

刘宇扬
刘宇扬建筑事务所 创始人 设计总监

刘宇扬

毕业于美国哈佛大学建筑设计学院，师从荷兰建筑家库哈斯，完成中国珠江三角洲城市化的研究，并于1997年参加德国卡塞尔第十届文件展。曾任教于香港中文大学，韩国艺术大学建筑系评鉴委员，2007年受邀担任深圳香港双城双年展策展人之一。现为上海刘宇扬建筑事务所主持建筑师、香港大学建筑学院荣誉副教授、上海青浦区规划局顾问建筑师。完成作品包括上海当代艺术馆、上海南京路步行街行人服务亭、香港九广铁路“连线城市”规划研究、韩国“汉江计划”行人隧道景观设计等一系列在中国及亚洲城市中具有前瞻性和研究性的公共项目。

讲座与获奖

香港大学建筑学院讲座，2008
密西根大学建筑与城市学院讲座，2008
台中城市论坛，2008
韩国国立艺术大学-原都市建筑研究所讲座“香港-深圳：Recipro-City”，2006
台北市立美术馆 普立兹克建筑奖讲座，“Herzog de Meuron：物质（改变）文化”，2005
英国伦敦城市大学建筑学院 国际论坛 特邀讲座 ，2005
台湾集集地震纪念公园 建筑与景观设计（国际竞赛第二名）2003-4
纽约苏和区剧院设计（国际竞赛优异奖）1999
香港1997纪念碑设计（国际竞赛入围奖）1997

出版

深圳商报 文化版万象专栏 2007
“实验城市：建筑教育与城市状态”，《时代建筑》杂志，2007年3月

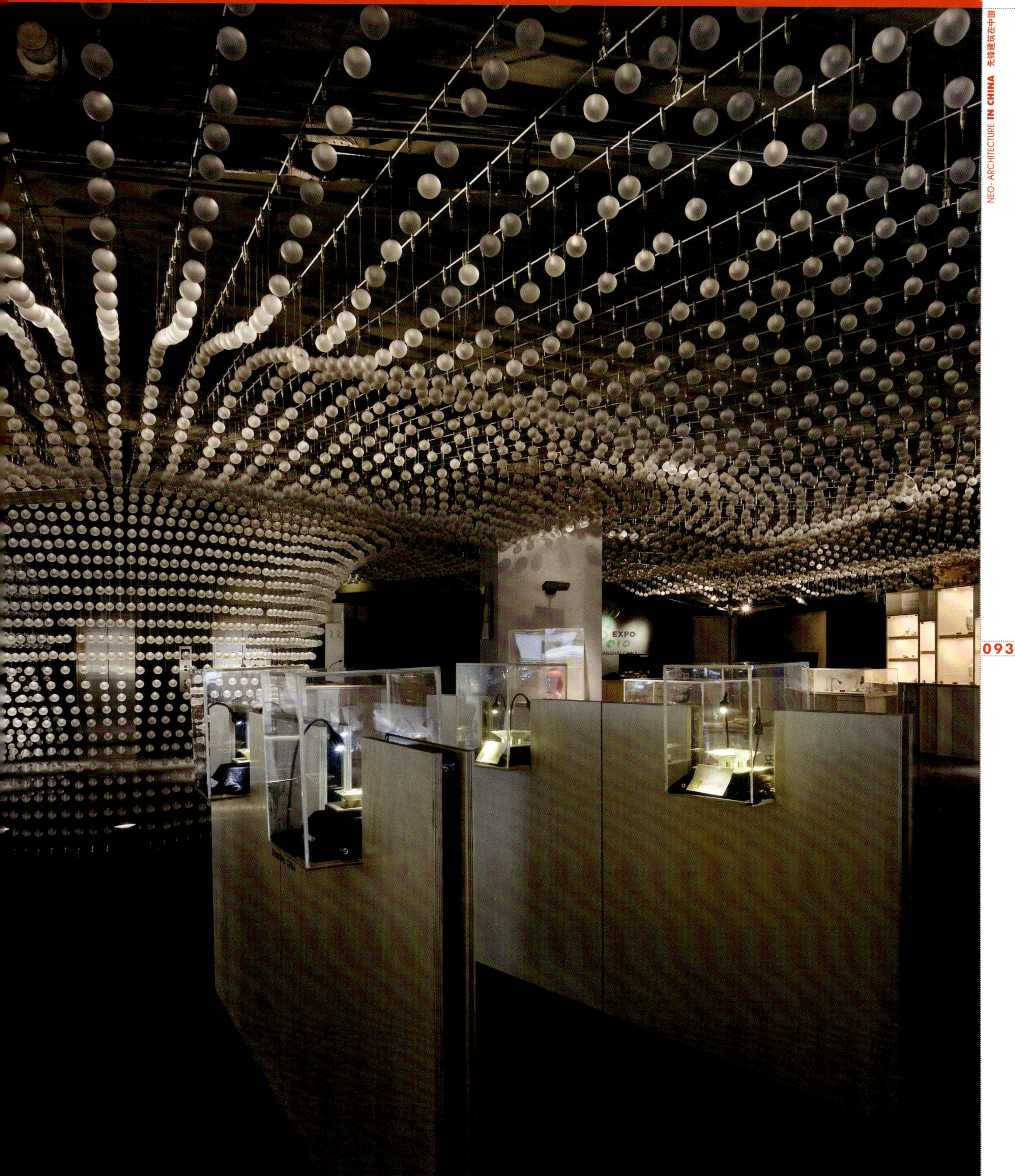

Born in Taiwan, Mr. Liu received his Master Degree of Architecture from Harvard University and Bachelor of Arts from the University of California, San Diego. His published works include the "Great Leap Forward" with Prof. Rem Koolhaas on emerging urban conditions of China's Pearl River Delta (PRD). Since 2001, Mr. Liu has served as an assistant professor at University of Hong Kong and an external examiner for the Korean National University of Arts. At the invitation of the Li Ka Shing Foundation, Mr. Liu also designed the Shantou University campus master plan.

Since founding his practice: Atelier Liu Yuyang Architects, Mr. Liu has conducted numerous significant projects such as the Shanghai Museum of Contemporary Art (MoCA), the Han River Renaissance urban and landscape design in Seoul; the Yellow Box exhibition and installation at the Taipei Fine Arts Museum and Qingpu, Shanghai; Linear City, a Kowloon-Canton Rail sponsored urban research, and the Chinese University campus master plan. In addition, Mr. Liu has completed a number of exclusive residential and commercial interior projects in New York, Hong Kong, Beijing, among other cities.

Prior to moving back to Asia, Mr. Liu had taught at Harvard and practiced with Leers Weizapfel Associates in Boston and Skidmore Owings Merrill LLP in New York, where he designed a 50-storey headquarters building for a global investment bank in Manhattan. Mr. Liu has recently been commissioned as a head curator for the 2007-08 Shenzhen-Hong Kong Biennale on Architecture and Urbanism.

ABOUT US

Established in Hong Kong and Shanghai, Atelier Liu Yuyang Architects (ALYA) works to improve the built-environment in an honest, meaningful and sustainable way. Equipped with global perspective and local know-how, we believe that sound research forms the basis for intelligent design, and through design excellence we add value to our clients and to the society at large. Our design portfolio includes the acclaimed Shanghai Museum of Contemporary Art (Shanghai MoCA), the "Han River Renaissance"—a series of pedestrian tunnels in Seoul, Korea, high-end residential interiors in Hong Kong, storage and manufacturing facility in the Pearl River Delta, and most recently a set of kiosks design for Shanghai's Nanjing Road Pedestrian District.

《DOMUS与中国78建筑师/设计师》，中国建筑工业出版社，2007

"场所、意图、与 建筑" 《社会科学的可能》，香港中文大学出版社，2006

"城中村研究" 《住区》杂志，中国建筑工业出版社，2006年4月

"为香港设计新的脸孔" 《亚洲周刊》，2003-06-09

《大跃进》(Great Leap Forward) 伦敦 TASCHEN PUBLISHERS，2001

展览

密西根大学建筑与城市学院 China Near Now 作品展 2008

2007深圳·香港建筑与城市双年展 2007

上海青浦黄盒子艺术展 2006

台北美术馆黄盒子展览设计 2005

首届深圳城市与建筑双年展 2005

第十届德国卡塞尔文件展 1997

公司简介

在我们每天的工作中，我们追求真诚的、有意义的、可持续的建筑与环境。公司成立于上海及香港，并在伦敦及首尔有合作事务所。我们的理念是扎根本土、面向世界，以研究为设计之本，通过高品质的设计为客户及社会创造更高价值。在2003至2005年期间，我们设计了上海第一座由私人基金会资助的"上海当代艺术馆"，并获得国际艺术机构的一致好评。近年来我们积极参与在亚洲城市中一系列具有前瞻性和研究性的公共项目，其中包括香港九广铁路"连线城市"规划、韩国"汉江复兴计划"行人隧道设计、厦门"气候变迁"研究。事务所同时透过设计来关注当代城市中的微观议题，代表作品有东莞玩具工厂、上海南京路步行街行人服务亭等。

城市 让生活更美好
Better City,Better Life
EXPO

EXPO
2010
SHANGHA CHINA

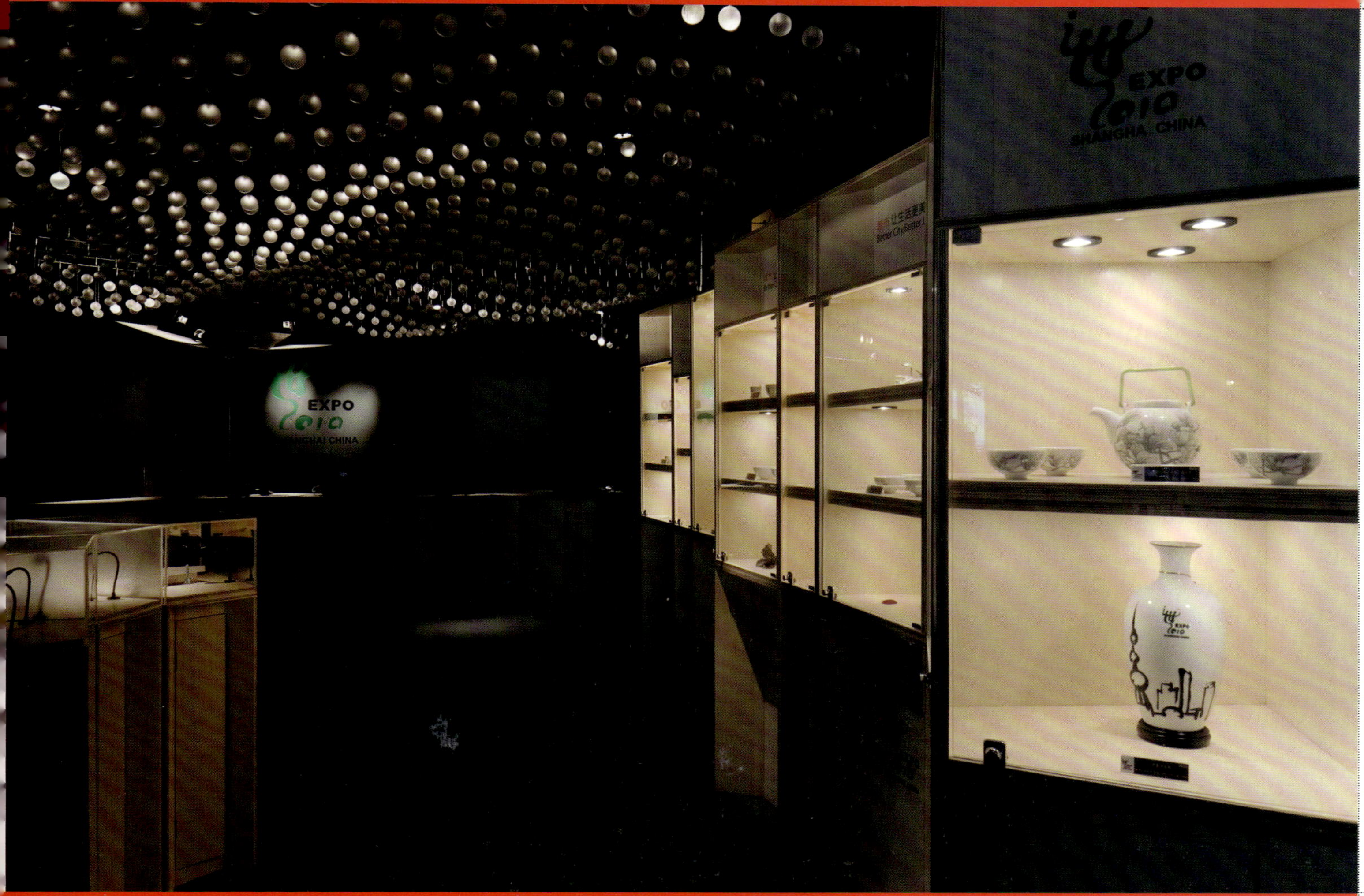

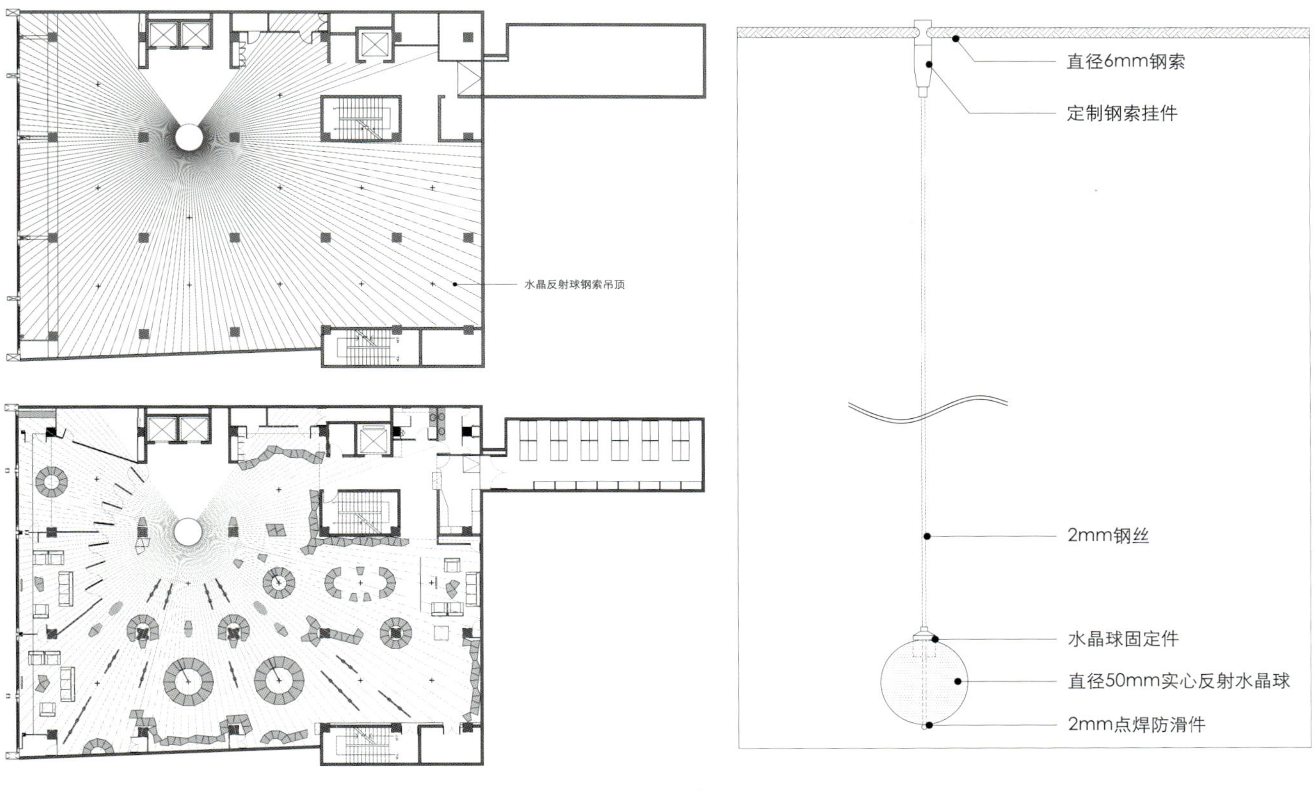

水晶反射球钢索吊顶

直径6mm钢索
定制钢索挂件
2mm钢丝
水晶球固定件
直径50mm实心反射水晶球
2mm点焊防滑件

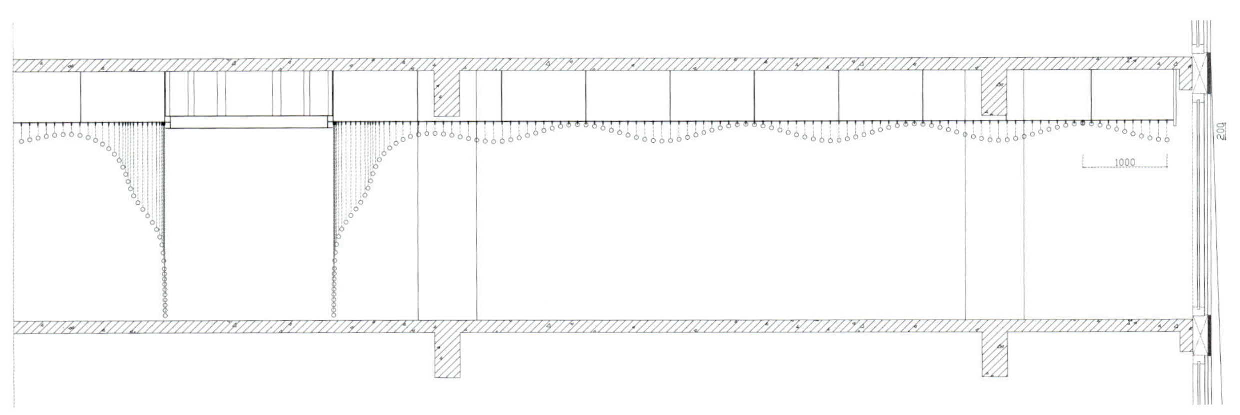

1000
200

Dongguan Toy Warehouse
东莞玩具仓库

设计单位：刘宇扬建筑事务所
设计团队：刘宇扬、卢小乾、冯国安、温茹、蔡春雅
项目地点：东莞塘厦镇
项目功能：仓储
建筑规模：10 800 m²
设计／建成：2006年／2008年

Design firm: Atelier Liu Yuyang Architects
Design team: Liu Yuyang, Lu Xiaoqian, Philip Fung, Wen Ru, Ciciya Cai
Location: Dongguan, Pearl River Delta
Program: Storage
Scale: 10 800 m²
Design/Built: 2006/2008

巨大而单一的建筑量体与工业区周边典型而多重的城乡建筑形成了强烈对比。仓库本身仅是包了一层铁皮的容器，但透过室内空间的分隔组合，它成为物流过程中的“整流器”。屋面锌板和采光板的错位排列亦令它成为当地的新城市地貌。

The large singular massing of the warehouse forms a stark contrast with the multiplicity of this typical industrial neighborhood. Merely a container clad with a layer of metallic skin, the building becomes a logistic "transformer" through a careful spatial arrangement.

Dongguan Toy Factory
东莞玩具工厂

设计单位：刘宇扬建筑事务所
设计团队：刘宇扬、蔡晖、林秋雷
项目地点：东莞塘厦镇
项目功能：车间、生产线、仓储
总建筑规模：15 000 m^2

Design firm: Atelier Liu Yuyang Architects
Design team: Liu Yuyang, Larry Tsoi, Charles Lam
Location:Pearl River Delta Dongguan,
Program: Manufacturing, assembly line, storage
Scale: 15 000 m^2

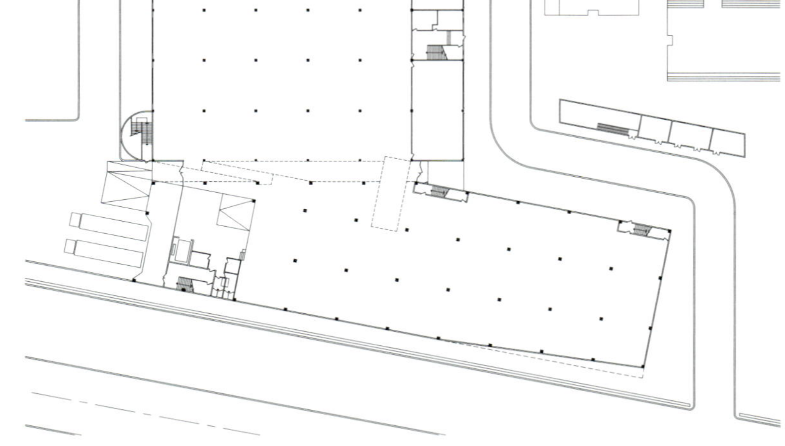

本项目为一家世界级的玩具制造厂提供一栋五层楼的装配与储存空间。基地位于具有"世界工厂"之称的东莞。设计的挑战性在于：建筑需兼备趣味性、实用性、耐久性，而且要符合工厂的整体形象——务实的管理层和熟练的工人所组成的团体，并维持每平方米1000元人民币的低廉造价。

作品探讨珠三角工业城市中通属建筑的可能与变奏。外立面使用的是极为普通的面砖，但透过在颜色和排列上的差异性，转换对廉价材料的既有印象。同时，新旧厂之间的连接天桥和斜角阳台扰动了原有的矩形结构，为工业厂房重新植入流动、停顿、和随着自然光变化的空间韵律。

The project investigates the possible mutations of generic industrial architecture in the Pearl River Delta. Exterior walls are clad with typical tiles, through colors and pattern variations, transforming the perception of cheap materials. A new sky-bridge diagonally inserted between the old and new part of the factory results in an interstitial outdoor balcony with acid-etched glass floor, in-planting in the rational structure momentous flow, suspension, and spatial rhythm that changes with the natural light.

Xinyu Science Museum
江西新余自然科学博物馆

设计单位：刘宇扬建筑事务所
设计团队：刘宇扬建筑事务所（刘宇扬、范芷康、林一麟、刘烨、蔡春雅），CHORA（Raoul Bunschoten、Ana Zazo、Alberto Alvarez），上海现代集团都市设计院
项目地点：江西新余
项目功能：展览、剧场、会议、研究、办公、餐饮
总建筑规模：50 000 m²
结构顾问：Structured Environment（Alan Burden）
环保顾问：Zero Energy First（Rabih el Fadel）

Design firm: Atelier Liu Yuyang Architects With CHORA Architecture
Design team: ALYA (Liu Yuyang, Mavis Fan, Lin Yilin, Liu Ye, Cai Chunya), CHORA (Raoul Bunschoten, Ana Zazo, Alberto Alvarez), Shanghai Xiandai Group Urban Design Institute
Location: Xinyu, Jiangxi
Program: Exhibition, IMAX theater, convention center, research center, office, cafe
Scale: 50 000 m²
Structure consultant: Structured Environment (Alan Burden)
Environmental consultant: Zero Energy First (Rabih el Fadel)

这是一个回应“气候变迁”议题的博物馆设计。主要的概念介由创造一个可成为“能量农场”的屋顶平台，而达成零碳排放的建筑环境。在此平台之下，两个不同的博物馆：科学技术和自然历史博物馆，在楼层上分开，但在空间上交织起来，不同的展厅和功能区由坡道、楼梯间、电梯和空间的视角来编织。这座博物馆中丰富的空间体验与线性的楼层组合起来，使潜在自由的游览流线贯穿于历史与创新进化之间。

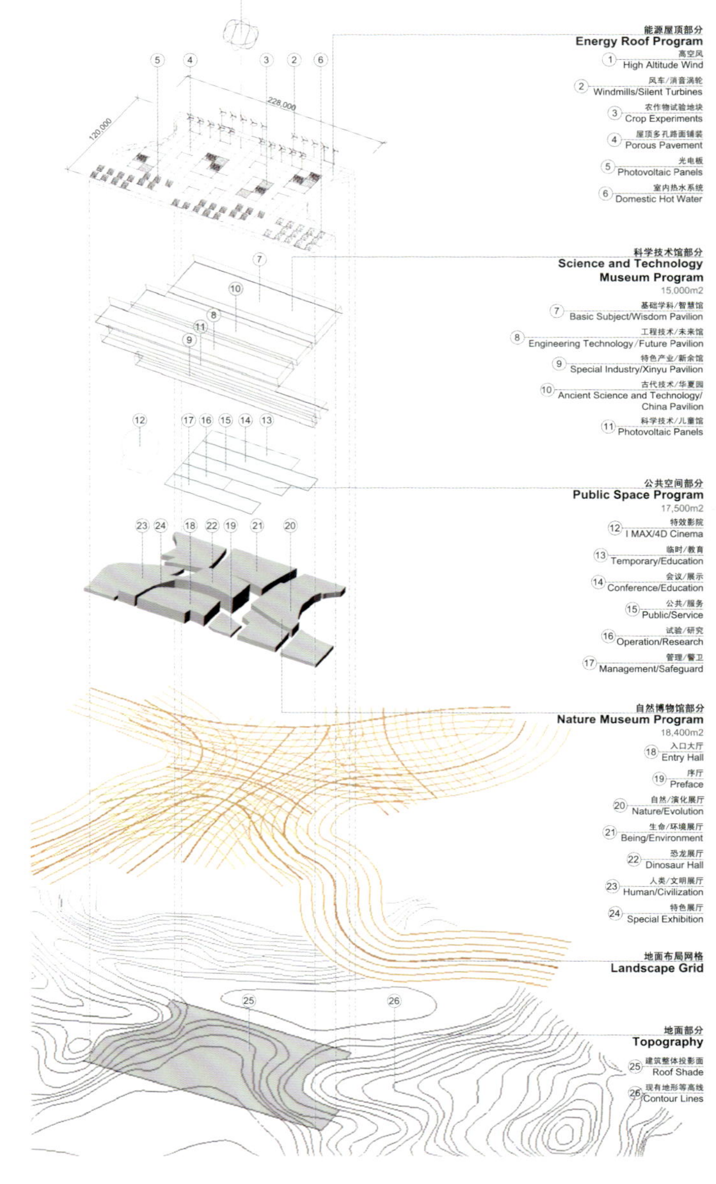

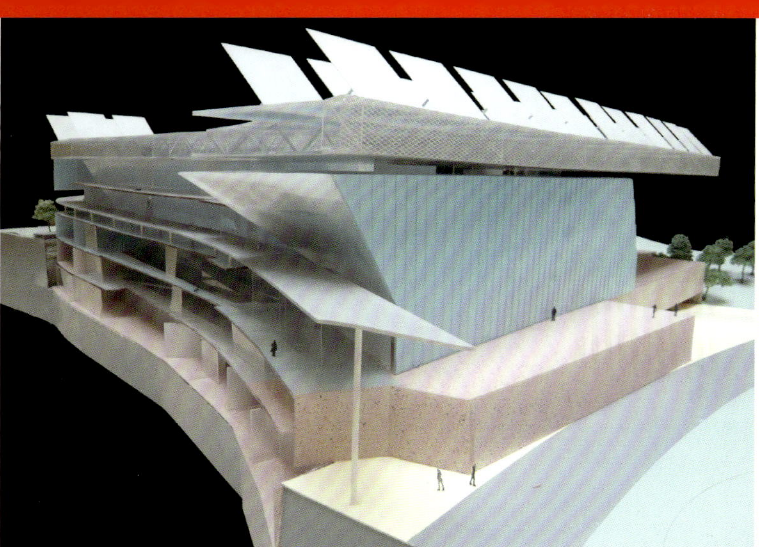

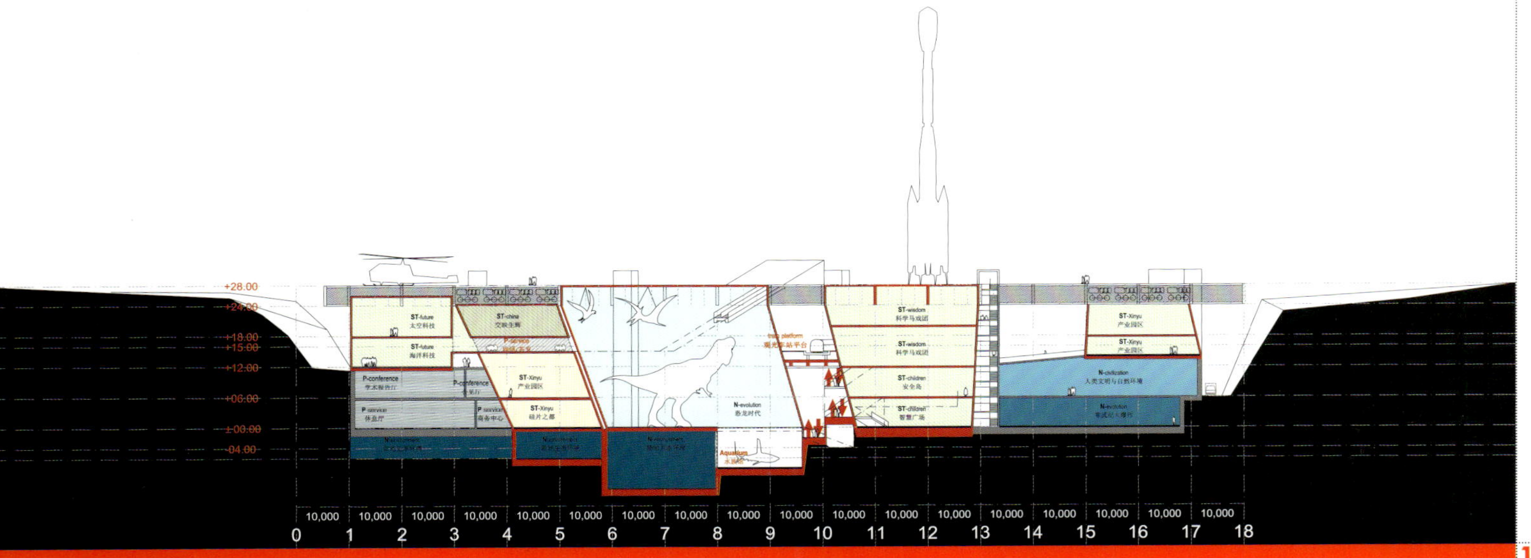

The design responses to the issue of "climate change" and proposes an "energy farm" on a gigantic roof structure, making it a zero-carbon museum. Underneath this platform, two museums: technology and natural history, are separated in stories but spatially interwined. Like fabric different exhibition galleries and programes are stitched together by ramps, staircases, elevators and spatial views. The museum is a rich spatial experience combining linear story lines with the potential to roam free through history and innovation.

Shanghai Museum of Contemporary Art
上海当代艺术馆

设计单位：刘宇扬建筑事务所
设计团队成员：刘宇扬、余振明、周天朗、蔡晖
改造前名称：人民公园花卉馆
地点：上海市人民公园内
合作单位：结构：Ronan Collins/机电：李德明（Perry Lee）
业主：龚明光基金会、上海当代艺术馆
基地面积：1 800 m²
建筑面积：3 900 m²

Design firm: Atelier Liu Yuyang Architects
Design team member: Liu Yuyang, Keith Yee, Tynnon Chow, Larry Tsoi
Project name before modification: Flower Pavilion at the People's Park
Project name after modification: Shanghai Museum of Contemporary Art (Shanghai MOCA)
Address: Shanghai, People's Park
Cooperation company: Structural: Ronan Collins/ Electrical & Mechanica: Perry Lee
Owner: Samuel Kung Foundation, Shanghai MOCA
Basic area: 1 800 m²
Construction area: 3 900 m²

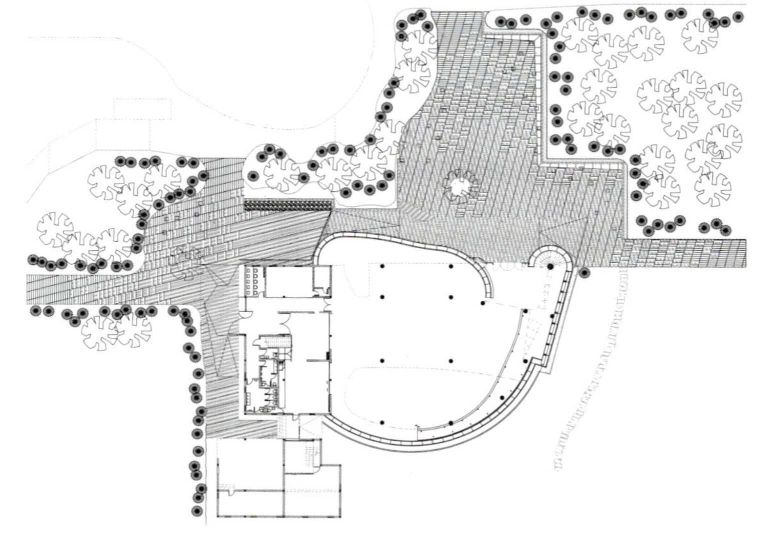

这是一个如何把城市建筑的“灰姑娘”转变为当代艺术“公主”的故事。在这个故事里，建筑设计者的角色更像是一名建筑“化妆师”。原本的建筑体由于政策考量不好拆。但是，每个参与的人都希望看到一座被重新赋予生命力的建筑。

“上海当代艺术馆”的设计并不想要一个“宣言式”的建筑，而更多的追求是其建筑语汇的“双重性”（duality）。它是一座介于现有和新造的建筑。首先，在原入口和三楼加建的部分，新的设计加入了数个比较突出的几何玻璃体，来“融解”旧玻璃房原有的外形。在原水泥房的部分，外墙以斜著排列的“蒙古黑”花岗岩配合了同样斜列的不锈钢窗框，体现出一种含蓄却与众不同的外观。既不是仅仅的装修，也不完全是单纯的加建，而是在保留原结构体的条件下做彻底的改头换面。

新“艺术馆”的功能必须兼顾艺术展览空间—所谓的白盒子的要求，又欲求体现其建筑本质上的意义—无论是建构、空间、结构、材料等方面。其中，斜坡桥的设计可以算是一个例子。藉由电脑结构模型的辅助，斜坡桥的设计用最少量的钢材（不到三吨）和最大的跨距（近三十米）连接了两个主展览层。弧状的钢结构体从不同切面穿过有如树林般的混凝土柱，提供了参观者从不同定点与高度观看大型艺术装置的可能性。

新“艺术馆”是一座介于园林和都市的建筑。由于它特殊的地理位置，人们先穿越绿意盎然的人民公园，再抵达这座更近乎于当代城市脉搏的建筑。从展馆的主玻璃体内和三楼的大阳台向外望，参观者得到了园林与都市的双重印象。在此，原“花卉馆”的功能得到了再生。人们不再只是欣赏馆内的花，而是从这里可以欣赏公园里所有的花草。

新“艺术馆”是一座介于隐喻与现实的建筑。说它是一颗黑钻石也好、一架隐形轰炸机也好，或者是解构主义遇上了简约主义也好。然而，更有意思的可能是这栋建筑所呈现的现实景象。事实上人们将可看到的是个多重现实景象：花枝招展的艺术品、火热兴建中的城市、偷得浮生闲的花园。当这栋建筑已成为这个城市的一部分的时候，艺术如何走入生活，就不仅限于狭义的硬体空间或“展览”空间。这栋建筑所能提供的，除了遮风避雨外而更多的是这个建筑所传达给这个城市的讯息、所提供的活动、所创造的文化。

The story of the Shanghai MOCA is about how the architectural "Cinderella"—an abandoned flower pavilion—was transformed into a "Princess" of contemporary art. The role of the architect in this case was more akin to that of a "make-up artist".

The design of the Shanghai MOCA was so not much about establishing a new manifesto, but instead to exploit the notion of duality, mediating between an existing form and new intentions. The original structure was an un-utilized but structurally in-tack glass and concrete building. A series of geometric glass volumes were introduced to replace the main entrance and to extend part of the third floor, dissolving the predictable form of the original glass pavilion. The diagonally-laid "Mongolian Black" stone cladding over the existing concrete building gives a much subdued yet differentiated expression, highlighted by the deep-recessed stainless steel window frames that are intentionally mis-aligned. The resulting work could neither be defined as a new building, nor a mere addition.

The new program mediates between the requirements for art exhibition—the need for a generic white box, and the desire for an appropriate architectural expression—one which celebrates the intrinsic quality of architecture, be it tectonic, spatial, structural, or material. The design of the ramp is one such example. Thanks to an elegantly resolved structural model, the ramp connects the two principal exhibition floors at a maximum span with a minimum usage of steel (just under 3 tons), producing a sweeping curvature that "dances" through the existing reinforced concrete columns in different tangential relationships, and allows for a circumscribed and ascending viewing of large-scale installations placed in the center of the main exhibition space.

The new museum mediates between landscape and city. Because of its unique location within the People's Park, visitors are required to meander through the 'garden of the proletariats' before arriving at the institution that is paradoxically more akin to the consumerist nature of the city outside. The largely unobstructed glazing of the glass pavilion and the roof deck of the third floor bring together a view of the park with the images of the city. Here the former function of the building as a flower pavilion is somewhat re-incarnated; instead of housing the flowers, the new building affords the visitors a view of the Park's lush vegetation from its galleries, café, and sun deck.

The building mediates between metaphor and reality. A gem, a stealth bomber, a collage of deconstruction meets minimalism; these are some of the possible metaphoric descriptions of the project. However, it is far more intriguing to adopt the views of a reality that is emerging through the building itself. There is in fact a multiple reality, with apertures to the art exhibited, the city being constructed, and the garden to be sought refuge in. When the building finally becomes a part of the city, how the art affects

one's life is no longer limited to the physical "exhibition" space. Rather, it's how the museum as an institution lays the ground for a new culture of the city. What the building can provide, besides a shelter for rain and sun, is the possibility of the events and the creation of a genuine culture.

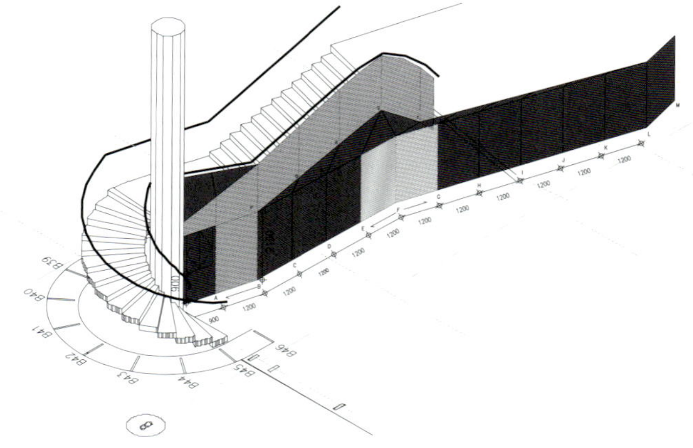

Zhujiajiao Art Museum
朱家角人文艺术馆方案

设计单位：刘宇扬建筑事务所
设计团队：刘宇扬、范芷康、刘烨、林一麟、Tim Brock
项目地点：上海青浦区朱家角镇
项目功能：展览、仓储
总建筑规模：2 500 m^2
设计时间：2008年

Design firm: Atelier Liu Yuyang Architects
Design team: Liu Yuyang, Mavis Fan, Chaton Liu, Lin Yilin, Tim Brock
Location: Qingpu District, Shanghai
Program: Exhibition, storage
Scale: 2 500 m^2
Design date: 2008

基地位于古镇风貌区的界限边。方案尝试从屋顶形式和传统符号如山墙、漏窗等建筑元素的转化，提出适合古镇的新建筑语汇，并介由视线、动线和光线上的安排，传达具有人文底蕴的建筑意境。

Located on the edge of the historic protection zone, the scheme attempts a new architectural language fit for the old town by re-interpreting the roof-scape and traditional motifs such as the "mountain wall" and "hollow window". Through the careful re-arrangement of the viewing angle, circulation, and light path, the design expresses a humanist approach to architecture.

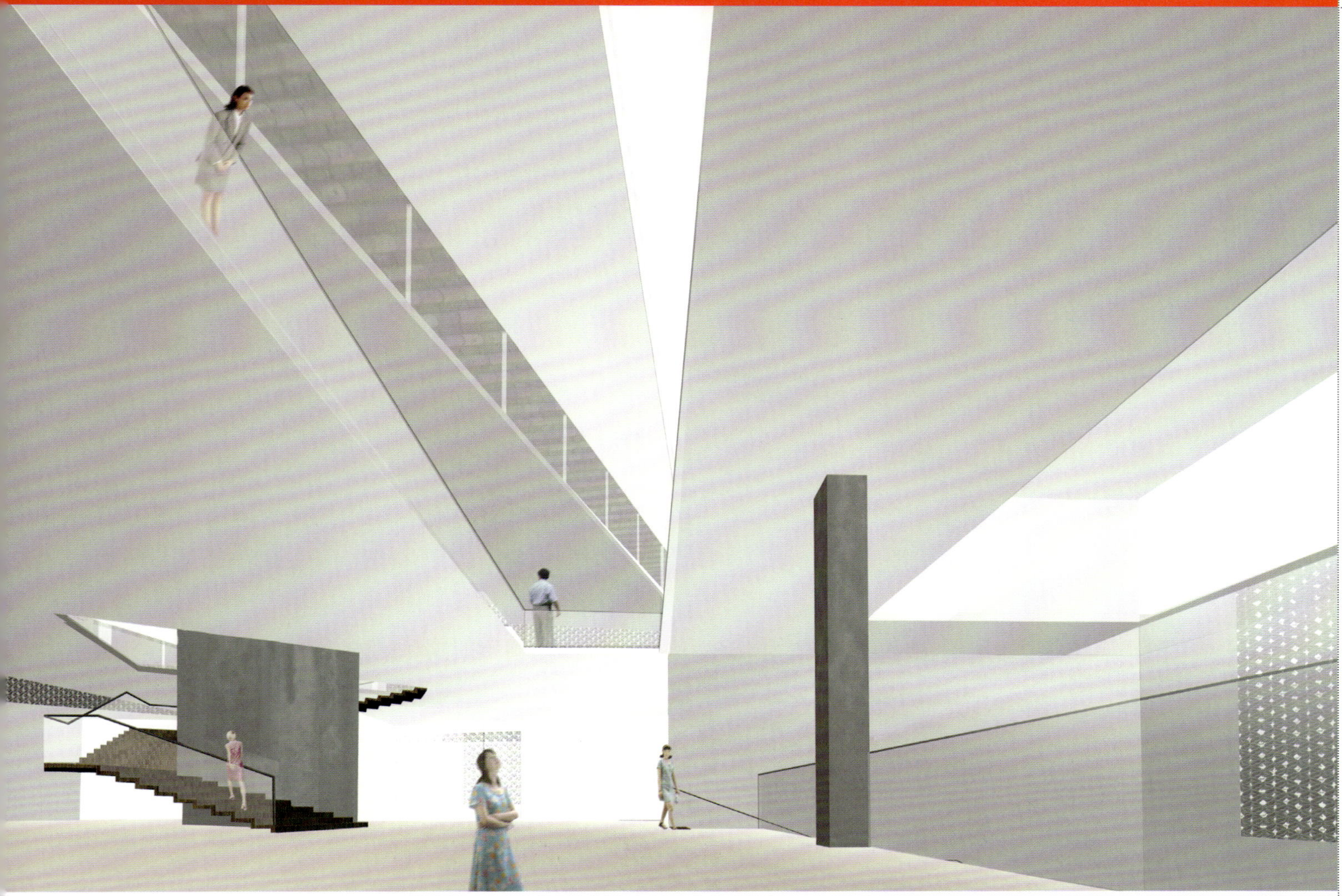

Ten Cultural Venues Of Laibing, Guangxi

广西来宾十大文化场馆

设计单位：美国DF国际建筑设计有限公司
主设计师：刘晓逢

Design firm: U.S. DIFFER International Architecture Design INC.
Lead designer: Liu Xiaofeng

作为建筑师，面对建筑群的规划设计，总会遇到比独立建筑设计更多的难题，广西来宾十大文化场馆也不例外，用地、个性与差异、建筑的经济效益、视觉影响力都是需要仔细研究考虑的环节，在经过反复的衡量和研究之后，我们决定运用入地、拔高、交叉共享、分割等多种设计技巧，在保证功能的情况下，做到收放自如，解决了用地紧张的问题。又通过建筑的不同体形与服饰（也即形体和外部材料）等建筑语言来表达同中有异、整体和谐的意向。

设计过程中我们始终遵循着三大原则：

1. 开放性和人性化：足够的开放性使人们可以轻松介入到各场馆的文化活动中来，同时通过电梯、坡道等的设计实现无障碍交通。
2. 生态节能：多层次的立体空间绿化结构反映了生态环保的理念，同时提供了一个绿色景观场，还可以通过许多新材料、新技术来达到节约能源的目的，如局部采用遮阳百页，设置内院形成自然拔风等方式。
3. 文化传承和前瞻新颖的原则：形式上的现代其实不能掩盖内容上对来宾民族文化的传承，文化上的传承是通过文化符号的意向来实现的，如白色文化石，深色文化石，红、白、灰、黄等壮族传统色彩，灰色瓦片贴墙，如同壮锦，中国式的红格墙等形式都传承了一定的文化意义。造型上具有前瞻性，意在未来几十年内，要有足够高的建筑设计水准，来引导来宾市的城市建设，使得来宾市能够在将来顺利接轨国际化、未来化的城市新格局，而这一点必须从现在的标志性建筑做起，才能引导其他建筑的设计，从而在建筑的标志性上提升来宾市的知名度。

总平面图

Liu Xiaofeng
Class 1 National Registered Architect
General Manager of U.S. DF International SZ Architecture Design INC.

刘晓逢
中国一级注册建筑师
美国DF国际建筑设计有限公司中国分公司总经理

个人主要作品：深圳购物公园南区、深圳市大中华TIME现代城、深圳坂田商贸城、深圳南海玫瑰园二期外观、成都锦江科技大厦、江苏扬州华泰130地块项目、四川万景国际项目、浙江华立天润凤凰城、重庆金洲港湾小区、安徽国电明园项目、天健黄阁路项目、东莞文化之都规划、防城港工业区规划、湖北省汽配城规划、长春市启明软件科技园、山东滕州行政商务办公区规划、深圳南澳珍珠岛旅游度假区规划、武汉月湖文化艺术中心、长沙市烈士公园新规划、汕尾大中华品清湖小区、湖北昌盛领秀中原项目、东湖国际大酒店、福建仁文大儒世家小区（国家康居示范小区）……

Major personal works: Southern Area of Shenzhen Shopping Park, Shenzhen Dazhonghua TIME Modern City,Shenzhen Bantian Commercial Centre,Second Phase Appearance of Shenzhen Nanhai Rose Garden, Chengdu Jinjiang Science and Technology Building, Jiangsu Yangzhou Huatai No. 130 Land, Sichuan Wanjing International Project, Zhejiang Huali Tianrun Phoenix City, Chongqin Jinzhou Harbor Residential Area, Anhui Guodian Ming Garden Project, Tianjian Huangge Road Project, Planning for Dongguan Cultural City, Planning for Industrial Area of Fangcheng Port, Planning for Hubei Autoparts City, Changchun Qirning Software Technology Park, Project Planning of the Government Commercial Office Section of Tengzhou, Shandong, Planning for Shenzhen Nanao Pearl Island Tourist Resort, The Moon Lake Culture and Art Area in Huhan, Re-planning for Changsha Martyr Memorial Park, Shanwei Pingqin Lake Residential Area, Hubei Lingxiuchunyuan Residential Area Project, East Lake International Hotel, Fujian Renwen Darushijia Residential Area(National Kangju demonstration district).

For an architect, there are always more difficult problems to be solved in the designing of an architectural complex than an independent building, and this is also the case with the ten cultural venues of Laibin. Land use, individuality and diversity, economic effects of the buildings, optic influences are all sections that deserve careful study and consideration. After repeated measurements and studies, we cracked the problem of limited usable land and achieved natural contraction and relaxation through the use of a number of design skills such as undergroundization, elevation, cross share, fragmentation and so on. Meanwhile, we give expression to the intention of coexistence of commonality and diversity and overall harmony by using the architectural language of different body types and clothes (or the shape and outer material) of the buildings.

Three principles are all along followed throughout the design:

1. Openness and humanization: sufficient openness enables people to easily participate in the cultural activities of all venues and meanwhile, elevators and ramps provide them with barrier-free access.

2. Ecologically energy-saving: multi-layered spatial greening structure reflects the ecologically environmental-friendly idea and provides a green landscape. A number of new materials and skills, such as partial application of blinds and designing courtyards for natural air draft, can also be used to achieve energy saving.

3. The principle of cultural transmission and predictability and novelty: the modernization in form should not mask the transmission of Laibin culture in substance, which is to be realized through its cultural symbols such as white cultural stones, fuscous cultural stones, conventional colors of red, white, grey and yellow of Zhuang ethnic group, grey tiles for wall covering, Zhuang brocade-like patterns, Chinese red grid walls and so on. The predictability in form means the architectural design level should be high enough to lead Laibin's city construction in the coming decades and bring Laibin successfully in line with a new city order featuring internationalization and futurism. Only by starting from present symbolic buildings can we reach this goal and lead the design of other buildings, thus enhancing Laibin's popularity in terms of architectural symbolism.

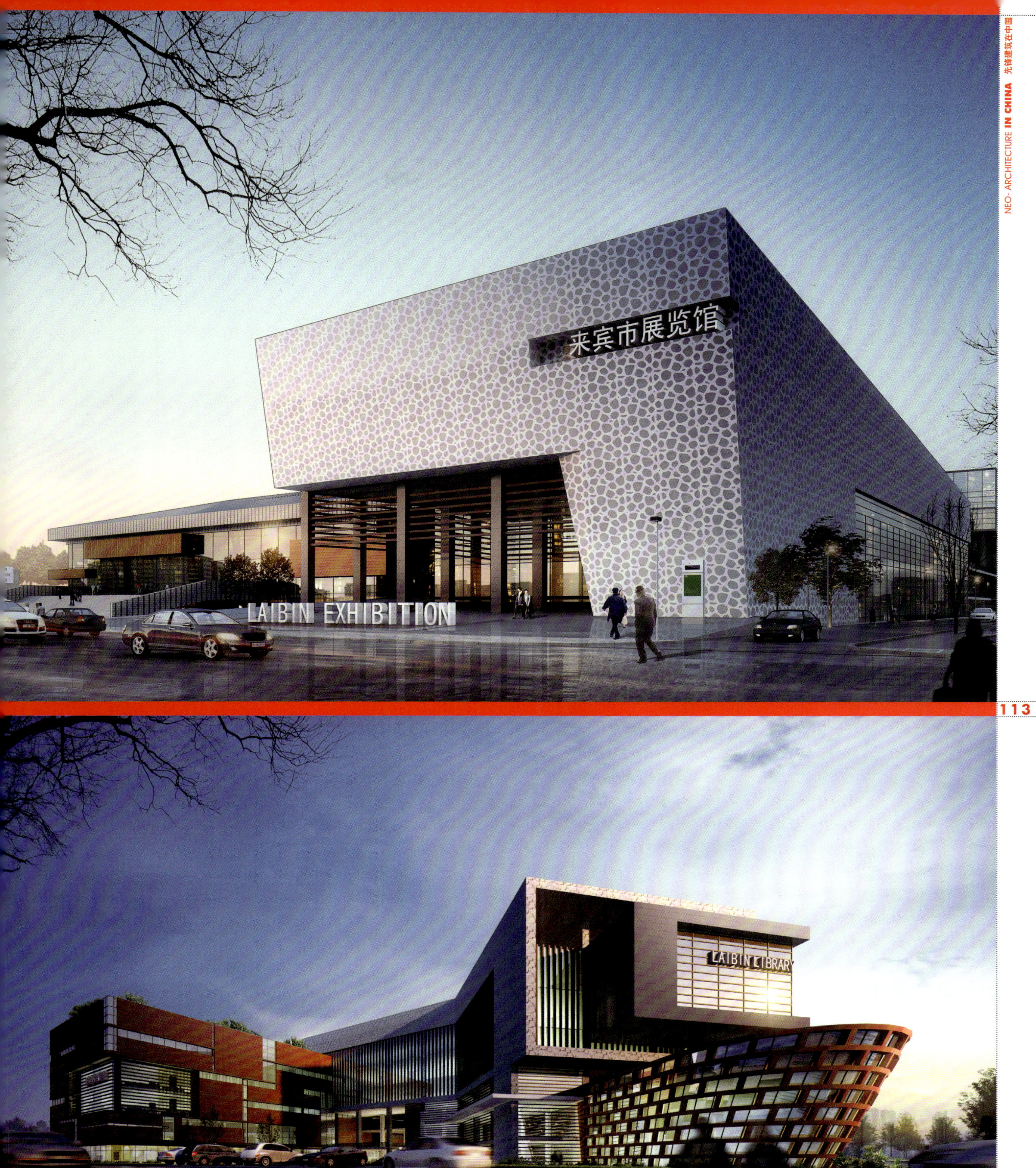
来宾市展览馆
LAIBIN EXHIBITION
LAIBIN LIBRARY

来宾市档案馆

来宾市博物馆

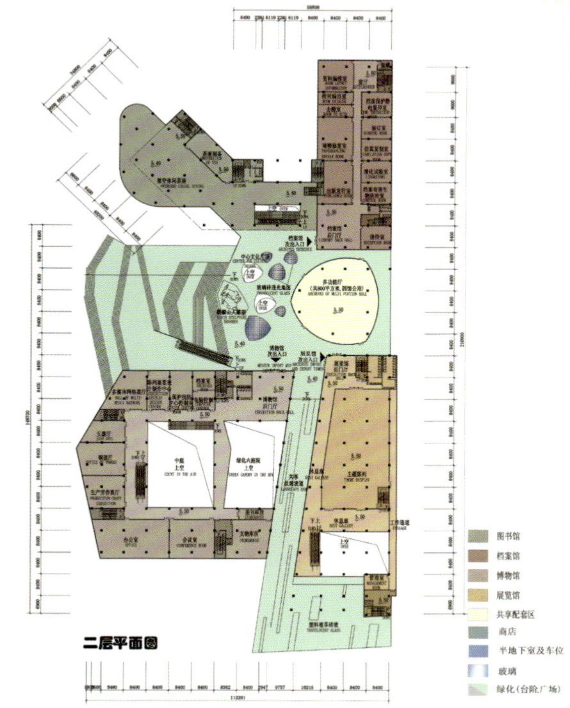

二层平面图

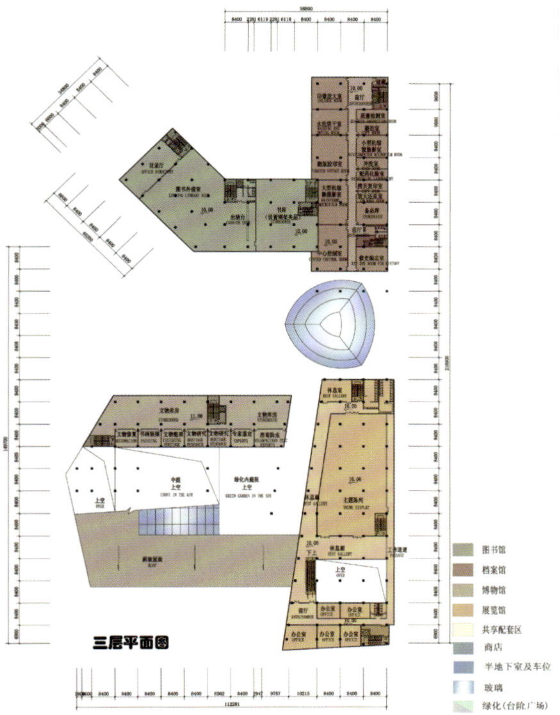

三层平面图

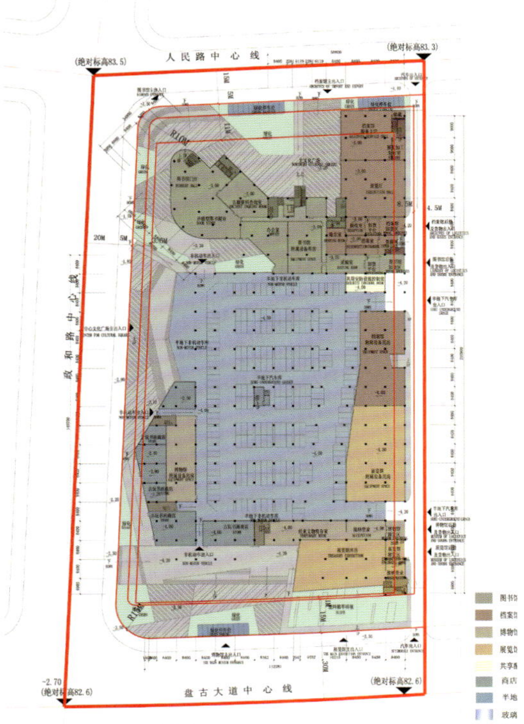

负一层平面图

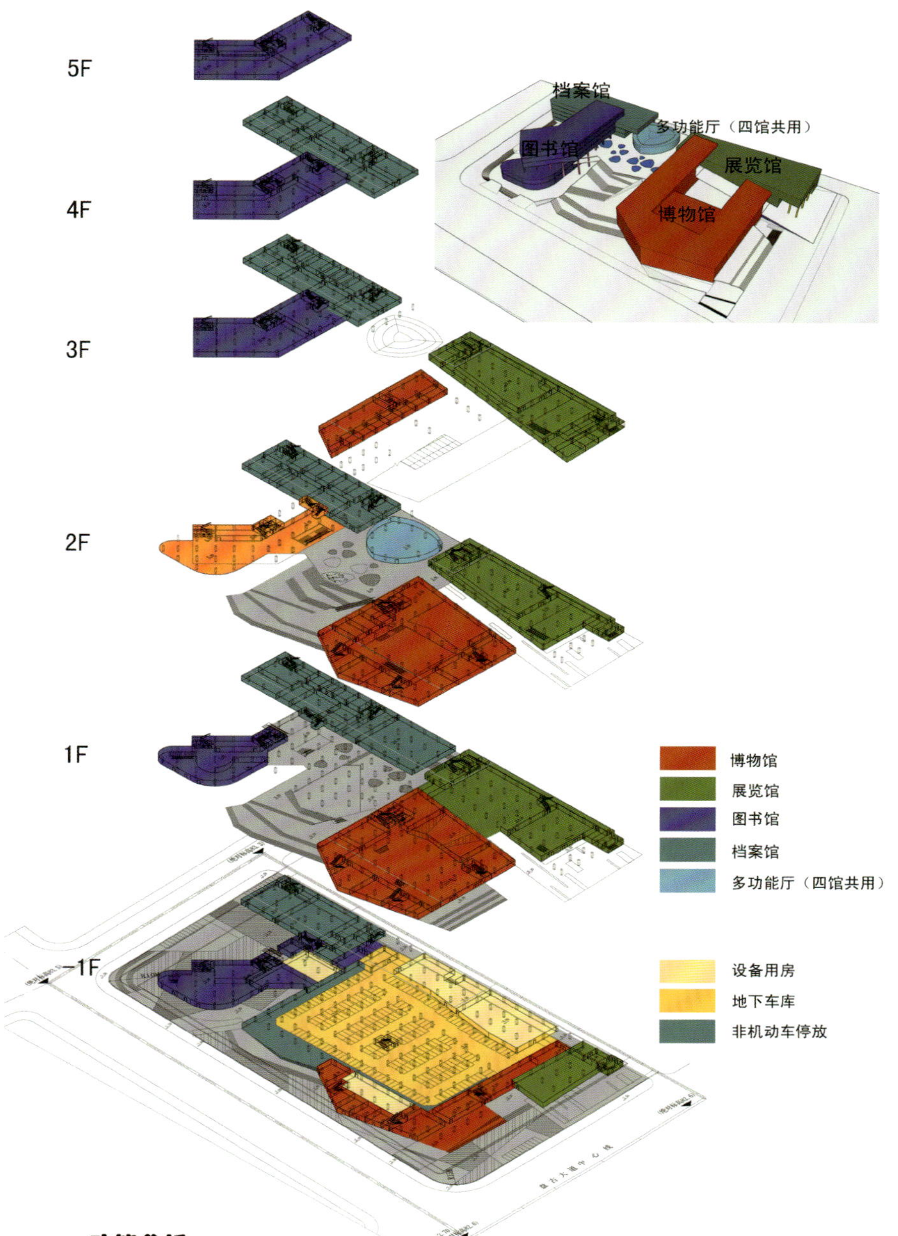

功能分析

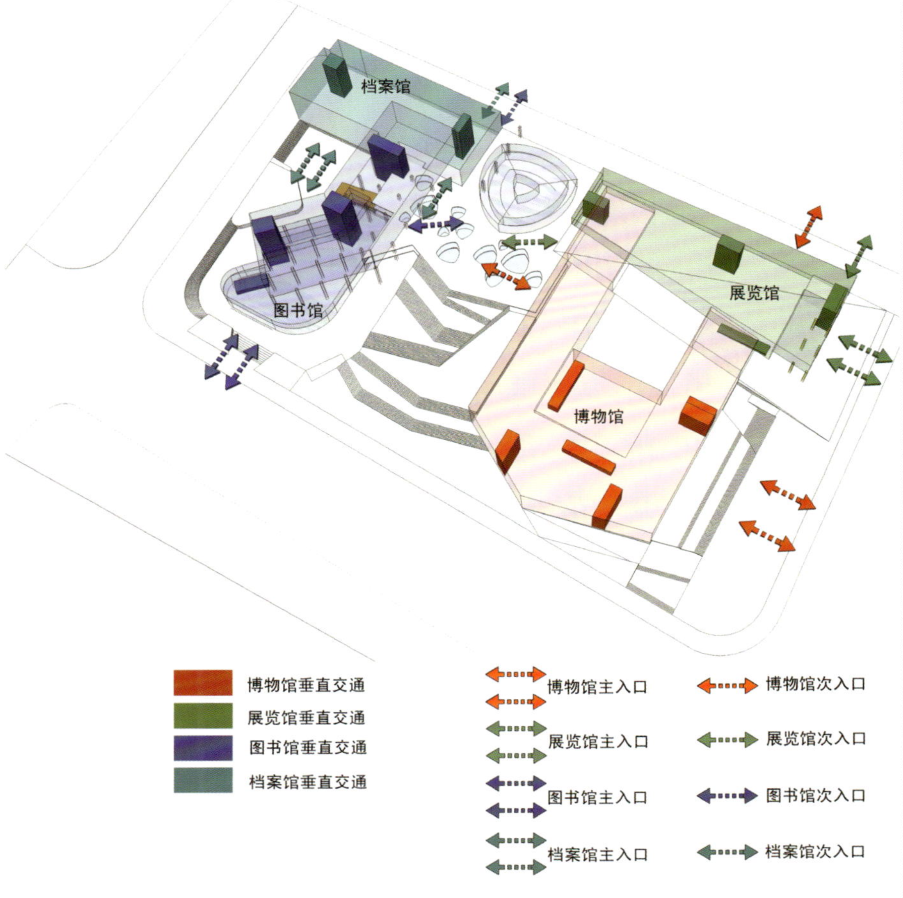

交通组织分析图

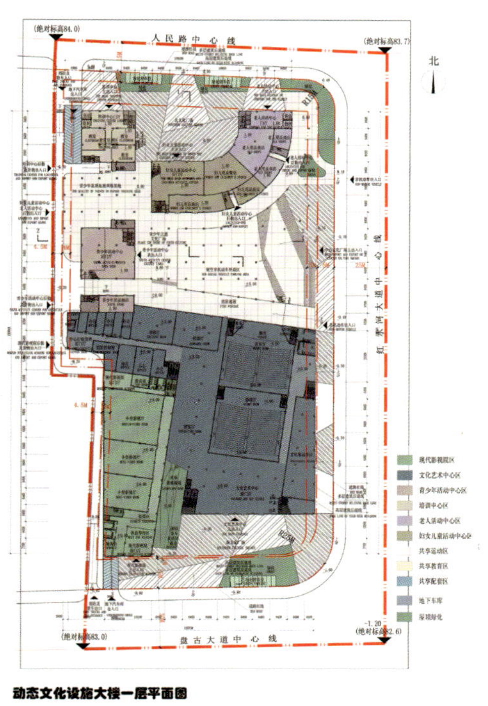

动态文化设施大楼一层平面图

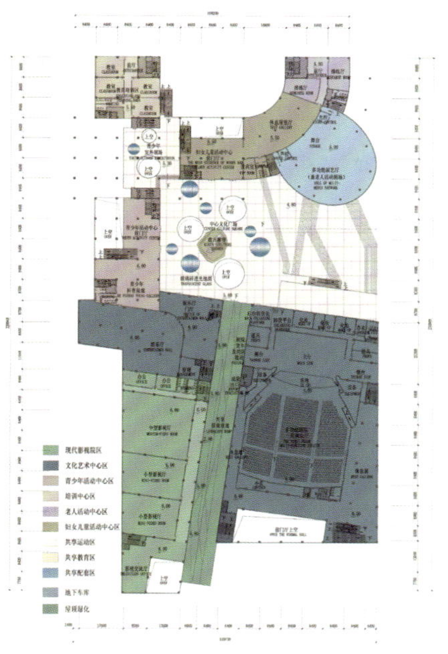

动态文化设施大楼二层平面图

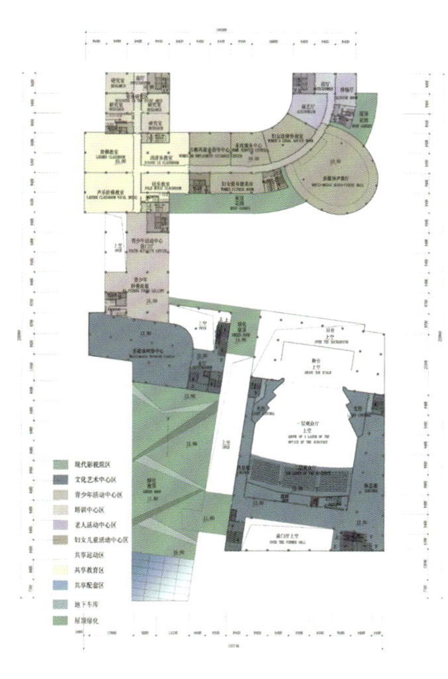

动态文化设施大楼三层平面图

培训中心
共用空间
青少年活动中心
妇儿中心
老年活动中心
影剧院
文化艺术中心

8F
7F
6F
5F
4F
3F
2F
1F
-1F

影剧院
青少年活动中心
培训中心
文化艺术中心
妇儿中心
老年人活动中心
文化艺术中心
影剧院
青少年活动中心
妇儿中心
老年人活动中心
培训中心
文化艺术中心主入口
文化艺术中心次入口
影剧院主入口
影剧院次入口
青少年活动中心主入口
青少年活动中心次入口
培训中心主入口
培训中心次入口
妇儿中心主入口
妇儿中心次入口
老年人活动中心主入口

交通组织分析图

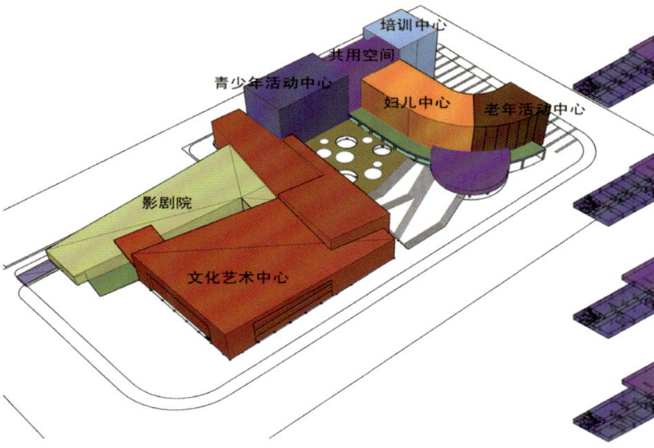

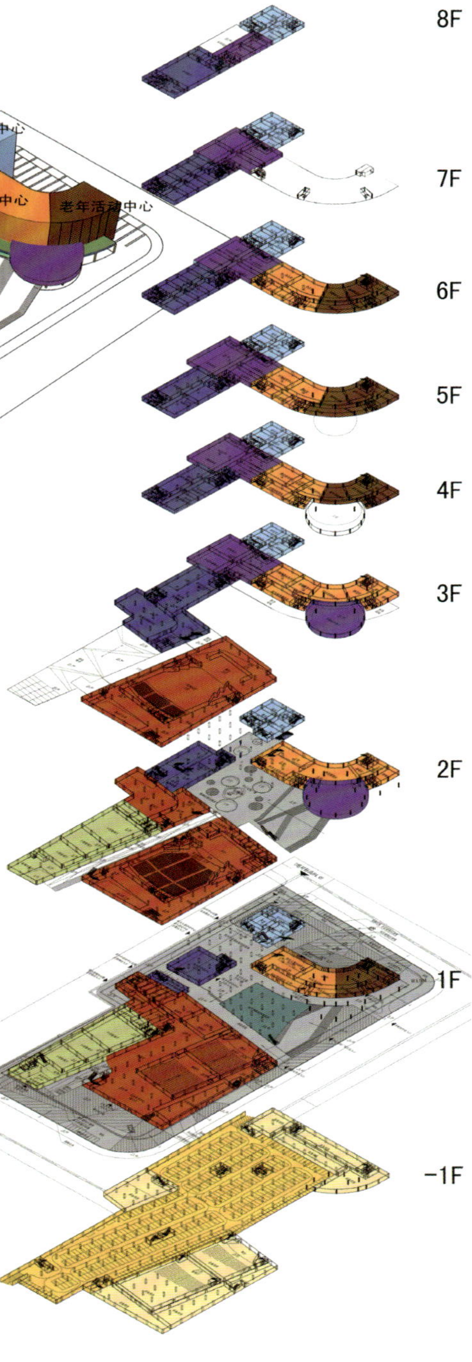

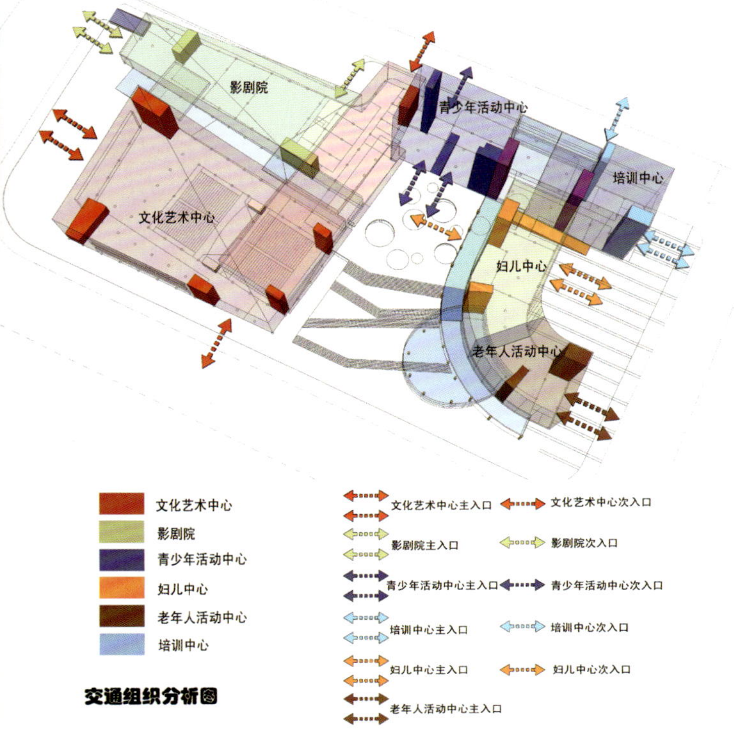

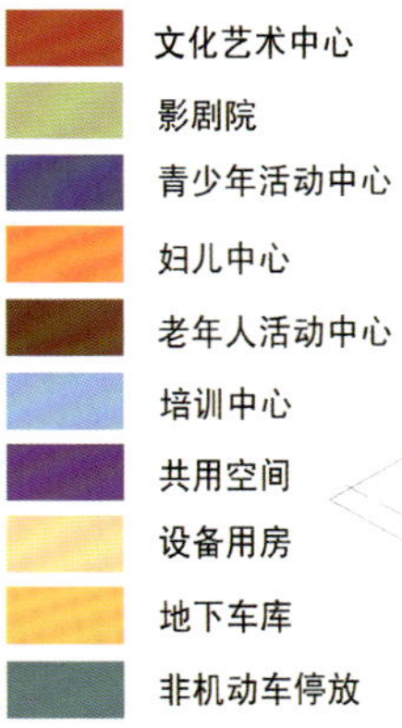

文化艺术中心
影剧院
青少年活动中心
妇儿中心
老年人活动中心
培训中心
共用空间
设备用房
地下车库
非机动车停放

功能分析

Shanghai World Expo 2010: The Shanghai Corporate Pavilion Design

2010年上海世博会——上海企业联合馆

设计单位：非常建筑
主持设计：张永和
项目负责人：臧峰
室内建筑师：刘鲁滨、沈海恩
项目团队：王兆铭、王宽、仇玉、梁小宁、王琳、吴瑕、张明慧、邓鸿辉、吴杰、陈冠楠
专业咨询：总装备部设计研究总院
结构材料：钢
建筑面积：4 949 m²
设计时间：2008年–2009年
施工时间：2009年–2010年

Design firm: Atelier Feichang Jianzhu
Principal architect: Yung Ho Chang
Project architect: Zang Feng
Interior architects: Liu Lubin, James Shen
Project team: Wong Siuming, Wang Kuan, Liang Xiaoning, Wang Lin, Wu Xia, Zhang Minghui, Wu Jie, Chen Guannan
Consultants: Center for Engineering Design and Research under the Headquarters of General Equipment
Structure material: Steel
Building area: 4 949 m²
Design period: 2008–2009
Construction period: 2009–2010

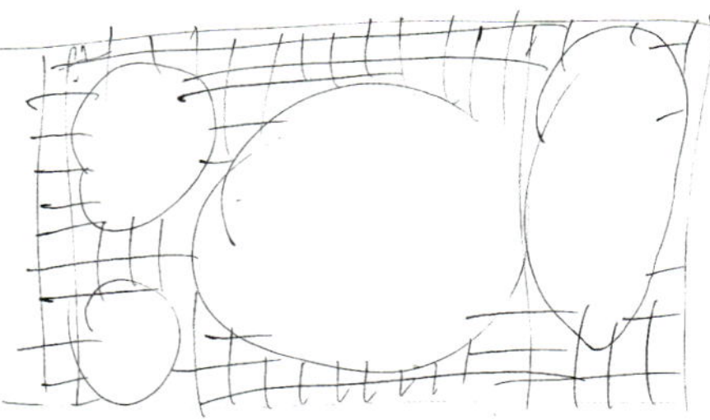

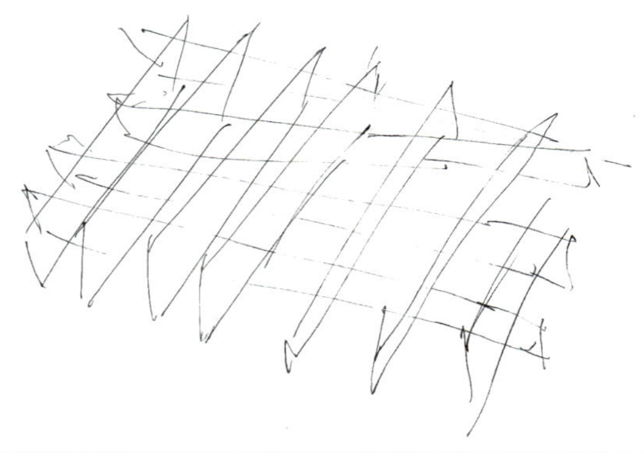

Yung Ho Chang
Atelier Feichang Jianzhu

张永和
美国注册建筑师
非常建筑工作室主持建筑师
美国麻省理工学院建筑系教授

1956年出生于北京，曾在中国和美国求学，于1984年获得伯克利加利福尼亚大学建筑系建筑硕士学位。自1992年起开始在国内实践，并于1993创立非常建筑工作室。他曾荣获诸多奖项，如1987年荣获日本新建筑国际住宅设计竞赛一等奖第一名，美国"进步建筑"1996年度优秀建筑工程设计奖，2000年获联合国教科文组织艺术贡献奖，2006年获美国艺术与文学院的学院建筑奖。至今为止出版发表 8 本书籍和专著，包括英法双语图书《Yung Ho Chang / Atelier Feichang Jianzhu：A Chinese Practice》（《张永和／非常建筑——一个中国建筑师的工作室》）以及意大利语图书《Yung Ho Chang：Luce chiara，camera oscura》。他曾多次参加国际建筑及艺术展，从2000年起先后五次参加威尼斯双年展。曾在美国和中国的建筑学校任教，曾任2002年美国哈佛大学设计研究院丹下健三教授教席，2004年美国密歇根大学伊利尔・沙里宁教授教席。他是北京大学建筑学研究中心教授、创始人。

Born in Beijing and educated both in China and in the US, Chang received Master degree of Architecture from the University of California at Berkeley in 1984. He has been practicing in China since 1992 and established Atelier Feichang Jianzhu (FCJZ) in 1993. He has won a number of prizes, such as First Place in the Shinkenchiku Residential Design Competition in 1987, a Progressive Architecture Citation Award in 1996, the 2000 UNESCO Prize for the Promotion of the Arts, and the Academy Award in Architecture from American Academy of Arts and Letters in 2006. He has published eight books and monographs so far, including one in English/French entitled *Yung Ho Chang / Atelier Feichang Jianzhu: A Chinese Practice* and one in Italian entitled *Yung Ho Chang: Luce chiara, camera oscura*. He participated in many international exhibitions of art and architecture, including five times in the Venice Biennale since 2000. He has taught at various architecture schools in the USA and China; he was the Kenzo Tange Chair Professor at Harvard in 2002 and the Eliel Saarinen Chair Professor at Michigan in 2004. He is a Professor and Founding Head of Graduate Center of Architecture at Peking University.

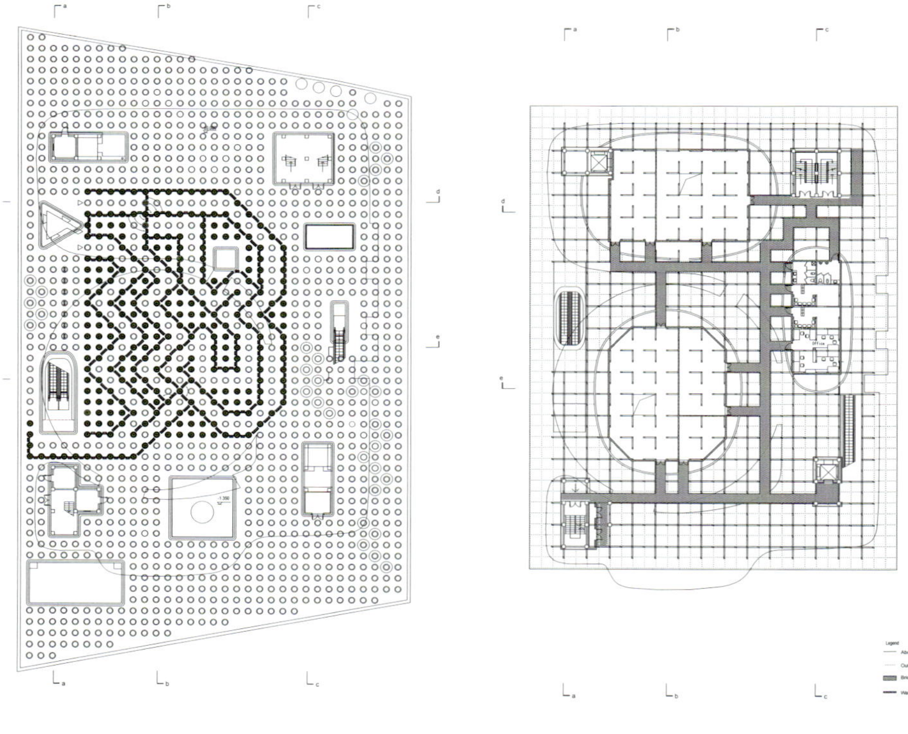

1976年，由伦佐·皮亚诺与理查德·罗杰斯设计的巴黎蓬皮杜中心建造完成。整栋建筑的内部结构完全暴露在外，并将纵横交错的管道系统作为建筑表现形式。凭借该史无前例的未来主义设计，蓬皮杜中心成为了建筑领域的重大突破。

至2010年，我们经历了一段长时间的高速技术发展，建筑内部的大量技术组件将会成为建筑的基本元素。我们希望将这一观察应用到世博会上海企业联合馆的设计中去：上海企业联合馆是一个自由、流动的空间，它不只是由墙围合界定形成的，而更是由密集的技术网络立方体包裹而成。在这个技术网络立方体中，内装LED塑料管与喷雾系统可以依照电脑程序的控制，不断改变建筑的外观。

不过，企业联合馆的建筑设计并不是"为技术而技术"。首先，我们希望通过这些复杂的技术和外观变化，在视觉上向人们传达上海企业联合馆的精神和人们对美好未来的梦想。技术不仅凝结着丰富的想象力，还象征了上海工业与工业精神。其次，我们还希望通过技术来探究和解决日益严峻的能源和可持续发展问题，例如：新型塑料材料的使用，以及太阳能和雨水的采集。

世界博览会是通向未来的窗户。作为国际化大都市，上海不但传承了历史辉煌的荣耀，也在经历着飞速的发展，而且始终保持着一种面向未来的乐观主义精神。借2010年世博会之机，上海企业联合馆将通过设计来诠释上海——这座21世纪伟大城市的独特魅力。

环保技术应用

1.能源利用全新途径——太阳能热水发电

上海企业联合馆在建筑屋顶上布置了1 600 m²的太阳能集热屏，收集太阳能生成的95° C热水，通过超低温发电新技术发电。这个技术开辟了利用太阳能发电的全新途径。这些电能可供建筑展览和日常用电。

2.可循环材料再生利用——再生塑料

据不完全统计，上海每年产生的废旧光盘在3 000万张以上，却只有25%得到了回收与再利用。如果将这些光盘回收清洗，可以再造出新的塑料（聚碳酸酯）颗粒。上海企业联合馆的外围立面材料采用聚碳酸酯透明塑料管，将各种技术设备管线容纳其中，共同构成建筑虚幻隐约的外立面。当世博会结束后，这些塑料管也很容易进入到再生

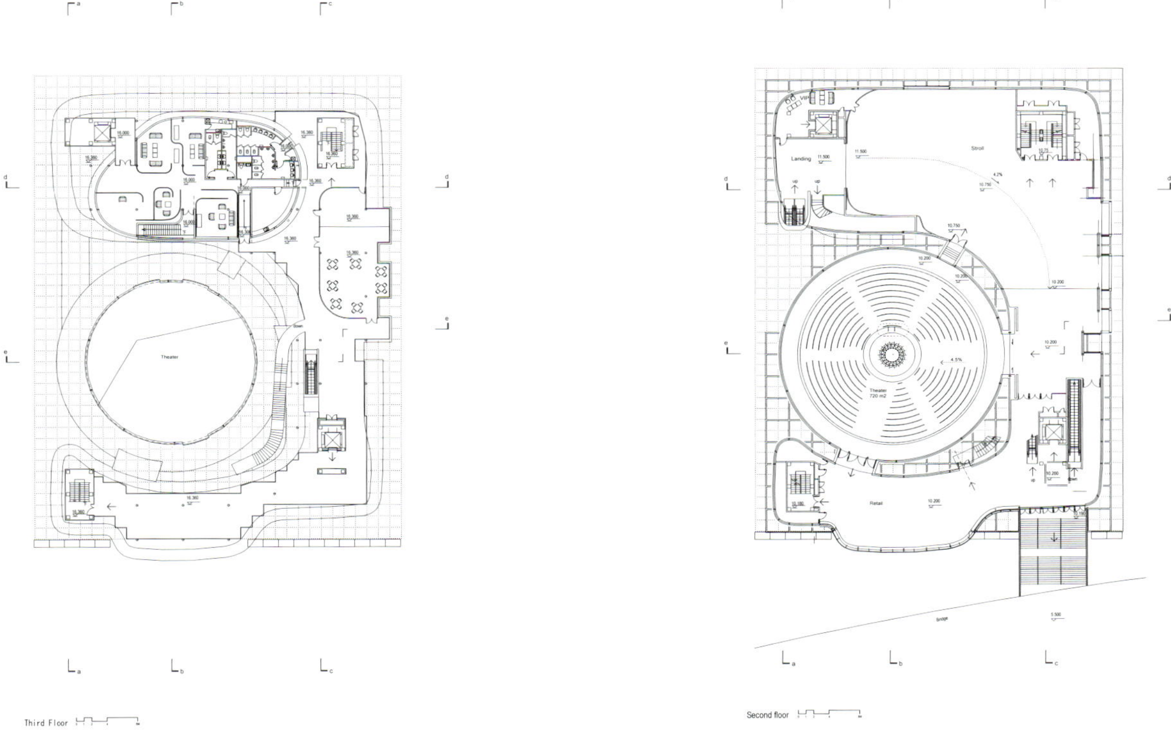
Third Floor

Second floor

In 1976, Centre Pompidou in Paris, designed by Renzo Piano and Richard Rogers, turned the building inside out and made utility ductworks part of the architectural expression. It was unprecedented thus a breakthrough in the field of architecture.

In 2010, we have gone through a long period of rapid technological advancement and the amount of infrastructure in a building has dramatically increased to the point that technologies are today's basic building blocks. For Shanghai Corporate Pavilion at the World Expo, we would like to manifest this observation in our design: the interior spaces of the Shanghai Corporate Pavilion, which are shaped as a series of free, flowing forms, will not only be enclosed by walls of the static kind but also a dense, cubic volume of infrastructural network, including LED lights and mist making system, which are capable of changing the appearance of the building from one moment to another as programmed through computer.

However, our design is not embracing technology for the technology's sake. Rather, we like to convey visually the spirit of the Shanghai Corporate Pavilion, the dream of a brighter future, through sophisticated technologies. Technology is about the enrichment of imagination and symbolic of the industry and industrialism of Shanghai. Also through technology, we like to address the pressing issue of energy and sustainability. A part of the architectural infrastructure is designated for the solar energy harvesting and rain water collecting, and the external facade will be made of recycled polycarbonate(PC) plastic.

World Expo is always a window to the future. Shanghai, as a historically progressive yet still fast developing international metropolis, has been all along the embodiment of this forward-looking optimism. As architects, we take the special occasion offered by the World Expo 2010 to solute Shanghai, a great city of the 21st Century, through our architectural design.

Application of Environmental Protection Technologies

1. Solar Energy System

The Shanghai Corporate Pavilion features a 1 600 m^2 area of solar heat-collecting tubes on the roof. These solar tubes can collect solar energy to produce hot water up to 95°C. Ultra-low temperature power generation techology, is a new, highly efficient approach to harvest electricity through solar power. The power generated using this technology can be used for both the exposition and everyday life.

2. Recycled Plastic Material

Shanghai produces nearly 30 million of waste CDs every year, and only 25% of them are reclaimed and recycled. If these CDs were reclaimed and washed, they could be

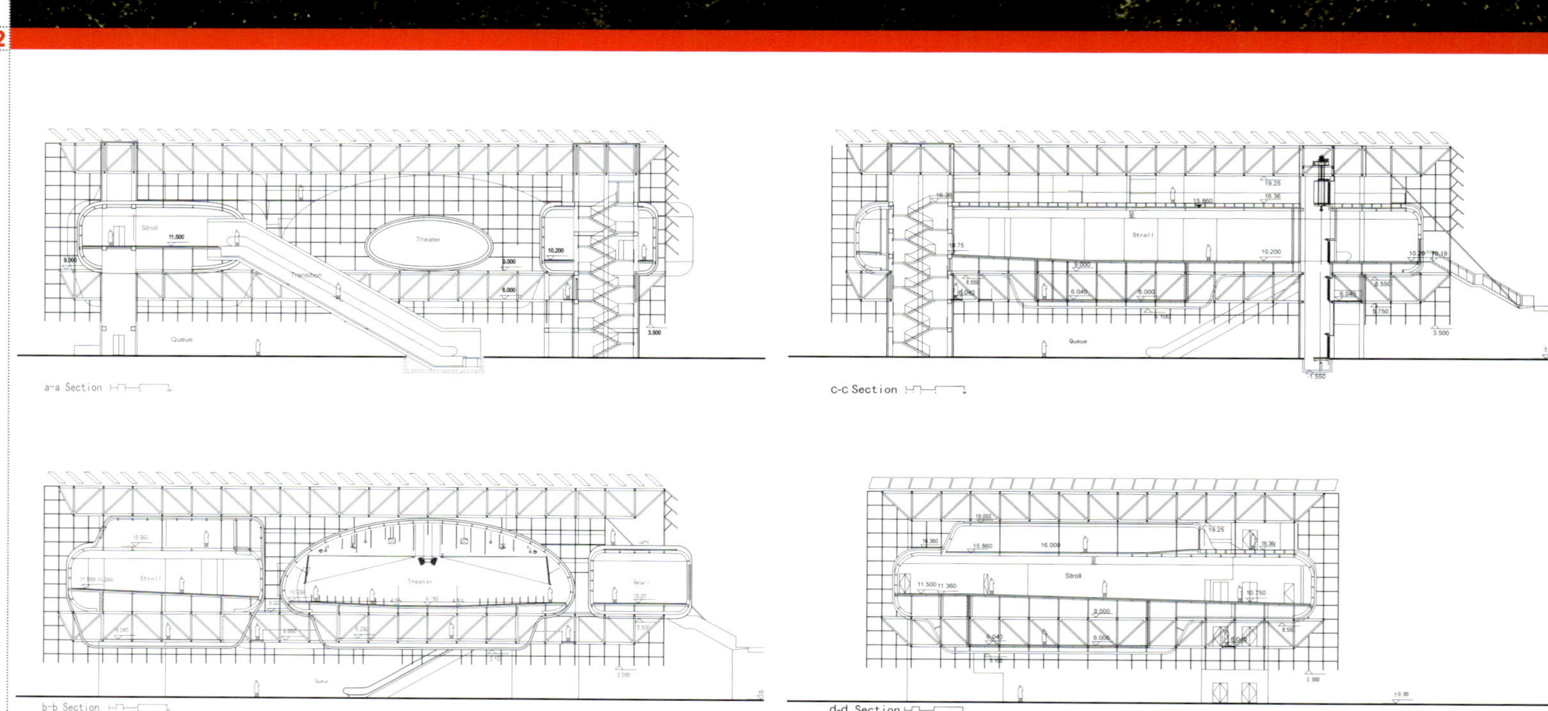

循环体系之中，节省社会整体能耗。

3.充分利用自然界资源——水/雾

上海企业联合馆场地范围内的雨水将得到回收，经过沉淀、过滤和储存等技术处理之后，可用作场馆内的日常用水，更可以为喷雾方案提供水源。喷雾方案不仅能够降低局部环境温度、净化空气、带来舒适的空间小气候；更能按照程序的控制，在建筑底层形成丰富多样的喷射图案，令企业联合馆的整体外观呈现出多变、飘逸的特点。

used to produce polycarbonate granules and manufacture more polycarbonate plastic products. The external facade materials of the Shanghai Corporate Pavilion will use polycarbonate transparent plastic tubes to create its dreamlike appearance. After the Expo, the plastic tubes can also be easily recycled to reduce social wastage.

3. Water/Mist System

For the Shanghai Corporate Pavilion, rainwater will be collected and recycled. After such treatments as sedimentation, filtration and storage, rainwater can be used for daily purposes at the pavilion and for the mist spray in particular. The mist can lower the temperature, purify the air and create a comfortable micro-climate around the pavilion. The mist spray can also be used to form various patterns under the ceiling of the entrance hall and make the overall appearance of the Shanghai Corporate Pavilion fresh and elegant.

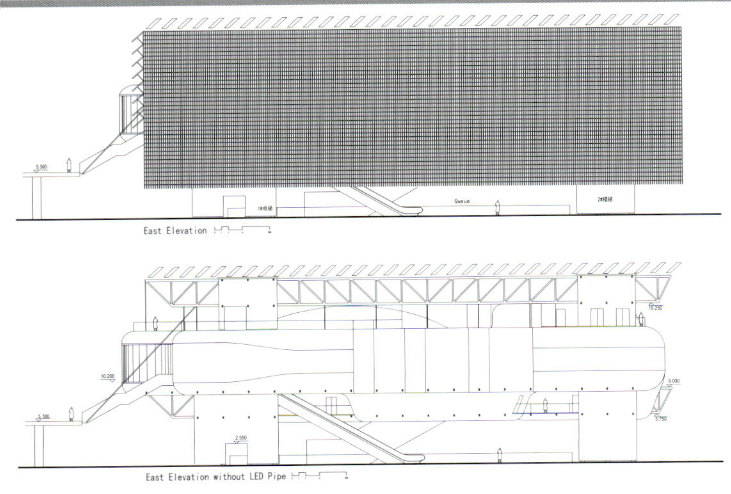
East Elevation
East Elevation without LED Pipe

Ordos Protestant Church

鄂尔多斯基督教堂

设计单位：北京三磊建筑设计有限公司
设计总监：张华
设计师：周厚陶
设计时间：2009年
建筑面积：3 000 m²
高度：37m
业主：鄂尔多斯市规划局

Design firm: Beijing Sunlay Architectural Design Co.Ltd.
Chief designer: Zhang Hua
Designer: Hotao Chow
Design date: 2009
Building area: 3 000 m²
Client: Ordos City Planning Administration Bureau

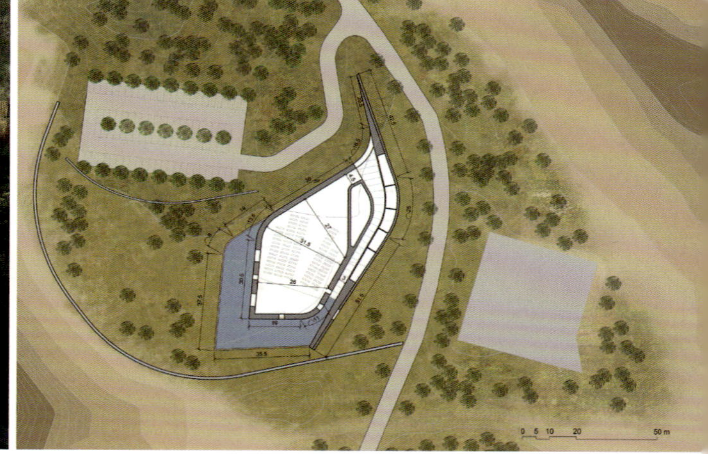

Zhang Hua
Beijing Sunlay Architectural Design Co.Ltd.

张华
北京三磊建筑设计有限公司 设计总监

张华先生介绍

三磊总裁及设计总监张华，1991年毕业于清华大学建筑学院，获博士学位，国家一级注册建筑师，香港建筑协会会员；于1994年创立北京三磊建筑设计有限公司。

十几年来，张华与三磊同事完成了大量城市设计、公共建筑、住宅建筑的设计工作，其中宁波交通银行获浙江省优秀设计奖，宁波建设银行获建设部优秀设计奖，北京西单光大银行与民生银行大厦获北京市优秀设计奖。张华主持完成的作品还包括：北京来福士广场、北京国瑞城、当代万国城、丽都水岸、橘郡、龙湖滟澜山等。近几年来，通过参与Moma系列建筑的设计实践以及北京旧城改造和廊坊生态城的规划设计工作，张华及三磊同事将技术、环境、人文因素统一整合，致力于可持续发展的城市建设研究。将业主的利益、公众的利益以及建筑师的社会责任放在首位，在解决每一个具体而复杂的问题过程中寻求三者平衡，渴望对每一个具体问题找到一个至臻完美的答案，从而创造出有效、适用、令人向往的人类生存空间。

公司简介

北京三磊建筑设计有限公司是国家建设部直属最早实行股份制的设计公司，始建于1990年，1994年获得国家综合甲级设计资质，2005年获得ISO-9001质量体系认证。经过十几年扎实、稳定的建设与发展，三磊公司已成为一个拥有近二百人设计团队的综合性设计公司，并广泛获得同行与客户的好评。

北京三磊建筑设计有限公司是一个充满活力与合作精神的集体，公司设计骨干来自知名的设计院校、优秀设计院和海外留学归国群体，他们有着优秀的教育背景和实际工程经验，并共同努力逐渐形成了独特的三磊设计文化，即富于创新精神与优雅的设计品味，有高度责任感的从业品德和严把

质量的设计品质。三磊公司在发扬与建设自身文化的同时，始终保持着开放与吸纳精神，扎实而稳定地扩大公司规模，并与境外十几家国际知名的设计机构有着学术与业务合作关系。

三磊公司关注绿色建筑：完成以及正在设计中的绿色建筑包括北京当代MOMA、万万树MOMA、太原MOMA、杭州西溪湿地、廊坊万庄生态城、北京金融街大屯综合楼、青岛大荣世纪综合楼、北京海淀图书城等。

十几年来，三磊公司的客户包括海内外各类投资机构、发展商以及政府机构，已有大量建筑实施建成。我们象珍惜生命一样看待公司的信誉，随时准备接受新的挑战，给客户提供超值的设计作品。

Zhang Hua graduated from School of Architecture, Tsinghua University in 1991 and received the Doctor Degree. He is the National Registered Architect as well as member of Association of Hongkong Institute of Architects. He founded Sunlay Design in 1994. For more than 15 years, Zhuang Hua and his team has done numerous works, including Xidan Zhongwu Complex, Beijing Wanguocheng MOMA, Taiyuan MOMA, Beijing Raffles City, Tianjing Bridge Cultural Museum and Ordos Protestant Church. Zhang Hua and his team concern about Sustainable City and Architecture.

《圣经·创世纪》中被洪水淹没，留在方舟里保全生命的诺亚，一天放出鸽子去探测洪水是否已经退去，当鸽子回来时，嘴里衔着一个新拧下的橄榄枝子，诺亚就知道地上的洪水退了。后来人们就把鸽子和橄榄枝当作和平的象征；基督教传入我国以后，也有用和平鸽作为装饰纹样的。

坐落于鄂尔多斯一座小山上，这座基督教堂的设计灵感之一来源于其地形。设计师首先从地形作为设计的出发点，结合鄂尔多斯实际的气候特质：鄂尔多斯总是阳光明媚，天总是比别的地方显得高一些，这些都被带入设计灵感中。周围的环境色彩对比强烈，蓝天和褐土对比产生出强烈的视觉效果，为教堂产生了完美的周边环境。营造出了丰富的昼夜背景变化。它形成了对于鄂尔多斯这座城市而言，独特的教堂景观。

方案命名为"和平鸽"，通过重新诠释和平鸽用喙衔回橄榄枝的故事，赋予了教堂新的寓意和诗意。本教堂是混凝土结构，外立面为白色涂料表面。其流线的外形同时顺应了地块周边的道路走向。其内外空间关系是通过对光线和阴影的描写，深层次解读教堂的空间。其设计元素是为了表现出教堂文化的和谐和平静。

白鸽，一种和平的象征，同时也代表飞翔、轻盈、优雅和平静，它可以和谐地融入周边环境。在国外，教堂是宗教的象征，它代表了宗教的权力，同时也是人类跟上帝沟通的地方，天堂和人间沟通的地方，这也是为什么以前的教堂不断挑战建筑极限，越建越高的原因。

三磊设计的鄂尔多斯基督教堂，既传承了传统的教堂文化，又融入了新的设计元素。柔美的建筑线条加上微妙的光线关系处理，营造出了全新的供人们祈祷以及庆祝的空间，三磊的这个方案旨在营造鄂尔多斯新的身份，营造一个现代感十足而又不失传统文化底蕴的一座建筑，因为我们相信，未来总是基于今天基础之上的，铭记历史轨迹非常重要。

Located on top of a hill of Ordos, planned as a green open space for the city, the project takes its inspiration from the topography of the land. The surrounding landscape offers a strong contrast of colors and depth, creating a rich changing background from day time to night time for the church's settlement. It sets framed views of the church in a characterized landscape of excavated rocks proper to a city like Ordos, in Inner Mongolia.

The scheme, named "Dove of Peace", gives its metaphor and poetry to the church by re-interpreting a contemporary and abstract silhouette of the bird caring a branch of Olive in its beak. The Church has a concrete structure and uses white crepi finish for its facades. Its dynamic shape follows the adjacent curved road that crosses the site. The dialogue between the outside and the inside space is emphasized by the play of shadows and light that creates complexity and depth in the reading of the space. Its elements are thought to reflect harmony and tranquility in this place for prays and celebration.

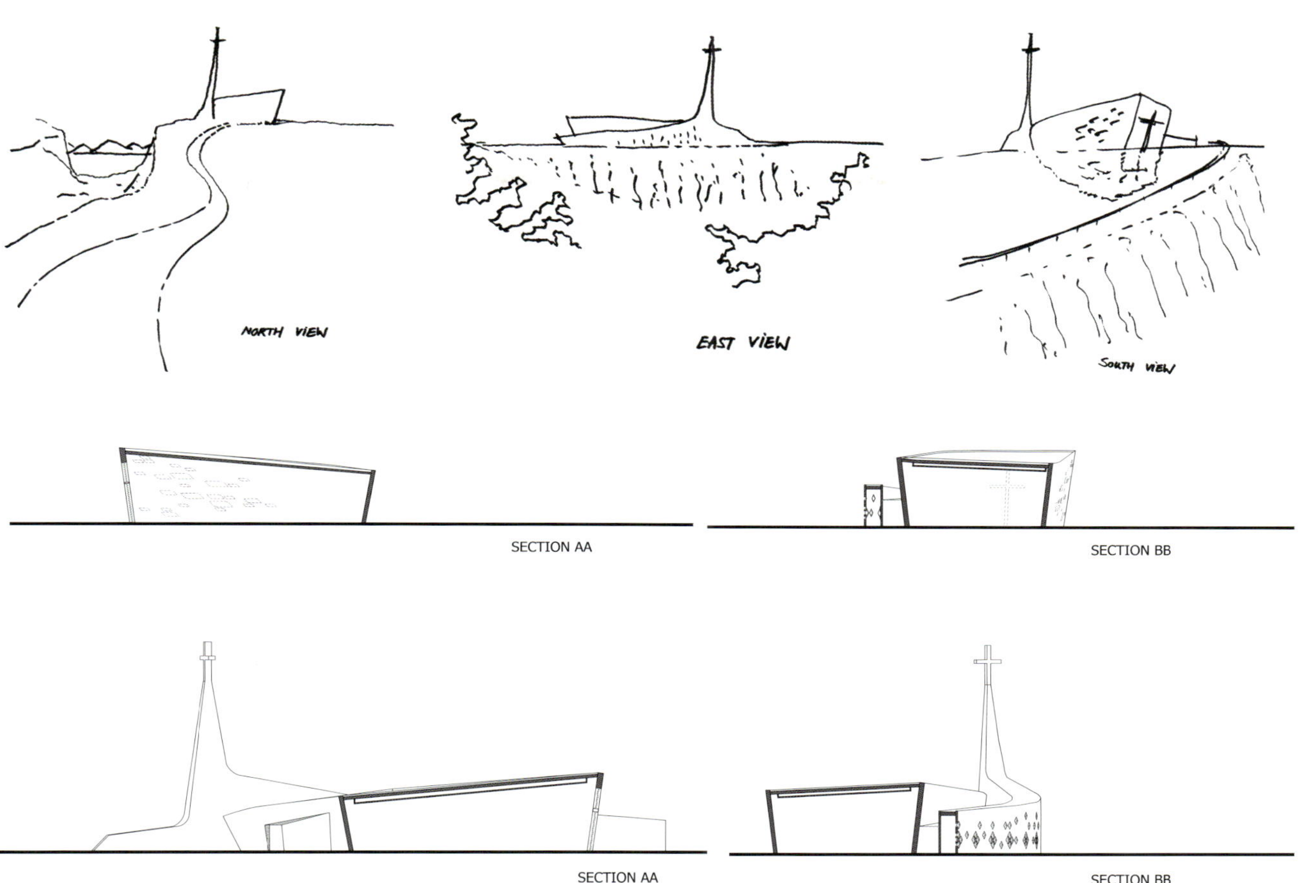
NORTH VIEW
EAST VIEW
SOUTH VIEW
SECTION AA
SECTION BB
SECTION AA
SECTION BB

Qingcuiyuan Club House

晴翠园别墅小区会所

设计单位：北京三磊建筑设计有限公司
设计总监：张华
设计团队：范黎等
落成时间：2008年
建筑面积：2 400 m²
业主：北京丰联房地产开发经营有限公司
照片摄影：舒赫工作室

Design firm: Beijing Sunlay Architectural Design Co.Ltd.
Chief designer: Zhang Hua
Design team: Fang Li
Design date: 2008
Building area: 2 400 m²
Photography: Shuhe Photographer

晴翠园别墅小区会所位于温榆河西岸，蜿蜒而至的温榆河在这里变宽；会所面向河中的小岛，岛上覆盖着密集的树木。第一次看场地便被这里的绿色打动。这样的特定场所决定了位于此处的建筑应是既独立站立的物体，又能融入并更好地体现它所在场所的意境。

时空交融在这种容纳性极强的场地中，鉴于会所所服务的多文化背景的人群，建筑被定位为冲撞与交融：多元文化、风格的碰撞；划时空的交融。它是温和并且自然的。它讲述一个古老与现代的故事，两种美学世界之间的相遇。

红砖墙体与玻璃虚空 会所地处斜坡上，结合地势，由坡上西面入口进入会所首层，地下一层东面的阳光餐厅则位于河岸之上。建筑主体由南北两个体块斜向构成，在平面布局上具有古典建筑语言所强调的轴线感与对称性，在空间上则呈现出现代建筑语言所追求的空间流动感与内外一致性。红色的亭泥砖砌成的厚墙构成会所的主体，其断裂、开孔处则为玻璃虚空。它们一并构成凝固的实体与流动的空间。建筑内外空间均在寻求与场地的对话，精心引人的阳光与景色形成生动的室内空间。不同的开窗方式形成多样化的光线，光影和空间交织出特有的节奏。建筑空间与外部自然风景交替呈现。首层的入口大厅、娱乐室、健身房、更衣室，地下一层的酒吧、阳光餐厅，二层的游泳池、阅览室、屋顶花园，为进入其间的人们提供多样的、不同的空间感受，体会行于其间、停留于其中的乐趣。

内庭院建筑的缝隙营造出会所中心的内庭院。它为入口大厅提供迷人的对景，引入光线，使整组建筑层次更丰富，更有深度。宜人尺度的内庭院构成会所的中心，它与地下一层阳光餐厅中的室内植物园、向外延伸的露天咖啡、会所周边所营造的绿化景观、水系以及原有的自然景观完美结合，使绿色景观渗透于建筑之中。

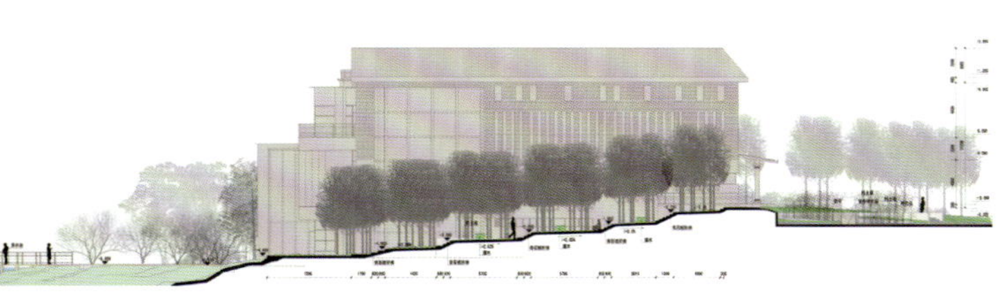

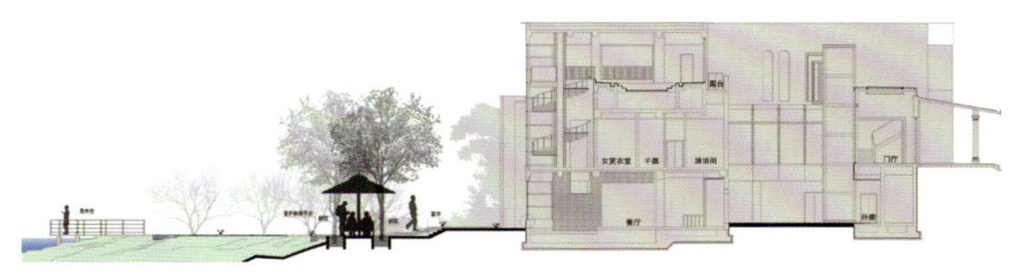

Qingcuiyaun Club House is located on the west bank of Wenyu River, Chaoyang District, Beijing, which has excellent condition of graceful natural landscape. The design concept is not only to create a unique building, but also to integrate it into this attractive landscape environment.

Qingcuiyaun Club House shows two topics, Collision and Blend, the collision of different cultures and styles, the blend of time and space. It is telling a story which is ancient and modern. It is describing an aesthetics encounter between east and west.

Hitectural design scheme considers `axis and symmetry' which are emphasized by classical architectural language, `fluxion and consistency' which is sought by modern architectural language. Red brick walls and transparent glazing are employed to create coagulated building mass and flowing spaces. Inside courtyard with comfortable scale is the continuation of greening, water scene and original natural landscape.

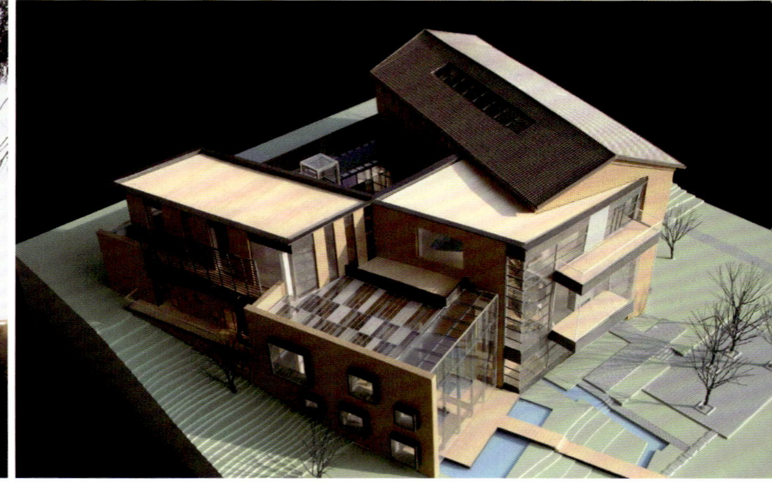

Tianjing Bridge Culture Museum

天津桥园桥文化博物馆

设计单位：北京三磊建筑设计有限公司
设计总监：张华
设计团队：范黎等
建筑性质：公共综合建筑
建筑面积：2 220 m^2
业主：天津市环境投资有限公司
照片摄影：舒赫工作室

Design firm: Beijing Sunlay Architectural Design Co.Ltd
Chief designer: Zhang Hua
Design team: Fan Li
Type: Public and Mixed-use
Building area: 2 220 m^2
Client: Tianjin Environment Development Investment Co.,Ltd.
Photography: Shuhe Photographer

天津园桥文化博物馆是一座公园之中的博物馆。

它位于天津桥园公园的中心位置，处于主入口相对应的中轴线上。它是桥园公园的"点题"主体建筑和区域标志。由于它所处的特殊场地，我们将它定义为"休闲型展示空间"，满足人们"看"的欲望：在"看展示"的同时，也能"看外面风景"。

三磊介入设计时，此项目的主体结构已施工完成。须在原有的结构基础上进行设计调整，重构建筑轮廓，使人们无论近观远眺，均能感受到建筑本体构思的起源——开启桥。

我们将它设计为一个"散步建筑"，随人们行走的路线，外部与内部空间的转换，建筑与所处场地的空间关系随即在眼前展开，充满了丰富的变化，在空间的运动使我们的视觉系统不断的感觉期待与惊奇。插入建筑间的钢桥引导人们走近展馆，眼前展现的仍是满眼绿色；建筑底部被设计为多变的折面，形成被穿越的宜人灰空间；原有繁多的十六根结构柱被多手法处理，以达到减量与弱化的目的；呈折线而起的建筑体、U形围合空间、自内向外延伸的咖啡平台、室内外空间的框取渗透……，使建筑得以有机地契入场地。

对建筑的欣赏源于对它的体验。桥文化博物馆是可以被"通过"和"穿越"的，无论是在内部还是在外部：是与人们形成互动关系的建筑。建筑主体和陈列主题相辅相成，如同一个不可分割的整体。进入建筑内部，展览的交通以线性展开。通过动态的流线，折线坡道和台阶有机结合设计，以建筑自身作为展览结构承载，积极地引导着空间元素与展示的交织，引导参观者选择自己的观展路线，避免了传统空间的单调死板，同时也与建筑外部的空间形态相一致。

墙、窗以及从天窗注入室内的阳光所设计的黑白分明的影、窗洞透视出了室外的景色，建筑与自然相互协调，浑然一体；墙体在这里被虚化，一方面，利用墙体片段式的大玻璃窗将建筑外部形体引入内部，并提供开敞的视野，使外部绿色景观也如同被剪辑过的布景，穿插与内部空间之中，建筑内部空间成为公园景观空间体验的构成元素；另一方面，建筑的通透性使人们从外部也能感受室内空间，从而达到建筑内外空间与景观品质、尺度以及使用方式上的协调，与公园一起组成有机体。

The Bridge Culture Museum is located at the centre of the QiaoYuan Park, Tianjin. Because of its special location, on the central axis facing to the main entrance, it is supposed to be the landmark of the Bridge Park. This area is designed as a leisure and exhibition space in order to meet people's needs of 'pleasurable show space'.

The origin of our design concept is 'operable bridge'. Steel bridge, folded surface, variable structural columns, U-shape enclosed space and extended platform, all of these create a 'Building for Strolling'. This building is 'accessible and passable'. It brings people exciting and surprising experiences because of the conversion between interior and exterior spaces. The steel bridge between the buildings leads people to the exhibition space, which is all green; the bottom of the building is multidimensional surface, which is accessible for people to go though; the sixteen structural columns have been treated in different ways to distract people's sight; the Z-shaped building, U-shaped enclosed space, the coffee break deck and the combination of the interior and exterior spaces merge the building into the site.

One can find attraction of the building through their own experience to it. The 'accessible and passable' Bridge Culture Museum is interactive for people both in interior and exterior.

LangFang Eco-city
廊坊万庄可持续生态城

设计单位：三磊建筑设计
设计总监：张华
主创设计师：范黎
建筑面积：370 900 m²
业主：廊坊上实生态城投资发展有限公司（上海上实集团）

Design firm: Beijing Sunlay Architectural Design Co.Ltd.
Chief designer: Zhang Hua
Lead designer: Fan Li
Building area: 370 900 m²
Client: Langfang Eco-city Investment & Development Co.,Ltd. (SIIC)

“建筑如同植物一样，是地面上一个基本的、和谐的要素，从属于环境，从地里生长出来，迎接太阳。”——赖特

城市规划与建筑形态脱离不开其所在地的环境、气候条件以及居住者的生活方式、意识形态、传统文化等因素的制约；反之，建筑形态与城市规划，又会潜移默化地影响居住者的生活模式。

廊坊万庄可持续生态城的规划设计理念是：以生态理念为出发点，营造一种理想的生活模式，使城市与乡村景观相辅相成，建造一个绿色、环保、温馨的可持续生态城市家园。

The LangFang Eco-city includes residential, retail, leisure, commercial, offices, educational traffic, parking spaces and public landscape design. Sunlay Design is doing the schematic design of the central part (341 800 m²) and the overall master planning.

As the first and largest eco-city of Northern China, many sustainable architectural technologies will be used, such as reflective shading system, atrium natural lighting system, passive solar technologies and three-dimensional greening system.

Wall's
Wall's

The Plan and Architectural Design Program for the Headquarters Base of Sichuan Chengxiang

四川呈祥总部基地规划及建筑设计方案

设计单位：北京清尚环艺建筑设计院有限公司
主设计师：张九郎

Design firm: Beijing Tshingshang Environmental Art and Architecture Design Institute
Lead designer: Zhang Jiulang

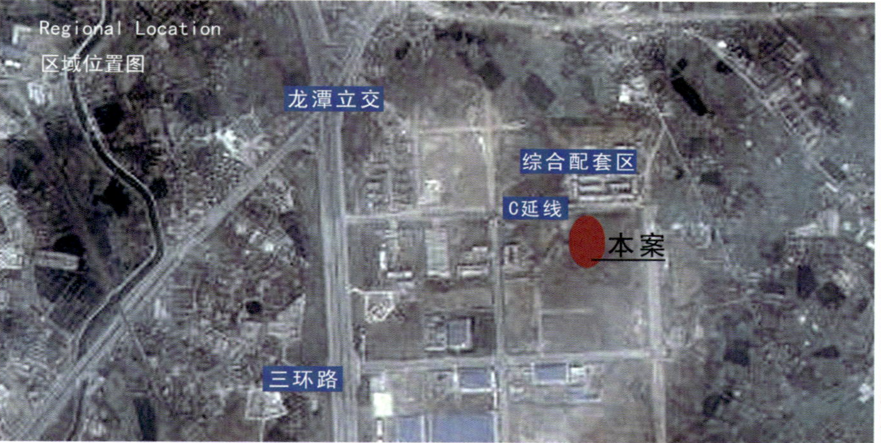

Zhang Jiulang
Beijing Tshingshang Environmental Art and Architecture Design Institute

张九郎
北京清尚环艺建筑设计院有限公司
第二设计所 所长

毕业院校

1997年7月毕业于 清华大学美术学院环艺系

2005年7月毕业于 同济大学建筑系 取得硕士学位

主要设计项目

上海国际影城

深圳世纪剧院

烟台玉森大酒店（五星级）

宁夏源泰大酒店（四星级）

内蒙古阳光大酒店（五星级）

河南锦鹏大酒店（五星级）

Graduated from:

Department of Environmental Art Design of Art & Design Academy of Tsinghua University in July, 1997

Department of Architecture of Tongji University in June, 2005 with a master's degree

Main programs:

Shanghai International Cinemas

Shenzhen Centurial Theater

Yantai Yuseng Hotel (five-star hotel)

Ningxia Yuantai Hotel (four-star hotel)

Sunshine Hotel of Inner Mongolia (five-star hotel)

Henan Jinpeng Hotel (five-star hotel)

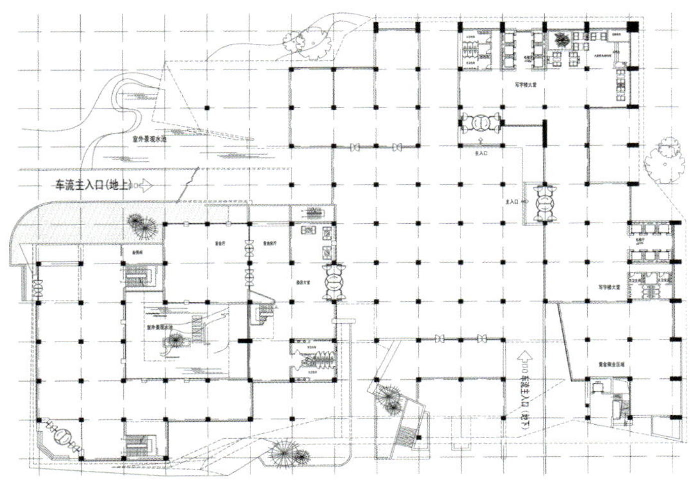

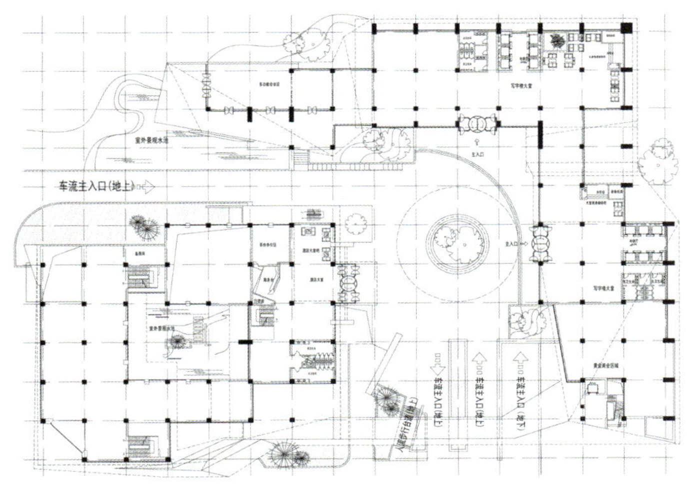

规划及建筑设计总说明：

国际大都市应有的文化追求：多样性、包容性、创造力。呈祥总部基地位于成都市龙潭工业园区内，总规划面积为25 333平方米，用地规则，交通便利，是园区较好的建设用地，但从大环境来分析，本地块目前周边商业及人流还不够成熟、完善。

因此，本案的设计目标：用后现代解构主义手法打造一个龙泽工业园地区的顶尖级办公、商业为一体的建筑综合体，并将其升华到当代建筑艺术与文化的高度，聚其精髓，傲视龙潭，镶嵌西南。

建筑设计

1.建筑布局

建筑布局的设计已经充分考虑了阳光辐射和视觉的因素。以规划路交叉口为视觉原点，将沿街商业、酒店、写字楼层层展开，而西侧的金属实墙的处理为大限度的屏蔽了夏季的阳光西晒，同时保证了节能的最大化。

2.景观设计

在有限的用地里内，地面的绿化面积受到极大的限制。本案在地面绿化的基础上发展竖向绿化，采用屋顶平台和顶面的绿化中庭，共同塑造出多层次、丰富的立体绿化体系。

3.交通分析

由于东西规划路无法设置机动车出口，所以在南北规划路建筑的西侧设置了两个机动车入口。靠南侧作为主入口将基地的车流直接引导到±5.000的内环平台上将人流导入各建筑的功能区，也可平行进入架空停车层或地下一层停车场，而沿建筑外围的环道则起到外围车流及消防环道的作用。

4.智能设计：

本案自动化功能的设计使其能够满足当今"智能大厦"的标准。大厦的控制系统将以一系列电脑控制的智能网络化的电子装置为基础，控制大厦的机械和照明系统，减少大厦的能量消耗和营运成本。温度调节装置以区域为基础，照明系统的控制由一套自动系统加以控制，或以负荷传感器、光敏探测器和定时器为基础对照明加以控制以减少光照的成本。

5.持久的环保型设计

建筑外墙的每片瓦愣形侧墙都是坚固美观的、高隔热的墙体，且减少了窗户的数量，

从而能够大大减少能量从大厦中流失。朝南幕墙的设计使得在冬季大厦能够尽可能采集到温暖的阳光。太阳能电池板将被安装在两座“塔楼”的顶部，从大厦底楼的路面和植物带，以及大厦顶部所采集到的雨水，将被收集过滤，并用来灌溉底楼的植物带和冬景温室花园内的植物，从而实现水的重复利用。

6．建筑功能分析

主要功能块为写字楼A塔，写字楼B塔及配套的多功能新闻发布厅和会议中心，沿街商业，配套的五星级酒店。其中餐饮部分：布置在沿街商业1–3层，包括中餐厅（可兼做宴会厅），写字楼A塔顶层由集团领导办公及集团接待商务会所组成，并配以顶层露天花园；本案通过整合国际顶尖设计团队，并结合地域特征，用后现代简约主义手法将呈祥总部基地打造成一颗镶嵌在龙潭工业园区的一颗璀璨明珠！

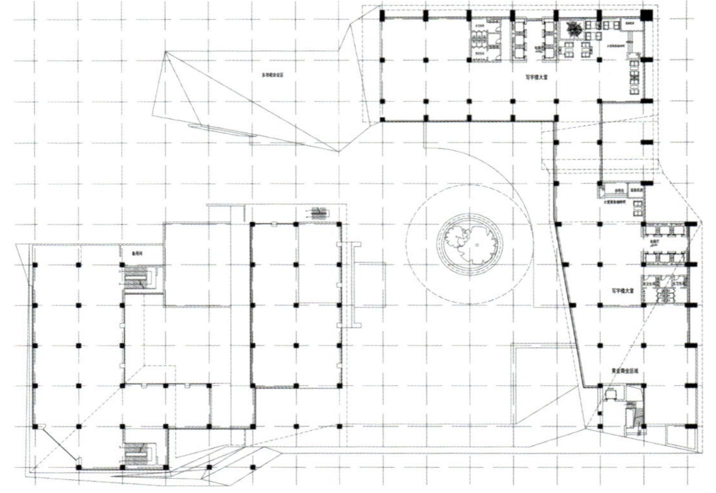

General specification for the plan and architectural design:

Diversity, capacity, and creativity are the cultural qualities that an international metropolis should possess. Located in Chengdu Longtan Industrial Park, with a planning area of 25 333 m^2 and convenient transport, the headquarters base of Chengxiang is a relatively good land for construction use in this park, but in terms of the macro environment, the business around and pedestrian flow through this land is immature and imperfect.

Because of this, the aim of this design program is: to create a top building complex that integrates work and business together in the Longze Industrial Park area by the application of postmodern deconstruction and to raise it to a height that gathers the essence of modern architectural art and culture and that stands out within the Longtan area and even shines in southwest China.

Architectural design

1. Building orientation:

Solar radiation and optical factors had been fully taken into account in the design of building orientation. With the crossings of planning roads being the ocular origin, street lined stores, hotels and office buildings were unfolded layer upon layer. A metal blind wall in the west keeps summer sunshine out and ensures maximum energy conservation.

2. Landscape:

The green area is greatly reduced because of the limited usable land. In addition to land greening, vertical greening was developed in this design program. A multi-layered and rich three-dimensional greening system was achieved by landscaping both roof terraces and central courtyards.

3. Traffic circulation:

Two entrances for motor vehicles were designed on the west side of the south-to-north planning roads because exits could not be made in the east-to-west planning roads. The southern one is the main entrance, leading the vehicles directly to the inner ring platform and the people into the domains of all buildings. It also leads to an overhead parking layer and the underground parking lot. And the circuit around the buildings serves for outer vehicle flows and fire fighting cars.

4. Intelligent design

The automation function design of the case is to meet standards of today's "smart building". The control system of the building is established on the basis of a series of smart networking electronic device controlled by computers, so that the machinery system and lighting system would be controlled and energy consumption and operating costs be reduced. Thermostat will be settled by regions, and lighting system will be controlled by an automatic system, or by load sensors, light-sensitive detectors, timers, to cut down the lighting cost.

5. Sustainable environmental design

Each tile-styled side wall of the building's outside walls are strong and beautiful and highly insulated, and these factors cut down the number of windows, consequently, greatly reduce energy losses from inside the building. The design of the south curtain wall is to make the building gather as much warm sunshine as possible in winter. Solar panels will be installed on the top of two "towers". Rain water collected from roads and plants on the ground floor of building and the top of building will be filtrated and used to irrigate the plants on the ground floor and the winter glasshouse garden so that water recycle is realized.

YG Art Center

YG艺术中心

设计单位：别人建筑工作室
主设计师：杨胤
用地面积：0.47公顷
地上建筑面积：50 233 m²
地下建筑面积：14 910 m²
总建筑面积：64 423 m²
容积率：10.7
设计时间：2009年

Design firm: Others Studio
Lead designer: Yang Yin
Design date: 2009
Land area: 64 423 m²

艺术展示类建筑可以有以下两种方式：
1.建筑以背景方式呈现，用以容纳、烘托展品。
2.建筑与展品共同表演，建筑融入到展品中——即具有强烈的个性、标志性、戏剧性，呈现出一种形体与空间的变奏，建筑是容器的同时也是展品。
此方案选择了后面的一种方式，它产生于这个喧闹的年代，躁动的都市，它不选择隐身，而是积极的参与，它要激活的不仅是一个区域、一个城市，更应该是一种创造性的心态和真实的人性的反思。

非匀质空间——建筑力求摆脱整齐划一的标准层模式，想法来自于人的生活本身就不应该是标准化的，在主体中，我们嵌入了尺寸、位置都不同的盒子空间，用这种方式打造不可预知的尺度变化，形成个性化的场所空间。

Yang Yin
Coparter of Others Studio

杨胤
别人建筑工作室

杨胤　1972年出生
　　1995年毕业于沈阳建筑大学建筑系 留校执教至今
　　1998年创立别人建筑工作室

工作室简介：
杨胤　1995年毕业于沈阳建筑大学建筑系
　　1998年创立别人工作室
高德战　1995年毕业于武汉工业大学建筑系学士
　　1999年加入别人工作室合伙人
张亦宁　1995年毕业于沈阳建筑大学建筑系学士
　　2002年加入别人建筑工作室合伙人
　　2005年毕业于同济大学建筑与城市规划学院硕士

我们总是在找不到自我的时候，想到别人，在别人的节日里寻找快乐。“在别人的思想中思想，在别人视线里生存。”——直到我们找到了自己的节日。那正是工作室成立之初的一种状态，所以我们命名工作室的名字为“别人”以纪念当时的心态。“别人”不是理论或口号，它是繁杂的交织在一起的建筑认识论和始终影响着我们创作心态的一个关键词，它时而是“地狱”，时而又成了“天堂”，它被解释的多样性正好说明了生活与建筑本身的多样性。

设计理念：
建筑设计时，不在考虑作品的内在含义，让体量与空间交织在一起，使形式变得鲜活，任由它们自在的表达。探索一种形式的语言，类似于在音乐中的连续性与音调的和谐，也类似于写作中的文字排列，在那里，各个元素都受到内部相互关系的严格限制。

Yang Yin
Born in 1972
Gratuated from Department of Architecture of Shenyang University of Architecture, then to be a teacher till now
Set up Others Studio in 1998

Brief introduction of the studio
Yang Yin
Gratuated from Department of Architecture of Shenyang University of Architecture in 1995
Set up others-studio in 1998
Gao Dezhan
Gratuated from Depertment of Architecture of Wuhan University of Technology in 1995
Joined of others-studio in 1999
Zhang Yining
Gratuated from Department of Architecture of Shenyang University of Architecture in 1995
Joined of others-studio in 2002
Get Master degree of college of Architecture and Urban Planning of Tongji University In 2005

We always think of others when we can't find ourselves, searching happiness in others' festivals. We "think in others' thoughts and live in others' sights"—till we find our own festivals. This is our state of mind at the start point and the reason why we named it "others". "Others" is not a theory or a slogan, but an architectural epistemology and a key word affecting our creational attitudes. Sometimes "others" is like "devil" and sometimes "paradise" . Its different interpretations just explain the diversities of life and building.

Design concept:
When designing, we don't consider the inherent meanings of our works and just express themselves freely on the base of the interchange of volume and space, which makes form real and vivid. Investigating one kind of formal language is like finding the harmony existing in musical works and the letters' arrangement of writing, where each element is strictly subject to the interior relationship of one another.

YG藝術中心

“建构”不仅显示结果，它更是一个过程，一个动词。我们的建筑突出体现了一个过程，强化了一种体块间的搭接，穿插的关系，还原建筑的本意。我们认为，过程永远重于结果。

关于景观：除了建筑给城市带来全方位的景观价值外，其内部空间同样运用景观设计手法，达成内与外、内与内的全景交融，建筑不仅是功能与雕塑形体调和的结果，同时也是各种具有空间张力的场景以空间序列的方式合理组织的结果。

关于流线：三种主要功能，五种流线相对独立，互不干扰，不仅是使用的需要，更是管理的需要。

艺术中心的展示空间分为上下两部分，顶部三层为永久展区，底部六层为临时展区，可根据面积、性质的不同需求灵活布展。

另外，在主体的1-2层设置了常年对外营业的画廊，在保障日常人气的同时，又可以分担一部分艺术中心的运营成本。

建筑以开敞的空间形态与原生态景观呼应，在原有植被全部保留的基础上，在树木间谨慎地设置铺装，水景，草地灯，座椅，雕塑等，使其具有足够的可进入、可停留性。

这片难得的宁静，不应该因为建筑的融入而被打破。

艺术中心入口空间采用雕塑手法，动显空间张力的同时，又有效的把基地西侧的原生态景观收纳其中，这也是建筑在设计之初的主要概念之一。

静逸的内部展示空间，建筑的外部形态与内部的空间感受完全契合，磨砂玻璃外墙均匀稳定了随时变动的日光，金属百叶进一步调整了照度，随墙而上的楼梯既提供了垂直动线，又活跃了空间本身。

There are two manners to design art exhibition buildings:

Buildings are backgrounds to contain and foil the items on display.

Buildings are showed with the items on display, which express intensive personality, landmark and dramatical effects. It is a kind of variation of form and space. Buildings are both items on display and containers at the same time.

This project chooses the later method, which is produced in this noisy time and restless city. It does not choose to hide itself but participates actively, which wants to not only activate the region and the city, but also cause a kind of creational attitude and the real human rethinking.

Non-homogeneous space — the project thrives to break away from the trim mode of standard level. This kind of thought comes from that the life itself shouldn't be standard. In the main space, we set in the box space with different sizes and positions to create unpredictable size change to form the site space with individuality.

"Tectonic" not only shows result, but course and action. The building embodies the course obviously and enforces the relationship between connection and intersection, showing the architectural original idea. We always believe that course is more important than result.

Landscape: Besides that the building brings full-oriental landscape values, its interior space also uses the method of landscape to reach the blended effect of inner space with one another, interior and exterior space. The building is not only the compromised results of function and form, but the results of reasonable arrangement by the spatial organizing landscape with space tension.

Circulation: three main functions and five circulations are noninterfering and independent from one another. It is not only the demand of application but more the need of management.

The exhibition space is divided into two parts of upside and downside. The top three levels are the exhibition hall perpetually and the lower six levels are the temporary exhibition area, which could be layout flexibly according to the different demands of area and function.

Moreover, we set up the corridor in one and two levels, which are opened perennially. This layout could maintain the daily people circulation and share the part cost of management of the arts center simultaneously.

The building's open space echoes the ecology landscape. On the basis of maintaining all of the whole vegetation, we carefully set up the small square, water, lawn lamps, chairs and sculptures etc., which make people enter and stay there freely. This silent area shouldn't be interrupted by the building.

展览
展览
5层
办公
13层
公寓
21层
展览
临时展厅上空
展览
展览
4层
办公
12层
公寓
20层
休息厅
临时展厅上空
展览
报告厅
3层
办公
11层
公寓
19层
办公
展览
临时展厅上空
展览
2层
办公
10层
公寓
18层
礼品店
办公区大堂
公寓大堂
临时展厅
画廊
画廊
1层
办公
9层
公寓
17层
设备用房
停车58
设备用房
停车43
-1层
办公
8层
公寓
16层
设备用房
停车58
设备用房
停车43
-2层
办公
7层
避难层
设备层
15层
设备用房
设备用房
-3层
展览
展览
6层
办公
14层

29层 37层 45层

28层 36层 44层

27层 35层 43层

26层 34层 42层

25层 33层 41层

24层 32层 40层

23层 31层 39层

22层 30层 38层

The entrance of the art center adopts the sculptural technique to the effect of showing the spatial tension and absorbing eco-landscape on the west of the site at the same time, which is one of the main conceptions at the beginning of the design. The building has silent interior exhibition space. The exterior form of the building and the interior space are correspondent completely. Its glass exterior wall makes the moving sunlight stable and the metal shutter adjusts the illumination better. The stair along the wall obtains the vertical circulation and activates the space itself.

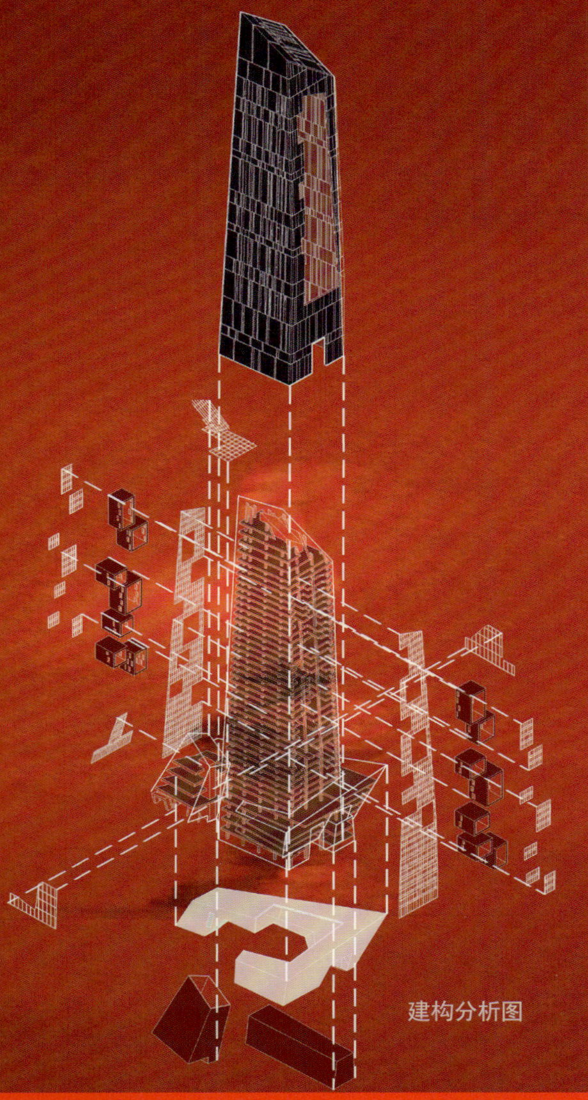

建构分析图

形体分析图

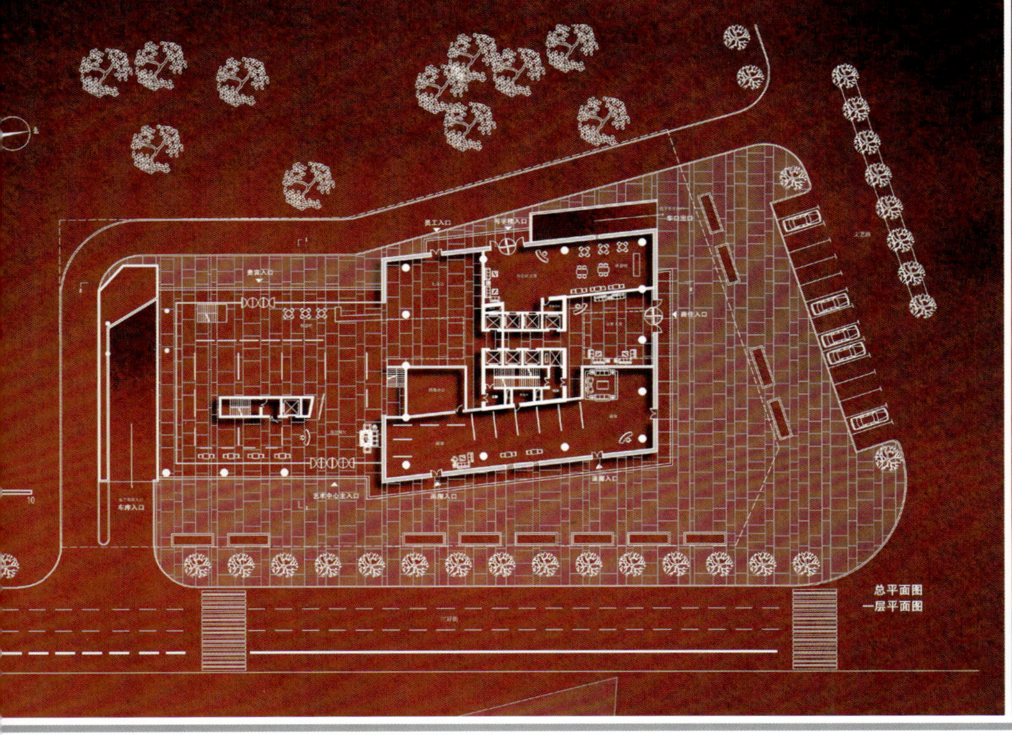
总平面图
一层平面图

Shenyang Culture & Arts Center Conceptual Design

沈阳文化艺术中心概念性设计

设计单位：别人建筑工作室
主设计师：杨胤
总建筑面积：42 000 m^2
设计时间：2008年

Design firm: Others Studio
Lead designer: Yang Yin
Design date: 2008
Land area: 42 000 m^2

设计概念

关键词：振颤、律动、轻盈、通透、开放

生命的律动：

人的生命源于心脏的跳动，而心电图则是生命延续的重要表征。通过心电图的引入，产生跳跃的、有节奏的生命动线，它时而舒缓、时而振颤，从而在浑河岸边、金廊大动脉上奏响"命运交响曲"。

动态系统：

1. 视觉动态循环系统：通过多维度、多方向的形态产生不规则的形态外表，而其形式却经过了高度解析。从城市各个角度，都能获得动态的建筑感受。
2. 动态流线系统：通过立体交叉的流线设计，产生连续、清晰的动线系统。
3. 动态空间系统：倾斜的墙面、屋面打破了传统意义对建筑边界的认识，内部空间与外部形态相互呼应，产生具有冲击力的空间体验。

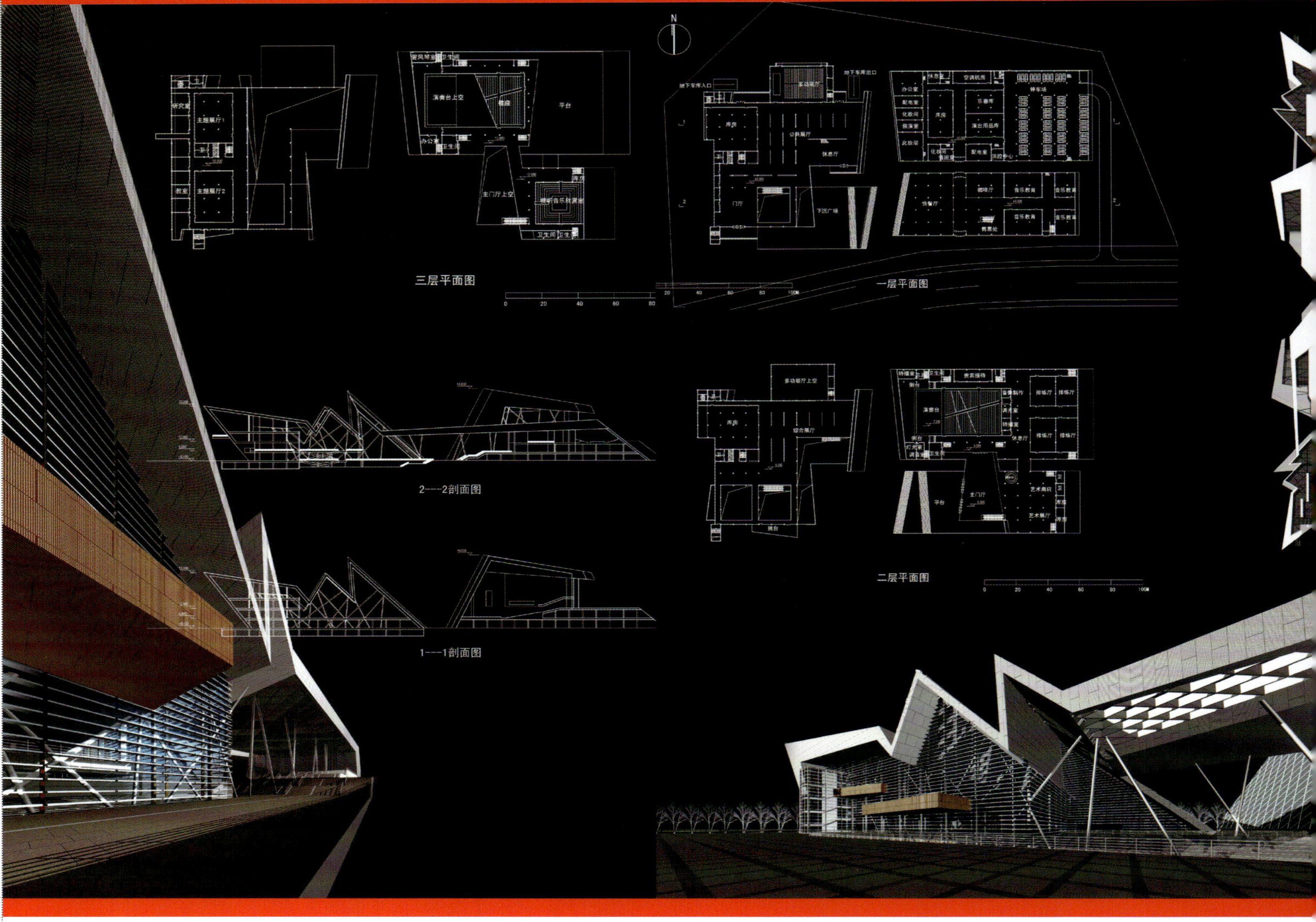

交叉意向：

功能交叉：文化艺术中心包含有音乐厅和美术馆两个大的功能板块，但又不是音乐厅和美术馆的简单集合，而是包含有多种公共文化设施的综合性文化场所。

音乐空间包括：舞台、观众厅、室内乐演奏厅等。

美术空间包括：各类展厅、美术研究等。

公共空间包括：内部——音乐展览、餐饮、音乐教育、音乐体验中心、音乐家工作室、视觉体验中心、美术家工作室、艺术吧等。

外部——下沉广场、入口平台、室外舞台等。

体积交叉：体积交叉与功能交叉相对应，音乐厅和美术馆两部分体积相互分离又相互交叉，共同形成起伏跌宕、错落有致、浑然一体的整体意向。

Design concept

key words: shake rhythm lightness penetration open

Rhythm of life:

Human life comes from heartbeat and the cardiogram is the important token of life continuing. According to the introduction of cardiogram, the project produces the jumping and rhythm life line, which is sometimes slow and sometimes jump to create destiny symphony on the side of Huhe River—the main artery of the golden corridor.

Dynamic systems:

1. Vision dynamic N-circles system: according to multi-dimensions, the form of multi-direction produces anomalistic appearance and its form was analyzed sufficiently. People can get dynamic feeling of the building from every viewpoint of the city.

2. Dynamic circulation system: on the basis of the solid crossed circulation, the building produces continuous and clear circulation system.

3. Dynamic space system: declining walls and roof goes against the understanding to the building's boundary in a traditional way. The interior and exterior space echo each another to produce the space experience of wallop.

Cross intention:

Functional intercrossing: the center of culture and art includes two main functional parts –odium and art gallery, but not their simple aggregation, which includes several public comprehensive cultural sites.

The musical space includes the following: stage, audience hall, interior performance hall, etc.

Art space includes: several kinds of exhibition halls, art research center etc.

Public space includes: interior–musical exhibition, dinning room, musical education and experience center, musician studio, visional experience center, painter studio and art bar.

Exterior—sunken square, entrance platform, exterior stage, etc.

Volume cross: the intercrossing of volume is correspondence with the functional cross. The two parts of musical hall and gallery are separated and intercrossed with each other, forming a whole feeling of undulated and ordered integration.

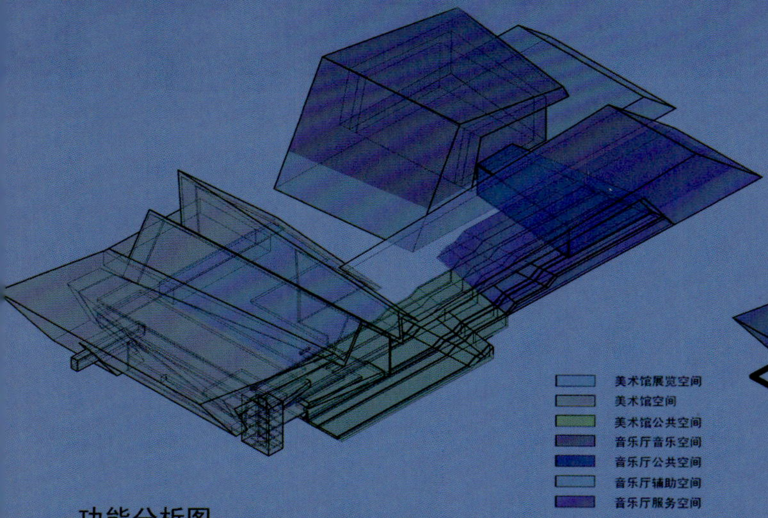

美术馆展览空间
美术馆空间
美术馆公共空间
音乐厅音乐空间
音乐厅公共空间
音乐厅辅助空间
音乐厅服务空间

功能分析图

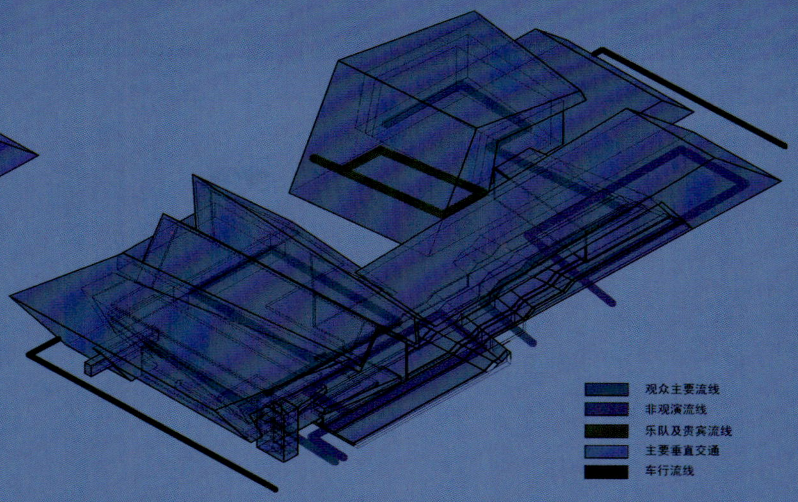

观众主要流线
非观演流线
乐队及贵宾流线
主要垂直交通
车行流线

流线分析图

Logistics Center of Modern Agriculture in Northeast China

东北现代农业物流中心

设计单位：北京龙安华诚建筑设计有限公司 SYN建筑师事务所（德国）
主设计师：邹迎晞
设计时间：2009年
基地面积：35 000 m²
总建筑面积：60 300 m²
绿化率：25%
容积率：0.92
建筑密度：37.9%
建筑层数：3层
建筑主体最大高度：22 m

Design firm: Beijing Long'anhuacheng Achitecture Design Limited Company/Syn Architecture
Lead designer: Zou Yingxi
Design date: 2009
Site area: 35 000 m²
Building area: 60 300 m²

Zou Yingxi
Beijing Long'anhuacheng Architecture Design Limited Company

邹迎晞
北京龙安华诚建筑设计有限公司

1973年5月 生于河南省郑州市
1987年 迁于北京
1993—1997年 就读于中央工艺美术学院 环境艺术设计系
1997—1998年 留校任职
1999年 荣获第二届中国室内设计大展金奖
2000年 赴德国留学 就读于柏林艺术大学建筑系
2004年 获得柏林艺术大学建筑学硕士学位
同年于柏林成立syn architects建筑师事务所(合伙人)
2004年—至今 北京龙安华诚建筑设计有限公司 总建筑师
2006年 作为创会会员加入世界华人建筑师协会
2008年 主创设计的中央美术学院燕郊校区经中国人居典范评审委员会评审荣获最佳设计方案金奖。
2009年 主创设计的东方宜家花园经中国人居典范评审委员会评审 获最佳设计方案金奖。
主创设计的韶关东堤路改造经中国人居典范评审委员会评审 获最佳设计方案金奖。

近期主要作品：
河南省移动通信郑州分公司郑东新区枢纽楼
广东省韶关市东堤路规划及建筑设计
中央美术学院北京燕效新校区总体规划及建筑设计
龙门石窟博物馆
法国工业园项目
宁波轻纺城
北京怀柔制片人总部基地
宁波九龙湖赛车场
国骅世纪宜家广场
北京南中轴线时尚商务中心区概念规划
曲美家居博物馆

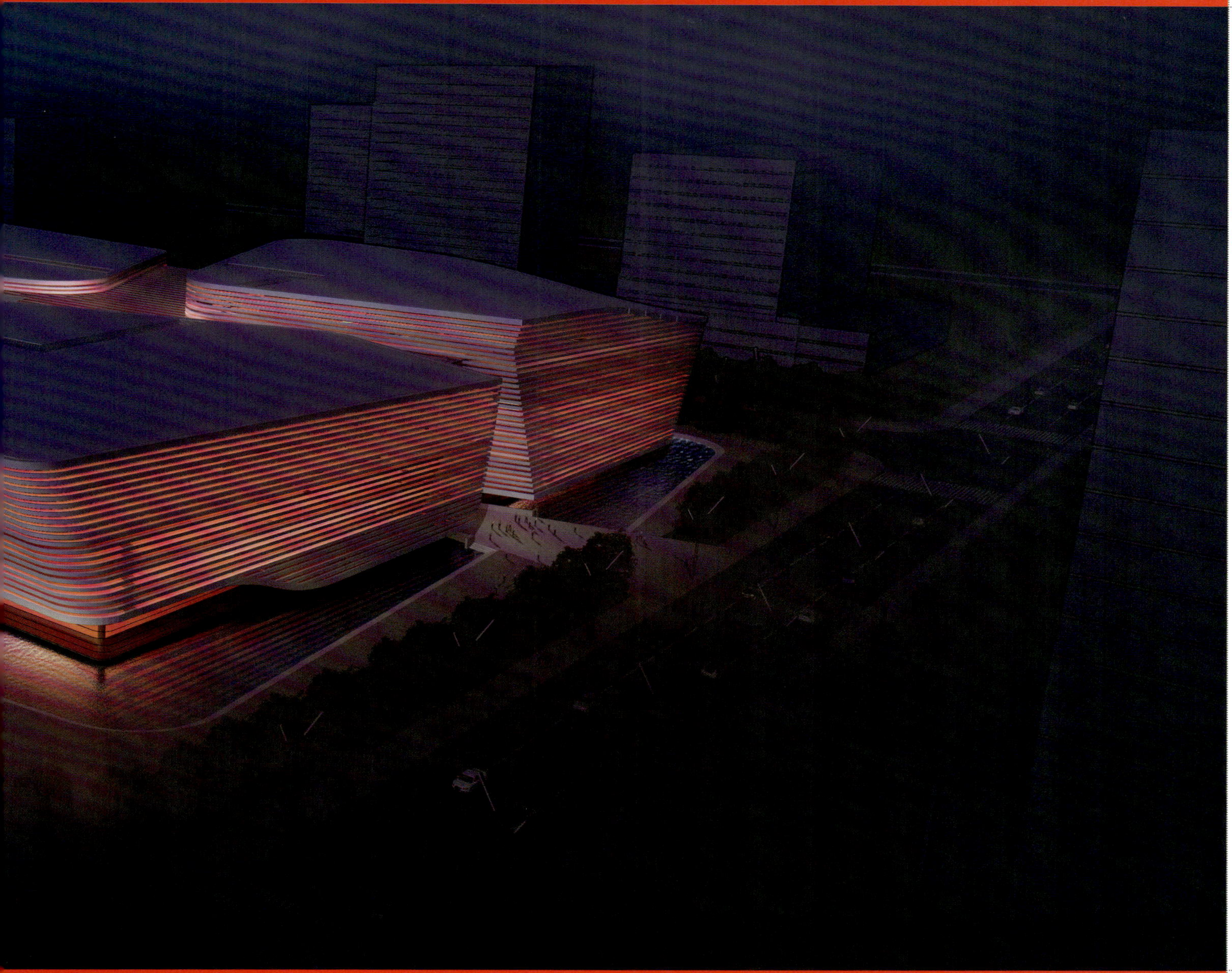

本项目位于东北铁岭新城——东北现代农业物流城。作为物流城中先行建设的项目，东北现代农业物流中心需要承担起新城的地标性作用。

The project is located at the town of Tieling—logistics town of modern agriculture in Northeast China. As one of the pioneering projects in the town, logistics center of modern agriculture has to fulfill the expectation of being a landmark.

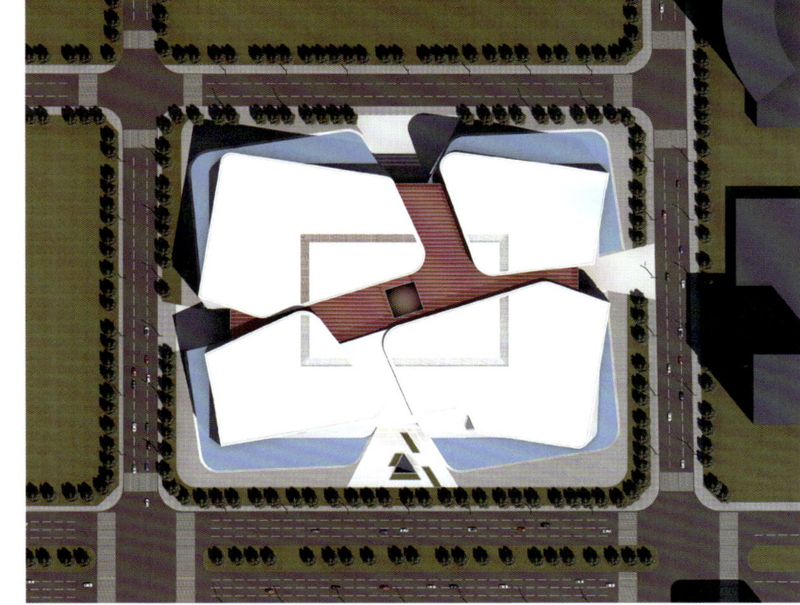

1973-5 Born in Zhenzhou, Henan Province

1987 Move to Beijing

1993~1997 Study in Central Institute of Arts and Crafts (i.e. Academy of Arts and Design of Tsinghua University)

1997~1998 Teach in Tsinghua University

1999 Win the Golden Prize for the 2nd Chinese Interior Design Exhibition

2000 Study in UDK Berlin, Germany, majoring in architecture

2004 Obtain Master Degree of Architecture from UDK.Found Synarchitects (Partner)

2004~present Practice in the field of architecture in China;Beijing Long' anhuacheng Architecture Design Limited Company, General Architect;
A founding member of World Association of Chinese Architects;

2008 Central Academy of Fine Arts Yanjiao Campus (main designer) wins the Golden Prize of the Best Design and Plan, according to Habitat Model Evaluating Committee of China

2009 The Orient IKEA Garden (main designer) wins the Golden Prize of the Best Design and Plan, according to Habitat Model Evaluating Committee of China;
The reconstruction of Dongdi Road in Shaoguan(main designer) wins the Golden Prize of the Best Design and Plan, according to Habitat Model Evaluating Committee of China.

Main works in recent period:

ww•Zhendong New Area Pivot Building of He'nan Mobile Zhenzhou Branch
•Planning and Architecture Design of Dongdi Road, Chaoguan, Guangdong Province
•General Planning and Architecture Design of Central Academy of Fine Arts Yanjiao Campus
•Longmen Grottoes Museum
•Industrial Park in France
•Textile City, Ningbo
•Orient IKEA Garden, Ningbo
•Orient IKEA Square, Ningbo
•Shiqi Office Building, Ningbo
•North River Ortles, Ningbo
•Health City, Hainai
•Producers' Headquarter Base, Huairou
•Nine-Dragon Lake Autodrome
•Tianbo City, Ningbo

"East Street" Project, Shaoguan, Guangdong

广东韶关"百年东街"项目

设计单位：北京龙安华诚建筑设计有限公司、SYN建筑师事务所（德国）
主计师：邹迎晞、丹尼尔·施瓦勃 （德国）
设计时间：2009年
建筑基地面积：36 000 m^2
建筑面积：145 000 m^2
建筑密度：36.5%
建筑层数：2~4层
容积率：1.6

Design firm: Beijing Long'anhuacheng Achitecture Design Limited Company/Syn Architecture
Lead designer: Zou Yingxi,Daniel Schwabe
Design date: 2009
Site area: 36 000 m^2
Building area: 145 000 m^2

项目位于韶关市中心东堤路，以清末岭南民居为主，总长1300米。历史上是孙中山北伐的起点，有多处历史文化遗迹。现状无序改扩建，以及滞后的经营模式，不合适宜的空间模式等。本项目改造完成后期望成为闻名全国的历史文化街区，韶关最有特色的历史文化街区，重要的市民文化休闲中心、文化展区。

坚持保护历史文化、以民为本的原则，在保留原有老街区风格风貌的基础上，统一规划，统一设计，统一市政配套建设，统一施工，把东提路打造成为集即可旅游、购物、享受特色餐饮，又可怀旧、亲水、休闲及融粤北地方风情为一体的商业街区。

历史街区应该是一个开放系统，它应是一个让市民，游客看得见、摸得着的客观存在，不断地从外界获得信息和能量，才有可能不停地向前进步。历史街区可以"修旧如旧"，但却不可以在发展机制中"守旧如旧"。设计一个商业、文化、居住互激的动态发展机制，调动公众参与的积极性，实现街区的自我更新。使商业、文化建立紧密的关联是整个机制的核心，以文化来吸引大众是大多数历史街区保护的主要商业目的和文化目的。以文化复苏商业，以商业反哺文化。

The project is set on the Dongdi Road downtown in the city of Shaoguan. The road is totally 1300 meters long, on which stand vernacular (Guangdong and Guangxi area) dwellings dated back to the end of Qing Dynasty. There are a lot of historical and cultural relics with one of which Sun Zhongshan started his Northwards Expedition. However, current situation here is unsatisfactory: rebuilding without order, lagging business models, inappropriate spatial patterns. This project when finished is expected to make a nationwide well-known historical and cultural street, the most special historical and cultural street of Shaoguan, an important culture and leisure center for citizens and cultural exhibition as well.

Sticking to the principle of history protection and people first, the project, planned, designed, constructed universally with government constructing faciliation, was going to make Dongdi Road without spoiling its original old features into a place where people enjoy not only traveling, shopping, and food of specialty but also nostalgic and leisure waterside views mixed with vernacular flavor of northern Guangdong.

A historical street should be an open system visible to all citizens and tourists, gaining information and energy from outside and developing constantly. It can be as old as it was after rebuilding, but it must not be keeping old in the dynamism of development. Therefore a dynamism involving business, culture, and habitation is developed to encourage people to participate actively and realize its renewing of its own. And the core of the dynamism is to build a close relationship between business and culture as it is both business and cultural purpose for most historical streets to attract people by culture. Culture revives business, while business funds culture.

COTSKY'S AT THE FAIR

DONGJIE
ONE WAY

PUMA

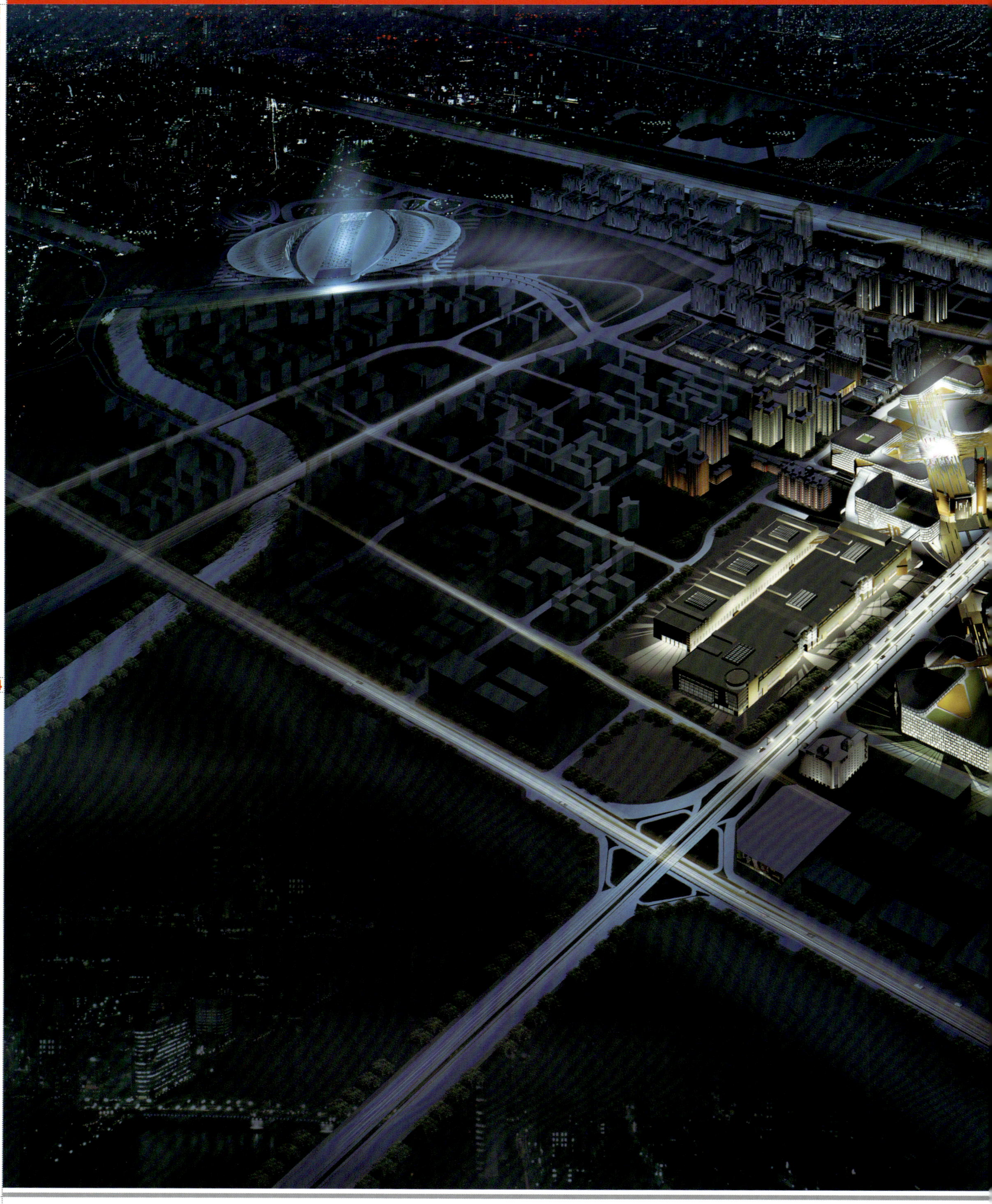

Conceptual Design for Fashion Business Zone, Beijing

北京南中轴线时尚商务中心区概念规划

设计单位：北京龙安华诚建筑设计有限公司、SYN建筑师事务所（德国）
主设计师：邹迎晞

Design firm: Beijing Long'anhuacheng Achitecture Design Co.LTD/Syn Architecture
Lead designer: Zou Yingxi

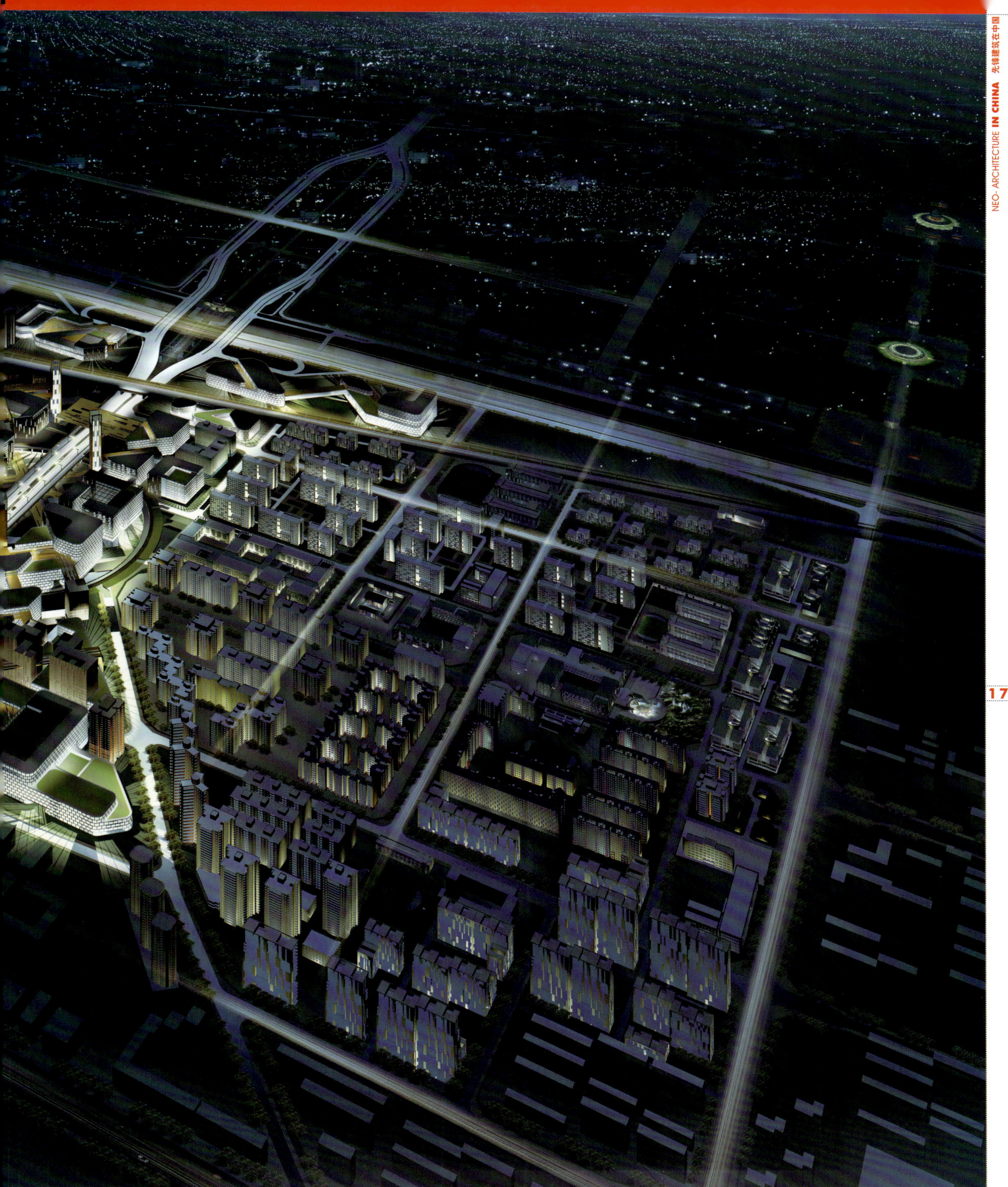

本项目位于北京崇文区永定门外，本规划的目的是给地方政府在土地开发时提供决策建议。

空间布局

一核两翼 中脉贯通

一核

时尚商务核心区：发展以商务为主的时尚产业集群，构建区域产业链发展核心。

两翼

南站商务区：结合车站经济特色，发展南站商务区，构建区域发展副中心，带动西侧区域的发展和价值提升。

景泰文化商旅区：与旅游资源有效结合，以商旅文化为主题，发展特色商旅文化区，打造东侧区域副中心，带动东侧区域发展和价值提升。

中脉贯通

实现一核两翼的关联和互动：革新路和安乐林路东西贯通，将一核两翼整体连通。

一核两翼过渡区为宜居住宅区，营造区域24小时活力，完善区域功能。

设计原则：畅通、高效、系统、人本、人文

畅通

——外部车行畅通

——内部车行畅通

——内部人行畅通

高效

——高效利用空间资源

——高效开发空间价值

系统

——系统完善的现代城市功能区

人本

——以人本化为基础

人文

——以人文化为灵魂

永外时尚商务中心
CODY BANKS

ATTACK
ESP
JEM
DON'T CALL IT
A CAR
IT GETS MAD

永外时尚商务中心

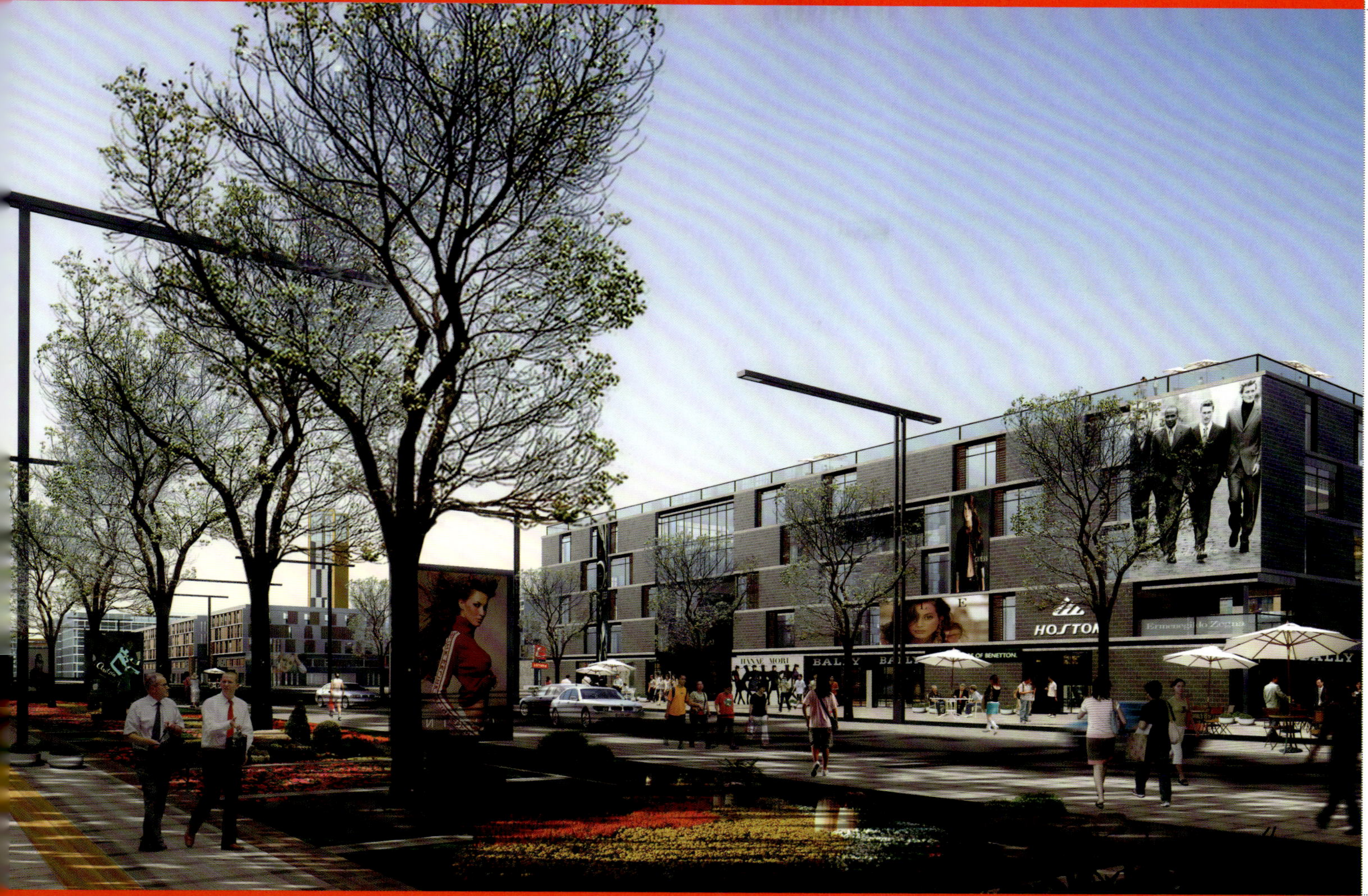
HOSTON
BALLY

IKEA
San Rem
OLDSTER PIPE

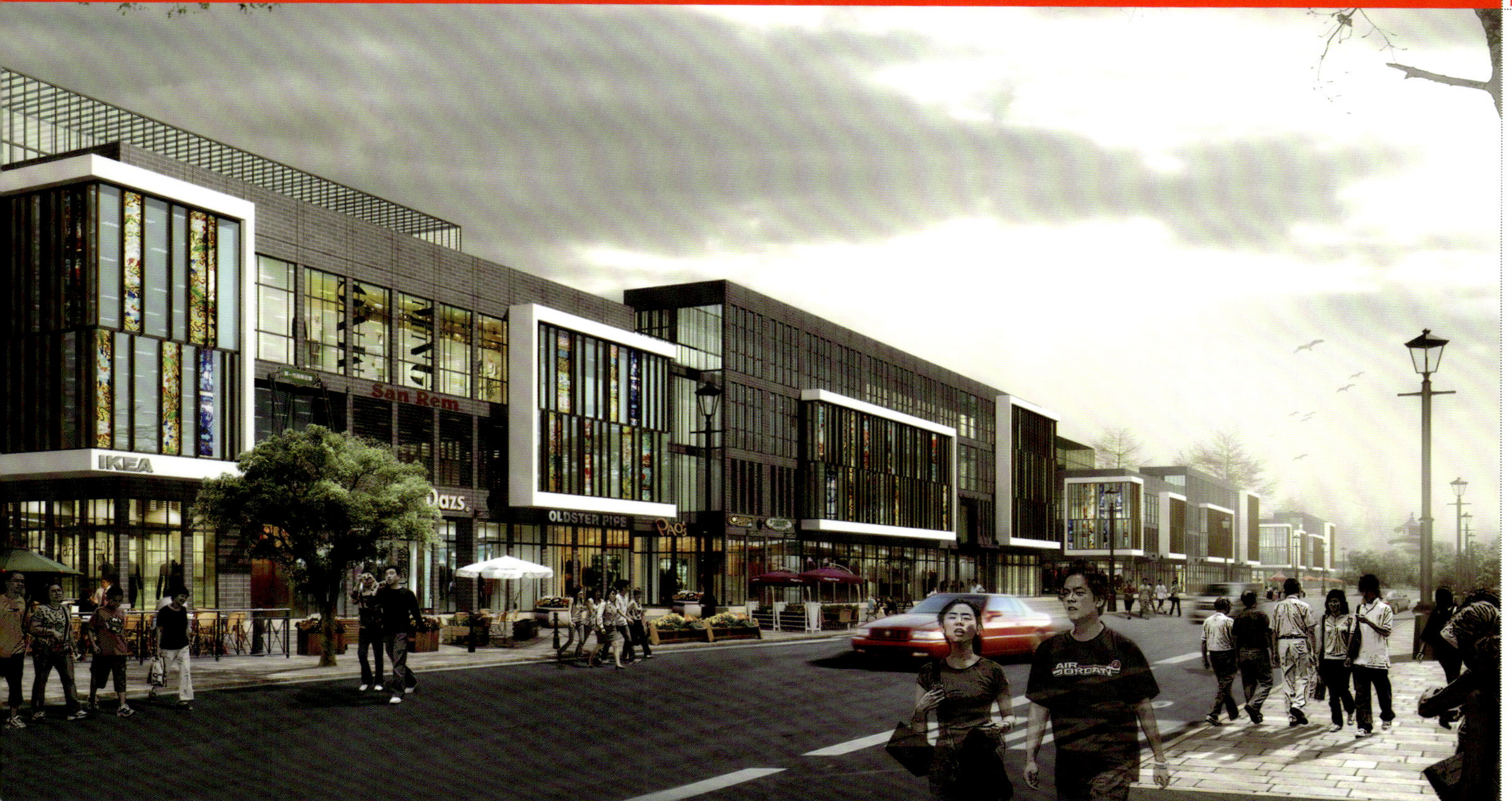

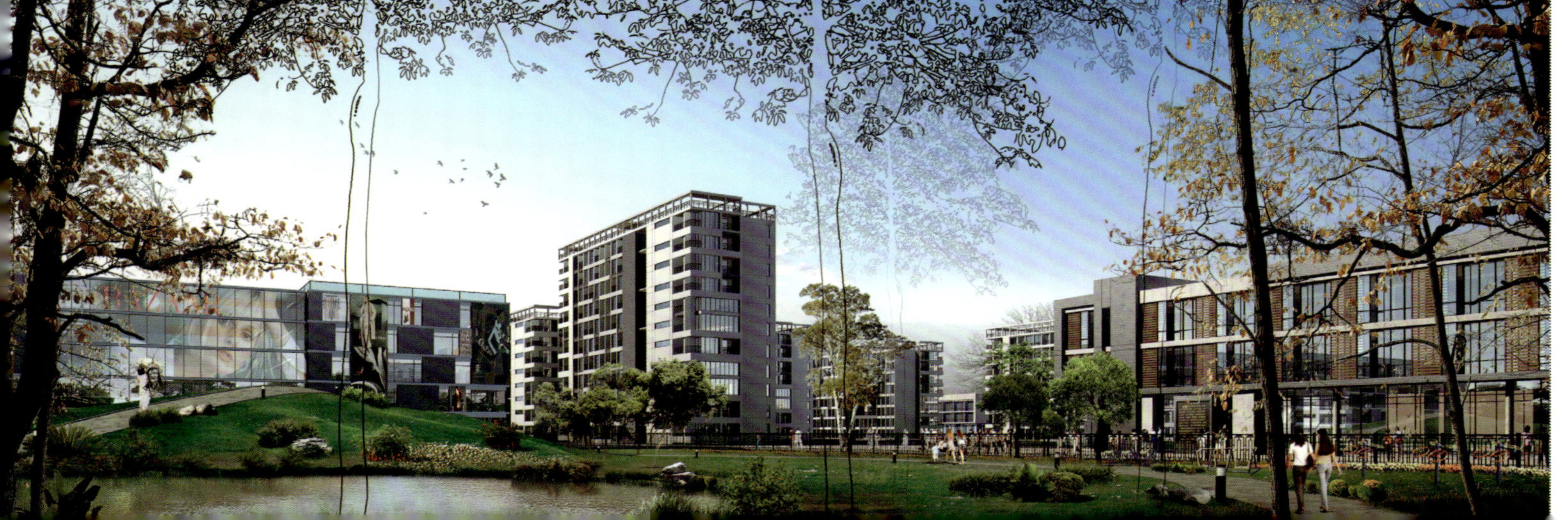

FASHION BU

AVENIR
PICARD
ATTACK
INTERNATIONA
FINANC

This project, outside of Yongding Men, Chongwen District, Beijing, is planned to provide suggestions for decision-making on land development.

Space Planning

One Core Two Wings Connected as a Whole

One Core

Core Zone for Fashion Business: it is developing fashion industry group and constructing industry chain.

Two Wings

South Station Business Zone: combined with economic features of station, it is being developed to be a sub-center and promote economic growth of western area.

Jingtai Cultural Zone for Business Travel: making good use of tourist resources, taking the theme of business travel culture, it is being developed to be the other sub-center and promote economic growth of eastern area.

Connected as a Whole

Connection and interaction between the core and two wings: Gexin Road and Anlelin Road are connected from east to west to make a whole of the core and its two wings. Between the core and its two wings are residential areas which provide energetic and perfect service for 24 hours.

Design Principles: smoothness, efficiency, system, people, humanity

Smoothness

- smooth stream of traffic outside
- smooth stream of traffic inside
- smooth stream of people

Efficiency

- efficiently exploiting spatial resources
- efficiently developing spatial value

System

- all wanted systems found in functional zone of modern city

People

- putting people at first place

Humanity

- considering humanity as soul

Longxing Commercial Center Ningbo

宁波隆兴商务中心

设计单位：北京龙安华诚建筑设计有限公司、SYN建筑师事务所（德国）
主设计师：邹迎晞、丹尼尔·施瓦勃（德国）
设计时间：2008年
基地面积：8 700 m²
建筑面积：149 000 m²
绿化率：30%
容积率：4.14
建筑密度：24.1%
建筑层数：28层
建筑主体最大高度：99 m

Design firm: Beijing Long'anhuacheng Achitecture Design Limited Company/Syn Architecture
Lead designer: Zou Yingxi, Daniel Schwabe
Design date: 2008
Site area: 8 700 m²
Building area: 149 000 m²

本项目位于宁波市鄞州区，现为甲方隆兴集团的厂区。近些年，宁波城市快速发展，本区域已从原来的城市边缘成为城市的中心区内，不再适合企业的生产功能。业主准备把现有生产区搬离市区，并在此用地上，建设总部办公，酒店，公寓等设施。

业主希望把本项目打造成宁波最有特色的商务中心区。因此，我们的目标是做宁波最有设计感，最有视觉冲击力的建筑群体。

考虑到用地的现状，在中心位置设置下沉文化广场，酒店，办公以及配套公寓，沿文化广场布置，共享景观之余，突出建筑群体感。建筑设计，以变化的曲线形体强调建筑的时代感，建筑的立面是隐框玻璃幕墙。

The project is set in the current premises of first party Longxing Group, in Yinzhou District, Ningbo. For recent years, the city is developing so rapidly that this site has been involved into center area and is not suitable for manufacturing. The client planed to get factory moved out of the city and build headquarters, hotel and apartments at current place.

The client hoped that the project would make the most distinctive business center in Ningbo. Our goal was to design a complex of novelist ideas and tremendous visual effect.

Taking account of the site conditions, we planned a sunken cultural square at the center where stood hotel, office and apartment buildings. In addition to sharing the view, the complex could be best represented as a whole.

As for the design, changing and curved shapes were used to emphasize current times with glass walls without frames.

Up-graded Project of Qingfang Town, Ningbo

宁波轻纺城升级项目

设计单位：北京龙安华诚建筑设计有限公司、SYN建筑师事务所（德国）
主设计师：邹迎晞
设计时间：2009年
基地面积：61 300 m²
总建筑面积：379 700 m²
绿化面积：51 800 m²
绿化率：30%
容积率：2.2
建筑密度：35.51%
建筑层数：15层
建筑主体最大高度：44.5 m

Design firm: Beijing Long'anhuacheng Achitecture Design Limited Company/Syn Architecture
Lead designer: Zou Yingxi
Design date: 2009
Site area: 61 300 m²
Building area: 379 700 m²

轻纺城项目位于鄞州区石碶街道，地理位置极其优越，交通便利。因原轻纺城的存在，石碶曾是鄞州区重要的商业中心。但随着鄞州中心区的崛起，奉化江对岸的石碶日渐落寞，商业发展缓慢，城建水平相对较低，现实状况与城市发展需要矛盾凸显。对于城市面貌改观的呼声越来越高，石碶新一轮的开发势在必行。

塑造城市肌理

鄞州区目前的城市发展格局可概括为"一心两翼"。"一心"指鄞州中心区，"两翼"分别为下应和石碶。本项目的开发将对石碶的城市面貌带来较大改观，为石碶成为宜居宜商的鄞州的重要一翼的助力。

重振商业繁荣

本项目作为在轻纺城基址上发展起来的城市综合体，其商业功能将得到突出，各种业态形式的引入、组合和全新的运营模式将把项目打造成区域内商业的旗舰品牌，再现原轻纺城昔日的繁荣。

促进区域升值

本项目作为大规模的商业综合体，将以其强大的商业功能与影响力，带动区域商业氛围进一步成熟，人居环境改善，最终促进区域价值提升。

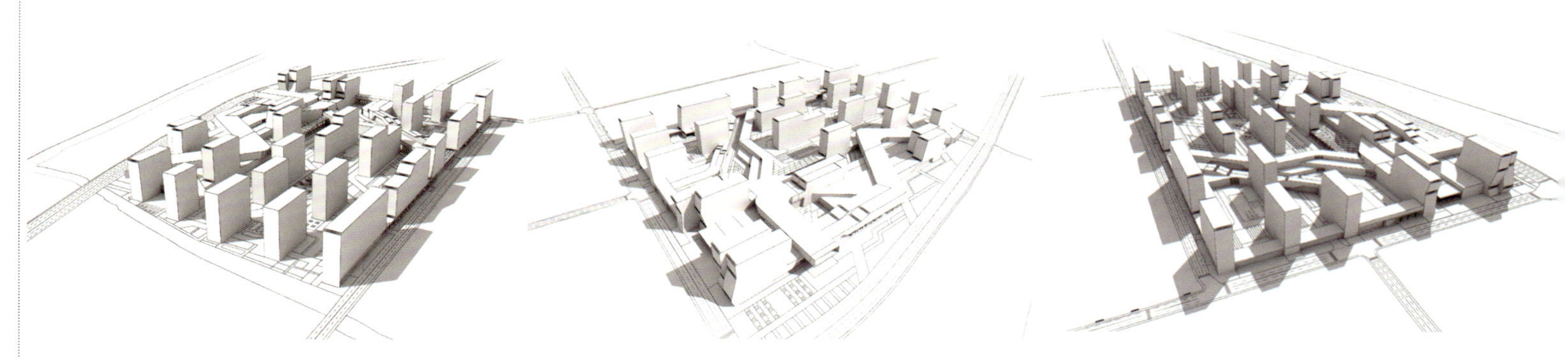

This project, set in Shiqi Street, Yinzhou District, occupies the most advantageous place with convenient transportation. Thanks to the Qingfang Town, Shiqi was an important business center of Yinzhou. However, with the development of the center area, Shiqi, on the other side of Fenghua River, was being depressed. Current situation is unable to catch up with the general development of the city, so improving city looks and a new round of developing Shiqi is necessary.

1. Shaping texture of the city

Current developing map of Yinzhou can be generalized as "one center and two wings". One center refers to the central area, while two wings are respectively Xiaying and Shiqi. The project is believed to be able to change the looks of Shiqi and help make an important wing of Yinzhou.

2. Reviving commercial prosperity

On the site of Qingfang Town, the project will highlight the commercial function with all kinds of management models brought in and make a business flagship in the area to have the golden old days once more.

3. Promoting economic growth

The project, as a wide-ranged business complex, will mature business environment around and improve living conditions with its strong commercial functions and influence.

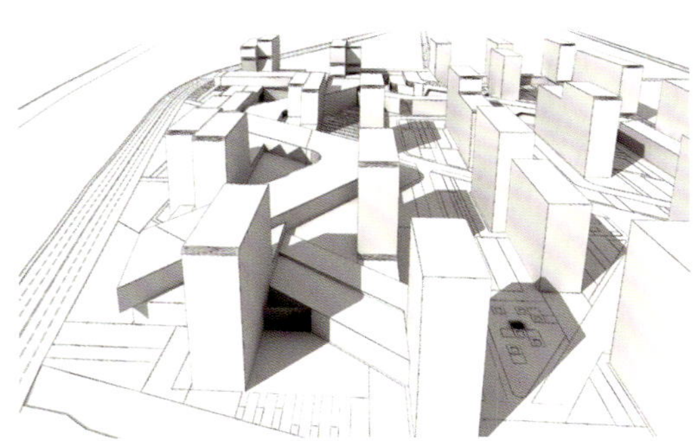

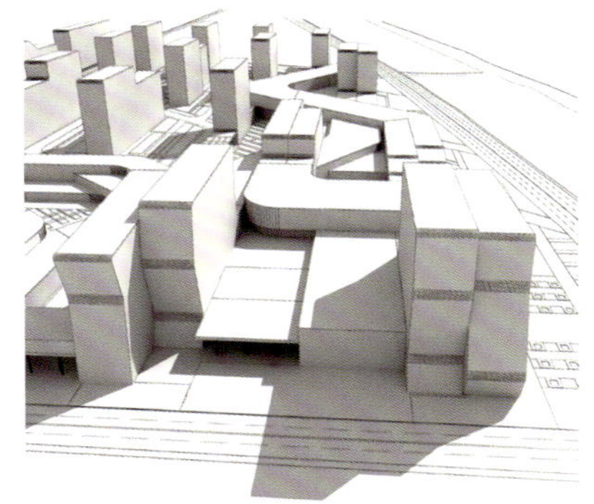

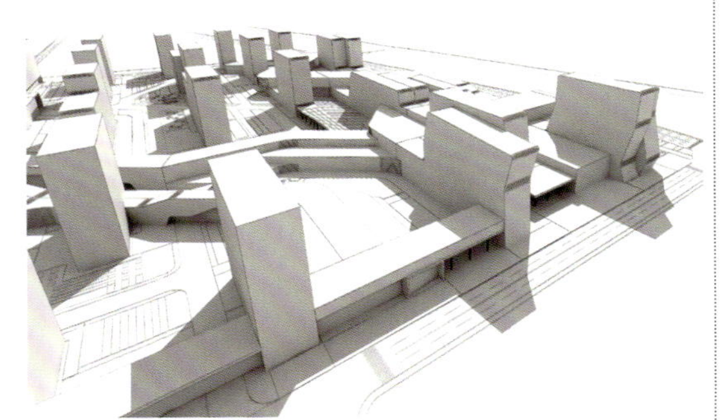

Museum of Longmen Caves

龙门石窟博物馆

设计单位：北京龙安华诚建筑设计有限公司，SYN建筑师事务所（德国）
主设计师：邹迎晞，丹尼尔·施瓦勃（德国）
设计时间：2008年
建筑物基底面积：4 328 m²
建筑面积：9 742 m²
建筑层数：三层（地上一层，地下二层）
建筑高度：9.60 m

Design firm: Beijing Long'anhuacheng Achitecture Design Limited Company/Syn Architecture
Lead designer: Zou Yingxi, Daniel Schwabe
Design date: 2008
Site area: 4 328 m²
Building area: 9 742 m²

1. "信仰的力量"
2. 空间是精神的载体
3. 龙门——无可替代性的空间
4. 可视世界与理想世界的过渡空间
5. 龙门石窟是反建筑的空间
6. 佛教哲学与艺术的"空、圆"

由于龙门的空间体现的是佛教信仰的力量，它是佛教精神的空间载体，决定了它从形式上的不可替代性，任何简单的模仿与拷贝都是浮于表面的。类似文物的赝品与真迹的对比一样，甚至更糟。龙门博物馆要将龙门的精神继承下来，并融进时代的特征，使其成为洛阳的新亮点，就要从空间与精神结合的切入点入手，创造出"形而上"的艺术空间，成为现实可视世界与佛教理想世界的过渡空间，使进入博物馆的每一个人都感受到龙门石窟背后的世界。

佛教哲学的"空"与"圆融无碍"正是空间与精神的完美结合。当我们越过建筑形式的束缚，看待龙门石窟空间的本质时，龙门是实体的石材与"性空"的佛教世界碰撞的产物。所以抓住龙门反建筑的"实"与佛教去除"实有"与"执著"的"空"相结合，就是龙门博物馆最终要表达的东西。

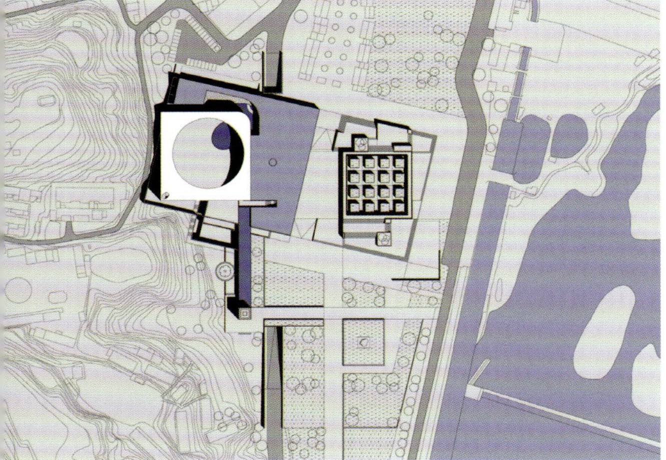

1. "The power of belief"
2. Space carries spirits.
3. Longmen—irreplaceable space.
4. Transitional space between visible and spiritual world
5. Longmen Caves are an anti-architectural space
6. Philosophy of Buddhism and "emptiness, roundness" in the art

As Longmen carries the spirits of Buddhism and reflects the power of belief, it cannot be replaced by any other simple and artificial copies and imitations. If Museum of Longmen wants to inherit the spirits of Longmen Caves and integrate with features of the times, it needs to start with combination between spirits and space to create a metaphysical art space which can be considered as transitional space between visible world and Buddhist and enable everyone entering into the museum to feel the spiritual world behind Longmen Caves.

The philosophy of Buddhism, "emptiness" and "roundness" are perfect combination between space and spirits. When we break the shackles of architectural forms and face to the nature of Caves' space, we found out that the Caves are the product of concrete stones and "vacant" Buddhist world. What the museum is trying to express is the combination between anti-architectural "concreteness" of Longmen and "emptiness" without "property" and "persistence".

-0.5层平面

-1层平面

1.5层平面图

2层平面图

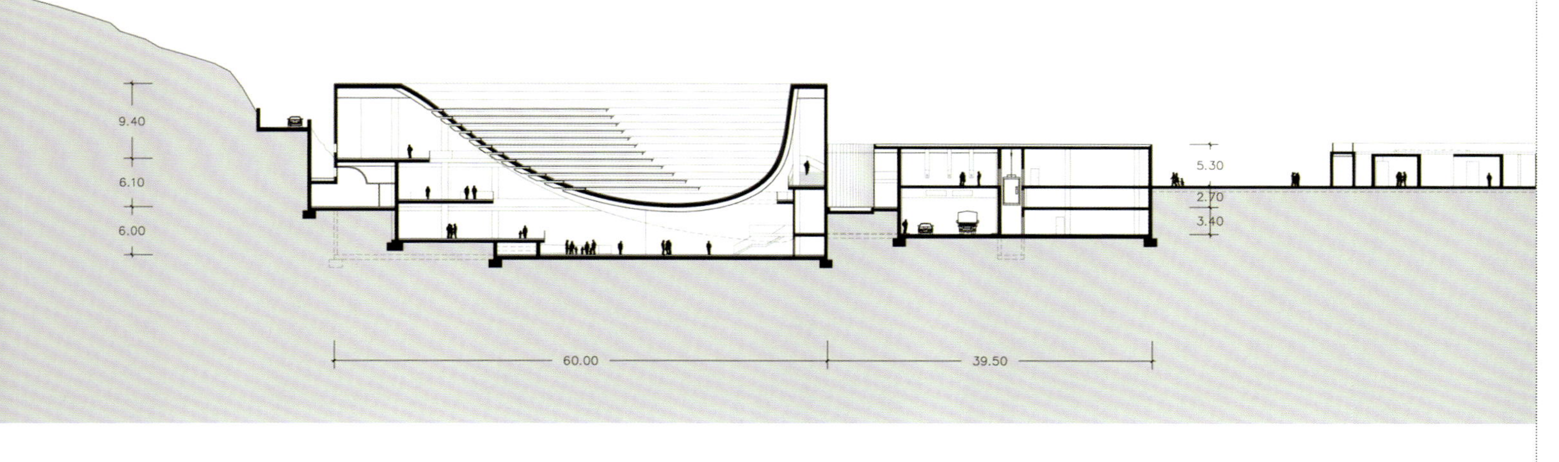
9.40
6.10
6.00
5.30
2.70
3.40
60.00
39.50

Yunnan Cultural Art Center – Yunnan Opera

云南文化艺术中心

设计单位：加拿大CPC建筑设计顾问公司
设计团队：Lisandro Ardusso、赵翀瀚
项目功能：剧院
用地面积：86 000 m^2
建筑面积：55 000 m^2
设计时间：2009年
开发商：云南文化艺术中心项目建设指挥部

Lead designer: Coast Palishade Consulting Gruop
Design team: Lisandro Ardusso, Zhao Chonghan
Site area: 86 000 m^2
Building area: 55 000 m^2
Design date: 2009

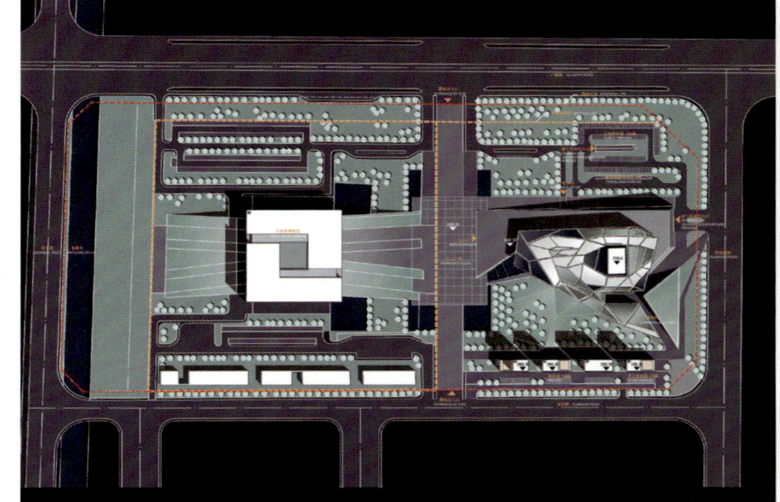

云南文化艺术中心地处昆明市新的城市中心，毗邻著名的高原湖泊——滇池。

这是一座真正意义上的无障碍建筑。大剧院作为一个为市民提供文化服务的场所和文化信息的载体，其设计强调市民和建筑空间的互动。观众可以通过盘旋而上的斜坡无障碍地到达剧院，欣赏歌舞、话剧、芭蕾等高雅艺术的演出。同样，这条路径还可以一直向上延伸直到屋面，饱览周边城市景观；再通过一侧的坡道与场地另一侧的商业街相连。这样的设计使得更多的公众可以通过这条路径参与建筑，融入建筑，使之真正成为人人可以参与的"民主"的建筑。

建筑的主体部分由相互交错的玻璃面所覆盖，仿佛一颗晶莹剔透的钻石。它既提供了对剧院厅堂的围护，共娱共乐，同时还为城市公众提供了一个相互交流、共同快乐的平台。将观众从广场引向入口大堂的斜坡和场地对面拟建的博物馆坡道相呼应，两条坡道均与中心文化广场相连接，形成两处文化设施共同的入口界面。而博物馆和文化艺术中心各自取意于云南的石林和高原梯田，勾勒出彩云之南的独特山水景色。

Qiu Jiang
Coast Palishade Consulting Gruop

邱江
加拿大CPC 建筑设计顾问有限公司总经理，总建筑师

学历：
1983–1988 年 北京清华大学建筑学士
1988–1990 年 加拿大不列颠哥伦比亚大学建筑学硕士

CPC于1994年在加拿大温哥华成立，自1995年起，CPC公司开始进入中国市场，为政府及房地产开发商提供城市规划、高端住宅设计、商业项目策划及设计、公共建筑设计、景观设计、室内设计等全方位的设计服务。随着工程项目的日益增加，2001年CPC公司将其在中国的办事处置于上海，以便更好地为业主提供即时的服务。

CPC公司拥有以北美为代表的境外建筑师和国内的优秀建筑师。CPC公司的建筑师在国内外高端住宅、大中型商业建筑等诸多领域内进行了深入的研究，积累了丰富的经验，这有助于CPC公司将先进的设计理念、规划思想及建筑技术运用于中国的建设项目，更专业地服务于国内的业主。

历史文脉

CPC公司在亚洲的建筑设计实践中试图做到尊重当地的历史文脉。我们不希望把我们的知识强加于人，而是与合作方共同分享我们的经验，以图创造出符合地方发展、符合业主既定目标的人文环境。

设计理念

优秀的建筑设计是由众多领域的专家通力协作的结晶：它功能合理、符合经济要求、美学上得体。这样的作品符合社会整体的价值观念因而具有生命力。建筑设计中有许多因素可以用技术或数值计量；而另一些则是主观的因素，需要设计师的素质、直觉以及不懈的执着才能得以解决。设计的过程要在主观与客观因素中找到这样的均衡：逻辑推理与设计师的直觉以及最终的设计需要满足使用者的要求，要对提高社会的品质做出贡献。

Design Philosophy
Good architectural design is a collaboration of many experts from different fields, with reasonable functions, in line with economic requirements and aesthetic decency. This kind of works is full of vitality because they accord with the values of the whole community. Some factors in architectural design can be measured by technology and amount; while some subjective factors need to be dug and solved by the designers with high quality, intuition, and relentless dedication. Design process is to be balanced between subjective and objective factors: logical reasoning and intuition of designers, the users' need to be met at last, the contribution to improving the quality of the community.

Practice in China
CPC has been designing for China for nearly 10 years, completed more than 20 million square meters involving planning, residential, commercial, hotel, office etc., and has made remarkable achievements including projects in a dozen domestic cities, such as Shanghai, Beijing, Chongqing, Chengdu, Suzhou and Dalian.

Cooperation with Arthur Erickson
CPC has been cooperating with Mr. Erickson since 10 years ago. We accomplished a number of architectural and planning projects together, some of which have been built in succession, such as Shenzhen International Convention & Exhibition Center, Hangzhou Culture Plaza, Suzhou Science and Cultural Art Center, Suzhou Jinji Lake Hotel, Dalian Development Zone Cultural Plaza, Kunming South City and West City, Dalian University Town, Beijing Willow Shopping Centre, etc.

Cooperation with Kisho Kurokawa
CPC has been working with Kurokawa, the international master of architecture, on a number of planning and architectural design projects through exchange visits. Cooperation projects are the Bund Number 15, Shanghai Jiading New Town, Shenzhen International Airport, Taiyuan administrative district planning.

Cooperation with the CMHC (Canada Mortgage and Housing Department)
CPC has been cooperating with CMHC for a long time, and has completed a series of urban planning, park planning and architectural design work in China. Since 2004, we have completed Shanghai Baoshan Gu village planning, Shanghai Nanhui residential area planning, Wuxi Zhongguancun Software Branch Park planning, etc. In 2007, these two groups accomplished the "Community Sustainable Development Planning Manual" for Shanghai Land Group. This manual has been introduced to the world by CMHC as a blueprint to promote sustainable development planning of communities.

在中国的实践

CPC公司在中国已有近10年的项目设计经验，已完成超过2000万平方米的各类建筑设计，项目类型涉及规划、住宅、商业、酒店、办公等，取得了令人瞩目的成就，工程项目遍布上海、北京、重庆、成都、苏州、大连等十几个国内城市。

与亚瑟·埃里克森先生合作

CPC公司与国际建筑大师亚瑟·埃里克森先生有着10年的合作历史，一起在中国参与了许多建筑及规划项目的设计，一些项目在陆续建成。合作项目有深圳国际会展中心、杭州文化广场、苏州科技文化艺术中心、苏州金鸡湖酒店、大连开发区文化广场、昆明南城西城、大连大学城、北京万柳购物中心等。

与黑川纪章先生合作

CPC公司从2004年开始与国际建筑大师黑川纪章先生就规划及建筑设计项目进行过多次合作，通过设计人员互访进行设计交流。合作项目有外滩15号、上海嘉定新城、深圳国际机场、太原行政区规划等。

与CMHC（加拿大贷款及房屋署）合作

一直以来，CPC公司与CMHC合作，在中国完成了一系列城市规划、园区规划及建筑设计的工作。从2004年至今完成了上海宝山顾村规划、上海南汇航头居住区规划、无锡中关村软件分园规划等项目的设计。2007年，CPC公司与CMHC合作，为上海地产集团编制了"社区可持续发展规划手册"。这一手册已作为CMHC推行社区可持续发展规划的教材蓝本在世界推广。

CPC was established in 1994 in Vancouver, Canada. CPC entered into Chinese market in 1995, and since then has provided full range of design services for the real estate developers and governments, such as urban planning, high level residential design, commercial project planning and design, public building design, landscape design, interior design. As the growth of the projects, CPC set up a China office in Shanghai in 2001, in order to better provide the owners with real-time services.

CPC has foreign architects represented by North American and excellent domestic architects working for him. CPC's architects carried through some deep research on high level residential, medium and large commercial buildings and many other areas in China and abroad, and it has accumulated rich experiences, which help CPC introduce advanced design concepts, planning ideas and construction techniques into China, and provide more professional services to domestic owners.

Historical Context

In the practice of the architectural design in Asia, CPC tries to respect local historical context. We don't attempt to impose our knowledge, but to share our experience with our partners, so that we could create a human environment that not only meets the local development but also accords with the demands of the owners' targets.

Yunnan Cultural Art Center is located in the center of the new city of Kunming and is adjacent to the famous plateau lake Dian Lake.

This is truly an obstacle-free architecture. As a platform to provide citizens with cultural services and information, the Opera emphasizes the interaction between the citizens and the architectural space. The audience can reach the Opera and enjoy refined art like dance, drama and ballet through a twisting slope without encountering any obstacle. This approach also provides access to the roof where the scene of surrounding city can be seen. The slope on the other side is connected with the shopping mall of the site. Such design enable more public crowd to join in the architecture and make it a democratic building to which every one can get an easy access.

The main body of the construction is covered by interveined glass facades, which make the building like a crystal clear diamond. It provides a protection to the hall as well as a platform for the citizen to communicate and share joy with each other. The slope to the entrance hall echoes the slope of the museum which will be built in the opposite. The two slopes are then connected to the Central Cultural Square, forming a sharing entrance interface. The museum and the Cultural Art Center take the flavor of the stone forest and the plateau terrace in Yunnan and form a unique scene of this mysterious province.

Talents Park. Shenzhen

深圳人才园设计

设计单位：库博事务所深圳立方公司
设计人员：邱慧康、涂江、ENRICO KREMP、郑敏莹、毕晓杰、林志杰
项目地点：深圳市福田区
设计时间：2008年
项目规模：79 372.4 m²
容 积 率：1.33

Design firm: Shenzhen CUBF Architecture Designing Office
Design team: Qiu Huikang, Xu Jiang, Enrico Kremp, Zheng Minying, Bi Xiaojie, Lin Zhijie
Design date: 2008
Construction area: 79 372.4 m²
Volume fraction: 1.33

深圳市人才园位于福田区竹子林片区，东侧隔规划路毗邻福田交通枢纽大厦，南临白石路，西侧隔红树林路毗邻地铁车辆段，北临深南大道，周边均属办公区。南面为红树林自然生态保护区及深圳湾，西北面为的园博园区，环境优美，咫尺可达。

设计构思

1.人才街道

设计引入了传统的街区概念构思，我们希望未来人才园不只是一个建筑单体，而是一个建筑群，一个城市综合体，一个人才 "mall"，利用"人才街道"这一建筑，对来访者进行有效的组织、接待、引导和分流，并贯穿南北，使其成为深南路至红树湾城市空间联系的纽带，并与城市公交节点紧密结合，以突显其城市性、开放性、亲和性的特征，寓意人才园拥揽八方人才之志。

2.创造"零台阶"式多层公共空间

为了强调公众来访的便捷通达，在公共裙房部分设计利用巨型折坡体系，模拟丘陵的起伏，不但提高空间形态的连续性，更重要的是让各股公共人流可以根据需求，轻松、安全又高效地到达不同标高的功能区间，且各流线、入口独立不交叉。其中整个裙房部分的首层、负一层、负二层与城市空间均实现了"零阶梯"衔接。

3.机场式人流立体交通处理方式

设计还在多处设置了自动扶梯、电梯、楼梯等垂直交通体，使人流能便捷地到达各个空间。

4.弹性设计

考虑到人才园使用功能的可变性及使用时间的交错性特点，设计保留了各公共空间、办公的公共服务部门与行政办公的完整独立性，以便于管理的同时，又强调其空间联系上的连续与紧密，以提高空间再利用、再划分的可能性，最终达到空间资源高效利用的目的。

Qiu Huikang
Shenzhen CUBE Architecture Designing Office

邱慧康
库博事务所深圳立方公司

邱慧康，1972年出生
1994年毕业于华中理工大学建筑学系，获学士学位
1997年毕业于华中理工大学建筑学院，获硕士学位
1997年至2001年任香港华艺设计顾问有限公司建筑师　高级建筑师、香港公司副经理
2009年获深圳市勘察设计行业首届十佳青年设计师
2004年9月，北京《新地产》杂志"中国最具影响力的建筑大师100"排名第39位
现任深圳市立方建筑设计顾问有限公司合伙人、执行董事、国家一级注册建筑师

5.内部引入城市型半地下道路

设计利用场地高差，地下首层车库实现了平层城市型半地下道路引入，架空生态车库的设计也将大量减少挖土方量，节约资金投入。办公部分的人车流与公共部分的人车流得到了有效的分隔，互不干扰。

6.“地毯式”生态建筑

首先，屋面及地面的巨型折坡体系形成一套沟渠系统，可收集雨水，进行再循环利用。其次，“地毯式”的屋顶花园也成为建筑生态固碳的有效方式。

7.生态庭院式的办公环境

人才园还具有重要的内向行政办公功能。为了给办公人员营造一个优美的办公环境，设计结合了深圳的地理气候特点，引入森林式内院以及立体式空中花园，两大生态绿色办公理念相结合，以丰富办公绿化景观系统的层次，多功能多方位地优化办公小气候，达到花园式办公的效果。另外，办公区的庭院景观有机地延续了基地北面的城市生态公园绿化景观，连成一体。

8.开放式的城市公园

在北部城市公园的设计中，顺应地形的自然坡度设计了大型且舒缓的斜坡广场，植被方面则用乔木及草地拼接成了点阵化的世界地图，寄寓人才园胸怀广阔，放眼世界。这幅抽象的地图同时也是一片森林，既创造了行人休憩的场所也丰富了城市肌理。同时通过广场铺地的变化，使公园场地与建筑内的空间相互渗透，完美相融。

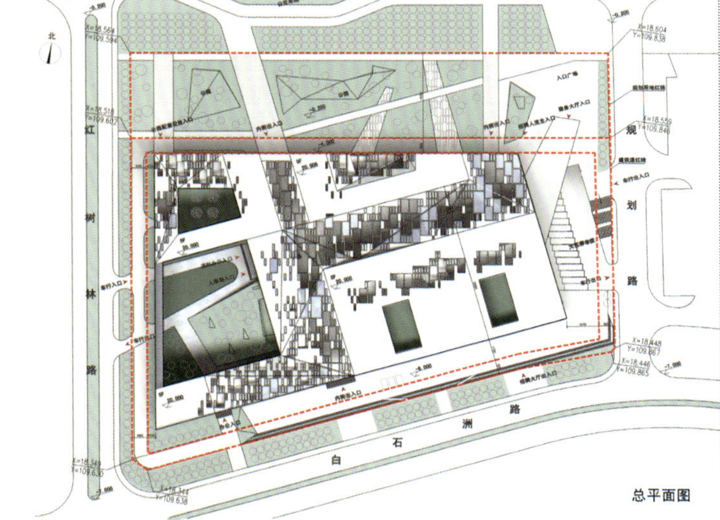

总平面图

Qiu Huikang

Male, born in 1972.

He got bachelor degree after graduating from Department of Architecture of Huazhong University of Science and Technology in 1994.

Got master degree after graduating from School of Architecture of Huazhong University of Science and Technology in 1997.

From 1997 to 2001, worked in Hong Kong Huayi Design Consultant Co. Ltd. as Architect, Senior Architect, and the deputy manager.

In 2009, he got one of the first top ten young designers in design industry by Shenzhen City.

Ranked the no. 39 in "China's most influential architect of 100" proposed by the Beijing's "new property" magazine on september in 2004.

Serving as Executive Director of Shenzhen Cube of Architectural Design Consultant Ltd., class 1 Registered Architect. Copartner of Shenzhen Cooper Architectural Design Studio, class 1 Registered Architect.

鸟瞰图

1. The elite street

Design introduces the concept of traditional block. We hope that the elite park is not just a single building, but a construction group, a city complex, an elite "mall". According to the "elite street" that is the gray space between building and outside space, we organize, accept, guide and divide the visitors. With this idea, we can highlight its urban, open and kindly features, which implicate the ambition of the park to embrace the elite from everywhere.

2. To create "no steps" type of multi-storey public space

In order to emphasize the convenience of the public visit, the design of public annex uses giant slope system, simulating rolling hills. This not only improves the continuity of spatial form, but also provides different ways for public flows arriving at function areas with different elevation easily, safely and efficiently by their own needs, and each flow and independent entrances do not cross.

3. Three-dimensional traffic-flow approach as an airport way

We also set up many escalators, elevators, stairways and other vertical transportation systems, so people can easily reach every space.

4. Flexible design

Considering the changeability of the function and the interleaving character of the using time in the elite park, the design retains public spaces and the full independence between public service offices, so that the management is more convenient and the continuity and compactness of spaces is emphasized to improve possibility of the spatial reuse and re-divide, and eventually achieve the purpose of efficient utilization of space resources.

5. Introducing the urban semi-underground roads to inner part

According to using the height difference, the garage of the first underground floor introduces the urban semi-underground road to the ground, and overhead ecological garage will also reduce the volume of excavated earthwork, saving capital investment. The flows of people and vehicles in office part and public part have been effectively separated from each other, which are not interfered.

6. Ecology Architecture like "Carpet"

Firstly, the giant turned slope system on the roof and the ground form a huge system of canals to collect rainwater for recycling. Secondly, the roof garden like "carpet" has become an eco-efficient way for building to carbon sequestration.

7. Ecological garden-style office environment

In order to create a beautiful office environment for office staffs , the design combines the features of geography and climate in Shenzhen, introducing a courtyard garden with forest-style and three-dimensional aerial garden. Two kinds of eco-green office concept are combined to enrich office landscape, optimizing office's micro-climate in multi-function and multi-faceted to achieve the goal of creating garden-office. In addition, the garden landscape of the office area organically continues the green scene of city's eco-park on the north of site, which seems to be a whole.

8. Open city park

The northern city park design follows the natural slope of the terrain and set a large slope square with small sloping angle. A lattice of mosaic map of the world is arranged with vegetation like trees and grass, implicating the elite's open mind and wide outlook. The abstract map is also a forest, creating a leisure space for pedestrian while enriching urban fabric. With the transformation of the plaza floor, the park ground and the architectural spaces penetrate into each other, blending perfectly.

GuanLing Five-star Hotel

北海冠岭五星级酒店

设计单位：库博事务所深圳立方公司
主设计师：邱慧康
设计团队：王新、亓红星、冯民兴、陆文健
设计时间：2009年
建筑基底面积：8 356 m^2
总建筑面积：37 820 m^2
容积率：0.15

Design firm: Shenzhen CUBF Architecture Designing Office
Lead designer: Qiu Huikang
Design team: Wang Xin, Qi Hongxing, Feng Minxing, Lu Wenjian
Design date: 2009
Site area: 8 356 m^2
Goross floor area: 37 820 m^2
Volume fraction: 0.15

北海冠岭项目五星级酒店（以下简称酒店）位于北海市冠头岭海滨，总建筑面积约为34 000 m^2，300间标准客房。建筑为一个平面S形，面海排开的8层分级跌落板式建筑，竖向稍有外倾。建筑设有二层面海开敞的半地下室，建筑高度约27.6 m，小于《高层建筑混凝土结构技术规程》适用的28 m条件。宽度为16 m，底层为10 m单跨斜撑大型平台支托。建筑高宽比最大为2:6，满足规范一般要求。建筑总长度约为300 m，直径约50 m两层高，大堂设于中部，上开18.5 m跨两层高弧顶大洞口，在四层方连为一体。七层屋面设有室外泳池。

The hotel project is located in North Sea Guan Lin Ridge coast, with a total floor area of approximately 34,000 square meters and 300 standard guest rooms. The architecture is a S-shaped and 8 floors plate construction with dropping in different level towards the sea, and has a slightly slope beyond the volume in the vertical.

Building has two-floor and semi-open basement towards the sea, with a building height of about 27.6 meters, which is less than the conditions of 28 meters in *Specification for Concrete Structures of High-rise Building*. The support flat is single bracing with width of 16 meters and 10 meters for the bottom floor. Maximum for the ratio of building height to width is 2:6, which meets the general requirements of the specification. The total length of the building is about 300 meters, and the diameter is about 50 meters. The two-level hall is laid out in the middle of the building, and in the top there is an 18.5 m high opening across two floors. Just from the 4th floor the building would be as a single entity. An outdoor swimming pool is set in the 7th floor.

Guang Xi Art and Design Gallery & Tonggu Museum

广西美术馆和铜鼓博物馆

设计单位：库博事务所深圳立方公司
主设计师：邱慧康
设计团队：黄燕翔、李捷、周青
设计时间：2009年

Design firm: Shenzhen CUBF Architecture Designing Office
Lead designer: Qiu Huikang
Design team: Huang Yanxiang, Li Jie, Zhou Qing
Design date: 2009

广西铜鼓博物馆位于五象新区规划地块南部，碧湖北岸，规划以自治区行政中心为核心，自北而南形成轴线，以轴线、水体、山峦串联城市规划展览馆，南宁市档案管理馆，位于山峦之上，周边山水相邻，景色优美。

出土的铜鼓

人类需要从自然中获取知识，这是传统的思维方式。在山水画中，人如何与一座山共同生存是被反复描绘的对象，山是中国人寻找失落文化和隐藏文化之地。

本项目5公顷的用地，大部分被一座山丘占据着，要么把山挖平，要么建筑退居边上。我们选择了后者。构思概念为一座即将出土的铜鼓。总体构成为铜鼓博物馆主体的一部分嵌入山体内，与山丘混为一体。体现出建筑对环境的一种谦让。

一座欣赏美景的看台

铜鼓博物馆连接山体，同时朝向五象新区规划中心主轴呈10° 倾斜，博物馆屋顶平台就像一座自然形成的看台，为从博物馆参观结束后的人们提供一个欣赏美景和休闲放松的地方。广西被称为各种类型铜鼓的荟萃之地，铜鼓数量众多，品类齐全，资料丰富，为世人瞩目。铜鼓的形态完满，圆润，充满了神秘的美感与艺术感染力，我们从铜鼓的基本特点中提出"鼓形"、"鼓纹"等要素作为本次铜鼓馆设计的出发点，同时赋予该建筑一些时尚建筑元素，使博物馆的造型亦民族亦现代，地方化国际化融为一体，让观者深深着迷。

铜鼓博物馆的外观造型由若干个彼此交织的部分组合而成，仿佛一部蒙太奇式的电影。部分清澈透明，轻盈且充满活力，部分呈重金属色，光亮，厚重且坚硬，有的覆盖着壮锦图案，仿若蕾丝般神秘，有的随光线的变化变幻出不同的色彩，形成一个略显陈旧却闪亮动人的丰富表面。

这座建筑有着被剪裁的轮廓，就像人的记忆，以片段的形式间断地展示出来，这是一种骨子里的铜鼓的印象。亦似铜鼓，亦不似铜鼓，难以捉摸。而铜鼓馆建筑表皮的处理，是对于广西民俗的最佳诠释。

流线设计

内观整个结构，包括一个入口处共享大平台，上部分为展厅部分，下部分为办公管理部分，以及屋顶花园部分。顺着螺旋向上的空间流线进入每层展示大厅，最后结束于屋顶的空中花园平台，参观者亦可自上而下进入各层展厅，欣赏各类广西民俗作品。

架空平台部分布置有演讲厅、图书馆、教学室、咖啡厅、休闲商店等多样性的活动展示方式和丰富的展示空间。

铜鼓博物馆首要解决的是广西民俗风情的展示问题。而当代版画艺术的展示，需要相当灵活的空间与之相适应，比如空间的尺度，照明以及气氛的可塑性。

本方案采用单元式模块的聚合方式，来营建博物馆的户内户外整体环境。把铜鼓博物馆塑造成一个具有丰富空间体验价值、可观可游、可分可合、适应多种类别和方式进行现代艺术展览活动的当代艺术场所。

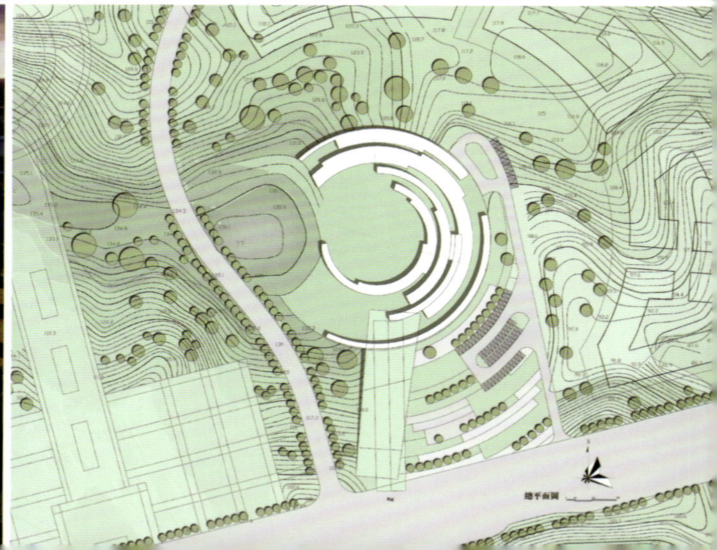

Guangxi Bronze Drum Museum is located in the southern part of Wuxiang New District, northern shore of Lake Bi. In the area, the municipality's administrative center was planned as the core, while an axis was set from north to south. Urban Planning Exhibition Hall and Nanning City Archives Museum are connected by axis, water and mountains. At the same time, they are on the mountains and surrounded by water with beautiful scene.

Bronze drum unearthed

The concept of the planning is a bronze drum to be unearthed. In the general constitution, one part of the main body is planned to embed in the mountain so that the museum and hills are mixed into a whole, which reflects modest attitude of building to environment.

A stand to enjoy the beauty

The Museum connects the mountain while tilting 10 degrees towards the planned central axis of Wuxiang New District. The flat roof serves as a natural formed stand for people to enjoy the beauty and a relaxing place after the visit to the museum. People face the main landscape axis of the core and natural environment with open view and good scenery.

Drum Museum's appearance is constituted of a number of interwoven parts, like a movie montage. Some parts are clear, light and full of vitality; some show heavy metal colors with bright, massiness and hard feelings; some are covered with zhuangjin patterns that are mysterious like lace, and some parts change with fantastic light in different colors, forming a slightly old but rich shiny surface. Bronze Drum Museum's skin treatment has the best interpretation to the folk-custom of Guangxi.

The figure of the building has been cut in the outline, like a man's memory, to display intermittently in a fragment form. This is a deep impression on drum instinctually, no matter what it looks like drum or not. The treatment to the Pavilion's skin is the best interpretation for the Guangxi folk-custom.

Circulation design

The whole inner structure includes a large shared platform at the entrance, with the exhibition part in the upper space, the management part in the lower space, and some roof garden. Visitors can approach the exhibition halls on each floor along the upward spiral circulation, ending visit on the roof garden, or enter into each hall from above to below to enjoy the works of various types of Folk Traditions of Guangxi. Aerial platform parts are arranged functional space such as lecture hall, library, teaching rooms, coffee houseand leisure stores.

Diverse ways of showing activities and rich exhibition space. The program adopts modular aggregation approach to construct indoor and outdoor environment as a whole. The museum was built into one contemporary art site which is rich of spatial experience, available to divide and combine, adoptable to multiple categories and ways to show contemporary art.

In the museum, visitors can experience various alternating spaces, which are open or closed, indoor or outdoor, bright or dim, private or public.

Shenzhen Higher Education Mega International Conference Center

深圳大学城国际会议中心

设计单位：库博事务所深圳立方公司
项目地点：深圳市南山区
设计时间：2008年
设计人员：邱慧康、张政强、黄燕翔、张宇、韩树勇、薛超
项目规模：13 265 m²

Design firm: Shenzhen CUBF Architecture Designing Office
Design team: Qiu Huikang, Zhang Zhengqiang, Huang Yanling, Zhangyu, Han Shuyong, Xue Chao
Gross floor area: 13 265 m²

方案构思

1.形态及表情

地块同图书馆相邻，为了尊重原规划和已建建筑，保证图书馆建筑嵌入到山体的纯粹感觉，我们将地块南边的山体延续下来，地块上形成坡状的覆土建筑。大部分建筑体块消失在自然地形之下，形成整个建筑底；完形的环状体量从覆土的部分升起来，是整个建筑的可视部分，整个建筑形成强烈的图底关系。圆形的点状同图书馆建筑的线状形成对比，和谐呼应。

2.轴线及视线通道

人们从城市沿着园区主要道路进入园区，在主要道路到地块开口处，穿过地块可以清晰地看到对面山上的西丽塔，我们的建筑形体没有遮挡住该标志塔，而是有意留出了这条视线的通道。

3. 色彩及标志

校园现有建筑多采用灰白色调，因此建筑色彩单一。项目处于园区的中心位置，我们给升起的圆环附上色彩斑斓的颜色，使之成为整个园区的点睛之笔。

空间分析

室内外空间的交融、渗透： 建筑空间布局上，形成内外二个广场，外广场半包围着建筑，而建筑围合出内广场，内广场是建筑的焦点，是建筑的户外舞台，建筑本身是个大的剧场。建筑的各功能空间分散布局，生态自然的室外空间包围着各种功能的室内空间。

立体、流动的绿化空间：覆土的屋顶绿化空间是地块北边山体的延续，而建筑的中庭绿化空间则是屋顶绿化空间的下沉，建筑的各功能空间就是被这些立体的流动的绿化空间所掩埋。

环境及广场景观

我们运用“拼图板”的方式完成我们的广场景观，使之同建筑及地块周围的自然环境形成一幅完整丰富的地景艺术。身处会议中心，你无法分辨哪儿是建筑，哪儿是景观，哪儿是屋顶，哪儿是广场。景观和建筑，屋顶和广场相互交织着，不分彼此。景观同建筑结合，一起创造出生态、惬意的工作环境；自由开放的交流场所；乐于表现的人生舞台。

Project Idea

1. Form and expression

As the land site is adjacent to library, in order to respect the original plan and built construction, ensure the pure sense of library building which is embedded into the mountain, we try to keep the mountain in the south of our site, and form a slope-shaped construction on the block. Most of the building body would have been hidden under the natural terrain, which create the base of building; complete ring-shaped body rise up from the earth part, which is the visible part of the building. Therefore, the whole building would create a strong figure-ground relationship and the dot shape also form a harmony contrast to the line-shaped library.

2. Axis and sight channels

People walk into the park along the main roads from city. Before they arrive our block from the main road through the opening block, Xili Tower would be visible. In our design, the sight channel to the tower as park symbol keeps reserved for passers-by.

3. Color and logo

The most existing buildings in campus always used the gray tone, so buildings are looked monotony in color. As our project is at the center point of the park, we try to attach colorful colors to the risen ring to make it the focus of the park.

Spatial Analysis

Blend and penetration between indoor and outdoor spaces:

There are two squares both inside and outside according to the space layout. The outside square surrounds the building half, and construction itself encloses the inside square, which is the focus of the whole building and the exterior stage. Then, the building would become a large theater. Different functional spaces are distributed, and indoor spaces are all surrounded by ecological outdoor spaces.

Tridimensional and flowing green space:

The green space on the earth-covered roof is a continuation of mountain in the north of our block, while the green atrium space in the building is the sunken place from green roof space. Different functional spaces of building are surrounded by such flowing and tridimensional green space.

The environment and square landscape

We use "jigsaw picture" to complete our square landscape, so to make it be a integrative ground landscape with the surrounding landscape, buildings and natural environment.

When you are at the conference center, it is hard to tell apart the construction, the roof and the square. Different elements such like landscape and architecture are integrated and become one, all which create an ecological and comfortable working environment, a free and open place for communication and a willing-to-express exhibition stage.

Shenzhen Mobile Dispath Center

深圳移动调度中心大厦

设计单位：库博事务所深圳立方公司
主设计师名称：邱慧康
设计团队：王新、黄梦春
设计时间：2009年

Design firm: Shenzhen CUBF Architecture Designing Office
Lead designer: Qiu Huikang
Design team: Wang Xin, Huang Mengchun

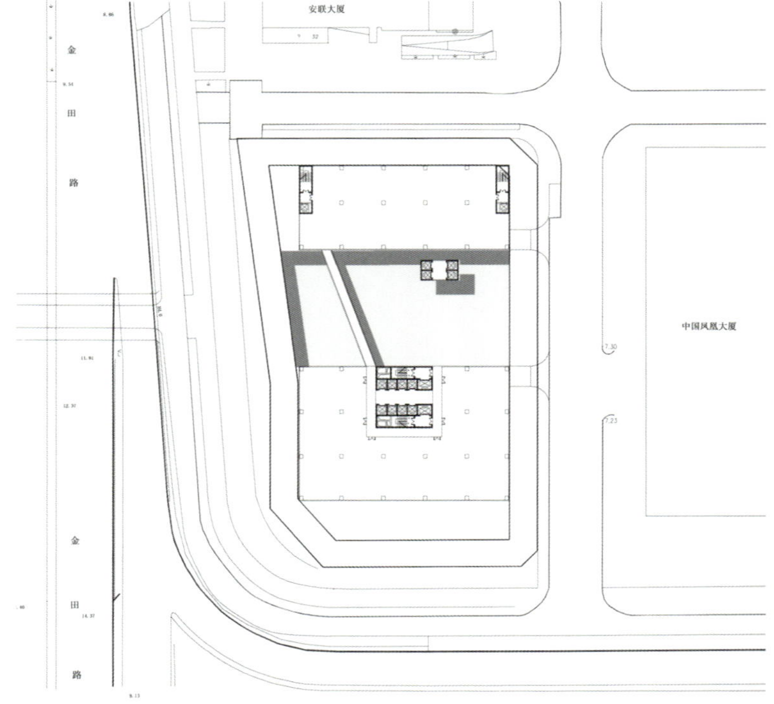

现状

深圳中心区的各种类型的高层建筑很多，但各建筑多为单一维度的各自发展，建筑内部的城市开放空间的设置很少，市民中心和会展中心前面虽有大片广场，但行人还是感觉缺乏场所感，缺少人体与城市空间互动的媒介。

垂直城市

中国移动提倡“互动”的商业理念，我们同时思考建筑在城市中的互动关系。在本项目中，我们在建筑的开放区和半开放区引入垂直的城市空间，试图给中心区单一维度的现状空间带来生机。开放的垂直空间，也同时带来了更多建筑单体与城市，市民与建筑之间互动的机会。

方式

通过功能分区，建筑分为南北两栋楼，单一的办公区设置在南楼，这里给办公室提供良好的朝向与景观，由体验中心，展示中心等组成的开放空间布置于北楼，两楼间通过公共电梯连接。南北楼因功能与使用方式的不同即相互独立同时又联系紧密。

Status quo

There are many types of high-rise buildings in center district of Shenzhen, but each building always developed in its own single dimension. Therefore the plan for urban open space in construction is few. Although there is a large square in front of the citizen center and exhibition center, the passersby still feel a lack of site sense, which is caused by the lack of medium of people interaction with the urban space.

Vertical city

China Mobile always promotes the business philosophy of "interaction", so we would think about the interaction between building and city. In this project, we try to introduce the vertical urban space to the open area and semi-open area of the building to bring vitality to the single dimension space in center district. The open vertical space would also bring more interactive opportunities between building and city, citizen and the construction.

Plan

The project is divided into two buildings in north and south by functional zoning. The south building is used only for office, which would provide a good orientation and

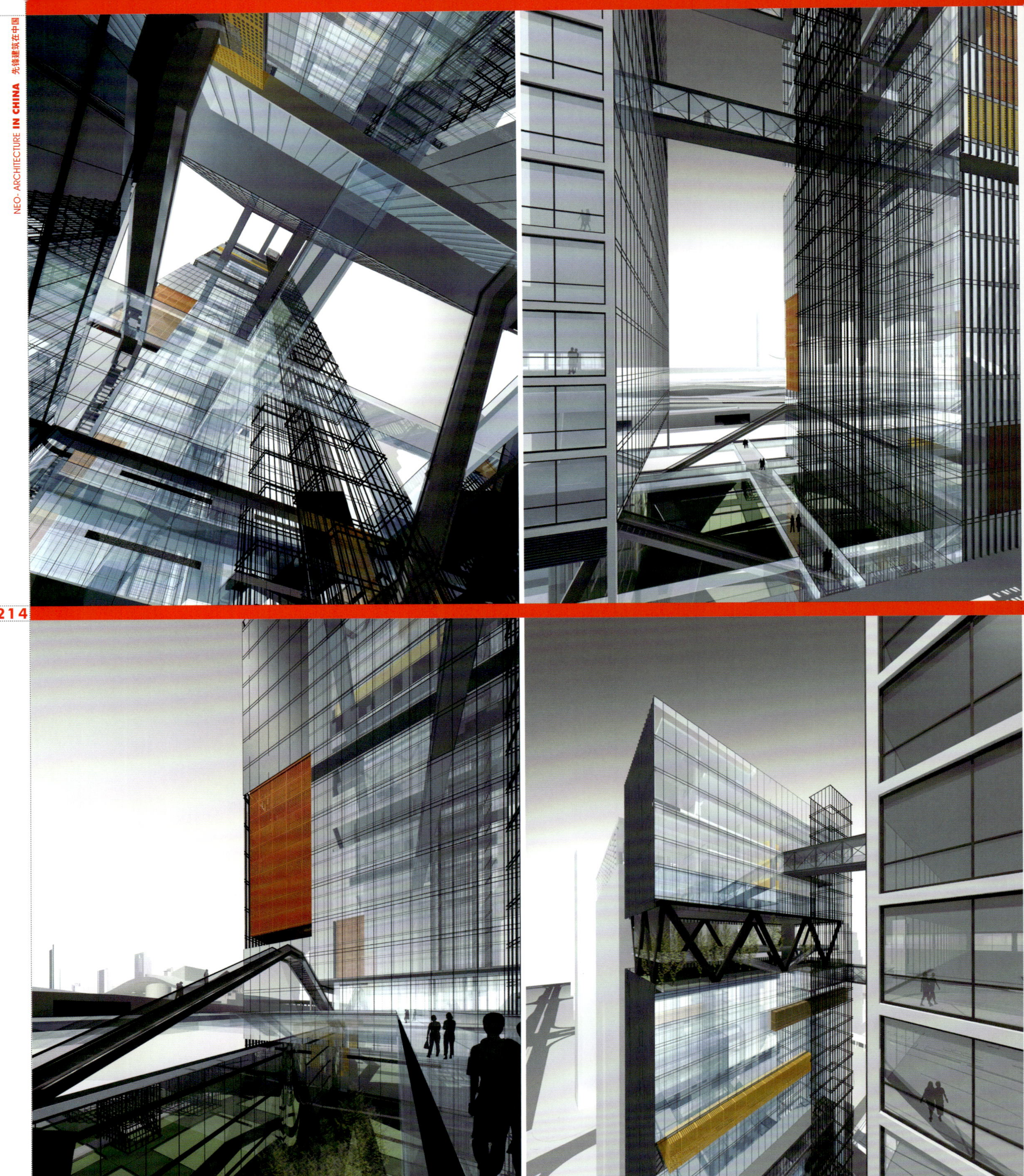

landscape. North building is composed of experience center, exhibition center and other open space. Two buildings are connected with public elevator, by which they become two different buildings for independent function and using mode, and would be closely linked at the same time.

Skyworth Semiconductor Design Centre

创维半导体设计中心

设计单位：库博事务所深圳立方公司
主设计师名称：邱慧康
设计团队：ENRICO、MICHAEL、黄梦春、张弓
设计时间：2010年

Design firm: Shenzhen CUBF Architecture Designing Office
Lead designer: Qiu Huikang
Design team: Enrico, Michael, Huang Mengchun, Zhang Gong
Design date: 2010

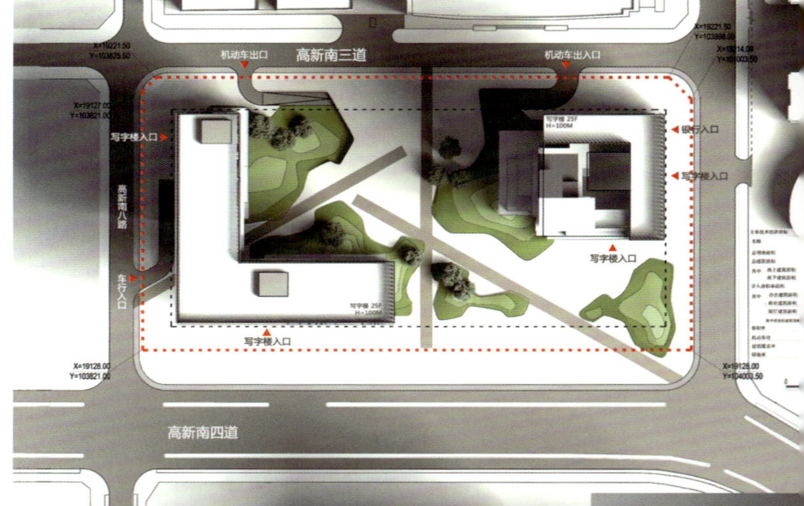

Architectural Design of Guangdong Xinghai Performing Arts Group Office Building in Ersha

广东星海演艺集团办公楼建筑设计

设计单位：广州天作建筑规划设计咨询有限公司
委托方：广东星海演艺集团
项目地址：广州市二沙岛
规划面积：7 325 m^2
建筑面积：13 623 m^2
实施情况：全国投标第一名，在建

Design firm: Guangzhou Teamzero Design & Planning Co., Ltd
The client: Guangdong Xinghai Performing Arts Group
Project address: Ersha Island, Guangzhou City
Planned area: 7 325 m^2
Building area: 13 623 m^2
Condition of implementation: The first in the national competitive bid, application of construction scheme

广东星海演艺集团办公楼位于广州市二沙岛晴波路与海山街交叉处西北侧地块内，毗邻星海音乐厅和岭南会，南隔晴波路眺望珠江水道，区位极佳，是二沙岛难得的南向珠江地块。用地为直角梯形，南北平均长约103 m，东西宽约87 m，其中南侧沿道路走向为一斜边，用地面积约0.73 hm^2。其周边多为低密度的文化公共建筑，环境优美、尺度宜人，是广州市民休闲、欣赏珠江夜景的理想场所。办公楼功能包括广州交响乐团排练用房、星海集团办公用房和辅助设施。总建筑面积约1.36万平方米，其中地下1层面积约3 880 m^2；地上6层建筑面积约9 743 m^2。

该项目位于广州的城市中心，是二沙岛上的标志性建筑——星海音乐厅的配楼，具有公共文化建筑的形态特征。方案的艺术构思源于中国传统山水画中“竹子”的形态。整体造型和立面设计以周边文化建筑区域环境为背景，重点考虑新建筑与星海音乐厅及珠江北岸建筑轮廓线的关系。造型上，和谐中求变化，统一中求创新，使新建筑与音乐厅相互依托、交相辉映。抽象而理性的构图塑造建筑的现代艺术气质，注重雕塑

Li Shaoyun
Guangzhou Teamzero Design & Planning Co., Ltd

李少云
广州天作建筑规划设计咨询有限公司

李少云简介：

广州市城市规划勘测设计研究院副总规划师、城市与建筑设计所所长、广州市天作建筑规划设计咨询有限公司设计顾问、高级工程师、国家一级注册建筑师、注册规划师。1994年获哈尔滨建筑大学建筑学学士学位，1997年获华南理工大学工学硕士学位，2004年获同济大学城市设计博士学位。长期以来从事城市规划、城市设计、建筑设计、旅游规划设计和风景园林规划设计工作，共主持和参加完成了100余个设计项目，多次在全国及国际投标中中标，并获得省部级优秀设计奖以及国际奖项。迄今已在国内重要专业期刊上发表了学述论文11篇，其中7篇发表在核心期刊，并于2005年10月在中国建工出版社出版个人专著《城市设计的本土化——以现代城市设计在中国的发展为例》。2007年获广州国际设计周全国十大杰出设计师奖。

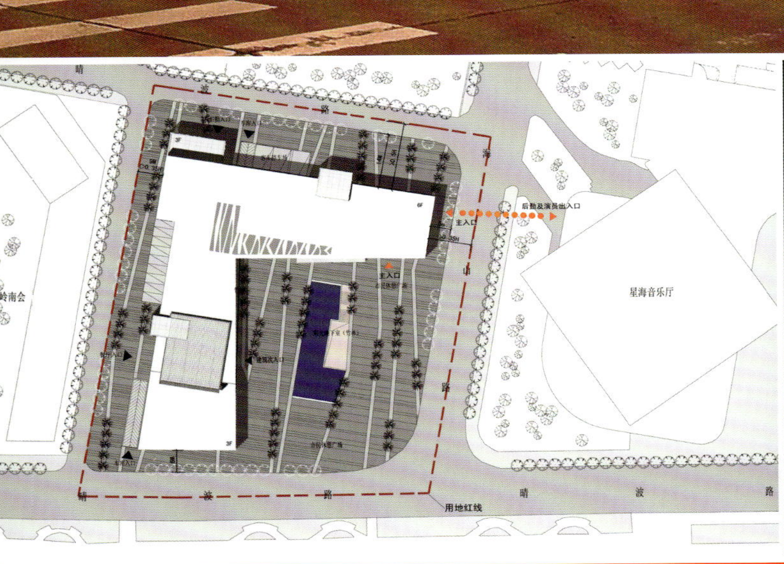

Li Shaoyun, who received the "Golden Goat Award" for the top ten young architects of China in 2007, has taken the degree of urban design DR. of Tongji University, architectural design post-doctor of South China University of Technology, senior engineer, registered planner, first grade registered architect, and is the chief planner of Guangzhou Urban Planning & Design Survey Institute, director of the Institute of Urban and architectural design, the design director of TEAMZERO Architectural Planning and Design Groups of the United States, and Guangzhou TianZuo Planning and Design Consulting Company.

He has engaged in fields of urban planning and design, architecture design, tourism planning and design, and landscape planning. He had presided over and participated in more than 80 projects, had been awarded in national and international competitions for many times, and received the Design Awards from the province and international. Up to the present, he had published 11 research papers in national important science journals, and 7 of them are in the core journals. In October of 2005, his individual monograph *Localization of Urban Design - Modern City Design in China as an example* was published by Chinese Construction Industry Press.

感，整体逻辑性强，虚实对比明确。设计上，注重形式与内容的统一、建筑群与建筑个体本身的高低错落、建筑表面与内部空间的关系，使建筑立面自然生成。选材上，力求朴素、经济，同时又努力创造优雅、清新、积极向上的演艺文化企业形象。连续、漂浮的实体的表皮取意于中国传统文人画竹子的抽象形态，形成强烈的标识性。遮阳板、百叶等要素的运用符合岭南气候特点，同时又使建筑呈现出特殊的气质和内涵。岭南庭院的布置手法的借鉴，形成内外、上下相互渗透的流动空间秩序。建筑的入口设计成通透的玻璃大厅，突出的入口架空层自然形成建筑的标志性雨篷，支撑立柱处理为多角度的柱群形式，也象征了竹林的形态。

办公楼的设计还充分考虑了城市空间关系，建筑布局强调与星海音乐厅在空间形态上的整体性，围合成界面完整清晰的开敞空间，并妥善处理新建筑与星海音乐厅之间的使用和建设间的协调关系。为增强外部广场空间的景观导向性，更好地引导人流，设计中恰当运用了铺地、花坛、竹林及水面的形态。

广东星海演艺集团办公楼可以说是中国本土建筑的现代化范本之一。设计在“反本土的本土化”理念的指导下，没有沿用中国传统建筑典型的装饰元素，但又不乏传统建筑意蕴，其诀窍在于建筑的色彩体系和建筑材料的文化特色。建筑色彩保留中国建筑的灰屋顶意象；沿江建筑立面的造型手法抽象地隐喻中国山水画中的竹子；园林设计中，通过竹林的平分布局形成和谐呼应的关系，通过灯光设计勾勒竹林的轮廓。相信这个以“丝竹”为创作灵感的建筑，未来会成为一道靓丽的滨江风景线。

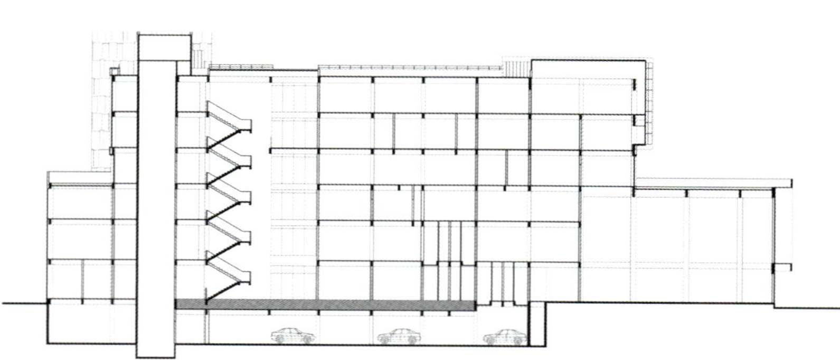

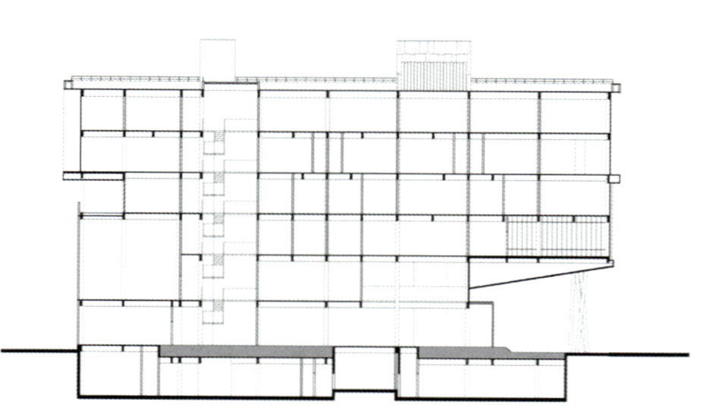

The new address of Guangdong Xinghai performing Art Group is located in the plot at the northwestern side of the infall of Qingbo Road and Haishan Street, Ersha Island, Guangzhou City.

The planning scheme is based on the art concept of "bamboo rhyme", starting from the general environmental texture in the design. It does not excessively apply the luxury material and does lay stress on the uniformity of form and content. The design tries to show the reality of the building and lays stress on the high and low interleaving of the architectural complex and the architectural individual, the relation between the surface and the inner space, to naturally produce the architectural vertical plane. The application of such factors as sunshade and shade and so on complies with Lingnan climate feature, and also makes the building display special texture effect and the vertical style simple and vivid.

The coordination relation of the use and construction among Xinghai music hall is well done in the design scheme. The Performing Arts Center serves as the supporting role but does not loose its distinction, and forms a relatively integrated spatial configuration together with Xinghai music hall. Taking the satisfaction with the reasonable and high-efficiency of work, rehearsal and reception as the precondition, the Performing Arts Center will satisfy the multi-functional requirements and promote the coordinated development of each aspect. In addition, the planning scheme increases the people stream in the external square space and the guidance quality of the landscape, properly manage the relation between the building and the environment. It specially emphasizes the spatial integrity with Xinghai music hall and surrounds the distinct wide space with complete interface.

Moreover, on the architectural image and vertical design, we use the environment of the building area of Ersha Island in the surrounding of the plot as the background, starting from the angle of the urban design, lay stress on considering the relation between the new building and Xinghai music hall and the contour line of the buildings on the northern side of Pearl River.

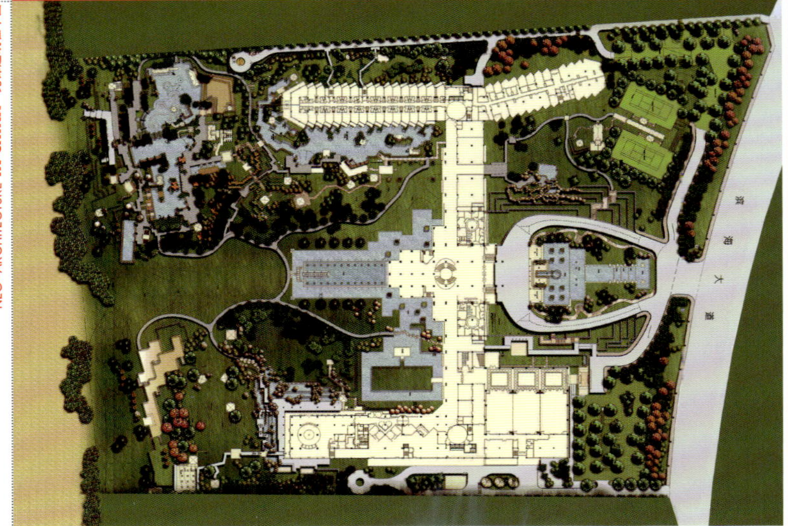

Sheraton Sanya Resort

三亚喜来登度假酒店

设计单位：北京市建筑设计研究院
主设计师：金卫钧、张耕、孙勃
设计团队：陈淑慧、胡光荧、徐聪义、赵毅强、王保国、沈玲
建筑面积：78 868 m²
建筑层数：地上8层，地下1层

Design firm: Beijing Institute of Architectural Design and Research
Lead designer: Jin Weijun, Zhang Geng, Sun Bo
Design team: Chen Shuhui, Hu Guangying, Xu Congyi, Zhao Yiqiang, Wang Baoguo, Shen Ling
Location: Hainan
Building area: 78 868 m²

三亚喜来登酒店位于海南三亚亚龙湾国家旅游渡假区，酒店总建筑面积为78 868平方米，共有500间客房，是一座以度假休闲为主兼具承接大型会议功能的五星级酒店。该设计充分尊重当地的自然和人文环境，结合原有地形地貌，对所处的生态环境给予最大的保护。为了保留南侧自然形成的沙坝，同时使游客步入酒店就能望到海面，酒店的主入口及大堂设于二层。从大跨度雨蓬起，酒店入口、大堂、落水台阶、大堂吧、天光水池，这一系列空间构成了最富特色的酒店公共空间。建筑采用分布式布局，尽可能地融于周围的植被之中。为了使建筑南北沟通，由东西两翼向中间逐级退台。同时，为了不对海滩及沙坝造成压迫感，建筑从北向南也采取了同样的手法。整个建筑采用U形对称平面。U形布局使酒店的海景客房达到了75%。酒店的园林设计刻意营造了许多阶梯式的地表特征，配以多种植物，使游客在步于其间时，永远不可能一览庭院的全局而产生枯燥感。

建成后以其朴素自然的建筑风格，宽松舒适的度假居住空间，独特的空间效果以及建筑与环境的渗透与交融等特点，尤其是充满整个酒店的浓郁的休闲气息深得业主和社会的好评。为海南三亚亚龙湾增添了一道亮丽的风景。

Jin Weijun
Beijing Institute of Architectural Design and Research

金卫钧
北京市建筑设计研究院一所所长

1981.9～1985.8 天津大学建筑系　获学士学位

1985.9～1988.4 天津大学建筑系　获硕士学位

1988.5～1988.9 北京市建筑设计研究院

1988.10～1996.12 北京市建筑设计研究院海南分院工作，先后担任海南分院副总建筑师、副院长、常务副院长等职。

1997.1～1998.4 北京市建筑设计研究院工作，高级建筑师、一级注册建筑师。在此期间，曾赴美国芝加哥与SOM建筑事务所工作。

1998.5～1999.10 入选《50名建筑师在法国》法国总统项目，注册“巴黎塞纳建筑学院”，并在让·努维尔建筑事务所工作。

1999.10～现在 现任北京市建筑设计研究院副总建筑师、一所所长、教授级高级建筑师。

主持设计了三亚喜来登度假酒店、神州数码软件研发中心、首都师范大学国际文化大厦、LG北京大厦（与美国SOM合作）、联想园区C座（与美国SOM合作）、京粮广场、海南三亚湾蓝波湾、海口体育馆、CMEC海南大厦、北京福景苑等多项大型工程。曾获国家优秀工程设计金奖、建设部优秀建筑设计一等奖、海南省北京市优秀建筑设计一等奖、中国青年建筑师奖及中国建筑学会建筑创作优秀奖，2006年北京市有突出贡献的科学、技术、管理人才等荣誉称号。专业刊物发表文章多篇。

1981.9 ~ 1985.8, Department of Architecture of Tianjin University, Bachelor's degree
1985.9 ~ 1988.4, Department of Architecture of Tianjin University, Master's degree
1988.5 ~ 1988.9, Beijing Institute of Architectural Design and Research
1988.10 ~ 1996.12, Hainan Branch of Beijing Institute of Architectural Design and Research, served as vice chief architect of Hainan Branch of Architects, Vice President, Executive Vice President and other staff.
1997.1 ~ 1998.4, Beijing Institute of Architectural Design and Research senior architect, class 1 Registered Architect. Worked for SOM Architectural Firm in Chicago during the period.
1998.5 ~ 1999.10, selected in the "50 architects in France," French President Projects, registered in " School of Architecture in Seine, Paris ", and Jean Nouvel Architectural Firm.
1999.10 ~ now the current vice chief architect of Beijing Institute of Architectural Design and Research, superintendent of First Design House, Senior Architect as Professor.

Jin presided over the design of the Sheraton Sanya Resort, Digital China Software R & D Center, Capital Normal University's International Culture Building, LG Beijing Tower (cooperated with SOM), Lenovo Park's C Block (cooperated with SOM), BGG Plaza, Sanya Blue Wave Bay, the gymnasium of Haikou, CMEC's Building in Hainan, Beijing Fortune Villa and many other large projects. He also won the National Excellent Engineering Design Award, first prize of excellent architectal design by Ministry of Construction, first prize of excellent architectal design by Hainan Province and Beijing, China's Young Architects Award and the Architectural Society of China Architectural Excellence Award, outstanding contribution in 2006 in Beijing science on technology, management and personnel, ect. Numerous articles are published in professional journals.

Sheraton Sanya Hotel lies in Yalong Bay National Tourism Resort Sanya Hainan. Total construction area of the hotel is 78 868 square meters, accommodating 500 rooms. It is a five-star hotel mainly for vacation and some large conferences. The design of the hotel fully respects the local natural and human environment, and combines the existing topography with the design so that the ecological environment is in maximum protection. In order to keep sand bar that has naturally formed on the south side, and to let the tourists could look over to the sea once they step into the hotel, the main entrance and lobby located on the second floor. From the big awning to the entrance, the lobby, the steps of falling water, the lobby bar, and the daylight pool, this series constitutes a most unique hotel public space. The building adopts a distributed layout, to fuse into the surrounding vegetation as much as possible. The east and west wings recedes gradually so that the north and south part of the building could communicate with each other. Meanwhile, in order not to cause a feeling of pressure to the beach and the sand bar, the same means is used from the north to the south of the building. The entire building shows a U-symmetry plane and rooms that can have a view of sea reach 75% of the whole rooms. The design of hotel's garden deliberately creates a lot of ladder-like surface features, together with various plants, in order that visitors wouldn't be able to see the whole courtyard with one glance when they stroll in it, so they wouldn't feel bored.

After construction, the hotel won a high reputation by the owners as well as other people by its simple and natural style, loose and comfortable vacation living space, unique space and the feature that the architecture and environments merge into each other, especially by its full-bodied sense of leisure. The project lends an additional beautiful landscape to Yalong Bay.

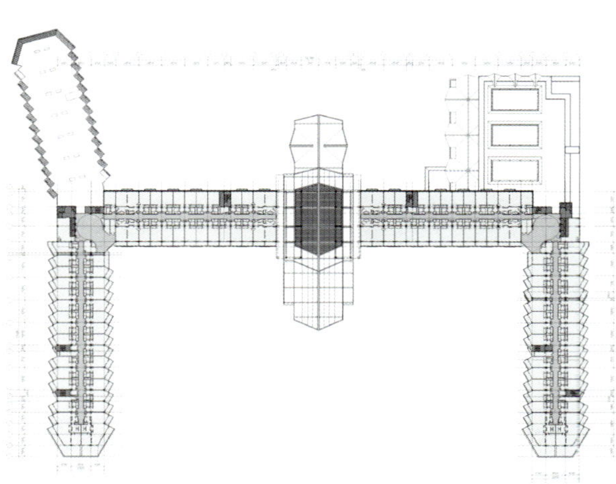

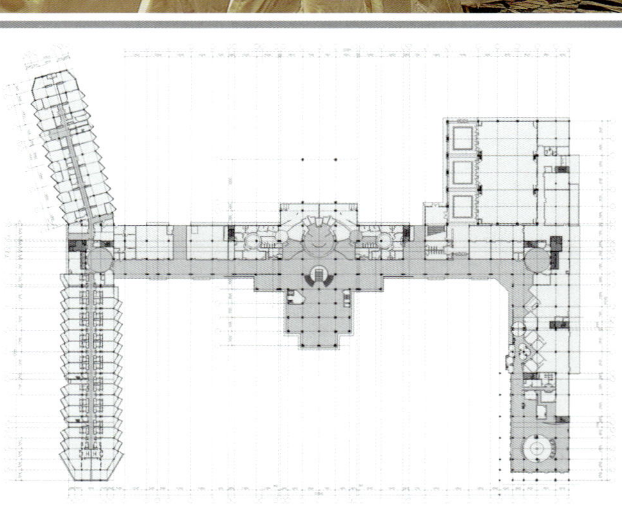

Palm Court

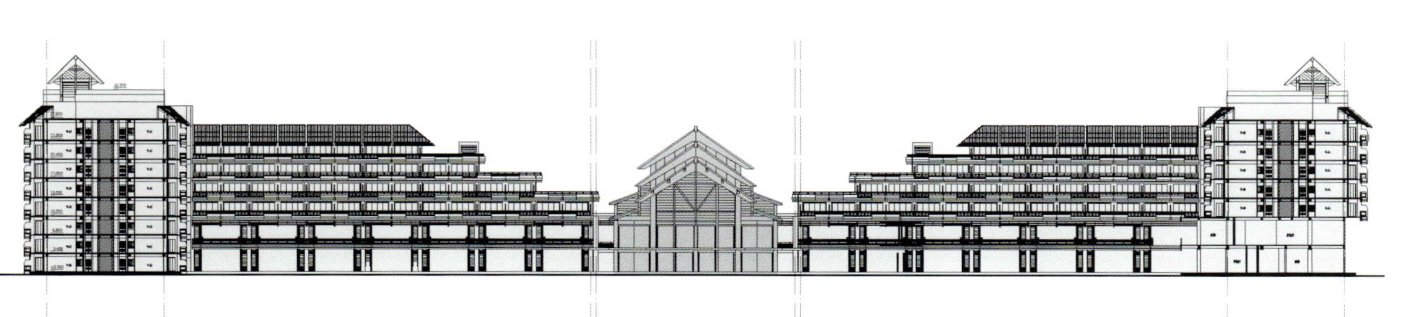

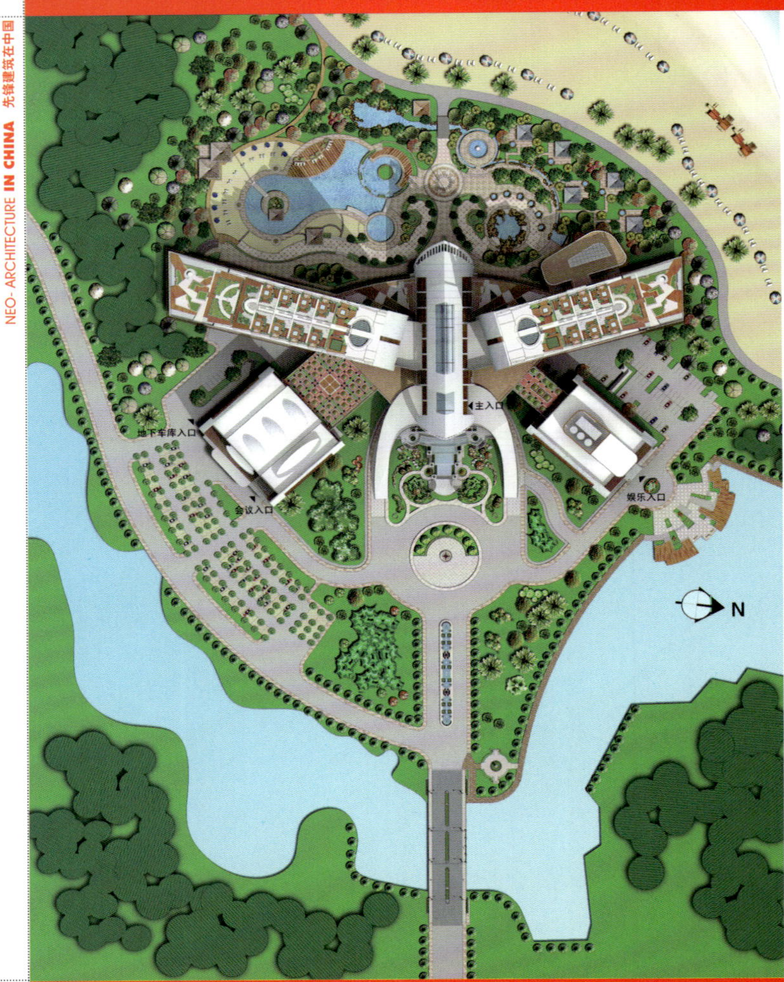

Jintai Sea-sight Hotel, Liaoning
辽宁金泰海景大酒店

设计单位：北京市建筑设计研究院
主设计师：金卫钧、孙勃
设计团队：姚建刚、于冬亮
建筑面积：63 607 m^2
建筑层数：地上9层，地下2层
建筑高度：47.5 m
设计时间：2008年

Design firm: Beijing Institute of Architectural Design and Research
Lead designer: Jin Weijun, Zhang Bo
Design team: Yao Jiangang, Yu Dongliang
Building area: 63 607 m^2
Design date: 2008

辽宁金泰海景大酒店位于辽宁营口经济技术开发区，西侧面向渤海，东侧、南侧为18洞高尔夫球场，景观环境得天独厚。

酒店大堂布置在建筑二层，充分利用室外良好的自然景观资源，提升室内空间的环境品质和内涵，以无框的点支玻璃幕墙体系来实现迎海面的“透明性”设计，使酒店大堂中的视野更加开阔，客人的视线可以不受任何阻挡地越过海边保护林带，欣赏到“西海落日”的壮观景色，同时，建筑距离海岸线比较远的不利因素也得以化解。室内圆形的大堂吧宛如漂浮在空中，与园林、沙滩、海面连为一体。客房部分平行海岸线布置，层层退台的形式充分利用了平台的景观优势。

港口城市的区域特点成为酒店形态的创作灵感源泉，构思是几条抽象出来的曲线，饱满而富有张力。建筑形态语言以更为雕塑感的形式出现，在大海、沙滩、高尔夫球场这些大尺度自然景观元素的包围中，建筑有与之和谐的体量和简洁大气的建筑语言，同时体现了度假酒店轻松悠闲的特点。

It is a Five-Star holiday hotel with 300 rooms and facilities, which locates at the Spanish Mackerel shore of Yingkou Economic Development Zone. The design utilizes the outstanding environment, seeking to make it a landmark of this area. The shape of the architecture is creative and unique, which is outlined by a couple of elegant, smooth and clear lines. These lines are graceful and of tension, romantic and of reason. The style of the architecture is very fresh, with a flavor of romance and matches the off-shore environment perfectly.

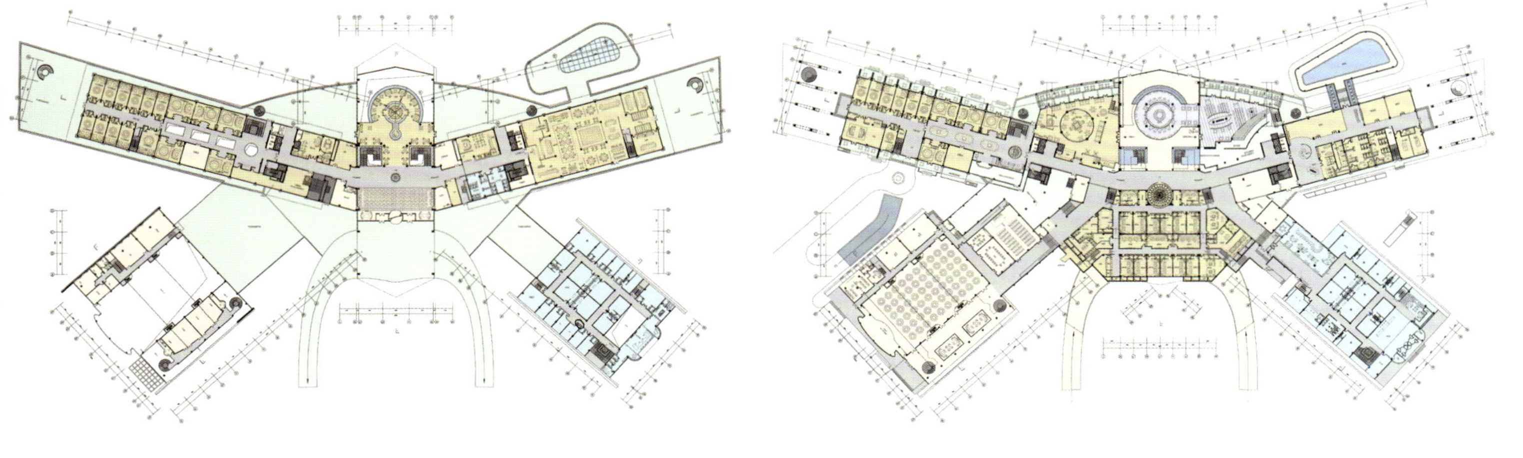

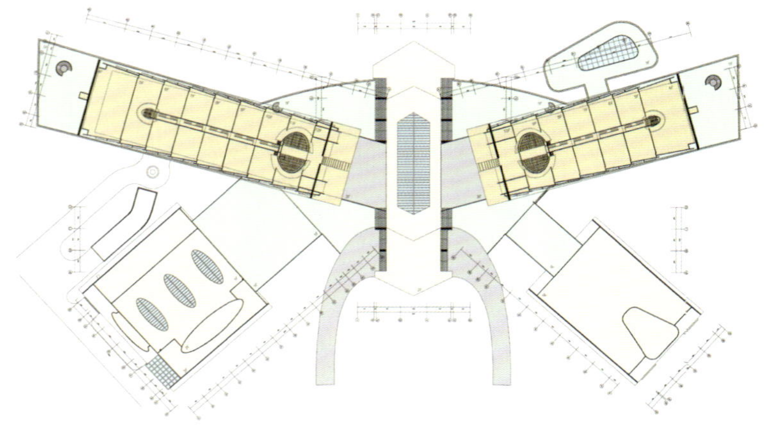

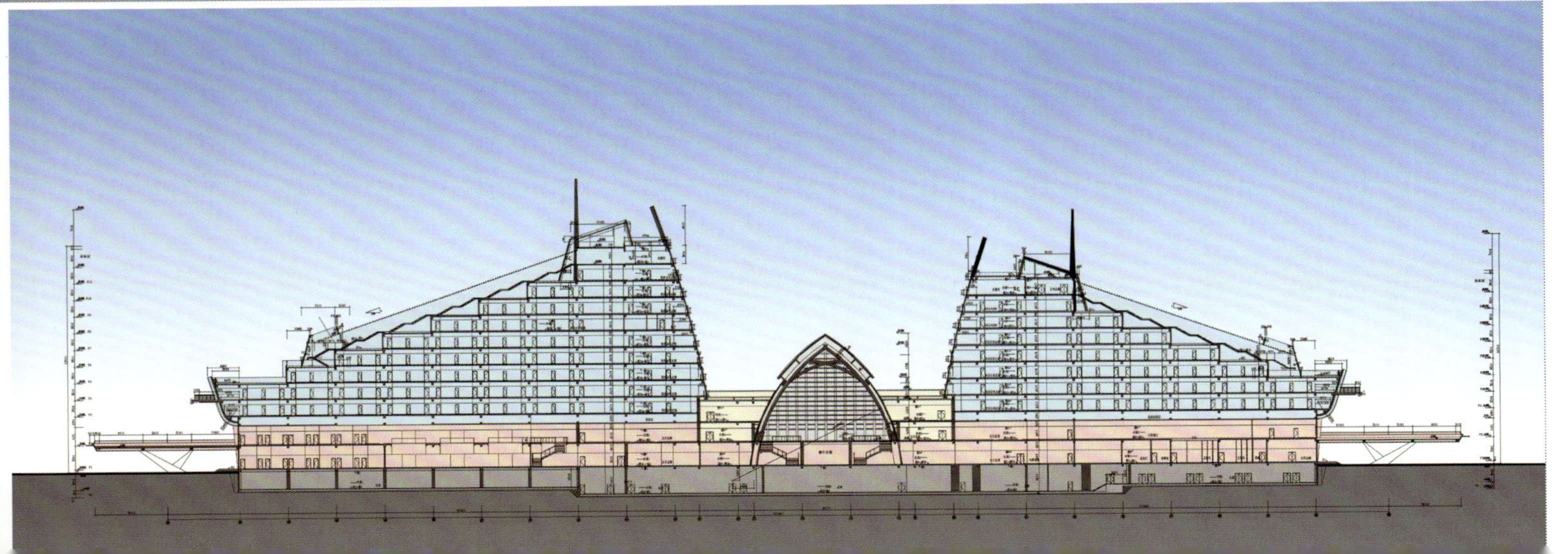

Shijingshan Tower, Beijing

北京石景山大厦

设计单位：北京市建筑设计研究院
主设计师：张耕、金卫钧、郭少山
设计团队：黄盛昕、周新超、郭毅、吕鹏骥
建筑面积：110 000 m²
建筑高度：100 m
设计时间：2009年

Design firm: Beijing Institute of Architectural Design and Research
Lead designer: Zhang Geng, Jin Weijun, Guo Shaoshan
Design team: Huang Shengxin, Zhou Xinchao, Guo Yi, Lv Pengji
Building area: 110 000 m²
Design date: 2009

首层平面

标准层平面

地块位于北京西五环和西长安街交界处，东邻石景山游乐园，西南为京燕饭店。因用地西侧和北侧住宅日照线的影响，使得建筑的体型只能控制在用地东侧从南向北逐渐高起的范围内。最后的造形是在满足日照、建筑充分采光及建筑功能的情况下通过富有逻辑的切割和划分而成。整体造型如不同形状、逐渐升高的水晶体排列而成，晶莹挺拔的建筑形象具有很强的地块标志性。建筑的中部开大的长方形过街楼以及南部向外悬挑，使城市绿地及内院园区景观连成一体。屋顶设计休息平台，提供健身、会议、商务等休闲空间。

The land lies near the cross of the West Fifth Circle and West Chang'an Avenue, while the Shijingshan Amusement Park to the east, and Jingyan Hotel to the southwest. Because of the limit of residential sunlight control line to the west and north, the body of the building is limited in the east and south of the land, and it has to rise from the south to the north. The final shape is cut and divided to meet the sunlight, ventilation and the function of the building. The overall shape, just like different shapes of gradually arising crystals being arrayed , became a prominent landmark. A large rectangular arcade is arranged in the center of the building and the southern part suspends in the air, so that the Greenland of the city immerges into the inner garden. Rest platform is set on the roof, providing leisure space for fitness, conference, business and so on.

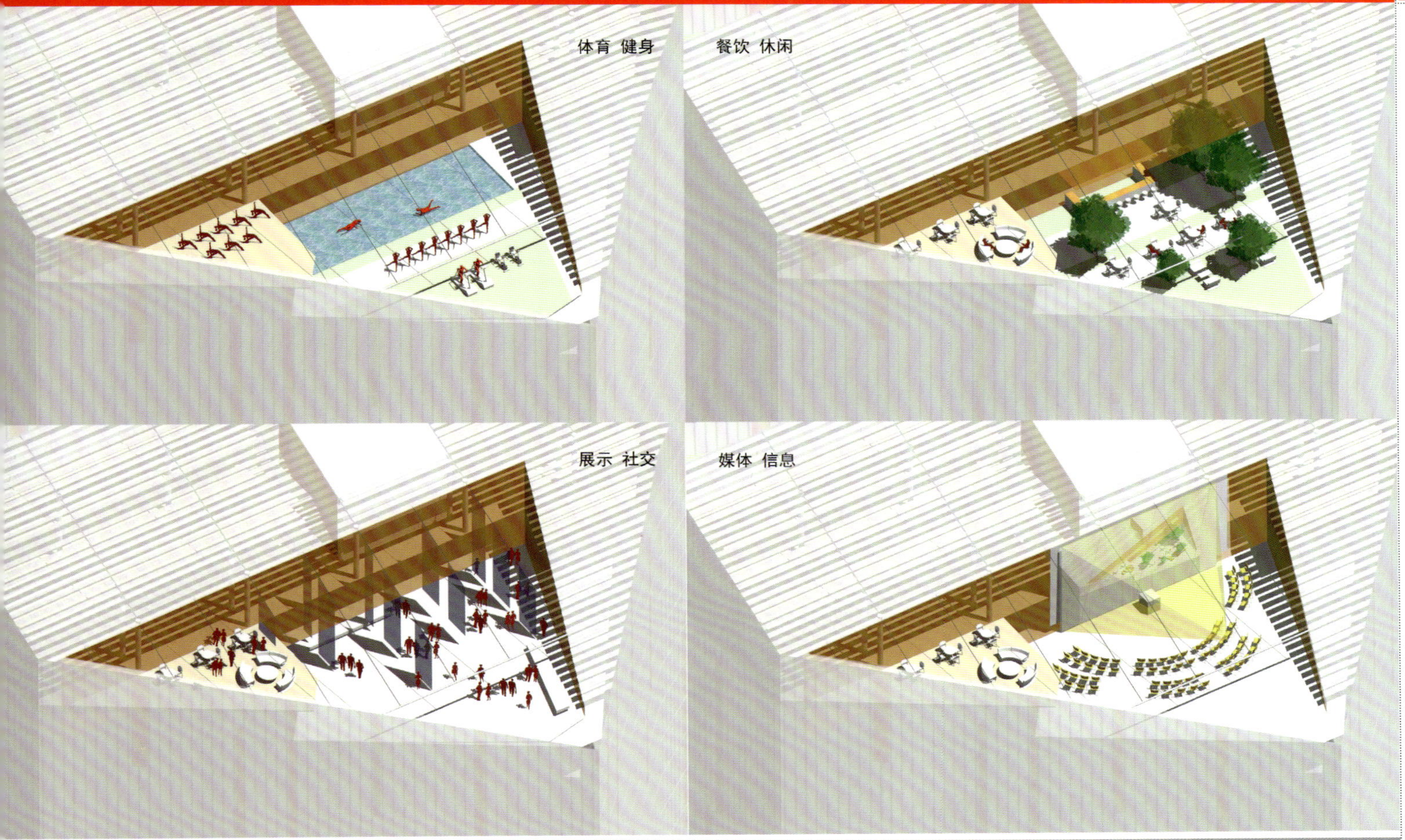

体育 健身

餐饮 休闲

展示 社交

媒体 信息

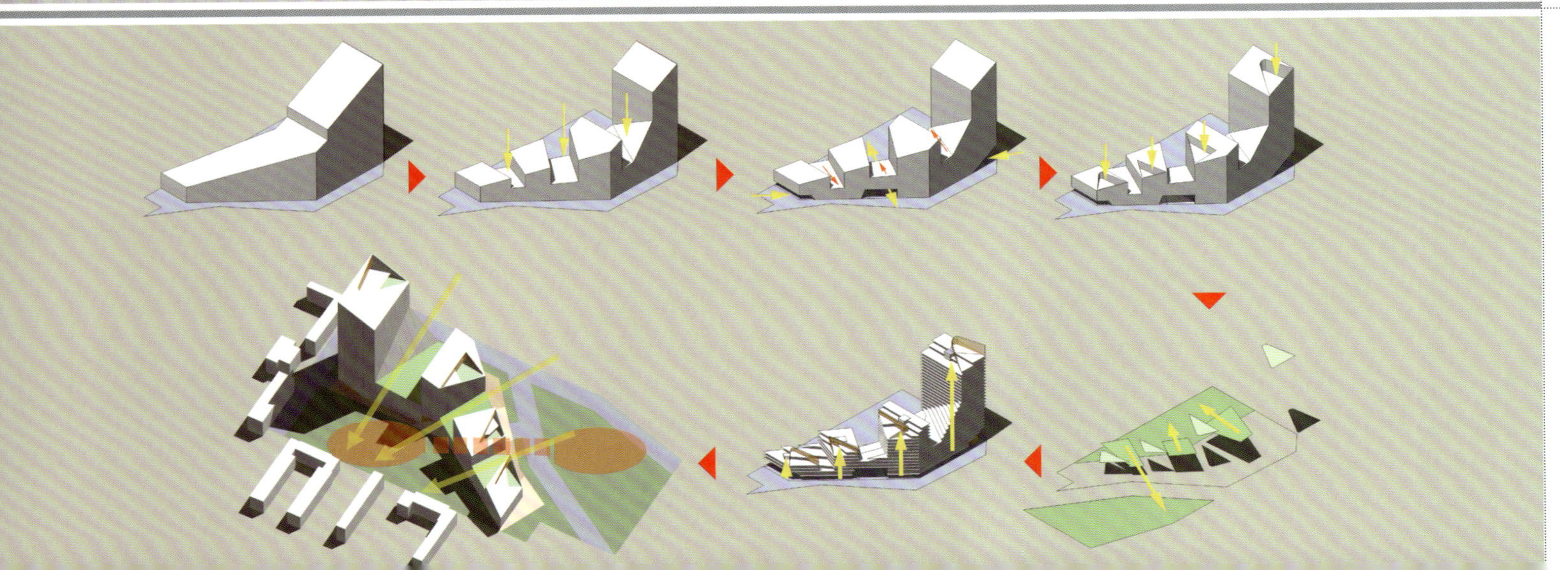

Art Academic Building of Beijing Institute of Fashion Technology

北京服装学院艺术教学楼

设计单位：北京市建筑设计研究院
主设计师：金卫钧
设计团队：吴剑利、李晓路、王征
建筑面积：31 600 m^2
建筑层数：地上9层，地下2层
建筑高度：45 m
设计时间：2009年

Design firm: Beijing Institute of Architectural Design and Research
Chief designer: Jin Weijun
Designers: Wu Jianli, Li Xiaolu, Wang Zheng
Building area: 31600 m^2
Building floors: 9 floors above ground, and 2 floors in the basement
Building height: 45 m
Design date: 2009

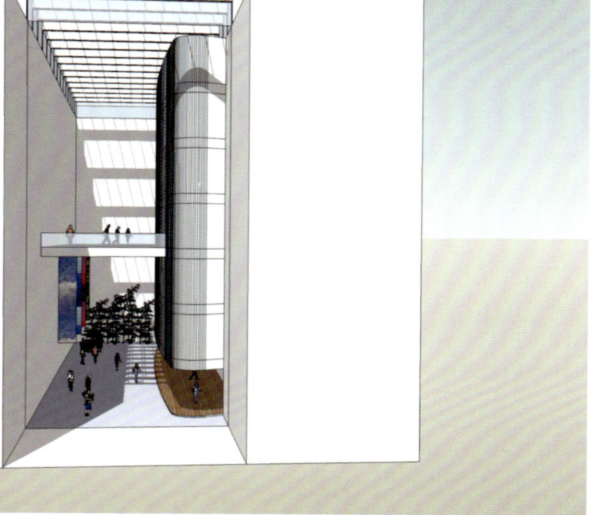

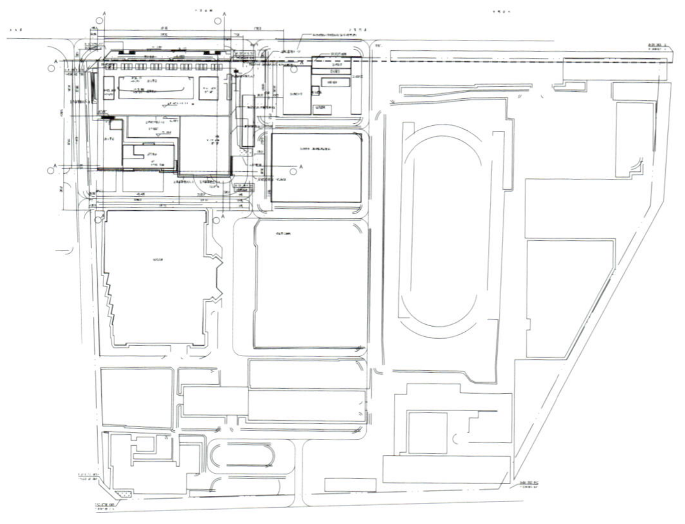

本项目位于北京市朝阳区樱花东街甲2号北京服装学院内，是一栋综合性服装、雕塑等艺术教学楼。设计的难点：与西南现有建筑结合问题，在用地限制的情况下，尽量大地使用系数以及低造价限制的情况下建筑的风格来符合艺术院校的特点。解决方法：建筑采用L形布局，和现有建筑的反L形成方形，中部形成内院；方正的体型有利于教室的排列；外立面以艺术视窗为构思，编织成整体，建筑语言纯净，格调朴实无华，具有内敛的艺术气质。外墙材料为清水混凝土预制板与涂料相结合，建筑色彩为黑白灰色调，与北京服装学院艺术院校的特点相吻合。主要功能为展厅、报告厅、表演厅、艺术工作室、文化创意产学中心、画室等。

This project is a general art academic building for clothing and sculpture, and it is located at the campus of Beijing Institute of Fashion Technology, NO. A-2 East Yinghua Street, Chaoyang District of Beijing. The design difficulties lie in: how to combine the new building with the existing building on the southwest direction; how to maximize the coefficient of land utilization when the land in use is constrained; and how to create the building style by conforming to the characteristics of an art institute when the project cost is low. To these difficulties, we have the following solutions: apply L-shaped layout for the new building to form a square with the existing building which is in a reverse L-shape, and the middle space in the square can become an inner courtyard; the square shape of the building is easy to align classrooms; the building facade is designed as view windows with artistic elements. Such pure and simple architectural language can demonstrate a sense of artistic quality. The exterior wall is made of fair-faced concrete precast slab and coating. The building appears in black, white and grey colors, echoing the features of an art institute. Major functional areas of the building include: Exhibition Hall, Lecture Hall, Performance Hall, Art Studio, Cultural Creation Center, Painting Workshops, etc.

Shenzhen Changfu Jinmao Tower

深圳长富金茂大厦

总用地面积：18812.7 m²
总建筑面积：206721.18 m²
容积率：8.60
建筑高度：303.8 m
主要功能：甲级办公，并含有部分配套商业设施
设计竞标：中标方案
客户：杨富实业（深圳）有限公司
在建项目

Land area: 18 812.7 m²
Building area: 206 721.2 m²
FAR: 8.6
Height: 303.8 m
Function: office (class A), commercial facilities
International bidding: winning project
Client: Yan Full Industrial (Shenzhen) Co.,Ltd.
Under construction

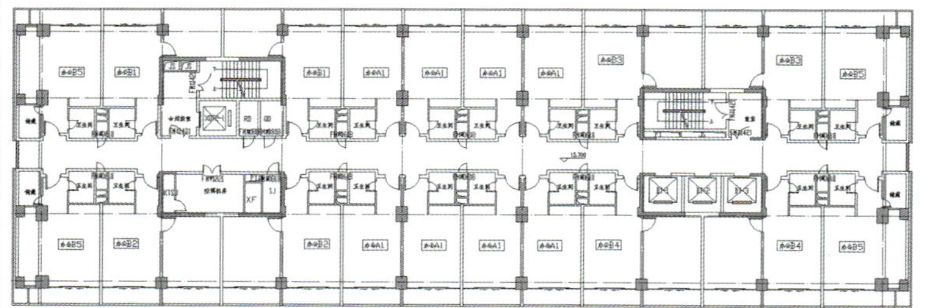

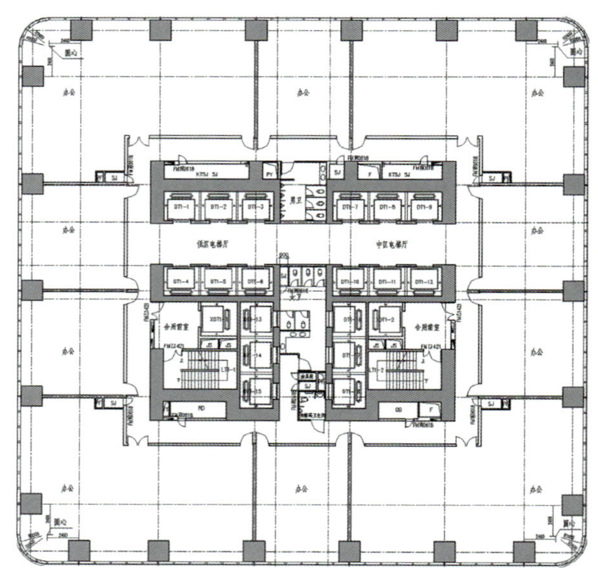

AUBE
www.aube-archi.com
法国欧博建筑与城市规划设计有限公司
深圳市博艺建筑工程设计有限公司
深圳市欧博设计有限公司

AUBE（欧博设计）团队由极具设计创意和专业技能、熟知中国市场规律的法国欧博建筑与城市规划设计公司、深圳市博艺建筑工程设计有限公司、深圳市欧博设计有限公司及中外设计师共同组成。

AUBE（欧博设计）的设计经验引导了规划、建筑、景观、工程领域。近年来，AUBE（欧博设计）中国区的业务范围立足于深圳，扩展到国内大中城市，并多次在国际竞标中胜出。代表作品有贵阳国际会议展览中心规划建筑景观工程设计、深圳长富金茂超高层建筑设计、深圳南油购物公园、深圳康佳研发大厦、深圳半岛城邦一期住宅区规划建筑景观工程设计、深圳北站交通枢纽中心景观工程设计、合肥澜溪镇建筑设计、华润置地成都翡翠城、深圳市华侨城生态广场、深圳华侨城中央教科所附属学校等。

AUBE（欧博设计）品牌的树立和发展，建立在设计师资源和设计平台协作共享的基础上，同时也建立在初始法国合伙人之间和陆续加入的不同国籍合伙人之间所表达的个人独立设计风格上。AUBE（欧博设计）的发展基于参与重要的国际竞赛和接受经过特别选择的委托设计。

AUBE（欧博设计）的多国设计师自1993年开始介入中国的重大建设工程项目。截止到目前，AUBE（欧博设计）参与和完成的中国重大设计项目近300余个。设计师的工作经历普遍具有国际化特征。AUBE（欧博设计）始终坚持"国际化经验、地域化实践"的设计理念，与每一位关注它的同仁共创、共享、共同发展。

AUBE CONCEPTION is constituted by AUBE Conception d'Architecture SARL, Shenzhen AUBE Design Co.,Ltd. and Shenzhen Boyi Constructional Engineering Design Co.,Ltd. It holds the qualifications of Type Class A in the field of architectural & engineering design in China and also in Europe. AUBE conception's designers have innovative ideas and outstanding professional skills and they are very familiar with China's market, although they come from different countries.

Finding a foothold in Shenzhen, radiating the whole country, Aube Conception plays a leading role in the planning, architecture, landscape and engineering design. Its representative works include Planning, Architecture & Landscape Design of Guiyang International Conference and Exhibition Center, Architecture Design of Shenzhen Changfu Jinmao Tower, Architecture Design of Shenzhen Nanyou Shopping Mall, Architecture Design of Shenzhen Konka R&D Tower, Planning, Architecture & Landscape Design of Shenzhen Peninsula Residential Community (Phase I), Landscape Design of Shenzhen North Station Traffic Terminal, Architecture Design of Hefei Nancy Town Residential Community, Architecture Design of CRL Emerald City of Chengdu, Landscape Design of Shenzhen OCT Ecological Plaza, Architecture Design of Shenzhen OCT Central Education and Research Institute Attached School, etc.

The establishment and development of the brand of AUBE CONCEPTION are based on a conjunct management of the designers' resource and design platform, and also based on the original and independent design styles of its founding partners and the other designers of different nationalities. The significant growth of AUBE CONCEPTION is derived from the practice and experience in the important international competition and the carefully selected projects.

Since 1993, the foreign designers of AUBE CONCEPTION started to participate in the important engineering construction projects of China, up to now, they have finished more than 300 important Chinese projects.

Consistently followed its design philosophy "international experience, regional practice" in its operation, human structure and design practice, AUBE CONCEPTION hopes to promote the mutual development with the clients and all the associates.

长富金茂大厦项目位于深圳市福田保税区核心地段，该地块位于城市主轴线的南尽端，交通便捷，位置显要，地块毗邻香港。中港双方对此区域未来合作开发的意向，为项目的定位和开发模式创造了新的机遇。

长富金茂大厦力创一座高效、全新、人性化的超高层建筑，充分尊重保税区的城市设计，同时创造具有相对独立领域感、结合经济性与自然生态于一体的多功能综合体。它将是公众喜闻乐见同时又提升城市文化的场所，与此同时又是新世纪保税区以及深圳市的标志。

建筑造型秉持修长挺拔的设计理念，两端小中间大，在方形平面的基础上，上下收分，在塔楼的顶部高度三分之一处为塔楼平面最大高度，依据黄金分割比塑造出更为高耸流动的上升动态，以玻璃为主的建筑群流光溢彩，恒远流传。303.8米的建筑高度使塔楼塑造了新的城市天际线，并成为城市景观的焦点。

Changfu Jinmao Tower is located in the core area of Futian Bonded Zone of Shenzhen. This area lies in the south of the city's main axis with convenient traffic and prominent position adjacent to Hong Kong. The future co-operational intention of this zone between China and Hong Kong has created new opportunities for the projects' orientation and development mode.

Changfu Jinmao Tower is meant to create an original humanized super-tall building with high-efficiency and a multifunctional complex building integrated economy and ecology with relatively independent sense. It fully respects the urban planning of Futian Bonded Area. It will be a landmark of the Bonded Area and Shenzhen, which will be welcomed by the public and promote the urban culture of Shenzhen.

The building is tall and slender, thin in both ends, plump in the middle; on the basis of square floor, frap the top and bottom. In the one third place of the top is the highest floor of the tower. According to the golden ratio, it is built to create an upward flowing dynamic. The architectural complex mainly made of glass is shining colorfully. The height of 303.8 meters has made the tower create a new skyline of the city and become the focus of urban landscape.

Urban, Architecture & landscape design of Nanyou Shopping Park, Shenzhen

深圳南油购物公园城市、建筑及景观设计

用地面积：12.69公顷
公园用地面积：8.76公顷
建筑用地面积：3.93公顷
平均容积率：8.48
总建筑面积：491 027 m²
建筑高度：150 m
主要功能：商业、办公、公寓、旅游社区
国际竞标：第一名
客户：深圳市金龙房地产开发有限公司

Land area: 12.69 ha
Park area: 8.76 ha
Building land area: 3.96 ha
Average FAR: 8.48
Total building area: 491 027 m²
Height: 150 m
Function: complex community of commerce, office, apartment and tourism
International bidding: 1st prize
Client: Shenzhen Jinlong Real Estate Development Co., Ltd.

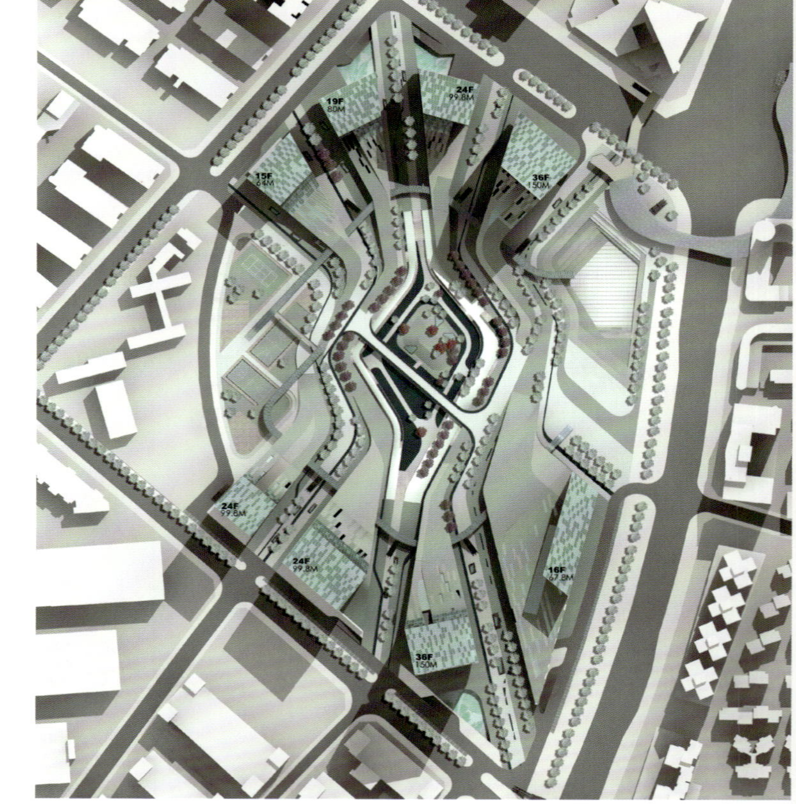

项目设计理念：

项目用地位于南山商业文化中心区域紧邻的城市核心地段，交错的道路、喧嚣的楼宇、繁忙的车流与宁静的大自然形成鲜明的对比。首先出于对自然与城市之间张力关系的判断，二者之间始终存在着此消彼长、相互侵蚀的态势。所以在设计上选择了自然由核心“外爆”的方式。一次对绿色自然能量的记录，由爆发到凝固，向外涌出的地面积聚了巨大的能量。在边界地带因受到建筑群的阻滞，进而向上延展，凝固为升起的绿色景观，形成了内低外高的碗状格局。

垂直体量后面拖曳的尾翼，在最大限度地向城市外延扩展的同时，吸纳了城市肌理向用地核心的渗透。之后，人得以进入，在这一片绿色自然能量集聚的地带，形成了以商业、办公、居住、旅游等为主的绿色生态综合社区。故从概念的根源来讲，自然与环境是优先于人进入这片土地的，自然是这里的主人。这里要做的不是人与自然之间一方对一方的驯服，而是二者之间的相互尊重。

项目规划结构：

1条横向文化轴：即东西向连接市民集会广场、中央生态公园和西侧学校、露天剧场、运动公园的文化轴线。

5条纵向商业轴：即位于8个分地块之间的南北向商业步行街。

2个同心商业环：即位于地表和地上6米标高的商业步行环线。

1个核心生态园：即中央水主题生态公园和公众水下美术馆。

1心、2环、6轴相互渗透交叉，向地下、地表和空中延绵开去，形成立体化的综合环境网络系统。

The project is located at the heart land of Nanshan District. Crisscross roads, multitudinous buildings, busy traffic and natural tranquility form a striking contrast. Between nature and city, it's like the ebb and flow of every relationship, so we selected the idea of "natural energy's explosion" as the design concept. Green nature explodes from the core and releases tremendous amounts of energy, which is obstructed by the surrounding buildings, rises into sky and solidifies out into risen landscape.

Through its tail, the building extends into the city and also integrates with the urban texture. Then, people could enter into the place where the green energy accumulates to form the natural and ecology community, which includes commerce, office, residence, tourism, etc. So, the origin of concept shows that the environment and nature have the priority over the people in this land, as nature is absolutely the host here. What we want to realize between the nature and human is not the inter-constraint, but mutual respect.

Planning structure:

1 horizontal cultural axis: from east to west, connecting Citizen Assembly Plaza, Central Ecological Park and school, open-air theatre and sports park.

5 longitudinal commercial axes: from south to north, the pedestrian commercial street in eight plots.

2 concentric commercial rings: the pedestrian commercial ring on ground and above 6 meters.

1 core ecological park: central ecology park of water theme and public art gallery blow water.

1 core, 2 rings and 6 axis spread to the underground, the ground and the air to form solid system with integrated environmental network.

景观生态水系分析
WATER SYSTEM ANALYSIS

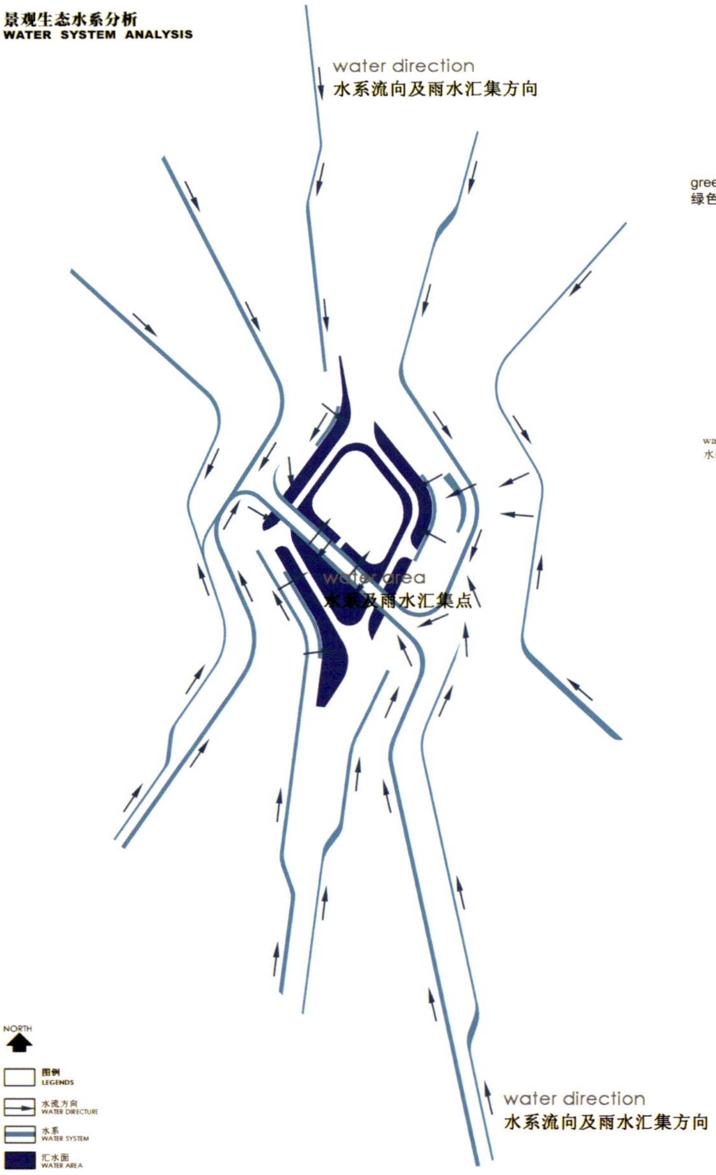

water direction
水系流向及雨水汇集方向

water area
水系及雨水汇集点

water direction
水系流向及雨水汇集方向

NORTH

图例 LEGENDS

水流方向 WATER DIRECTION

水系 WATER SYSTEM

汇水面 WATER AREA

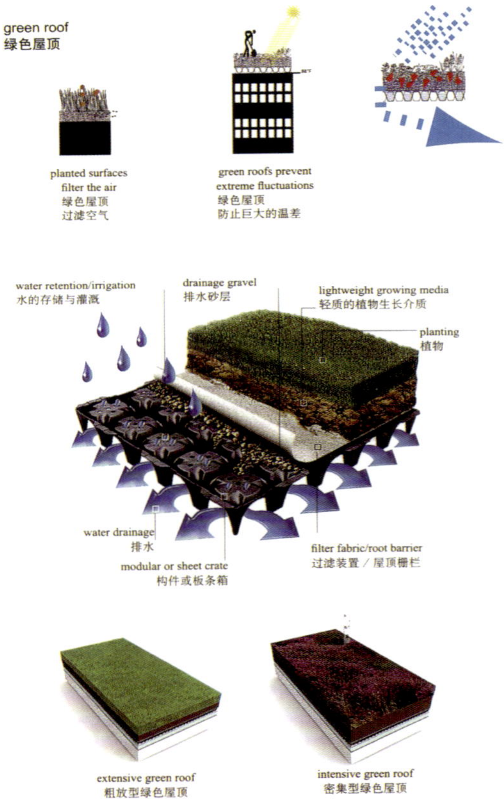

green roof
绿色屋顶

planted surfaces filter the air
绿色屋顶
过滤空气

green roofs prevent extreme fluctuations
绿色屋顶
防止巨大的温差

water retention/irrigation
水的存储与灌溉

drainage gravel
排水砂层

lightweight growing media
轻质的植物生长介质

planting
植物

water drainage
排水

modular or sheet crate
构件或板条箱

filter fabric/root barrier
过滤装置／屋顶栅栏

extensive green roof
粗放型绿色屋顶

intensive green roof
密集型绿色屋顶

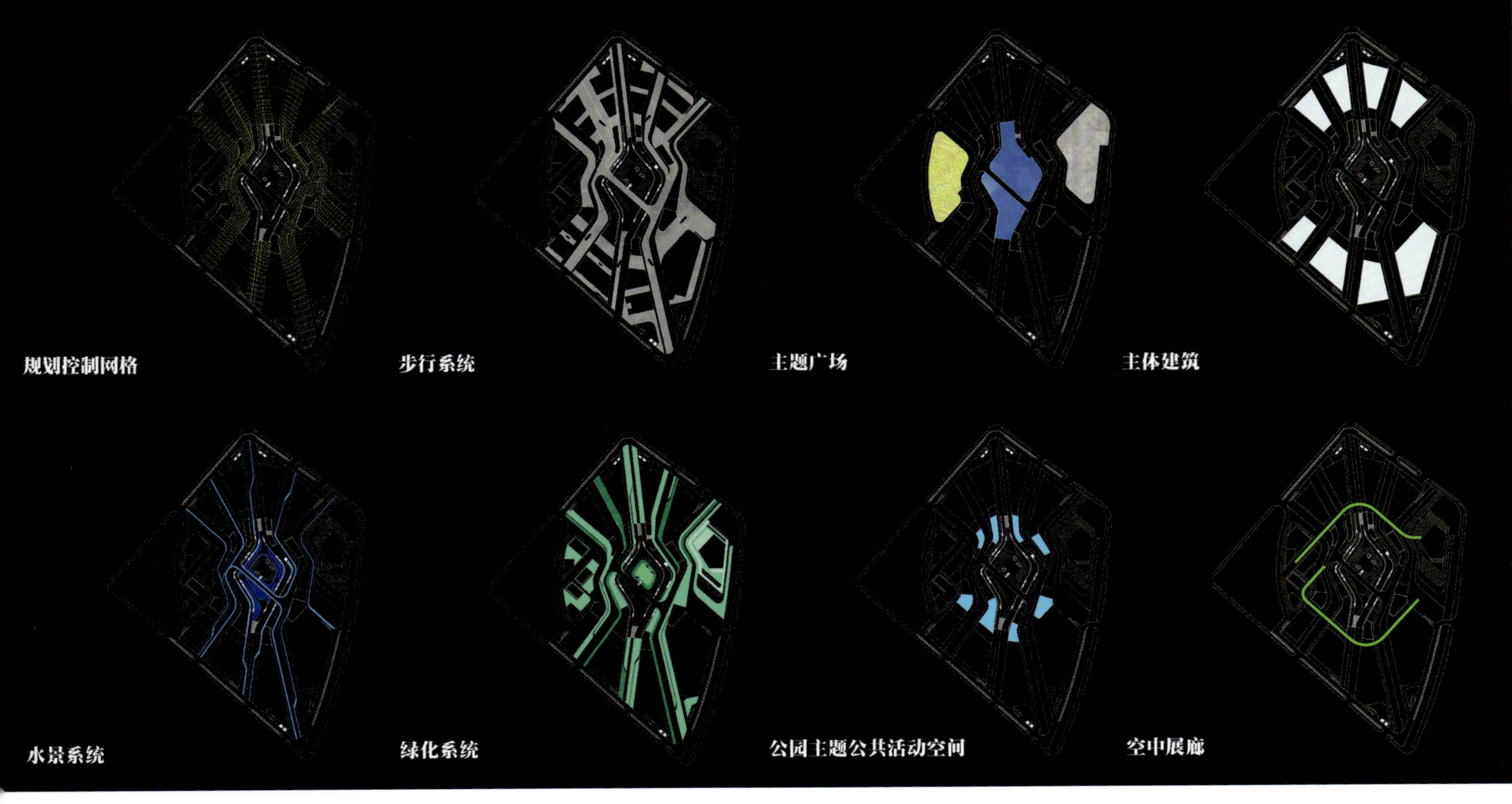
规划控制网格
步行系统
主题广场
主体建筑
水景系统
绿化系统
公园主题公共活动空间
空中展廊

Architectural Design of Konka Research Center in Shenzhen

深圳康佳研发大厦建筑设计

用地面积：0.96公顷
建筑面积：80 000 m²
容积率：8.3
建筑高度：100 m
主要功能：研发及办公
设计竞标：中标方案
客户：康佳集团股份有限公司
在建项目

Land area: 0.96 ha
Building area: 80 000 m²
FAR: 8.3
Height: 100 m
Function: R&D center & office
International bidding: winning project
Client: Konka Group Co., Ltd.
Under construction

总平面图

本项目所处的高新区南区为南海大道以东、深南大道以南的城市建设用地，地域条件优越，交通便捷，辐射范围广。本项目地处深圳市高新区南区东片，是园区的重要组成部分，通过现有道路网以及在建的地下交通系统，可方便到达深圳各口岸、港口、机场、火车站等交通枢纽。项目地块限制条件较多，地块平面呈现不规则的梯形，占地面积9 633.41 m²。高容积率、低限高、不规则的小型用地以及片区现有物业档次的参差不齐为项目的高端定位提出了难题。

我们将创造一座高效的、全新的、人性化的现代化高层建筑，充分尊重高新区的城市设计，同时创造具有独立领域感的城市空间，结合经济性与自然生态于一体的多功能综合体。它将是公众喜闻乐见同时又提升城市文化的场所，与此同时又是新世纪高新区以及深圳市的风景和标志。

别有天地：在处理与城市的关系上，我们一方面尊重城市的整体规划，另一方面积极创造独特的空间识别性和相对独立的内部公共空间，使人们一进入地段就会产生强烈的领域感。量体裁衣：设计结合城市空间规划结构和周边建筑环境和自然环境特色，采用切割的手法，在整体性的基础上，剪裁出符合东南西北各个朝向和功能需求的不同表情。大量的空中花园和共享空间穿插在建筑体量中各个切割后的开口处，为在这里工作的人们创造舒适的、易于交往的、贴近自然生态的空间，这本身也是康佳企业文化的一部分。一气呵成：遵循建筑景观的一体化设计原则，一张巨大的表皮伴随着挺拔清晰的线性肌理，从地面上升、变形、拉扯、回转，包裹了所有功能空间的同时，也生成大小不一的共享空间，最后又回到地面，形成景观系统，浑然一体，一气呵成。建筑从大地孕育而生，最后又回到大地，建筑和景观的界限被打破，连续动态的空间创造了活动和事件的舞台。城市名片：深南路一侧的立面被垂直分布的空中花园分割成若即若离的两部分，形成了一个字母“K”的意象，这是对康佳集团LOGO的一次建筑化转译，形成了一张巨大的城市名片，体现了康佳集团的品牌形象以及广告效应的设计理念。本设计是我们为康佳集团总部大楼项目在“此时此地”的一次量身打造，是与时代和地域的一次深刻对话。我们希望通过它继承昨天的传统，体现今天的形象，也适应明天的发展。

Our site is in the south of the high-technology zone which is located in the east of Nanhai Boulevard, and in the south of Shennan Boulevard. This site has extremely advantageous geographical conditions. The traffic is very convenient. The location of our site is very important in the high technology zone. Through the existing road network and the underground transport system, we can go easily to the ports, airports, railway stations and the other transport hubs of Shenzhen. The surface of the site shows irregular trapezoidal form and has a lot of restrictions. The total surface area of the site is 9 633.4 m^2. High FAR, low height, irregular small plots and property management give us a lot of difficulties to define this project.

We want to build up a modern, effective, humanized tower for respecting the urban design of the high-technology zone. We want to create an urban space with independent perception and multifunctions (economical elements and natural ecological elements). We want to create a public cultural space which could promote the city cultural level. We also want to create a landmark which could represent the high-technology zone and the Shenzhen city.

A PLACE OF UNIQUE SCENERY: on the one hand, we want to respect the urban planning. On the other hand, we want to create a unique and a relative independent interior public space which can give us a very strong territorial feeling. ACT ACCORDING TO ACTUAL CIRCUMSTANCES: the design is based on the planning structure, the buildings and the natural environment. Using 'cutting' technique to show the different appearances of different functions(east, west, south, and north). We create some comfortable, friendly and natural spaces for the employees of Konka by the air gardens and the common spaces which interlude in the tower. DONE WITHOUT ANY LETUP: we follow the integrative principle for the buildings and the landscape. The site is covered by a big entire skin which has a very clear linear texture. This skin goes up from the ground, transforms, turns back with all the function spaces, and at the same time creates different sized common spaces and landscape system. The whole process is done without any letup. The building is born from the earth and mate with the earth. There is no limit between the building and the landscape. All the activities and events are connected together by a continuous dynamic space. CITY CARD: the vertical air gardens divide the facade which faces the Shennan Boulevard into two parts. The building looks like a letter 'K'. The letter 'K' is the translation of Konka logo which could express the spirit of Konka group like a card of city. This is our design for Konka group according to actual circumstances. This is a conversation between the time and area. This design respects the old tradition, represents our age, and also fits for the future development.

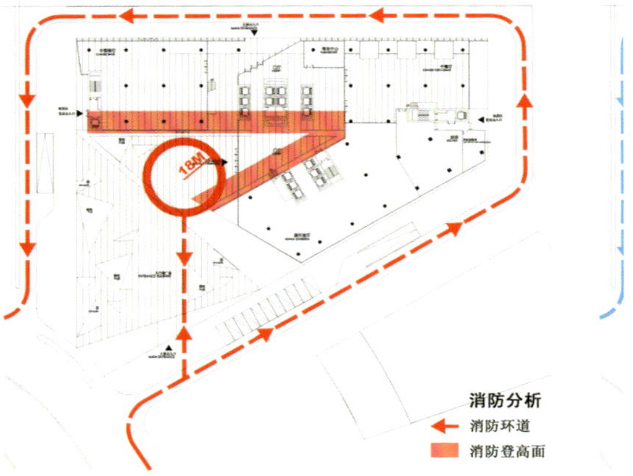

消防分析
消防环道
消防登高面

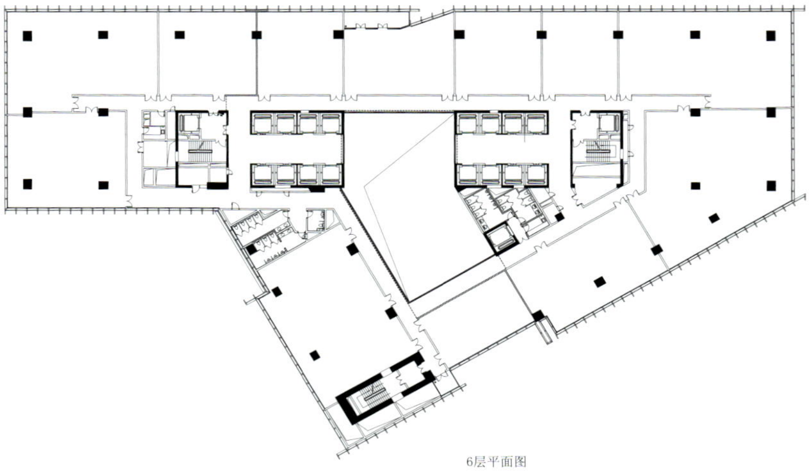

6层平面图

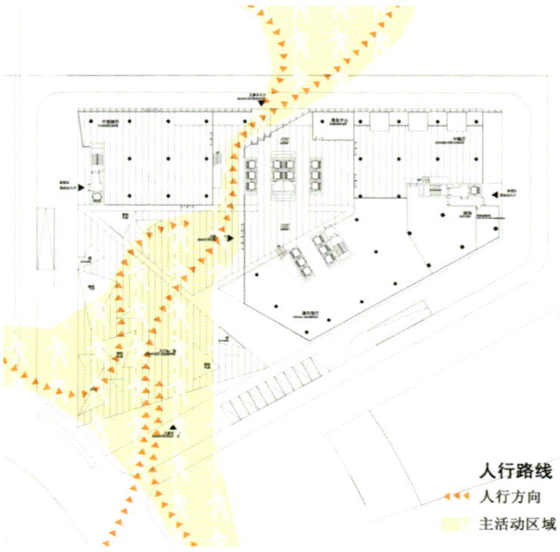

人行路线
人行方向
主活动区域

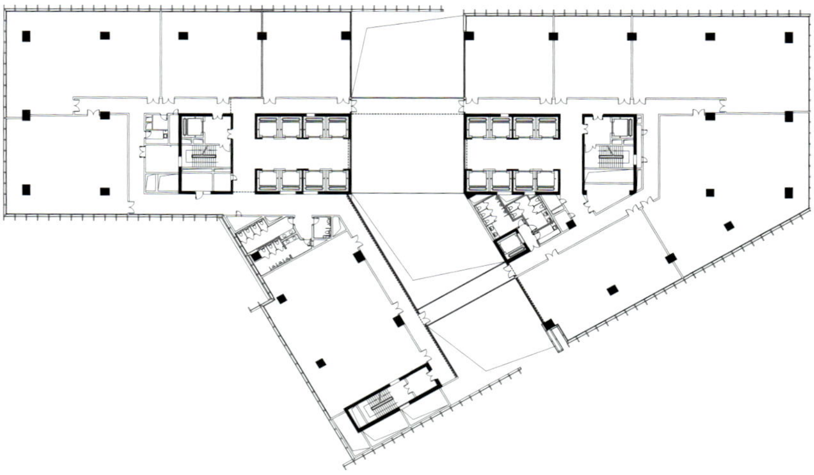

16层平面图

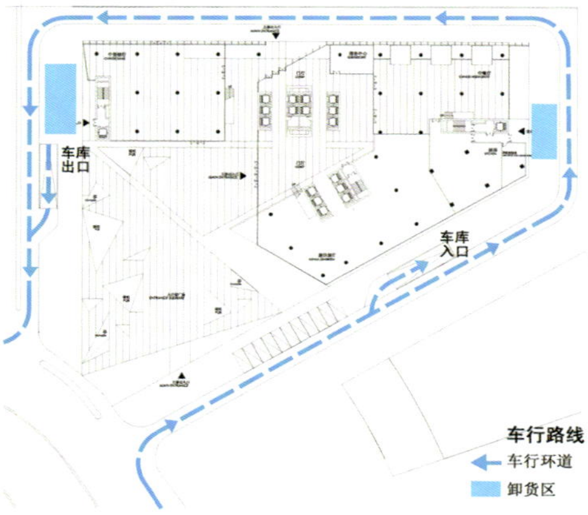

车行路线
车行环道
卸货区

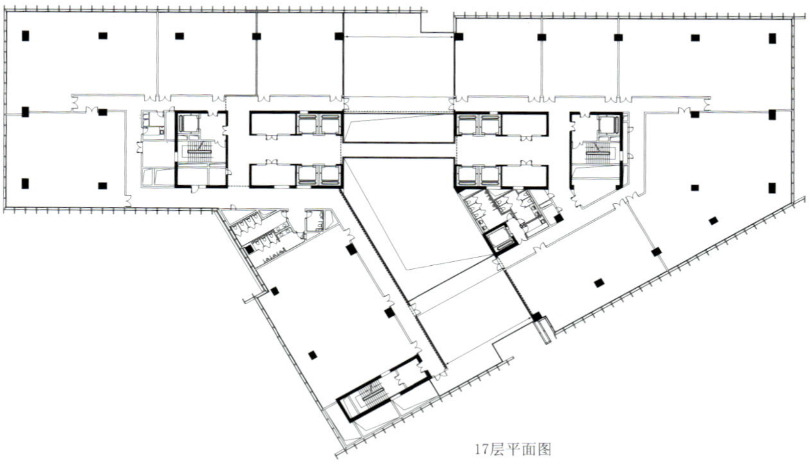

车库出口
车库入口

17层平面图

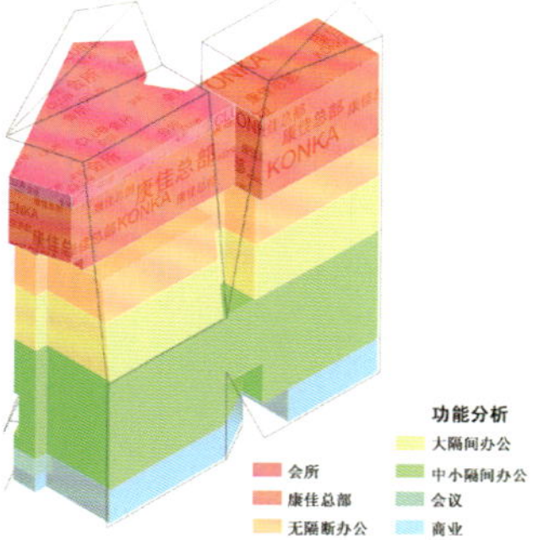
功能分析
会所
康佳总部
无隔断办公
大隔间办公
中小隔间办公
会议
商业

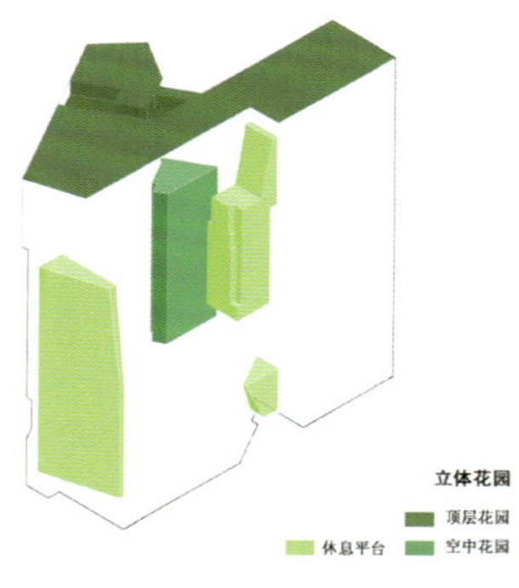
立体花园
休息平台
顶层花园
空中花园

共享大厅
一层大厅
总部大厅

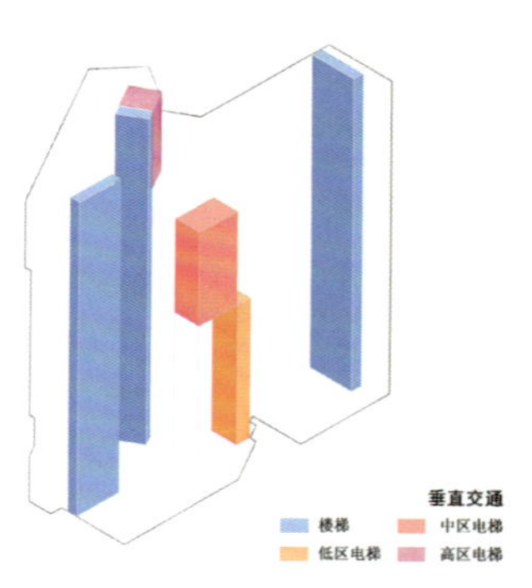
垂直交通
楼梯
低区电梯
中区电梯
高区电梯

Yiwu China Commodity City Huangyuan

义乌篁园中国小商品城

设计单位：杭州安道建筑规划设计咨询有限公司
主设计师：赵菊霞
建筑面积：75 566.65 m²

Design firm: A&I International
Lead designer: Zhao Juxia
Building area: 75 566.65 m²

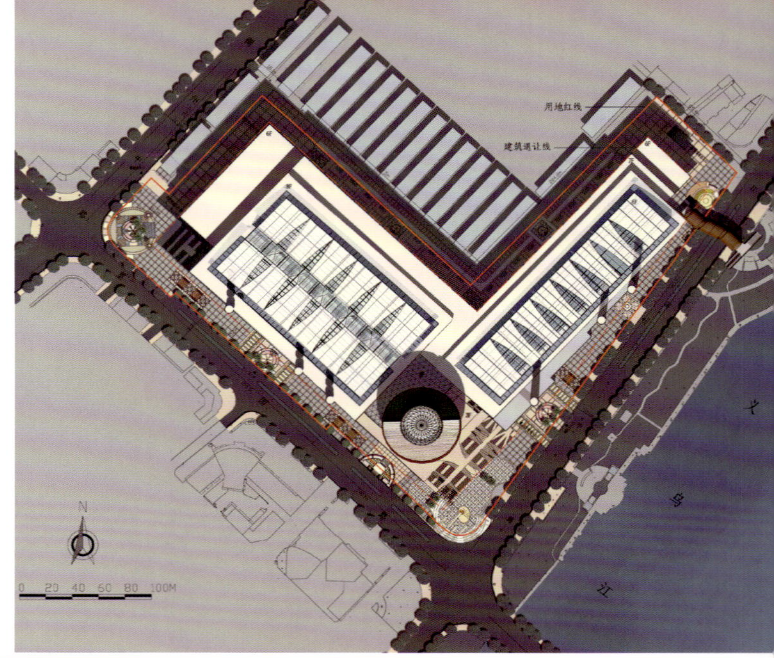

Zhao juxia
A&I International
Research & Development Center Majordomo
Project Leader
Graduated from Zhejiang University Of Technology.

赵菊霞
杭州安道建筑规划设计咨询有限公司
项目负责人
毕业于浙江工业大学

主创项目：
嘉兴·豪杰翡翠湾
海南天上人间
绍兴高级中学
南京江宁青年城
绍兴锦江半岛
万国首府广场
万国金色海岸
同曦大厦
义乌万商华府

Primary projects:
Jiaxing Haojie Green Bay Residence Community
Hainan Tian Shang Ren Jian Club
Shaoxing Senior High School
Nanjing Jiangning Youth City
Shaoxing Jin Jiang Peninsula Residence Community
Wanguo Capital Square
Wanguo Gold Coast
Tong Xi Building
Yiwu Wanshang Residence Community

本地块位于中国义乌核心商贸区块、市级商业中心，篁园路和江滨中路的交叉口。规划总用地约111亩，东临江滨中路，南靠篁园路，西临稠州路。地理环境优越，地貌平整。改建项目总用地面积：75 566.65 m²，地上总建筑面积约345 000 m²，市场主体建筑为地下2层，地上8层，约5 500～6 000个标准商位，配套以四星级商务酒店和市场交易服务用房等。场地区位良好，现有市场环境培育完善，认可度高，城市配套完善，与城市骨干道路联系较好。然而L形用地长度过长，单侧沿街界面对交通组织不利，不利于商业资源沿街面的充分开发，用地紧张导致绿地及开放空间较小，现状交通较为拥挤。由此结合城市总体规划与市场建筑形态的发展趋势，提出如下设计构想：在场地东南转角设计功能为全天侯展贸中心、商务信息型酒店的圆环形建筑作为核心爆发点，市场及各项配套设施向两翼延展，在两翼端部架空停车及车行出入口，形成"一心两体"的建筑组织结构。建筑沿篁园路和江滨中路沿街为连续商业界面，北侧、西侧与现状民房形成精致步行空间。结合两端及转角城市广场设计特色开放空间。在建筑处理上追求成为标志性特色建筑，设计以醒目、新颖、富有冲击力的形象展示在公众面前。建筑以高台、华冠、金鼎等特色语言为主要元素组织形体，形成乘风破浪航船形象，寓意改革开放30周年来义乌人屹立潮头，勇当市场经济弄潮儿的光辉历程。

It is located at the cross of Huangyuan road and Jiangbin road, which is in the central commercial area of Yiwu, China and also the commercial center on the city level. The total area of the item is about 7.4 ha, Jiangbinzhong road to the east, Huangyuan road to the south, Chouzhou road to the west, with excellent environment and flat landform. The project that is to be reformed has got a total area of 75 566.65 m^2, and the total building area is about 3 450 000 m^2. There are 8 floors on the ground and 2 floors below in the main building of the market, which contains about 5 500-6 000 standard shops, and a four-star business hotel and some trading service cells besides. The item has got a good location, where there are mature and well admitted market environment, comprehensive municipal facilities, and convenient transport system. However, the L-shaped land is too long, forming a one side interface along the street, which would be difficult to organize the transportation and also go against the full development of commercial resource along the street. The area is so narrow that the green area and open space is limited and the transport is jam-packed.

Therefore, combining the city's comprehensive planning and the developing trend of the commercial building form, we conceived our design like this: the south-east corner of the site is a cirque building as the eruptible core. The market and the affiliated facilities extend like wings to both sides of the corner. At the end of the wings are the aerial space for parking and the entrances of the traffic. These form the structure of "one core two bodies". The buildings along the Huangyuan road and Jiangbinzhong road make some continuous commercial interfaces, while the north and west part form some neat walking space with the existing houses around, and the both sides of the corner are designed as characteristic open space. The design of the architecture aspires after a figuration that is striking and novel to the public so that it could be the landmark of the district. High platform, coronet and ancient cooking vessel, as characteristic language, become the main organizing elements of the buildings, forming a sailing ship. This expresses the resplendent course that Yiwu people have gone through in the 30 years of reform and opening to the outside world.

WALT DISNEY
BOSS

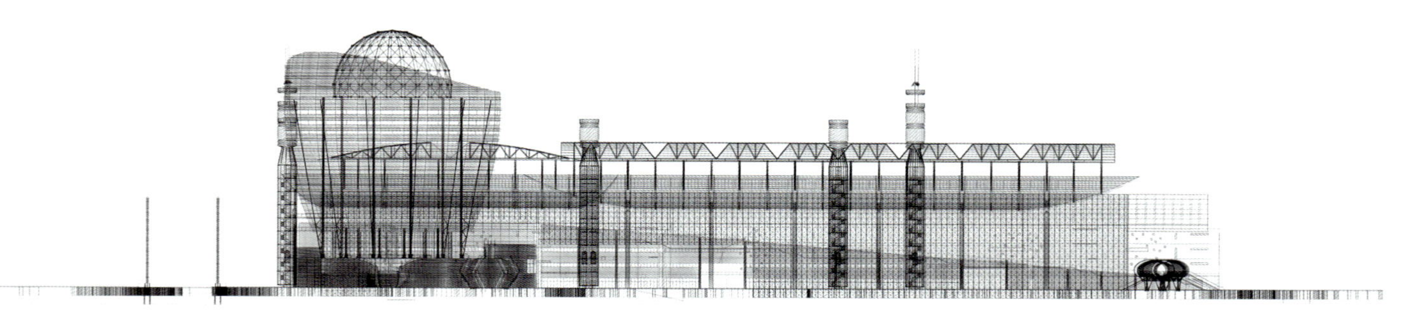

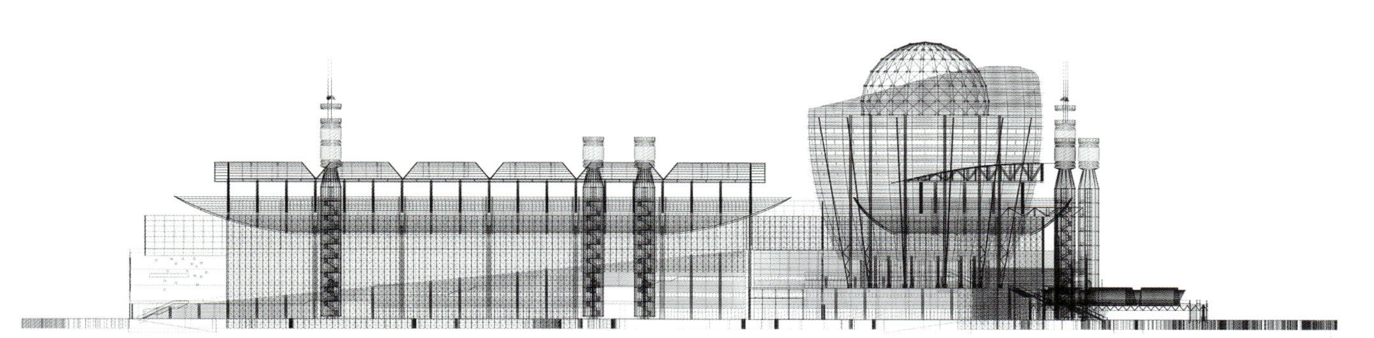

Grand Hill
观岭国际社区

设计单位：ECOLAND易兰（亚洲）
项目地址：成都

Design firm: ECOLAND
Location: Chengdu

易兰 ECOLAND

ECOLAND易兰（亚洲）

ECOLAND易兰（亚洲）作为国际知名规划设计事务所，在美国、香港、北京设有分支机构，是一支国际化的团队。具备先进设计理念同时拥有中国本土建筑工程甲级资质和景观设计资质，主要从事土地规划、城市设计、旅游规划、景观设计及项目设计管理等专业服务。项目类型包括生态系统与生态旅游规划、综合性土地开发规划、城市规划与设计、居住建筑及环境景观设计、公园及娱乐设施规划设计、酒店及旅游度假区规划设计等。

ECOLAND易兰（亚洲）由两百名来自北美、欧洲及中国本土的规划设计精英组成。凭借其国际化的视野、对国内市场运作规律的精准把握、卓越的设计团队、多国项目操作经验以及对中国文化理念的深刻理解，使规划设计充满了活力与创意。在综合运作能力上，能根据项目需求组织规划、建筑、景观、工程、经济、社会学、生态学专业的专家团队，可以胜任来自不同地区各个领域、各种类型的大型综合性项目。设计的项目得到众多客户好评并多次获得国际国内大奖。

ECOLAND易兰（亚洲）在为项目提供一流服务的同时注重生态保护和环境可持续性发展，把生态观念作为企业的职业追求与现实关怀。ECOLAND易兰（亚洲）倡导“大景观”的规划设计理念，强调总体的景观规划设计先行，强调城市规划设计过程中的整体性，消融了以往规划师、建筑师、园林师清晰分割的工作界限，促进城市空间的整体营建和良好环境氛围的形成。

ECOLAND is a leading planning and design firm dedicated to responsible land planning, landscape architecture, architecture and urban design. ECOLAND's central office is situated in Beijing, China, and is comprised of over 200 professionals. The expertise of our team encompasses a multitude of design types as well as experience within various geographic locations throughout the world.

The project extent of ECOLAND includes environmental planning and ecotourism, large-scale mixed-use development, urban planning and public open space, community planning and design, park and recreational facilities, hotel design and tourism planning.

As represented in our name, our incorporated mission is to shape the land with both ecological and economic consideration. We assure that each of our projects is carried out with imagination, technical mastery, intelligence and a strong environmental conscience.

观岭国际社区位于东方威尼斯——金堂新城区，南临唐巴公路，北临水景资源丰富的中河，并有十里大道连接金唐城区，享有金堂城区成熟配套。

ECOLAND易兰（亚洲）设计团队极为严格地遵循原生地貌结构，将一切设计融入自然，只为更大可能地拥有天然纯粹的景观与视野。4200亩的原生山水，1200亩天然浅丘果岭，10座高尔夫球道，无数高低错落的绿色山丘，十余个翡翠般温润的湖泊打造了观岭国际社区山水原生，丘陵起伏，河湖浸润，四季成荫的特点。

Next to the Tangba Road in the south and the rich Zhonghe River in the north, Grand Hill is located in New Jintang Town, which is called the Oriental Venice. With the Ten Li Road to the New Jintang Town, Grand Hill is equipped with all kinds of facilities.

ECOLAND team follow the original geomorphological structure strictly, and make all the design coupled with nature to reveal a pure natural landscape and vision. 4200 acres of native landscape, 1,200 acres of natural shallow, 10 Golf Road, numerous scattered high and low green hills, and a dozen jade lake has created a fantasy Grand Hill of native landscape, rolling hills, rich rivers and lakes and four shady seasons.

Raffles City Beijing

北京来福士广场

建筑、景观、室内设计：思邦建筑设计咨询有限公司
设计总监：Stephen Pimbley、 Jan Felix Clostermann
设计团队：Tan Ming Yin、 Sofia David、 Christian T ubert、 Gyn Kong、 Alvin Foo、 Nico Bornman、 Damian Chan、 John Curran、 Torrance Goh、 He Wei、 Ho Hsiu Yen、 Lee Si Hyung、 Victor Lee、 Peter Sim、 Sven Steiner、 Sun Penghui、 Jacqueline Yeo、 张桦、张宇、吴建云、李人杰
建筑面积：150 000 m^2
竣工年份：2009年6月
本地设计：三磊
开发商：凯德中国控股

Design firm: Sparch
Chief designer: Stephen Pimbley, Jan Felix Clostermann
Design team: Tan Ming Yin, Sofia David, Christian T ubert, Gyn Kong, Alvin Foo, Nico Bornman, Damian Chan, John Curran, Torrance Goh, He Wei, Ho Hsiu Yen, Lee Si Hyung, Victor Lee, Peter Sim, Sven Steiner, Sun Penghui, Jacqueline Yeo, Zhang Hua, Zhang Yu, Wu Jaingyun, Li Renjie
Building area: 150 000 m^2
Local design: Beijing Sunlay Architectural

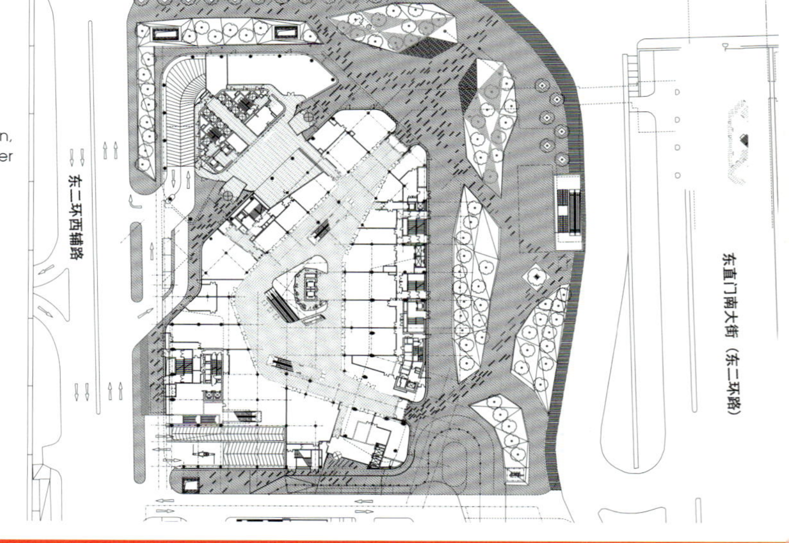

SPARCH

思邦建筑设计咨询（上海）有限公司

思邦是一家荣获多项国际大奖、在城市规划、建筑设计、景观设计及室内设计方面拥有丰富经验的国际性建筑设计事务所，25年来一直活跃于全球建筑设计领域。

在过去的10年里，思邦由一个源于欧洲的事务所迅速扩张成为国际化并引领新兴市场的知名设计公司。继近年来位于加拿大、新加坡和中国的多个主要项目的成功完成，思邦多元化的地标性项目已纵贯亚洲、欧洲和北美，并致力于打造其在独特性和可持续性设计方面所具有的良好声誉。

思邦透过分布于北京、上海、新加坡、马来西亚、阿布扎比和伦敦的事务所，呈献与众不同并获得高度评价的建筑艺术，在独创性和实践性方面倍受全世界的充分肯定。

SPARCH is an international award-winning architectural studio that has been designing and building worldwide for 25 years with proven experience in urban planning, architecture, landscape and interior design.

From its European beginnings, the studio has expanded rapidly into international and emerging markets over the last 10 years. Following the success of recent major built projects in Canada, Singapore and China, SPARCH is now delivering a diverse range of exciting landmark projects across Asia, Europe and North America, each seeking to build on the studio's reputation for delivering exceptional and sustainable design solutions.

From its studios in Abu Dhabi, Beijing, London, Malaysia, Shanghai and Singapore, SPARCH has gained worldwide recognition for originality and rich expression, through the delivery of distinctive and critically acclaimed architecture.

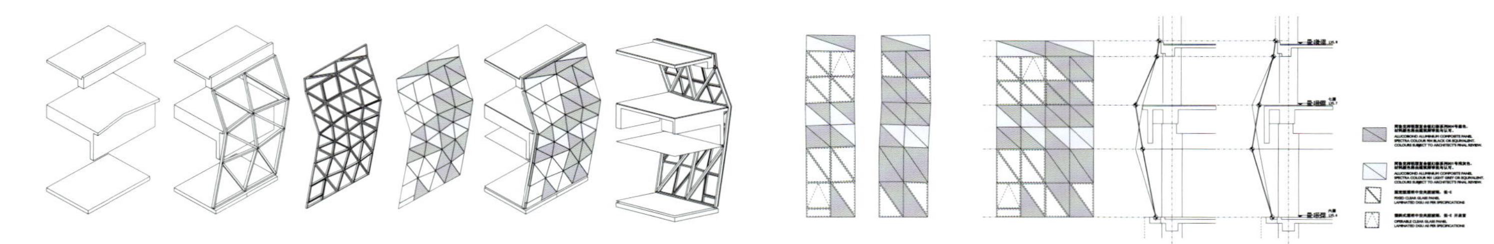
ALUCOBOND ALUMINIUM COMPOSITE PANEL.
COLOURS SUBJECT TO ARCHITECT'S FINAL REVIEW.
ALUCOBOND ALUMINIUM COMPOSITE PANEL.
SPECTRA COLOUR 901 LIGHT GREY OR EQUIVALENT.
COLOURS SUBJECT TO ARCHITECT'S FINAL REVIEW.
FIXED CLEAR GLASS PANEL.
LAMINATED DGU AS PER SPECIFICATIONS
OPERABLE CLEAR GLASS PANEL.
LAMINATED DGU AS PER SPECIFICATIONS

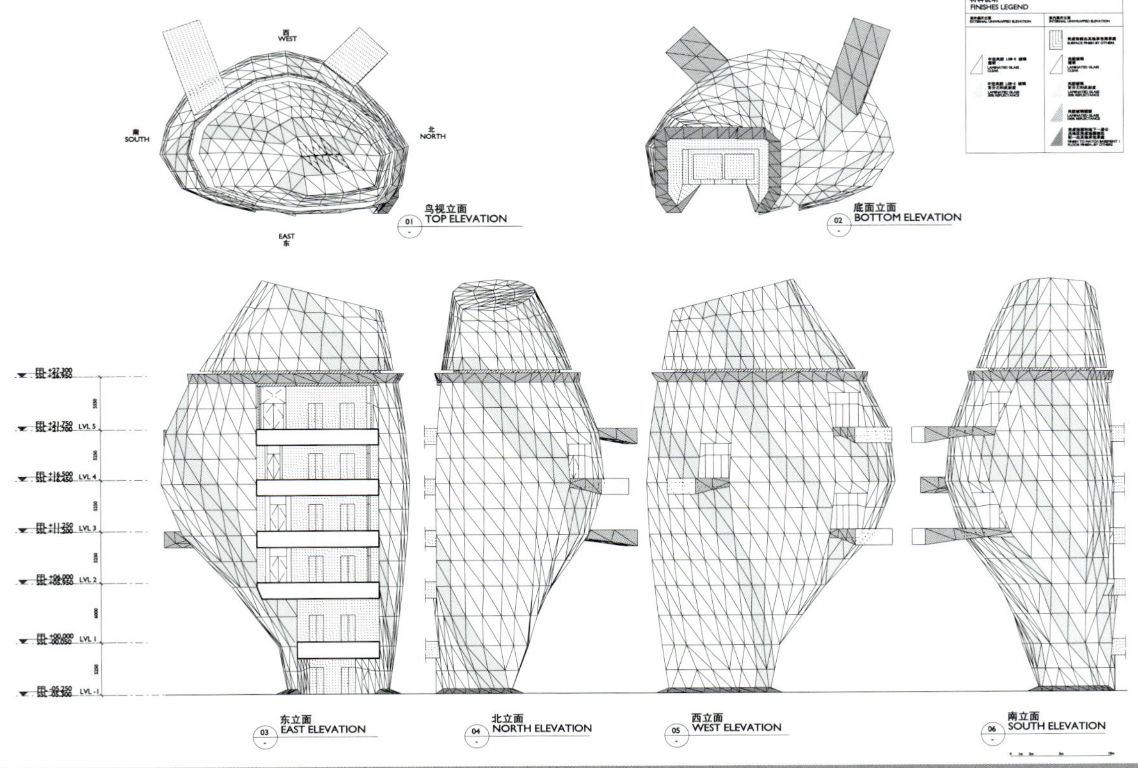

北京来福士广场，是思邦公司在中国完成的第一个综合商业项目，思邦在其他城市的项目将陆续完成。

（2009年9月30日，中国北京）国际知名建筑设计咨询公司思邦在北京的首个竣工项目——北京来福士广场将于2010年正式落成。

“北京来福士广场是我们秉承创新的设计及施工理念的一次验证。作为思邦在中国为凯德置地设计完成的第一个大型综合性项目，来福士广场的开业寓意非凡。”

“在中国我们有诸多正在施工中的项目，但作为在中国首都的第一个大型综合性项目，北京来福士广场奠定了思邦国际知名品牌的基础。在过去的很长一段时间里，我们一直捆绑于伦敦奥斯普工作室，所以公司的品牌知名度一直未得到提升。北京来福士广场向世人展示了思邦公司的设计实力，以及在非凡的业主支持下我们能够完成什么”，与思邦北京事务所主持人杨克共同设计完成北京来福士广场的思邦创始人史蒂芬•平博理这样说。

来福士广场总建筑面积150 000 m^2，坐落于北京东二环与东直门内大街的交界处，由一幢21层高的办公楼，一幢17层高的服务公寓和一幢15层高的住宅楼以及一幢5层高的商场裙楼组成，并且在地下与亚洲最大的交通港东直门交通枢纽完美连接。

2009年4月份开业以来，北京来福士广场一直吸引了众多顾客，并以其大面积的自然采光及独特的中庭悬臂式结构“水晶莲”而备受称赞。闪耀的水晶体结构从底层的食品区拔地而起，支撑起整个中庭的玻璃屋顶，内部还涵盖了电梯间。独特的镶嵌有玻璃带及块状镜面玻璃的水晶莲设计成为购物者及摄影爱好者的焦点。

北京来福士广场有着漂亮的黑白纹点式的彩釉玻璃幕墙。夜晚，面向主广场由多彩的块状屏幕组成的巨型LED显示屏使整幢建筑看起来更加生动。

新加坡开发商凯德置地于2005年5月委托思邦为其在中国的来福士品牌系列第二大综合性项目——北京来福士广场进行建筑设计。北京来福士广场于2006年7月开始施工，商场及写字楼部分分别于2009年4月及6月对外营业。

CapitaLand
凯德置地
Raffles City

Raffles City Beijing mixed-use development in Beijing a first for Sparch after projects in other Chinese cities.

(Beijing, China, 30 September 2009): International architecture firm Sparch's first completed project in Beijing – Raffles City Beijing – will be officially inaugurated in early 2010.

"Raffles City Beijing is a testament of our commitment to innovation in design and construction. Its opening marks an important milestone for Sparch as we completed our first major mixed-use project in China for CapitaLand."

"We have many projects currently under construction across China, but the first especially in the Chinese capital is very special given it marks the foundation of the Sparch brand internationally. We have, for too long, been coupled with the baggage of the Alsop London office which we (the directors of Sparch) left behind many years ago. Raffles City Beijing is a statement of who we are in our own right and what we are capable of doing with the support of an extraordinary client," says Stephen Pimbley, Sparch's founder and director who designed Raffles City Beijing with Jan Clostermann, Sparch's Beijing studio director.

Comprising a 21-storey office tower, a five-storey retail podium, a 17-storey serviced apartment tower and a 15-storey residential block, the 150,000 sqm development is located at the junction of Beijing's East 2nd Ring Road and Dongzhimen Neidaijie. It is well-connected via an underground link to Dongzhimen Transport Interchange, Asia's largest transport hub.

Since its opening in April 2009, Raffles City Beijing has been attracting crowds and acclaim with its sweeping day-lit enclosure and a glass cantilevering structure called the 'Crystal Lotus' at the centre of the retail atrium. This sparkling crystal structure encloses the main elevators as it rises spectacularly from the basement foodcourt to support a sweeping glass roof. The unique design of the 'Crystal Lotus' with its spiralling bands of glass and mirror panels is a cynosure for shoppers and photography enthusiasts.

Raffles City Beijing offers a stunning facade that is a pixelated pattern of black and white glass modules. At night, it is animated by a colourful play of light pixels framing a large public LED screen facing the main square.

Singapore developer CapitaLand commissioned Sparch in May 2005 to undertake the architectural design for Raffles City Beijing, the second Raffles City concept mixed-use development in China. Construction for Raffles City Beijing commenced in July 2006 with the retail and commercial components opening in April and June 2009 respectively.

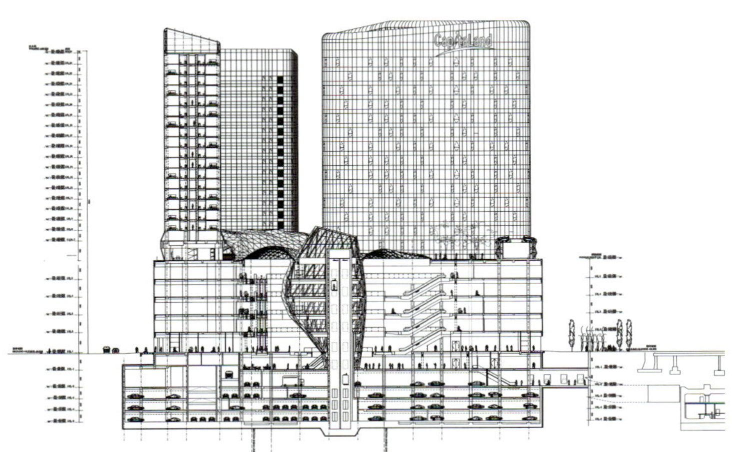

TEMPTATION
Food & Beverage
mötivi
LACOSTE
ZARA
X-MOOM
ORBIS
ZARA
ZARA

来福士说：
“越购物越时尚
越时尚

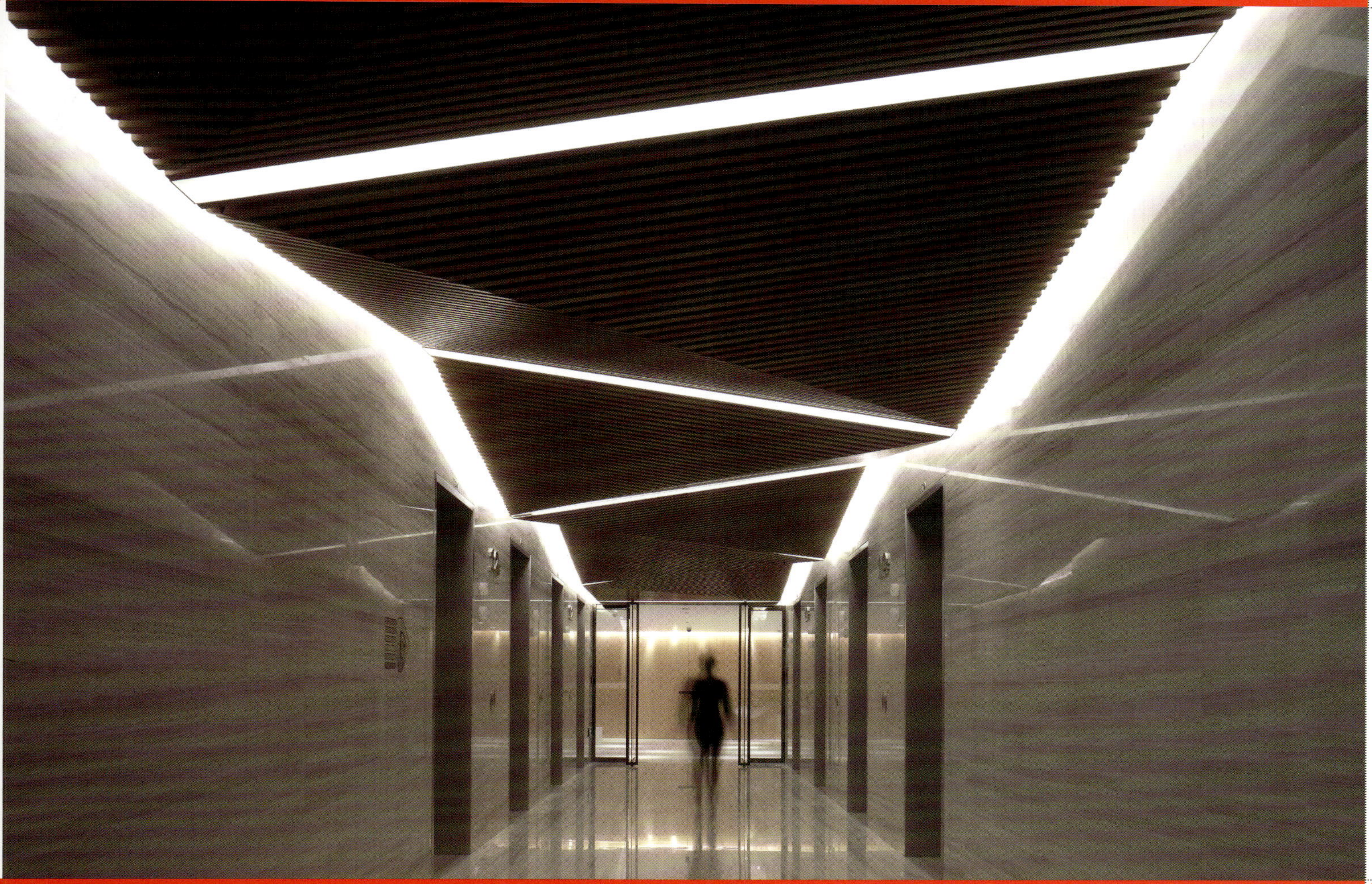

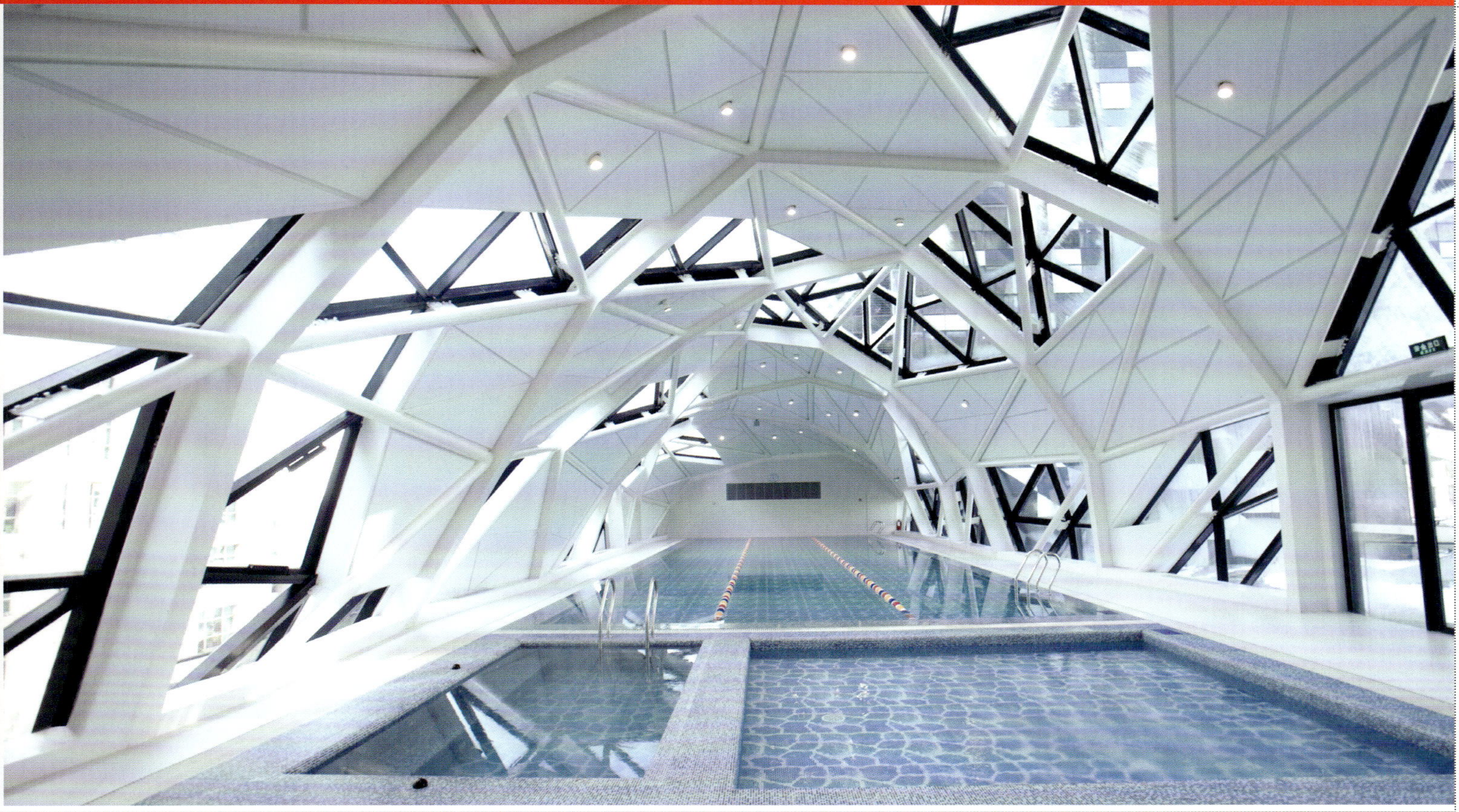

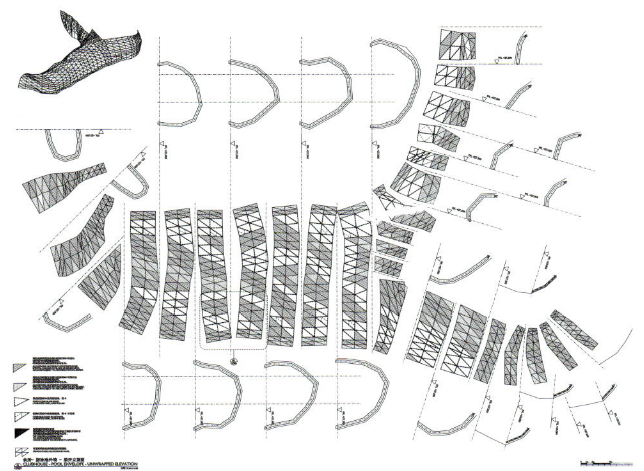

Cruise Termina Shanghai

上海国际港客运中心

设计单位：思邦建筑设计咨询有限公司
客户名称：上海国际港客运中心有限公司（国企）
项目地址：上海虹口区北外滩东大名路与高阳路交界处
建筑规模：260 000 m^2
地上建筑面积：130 073 m^2
总建筑面积（含地下面积）：263 448 m^2
项目完工：一期完工，岸边建筑：2009年10月二期完工，高层办公楼和文化中心：2010年4月
上海国际港配套设施：公共设施，娱乐，零售，餐饮，占总建筑面积20%
商业办公：占总建筑面积80%

Client: Shanghai Port International Cruise Terminal Ltd. (State-owned)
Project Address: Junction of Dong Daming Lu and Gaoyang Lu, North Bund, Shanghai
Size: 260 000 m^2
Project data: GFA (area above ground):130 073 sqm Total Area (including basements): 263 448 sqm
Project completion: Phase 1 Completion, Riverfront Buildings: October 2009
Phase 2 Completion, High Rise Tower and Winter Garden: April 2010
Cruise terminal support facilities: public facilities, entertainment, retail, F&B: 20% of Total Area
Commercial office: 80% of Total Area

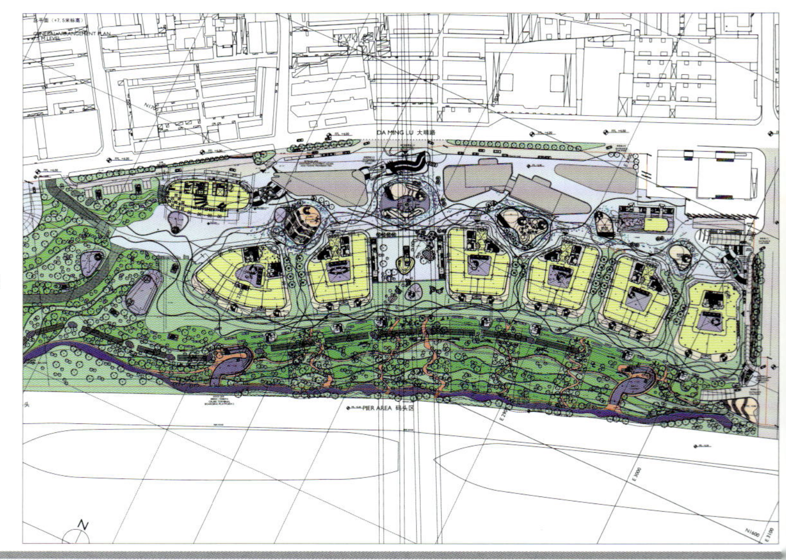

SPARCH（原英国斯凯奥斯普亚太区域公司）于2004年初赢得一个为新上海国际港客运中心提供总体规划项目的任命。这个项目将分成两个阶段完成，目前项目正在进行中。该项目总长度为800 m，地处历史悠久、通行极为方便的上海北外滩临江黄金沿岸区域（请参见城市地图）。项目建成后将成为一个全新的国际大都市的开埠口岸，在任一时间段都能停泊三艘八万吨级的游轮，预计每年旅客迎送量将超过1500 000人次。正是因为它无可比拟的优势，多家游轮公司纷纷争先恐后地要将上海国际港码头纳入到自己的东亚航行线路中。

上海市人口预计为2 000万（户籍人口为1674万人，流动人口为3 500万）相当于澳大利亚的全部人口，但是却被压缩在6 340平方公里的区域内。

上海市市政府曾一再强调在城市建设过程中，创建更多开放“呼吸空间”的迫切需要，并大胆制定了在2010年以“城市，让生活更美好”为主题的上海世博会之前，建造近30%的开放空间的目标，以供市民们尽情享用。上海国际港客运中心项目的远景是期望打造一个沿黄浦江岸边的绿色长廊，并且尽最大限度地让绿色走廊向南面位于卢浦大桥和南浦大桥之间的世博会址延伸部分。

上海国际港客运中心的建筑设计已经考虑到了今后码头船运的巨大吞吐量。整个建筑面积为260 000 m^2，而在项目任务书中更是要求50%的面积需要作为地下空间，包括为客运旅客设计的设施（码头建筑设计由Frank Repas建筑公司负责），然后敞开所有的场地作为绿色公园，层层叠叠地向黄浦江边推进。这里SPARCH的挑战是如何处理“地下世界”以及地上的建筑。对此，设计方案是运用向上开放的一系列蜂窝式下沉广场来创造模糊地平面的效果。建筑如同是从这些蜂巢状的洞口中生长出来的一样，从而为人们提供了更多的机会来探索地面和多层地下空间的联系。层层线性起伏的景观设计同样被引伸到建筑的幕墙设计中去（请参见概念模型）。我们为大楼表面提供了第二层幕墙，让朝南的商业办公空间免受强烈光线的影响，同时在两层幕墙之间设置了室外阳台空间以供人们可以俯视黄浦江景。入夜，栓系大楼表面的鲱鱼骨头般曲度精美的排排桅杆被城市的灯光所照亮，并映射在江面上。而在其中两栋大楼之间的空隙处——矗立着一个巨大的玻璃“桌子”，桌子里面悬吊着数个不规则造型的吊舱。这些吊舱悬浮在一个公共演出空间之上，位于桌子内部的一、二、四层，功能分别为咖啡馆、酒吧和餐厅。SPARCH的设计和上海的多元娱乐需求融为一体，最终将这一奇特的建筑变为现实。

公共活动领域

新建的上海国际港客运中心将成为上海黄浦江沿岸最能吸引眼球的地标之一。沿着400米长的步行街规划出一系列的下沉式广场，如同花朵盛放一样地形成不同的活动场所，这其中包括一个阶梯式演出剧场、一个可供节日采访的传媒中心和美食庭院。步行街从西端开始，一直延伸到东端的水景展览馆（请参见基地平面）。

音乐文化中心位于项目的中心地块，“桌子”底部40米通高的空间形成了通往公园与江边的入口，创造出一个激动人心的舞台，在节庆狂欢时可同时聚集上千人。入口一侧40米宽x30米高的网状结构形成巨大的屏幕，可以投射动态十足的数字影像。

绿色公园同时也是一个雕塑园，生动的艺术品陈列在空旷的草地与树木之间，并且在夜间被背投式玻璃射灯光线照亮而凸显于景观之中。

目前建设正在稳步进行中，大楼一期正面外立面已经建成。SPARCH目前正投入项目二期100米高的大楼的建设工作中，启动沿东大名路的第二阶段的开发工作。

环保创新——一个沿江冷却系统

所有的六栋办公大楼都包含竖向的中庭，顶部安装了能让光线通过的天窗。在季节转换的时候，空气可以通过外立面内作流通，并经过办公空间朝向中间的中庭，最后向顶端排出。外推式窗户布满外立面用以提供局部冷却的功效。南面室内可直接开门到室外的大阳台，在双层玻璃幕墙内俯视黄浦江景。双层幕墙结构阻挡了在夏日里UV射线进入大楼，同时在冬季起到隔热保温的功效。

Arup的工程师设计了一个在上海首次商业应用的“江水引入降温系统”，将从黄浦江中抽取江水，并通过HVAV系统进行热交换。这个系统将在夏季大量的降低大楼能耗。“光伏电池薄膜”将作为顶层天棚安置于办公大楼楼顶上，用以降低景观所需光照的能耗以及公共夜间区域光照的能耗。

通风和自然日光功效将被最大化，配合“江水降温系统”以及“光伏电池薄膜”天棚，并辅以繁荣的绿色公共园景，这一项目开发继承和发展了“环保及可持续发展”的理念，在最大程度上降低能耗及运营成本，让我们的客户成为21世纪绿色建筑项目开发的楷模。

bars and restaurants, hovering over a public performance space below. There is a symbiosis between Shanghai's fun loving desire for diversity, and SPARCH's approach to design, that has made this architecture a reality.

The Public Realm

The New International Cruise Terminal will be one of the most eye catching landmarks along Shanghai's waterfront. The brief programmes the site with public attractions along its 400 m long pedestrian street, a sequence of event spaces blossom from sunken courtyards, including a terraced performance theatre, a Media Garden for festival events and a Food Court. The pedestrian street flows from the west, leading to a Crystal Art Gallery at the east end (refer to site plan).

The Public Winter Garden forms the centerpiece of the site, its 40 m tall glass clad portal creates a dramatic stage addressing the public park and the waterfront, where thousands of people can gather to participate in festivals. The portal structure is designed to deploy a 40 m wide by 30 m tall gauze screen for digital projections.

The green public park is also a sculpture garden animated with artwork placed in the grass clearings between the trees, and illuminated at night by backlit glass prism skylights rising out of the landscape.

Construction continues at pace, the façades of the pavilion buildings are complete. SPARCH are now focusing on phase 2, the 100 m tall tower that forms the second layer of the development along Dong Daming Lu.

Environmental Innovation – River Water Cooling

All 6 Office Pavilions contain ventilated atria, topped with louvered skylights. During mid season air circulates through the facades, across the office spaces towards the central atrium where it exhausts at the top. Pixelated window openings across the office façades provides local comfort cooling. Large doors open onto generous balconies along the south side, within a double skin facade, overlooking the Huang Pu River. The double skin facade traps UV heat from entering the buildings in the summer, and acts as an insulating blanket during the winter.

Arup Engineers have designed a 'River Water Cooling System', a first in Shanghai for a commercial application, which will draw water from the Huangpu River and combine it, via heat exchangers, with the HVAC system. This system will greatly reduce the energy consumption of the buildings during the summer months.

The canopies hovering above the Office Pavilion roofs will be carpeted in a 'Photovoltaic Membrane', sized to offset the energy requirement of lighting the landscape and public spaces in the evenings.

By maximizing on natural daylight and ventilation, and introducing the 'River Water Cooling System', combined with Photovoltaic membranes on the roofs, in the context of a lush green public parkland, the development is following the philosophy of an 'Environmentally Sustainable Development', greatly reducing energy consumption and running costs, and rewarding the client with the credentials of a Green Development for the 21st Century.

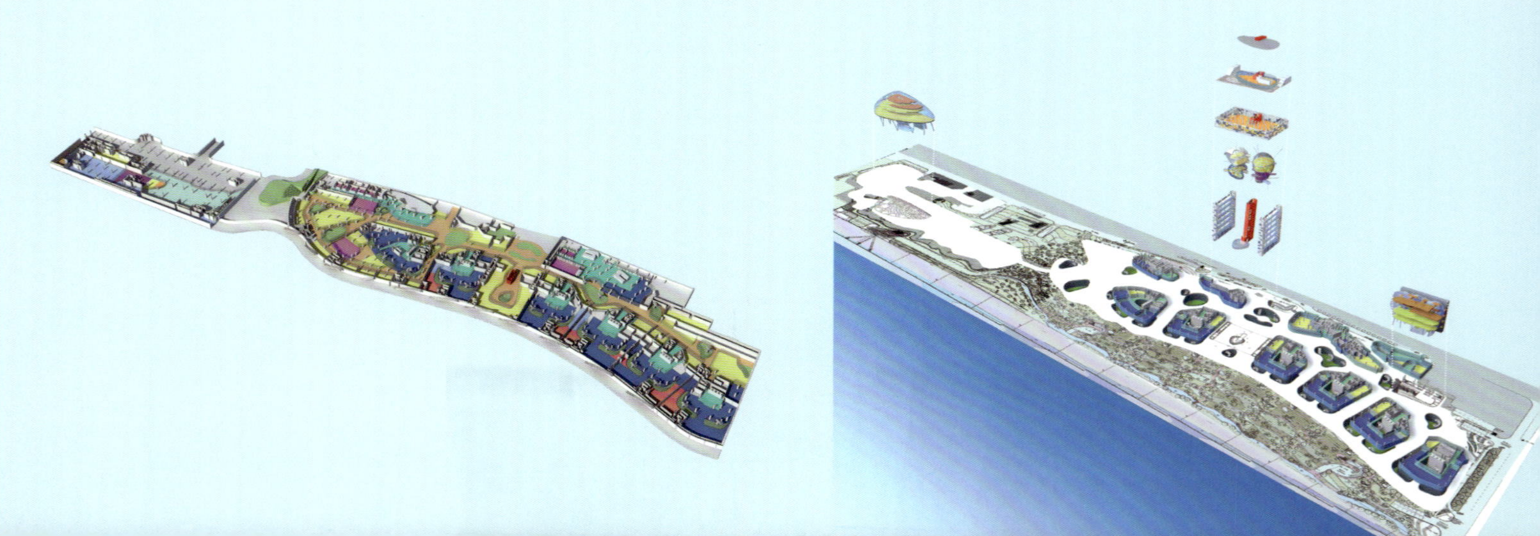

中海 中国海运 CHINA SHIPPING

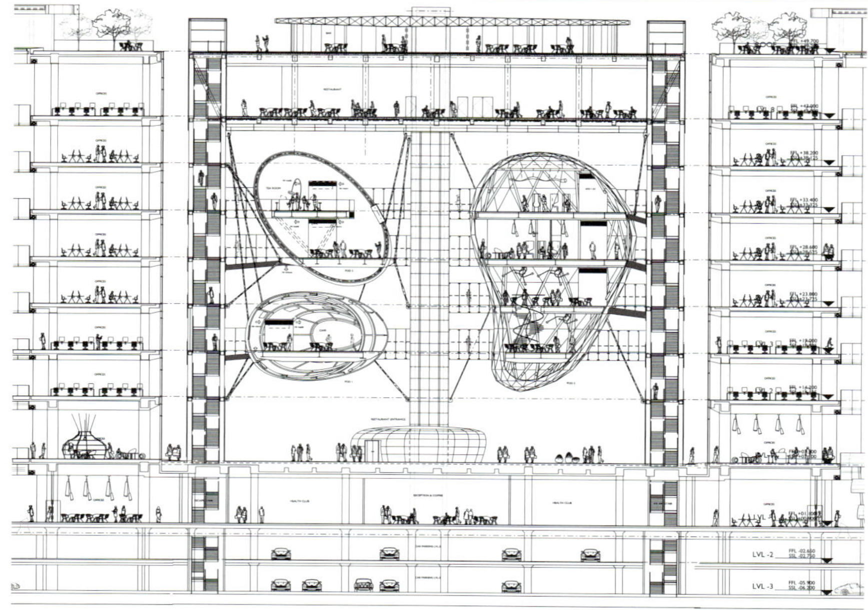
LVL-2
LVL-3

Plan and Design for Longtang Hot Spring,Changzhou

江苏常州龙汤温泉

设计单位：洲联集团
占地面积：4.3公顷
建筑面积：15 579 m²
合作单位：江苏华源建筑设计院有限公司

Design firm: Werkhart World Wide 5-star Alliance
Site area: 4.3 ha
Building area: 15 579 m²

本项目位于常州新北区河海东路。龙汤温泉以温泉为核心，是集温泉、SPA、餐饮、会议、住宿为一体的综合项目。规划上以“景观围绕建筑，建筑围合庭院”的布局原则。沿河海东路及四周的绿化带围绕着温泉接待中心、餐饮中心和温泉会所组成的一组建筑。同时这组公建和后面的汤宿区包围着室外温泉公园。使得建筑与景观相互渗透，互为景观。沿城市道路的公共建筑以金属和玻璃的纯净隐喻温泉的岩石和水，创造出一个富有创意的建筑造型，体现了“生态，自然，时尚，典雅”的创作主旨。

WERKHART WORLD WIDE 5-STAR ALLIANCE

洲联集团

洲联集团（WERKHART WORLD WIDE 5-STAR ALLIANCE）作为跨国机构，拥有多个子品牌：德国WLTK、五合国际（WERKHART）、北京华特（HUATE）、上海五合智库（WISENOVA）、刘力主创工作室（DRLIULI）、五合新力规划及红榜在线（INDEXRED）。凭借欧洲顶级高科技生态节能技术、中国甲级设计团队、丰富的大型工程施工图经验，以及优秀的策划实力和创意表现，整合城市规划、建筑设计、景观设计、室内设计、平面设计，外加市场研究与产品策划增值服务，为房地产业提供5+1项全程服务。

洲联集团在中国大陆现有员工500余人。在欧洲和亚洲已完成包括购物中心、酒店、银行及企业总部、飞机场、地铁站、音乐厅、教育研发等百余项大型工程。旗下的五合国际具备德国城市规划资质、建筑设计资质，成为境外驻中国第三大建筑设计公司，并获得众多奖项。集团于2007年并购的控股子公司——北京华特建筑设计顾问有限公司，具备工程设计甲级资质、工程咨询甲级资质和数百项工程业绩，旗下设计师 200余人，拓展业务范围并增强综合实力。集团全资子公司上海五合智库投资顾问有限公司（WISENOVA）为世界范围金融机构、投资商、开发商、政府部门提供城市开发，房地产市场及投融资方面的专业顾问服务。

洲联集团同德国著名的SOBEK结构工程设计、TRANSSOLAR生态节能设计、HENN工业研发设施设计以及JOI酒店商业室内设计优势互补，共同开拓中国市场。

洲联集团在业内率先提出“5+1”服务模式，整合规划设计、建筑设计、景观设计、室内设计、平面设计五大专业，并提供市场研究及产品策划增值服务；国际背景的核心团队，熟悉中国市场，特别在规划、酒店、商业、豪宅及高科技生态节能设计等方面独具专长，引领市场。

As a transnational agency, WERKHART WORLD WIDE 5-STAR ALLIANCE has a number of subsidiary brands: WLTK, WERKHART, Beijing HUATE, Shanghai WISENOVA, DRLIULI and INDEXRED. With its European top-level high-tech ecologically energy saving technology, China's first rate design team, rich experience in large project construction as well as excellent planning capacity and creative and expressive ability, it offers 5+1 full service in realty business by integrating urban planning, architectural designing, landscape designing, interior designing, graphic designing and value-added services of market research and product planning .

WERKHART WORLD WIDE 5-STAR ALLIANCE now has a staff of over 500 in China. It has completed more than one hundred large projects including shopping centers, hotels, banks, headquarters of enterprises, airports, subway stations, concert halls and educational research and development facilities in Europe and Asia. Its affiliated WERKHART, possessing a German certified qualification for urban planning and architectural designing, has become the third largest foreign architectural design corporation located in China and won a great number of prizes. In 2007, WERKHART WORLD WIDE 5-STAR ALLIANCE conducted the merger and acquisition of Beijing HUATE Architectural Design and Consultant Co. Ltd., which has a class A qualification for engineering design and consultation, hundreds of project achievements as well as a staff of over 200, expanding its business scope and enhancing its comprehensive strength. Its wholly-owned firm, Shanghai WISENOVA Investment Consultant Co. Ltd., provides professional services in realty markets and investing and financing for financial institutions, investors, developers and governments worldwide.

WERKHART WORLD WIDE 5-STAR ALLIANCE shares complementary advantages with German's famous SOBEK in structural and engineering design, TRANSSOLAR in ecologically energy saving design, HENN in industrial research and development facility design and JOI in hotel commercial interior design, exploiting Chinese market together.

WERKHART WORLD WIDE 5-STAR ALLIANCE is the first to put forward a "5+1"service mode within the industry, integrating the five specialties of planning design, architectural designing, landscape designing, interior designing, graphic designing as well as providing value-added services of market research and product planning. Its core team, with a international background, is familiar with Chinese market, and particularly, the team enjoys unique expertise in terms of planning, hotel, commercial, elite housing and high-tech ecologically energy saving designs and thus guides the market.

This project locates in the eastern Hehai road of new northern district in Changzhou. Longtang spring is one complex project with spring, SPA, dinning, meeting and lodgings, taking spring as core. Our planning regulation is "building is surrounded by landscape and yard is enclosed by building". This building clusters include reception center, dinning center and spring chamber, which are surrounded by the eastern Hehai road and the surrounding green belts. So, the buildings and landscape are penetrated each other and obtain landscape for one another. The metal and glass are very pure and they imply the stone and water of the hotspring. This project creates the building's sculpt with ideas and embodies the creational idea of ecology, nature, fasion and elegance.

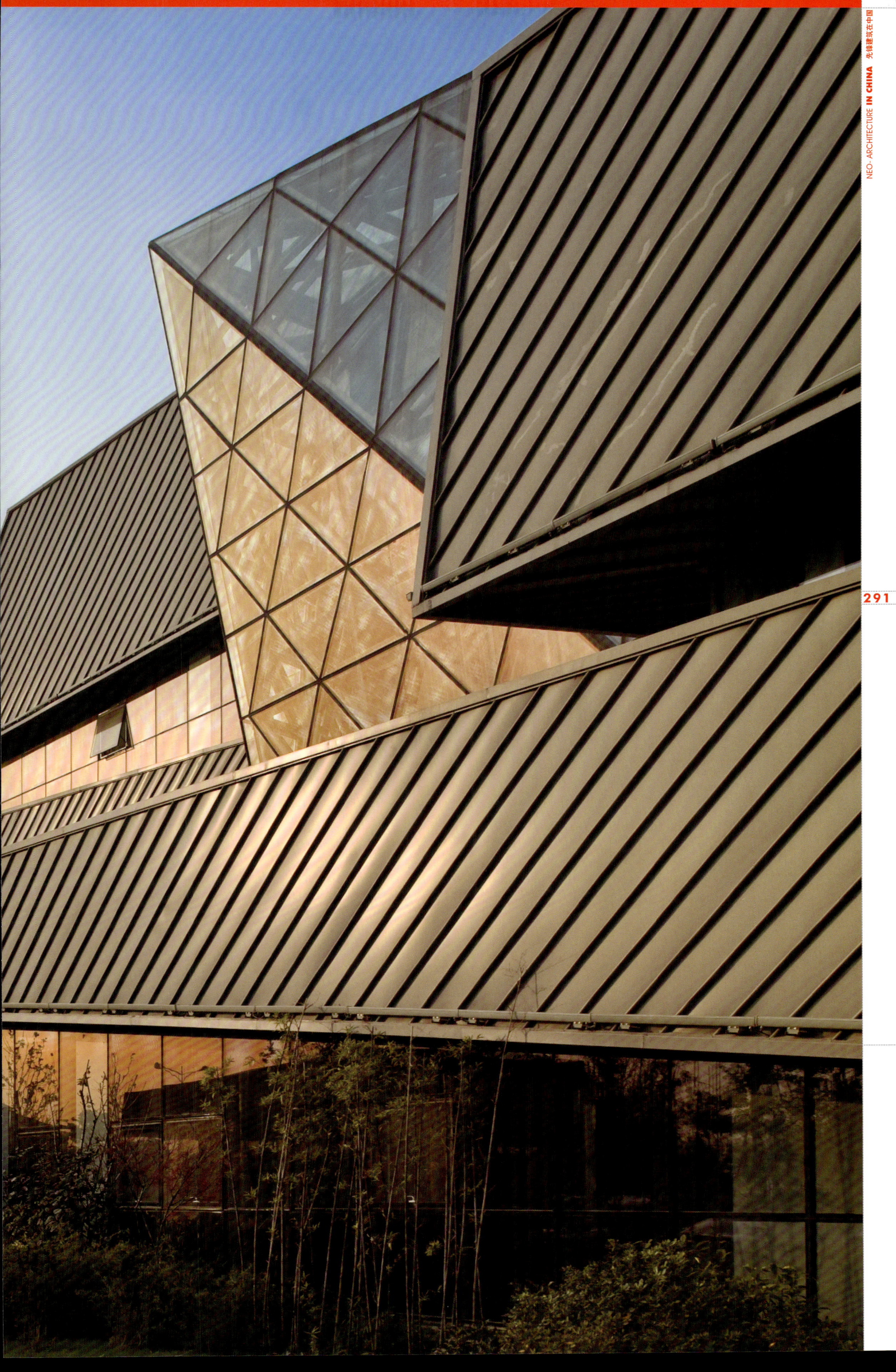

Bekaert Asia R&D Center
贝卡尔特亚洲研发中心

设计单位：AAI国际建筑师事务所
主要设计人员：Jan Benda、孙青、陆祎
项目地址：江阴市滨济开发区
规划用地面积：1.8 Ha
一期总建筑面积：20 413 m²
容积率：0.97
建筑密度：44.3%

Design firm: Allied Architecture International
Leading designer: Jan Benda, Sun qing, Lu yi
Address: Economic Development Zone, Jiangyin
Plan construction area: 1.8 Ha
First-stage overall floorage: 20 413 m²
Volume fraction: 0.97
Site coverage: 44.3%

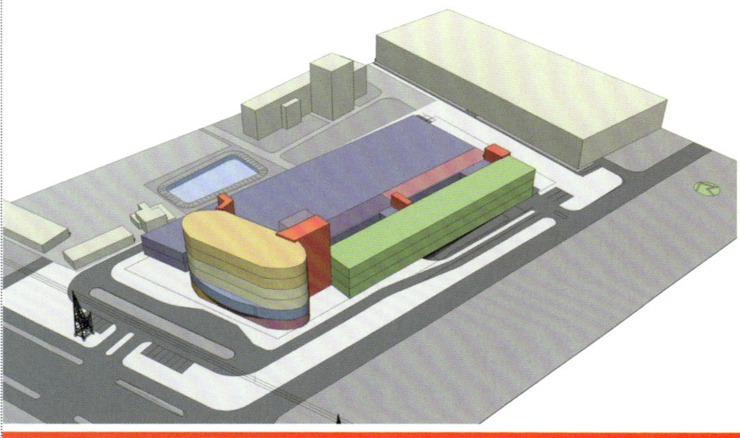

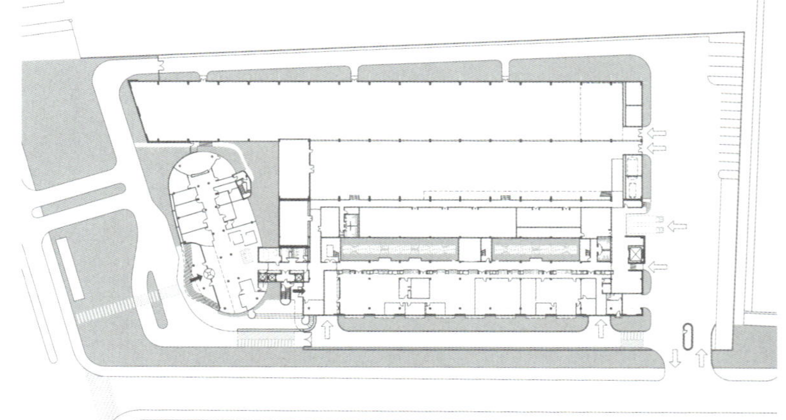

AAI
国际建筑师事务所 加拿大
ALLIED ARCHITECTS INTERNATIONAL

AAI国际建筑师事务所（加拿大）是一家立志于在中国长期发展的国际性设计机构，提供建筑设计、城市设计和城市规划等全方位的服务。事务所总裁及多位项目总监和设计总监均有在中国二十年以上的工作和合作经验，参与完成的项目超过200个。

事务所集中了来自于北美、欧洲和亚洲其他国家的执牌建筑师、建筑设计人员以及本地优秀建筑师。这样的综合性团队能通过与当地的顾问和政府部门的有效合作提供富于创造性和创新精神的设计作品，并保证实施力度。AAI不断扩展的设计发展综合服务和项目管理能力是帮助其取得建筑成就的重要因素。

2003年至今，在中国已设计和正在设计的项目规划面积累计已达4 000公顷，建筑面积超过1 200万m²。工程项目遍布上海、北京、天津、苏州、成都、武汉、三亚、青岛、杭州、宁波、呼和浩特等城市。

AAI出色的业绩和杰出的信誉为其在变化无穷的中国建筑设计领域赢得了领先地位。

Allied Architects International (Canada) Inc. is a dynamic firm of professionals licensed in Europe, North America and China focusing on China's long-term development. The Senior Management team has more than 20 years design experience and has completed more than 200 projects in China. AAI offers creative and innovative design solutions in the field of Architectural Design, Urban Design and Planning.

Our strategy is to have a project team comprised of experienced senior international designers and local architects. This combination of experience ensures design excellence while maintaining project schedules and ensuring efficient co-ordination with local consultants and government officials.

Our expanded design development package and strong project management skills are the final elements in achieving our goals.

From 2003, the planning area of our projects totals more than 4,000 Ha, with building area exceeding 12 million m^2. The project locations span the country in Shanghai, Beijing, Tianjin, Suzhou, Chengdu, Wuhan, Sanya, Qingdao, Hangzhou, Ningbo and Hohhot.

AAI is proud of its excellent professional reputation and experience in the constantly changing building industry in China.

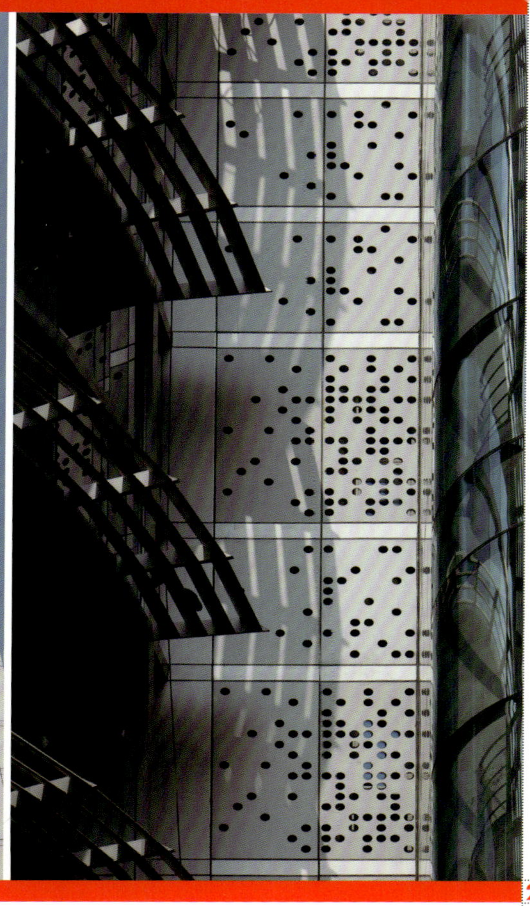

江阴贝卡尔特研究中心是贝卡尔特在本土比利时以外设立的第一个研究中心。贝卡尔特集团基于在金属变形以及先进材料、镀膜技术上的核心竞争力，在全球生产和销售一系列产品和系统并提供相关服务。为了满足亚洲市场的需要，贝卡尔特决定在中国设立一个国家级先进水平的研发中心。

在设计启动前，贝卡尔特的工程师和管理人员提出了四点设计标准：

1. 贯穿整个研究中心必须体现功能性和高效率
2. 确保研究成果及商业机密的安全性
3. 建筑风格符合亚洲公司的形象
4. 设计中符合生态节能原则

贝卡尔特江阴研究中心的设计最初希望参照比利时总部1960年建的研发中心为样本。然而鉴于研发技术，研发程序及测试设备在过去的半个世纪发生了巨大的变化，AAI的设计师必须说服甲方工程师们在此基础上探索更为科学合时宜的方法对研发中心的功能进行重新组织，最终建筑师和工程师们达成了一致。

建筑设计概念

建筑本身特殊的功能性决定了本项目设计策略有别于普通的建筑设计实践。在设计中必须保持对例如基地状况、不同功能分区恰当衔接的敏感度，这实际上是对我们能否平衡建筑设计、功能性、财务预算各方面因素的一场考验。

整个项目需要将以下三个功能分区经过设计有效地组织起来：研发办公、实验室、测试车间。从地块来看，按照传统设计方法在基地上安排三个功能区显得勉强，所以，AAI建立了一个垂直模型将三个功能分区有效地结合起来，同时确保了外观的统一性原则。设立中庭将实验车间与研发办公及实验室部分分割，内庭既成为阻隔噪音最有效的屏障，也成为员工休憩的场所，同时在有限的基地内增加了绿化覆盖。

贝卡尔特有三个生产基地分部在中国各地。所有生产基地都具有实用的外表但都不能体现贝卡尔特在市场上的定位，而江阴研发中心的建筑设计希望勾勒出企业在行业中的地位和企业想要表达的形象。在确保功能优先的原则下，最终确定将对外观的诉求更多地寄托在七层的研发办公楼上，建筑的形态、材质、选色和立面都做了最为细致的设计和选择，以确保获得包括客户、当地政府、规划部门及其他相关专家在内的一致认可。为了体现正在全球范围内革新的现代建筑发展趋势，一些新的元素被恰当地运用到建筑的细节中。在将合理性和美学因素结合的过程中清晰地勾勒出一个无论在结构上，外观上还是环境上都独一无二的建筑画面。另外，除了研发办公楼，其他部分也沿用主楼的风格，只是在材料的选用上更为节约。

Research centre in Jiangyin is the first Bekaert R&D facility set up outside Belgium. The company is manufacturing wires of all kinds, from the ordinary wires for everyday use, steel cord for the automotive industry as well as the hi-tech wire and other material used in the highly sophisticated machines and modern digital technology. In order to properly serve to its Asian clients, the company decide to invest into the state-of-art research facilities in China. A decision came after the business in the region grew enormously and proper testing and product development could no longer be carried out just form the Belgium base.

The four key design criteria were required by Bekaert team of engineers and managers for this project:

1. Functionality and efficiency of the completed R&D centre
2. Security of the research results and business secrets
3. Architectural appearance as the image of the company in Asia
4. Ecological approach to the design and energy conservation

The Bekaert R&D centre Asia in Jiangyin was primarily based on the experience from the same facilities in Belgium that have been set up in the 1960s. Since then the technology has changed substantially as well as the research procedure and testing equipment. Thus AAI designers have to in some cases convince the client's engineers for certain elements of the project that apart from the client's practical experience there might be other ways how to organize such facilities. At the end extremely good cooperation between the architect and the client teams resulted into a building complex that is appreciated by all people involved as well as by city residents.

Architectural Design Concept

A design strategy evolved around elements unusual for the normal architectural practice. The site condition and the proper relation of different functions were requiring a strategy that would be sensitive to all issues and aspects of the project. It was a balancing act in between the architecture, functionality and the budget that was given by the company executives before the real design was even started.

The program of this project calls for a design and organizing three main components of the R&D centre – the research and administration offices, laboratories and the test line facilities. The site appears to be too tight for the traditional set up of such facilities therefore AAI developed a vertical organization strategy consists of three main building blocks divided by an internal atrium in order to offset the noise and other disruptive aspects associated with the normal operation regime.

Bekaert has production facilities in three different regions in China. All of them have utilitarian look and do not reflect the position that the company has on the market. Architecture of this R&D centre is representing the image as well as unique position of the company in the territory. During the decision making process regarding the architecture and R&D appearance was stated by the client that the technology and research equipment should still be the main priority. Later on a decision has been made that the higher budget will be spent on the most visible part of the project – the tower. The building shape, material, colors and façade's elements have been carefully chosen to satisfy not just the client but also the local government and city planning officials as well as other authorities. By reflecting world-wide trends of digital age architecture some new elements have been used on the limited part of the building that are innovative and anchoring the building into the present times. The combination of the rationality and esthetics resulted into an image that is unique in its configuration, appearance and the environment. Other parts of the projects were complimenting the tower but materials used on the building were less expensive.

Hefei Grand Theatre

合肥大剧院

设计单位：上海秉仁建筑师事务所
主设计师：项秉仁
设计团队：秦戈今、缪琦、董屹、程翌、韩冰、滕露莹、吴波
建筑面积：60 034 m²

Design firm: DDB International LTD.Shanghai
Lead designer: Xiang Bingren
Design team: Qin Gejin, Miao Qi, Dong Yi, Cheng Yi, Han Bing, Teng Luying, Wu Bo
Building area: 60 034 m²

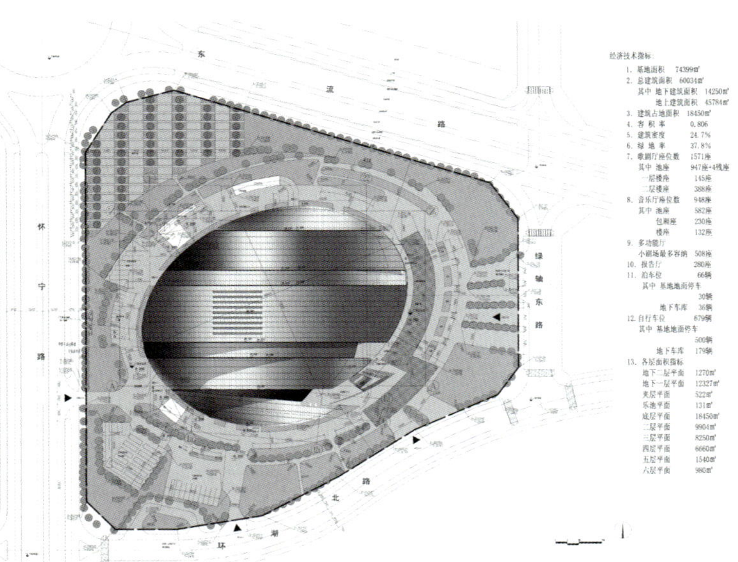

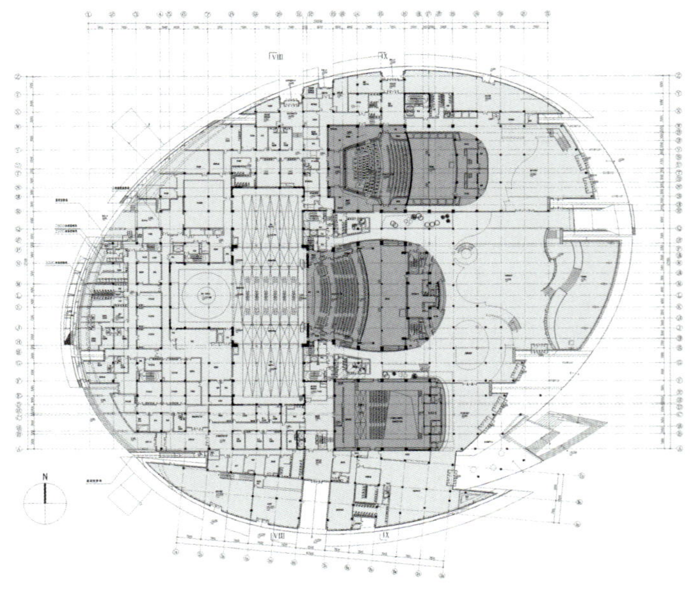

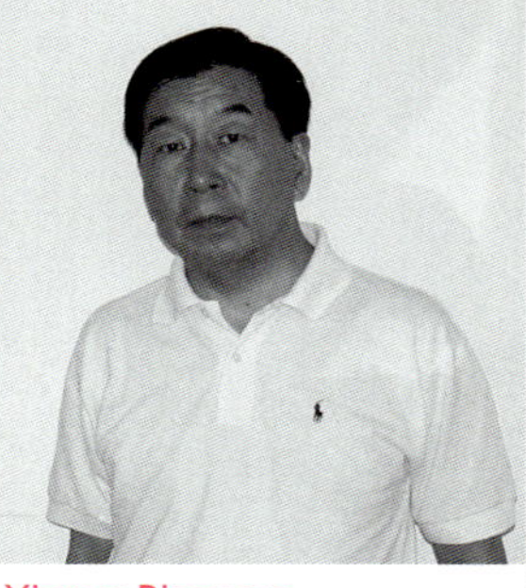

Xiang Bingren
DDB INTERNATIONAL LTD. SHANGHAI

项秉仁
上海秉仁建筑师事务所

上海秉仁建筑师事务所（DDB INTERNATIONAL LTD. SHANGHAI）创立于1998年。其前身为DDB INTERNATIONAL LTD. HONGKONG。公司设计主持人项秉仁教授为美国注册建筑师和中国一级注册建筑师，从事建筑设计40余年，包括在美国和香港逾十年的专业实践。

项秉仁
博士生导师，中国一级注册建筑师，美国注册建筑师，美国建筑师学会会员
1966年南京工学院（今东南大学）建筑学学士
1981年东南大学建筑学硕士
1985年东南大学建筑学博士学位
1999年返回上海同济大学城规学院，被聘为教授

DDB International Ltd. Shanghai grew out of DDB International LTD. Hongkong and was established in 1998. Its chief architec*, Xiang Bingren, registered architect of U.S.A and 1st-class registered architect of China, has been doing architecture design over 40 years, including over 10 years of practice in the profession in U.S and HongKong.

Xiang Bingren
1966 B. Arch. Southeast Univ.
1981 M. Arch. Southeast Univ.
1985 Dr. Arch. Southeast Univ.
1999 Professor & Doctor tutor, Architecture & Urban Planning college, Tongji Univ.
1st-class Registered Architect, China
Registered Arcitect, U.S.A
FAIA

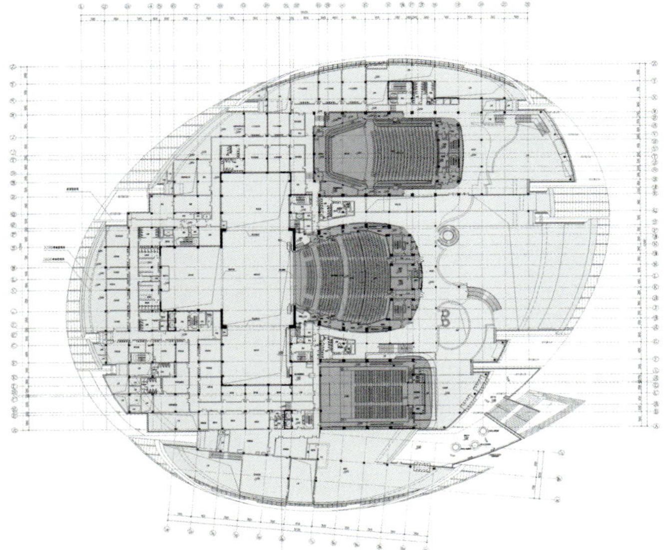

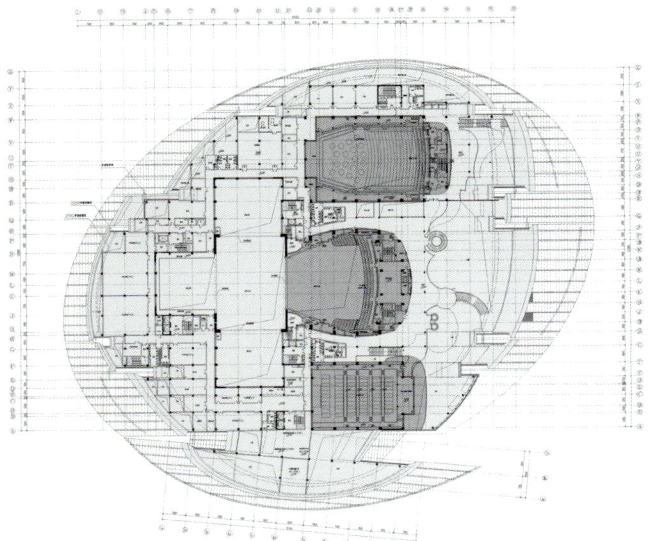

历经5年的修建，建于合肥市政务文化新区核心地段的合肥大剧院于2009年9月基本建成。这个耗资6亿元的大型演艺建筑，屹立在波光粼粼的天鹅湖畔，与不远处的政府办公大楼遥相呼应。在60 000多m^{2}的建筑空间里容纳了一个拥有1 517座席的歌剧厅，一个977座席的音乐厅和一个508座席的多功能厅，以及三个排练厅、地下车库、自行车库，公共服务空间和其他附属设施，从此结束了安徽省和城市缺乏现代化大型综合文化演艺中心的历史，极大地提升了这座城市的自信心，推动了社会文化的整体发展。

在总体设计中，设计师刻意解决了位于新区中心轴西侧的合肥大剧院与轴线东侧的综合艺术馆（待建）不同体量和形态的均衡性要求。在空间构图上和已建成的行政中心构成稳定的三角关系，塑造出开放而又具中心感的新区核心。

建筑立面造型的灵感源于天鹅湖的水纹，由“水纹”衍生出的柔性轮廓线，赋予建筑形态一种飘逸且沉静的效果，和天鹅湖畔静谧的自然环境相得益彰，宛如一颗熠熠生辉的“湖畔明珠”。

采用新材料、运用新技术以实现项目生态节能和可持续发展。设在顶层的屋顶机房可利用弧形屋面顶部的格栅及侧向百页解决通风的问题。高性能的玻璃幕墙有效地增加了自然采光，同时降低了空调能耗。此外，水源热泵处理系统的引入成为重要的可持续措施之一。

合肥大剧院的前厅空间开阔，层次丰富，高低错落，成为一个人们观看中庭空间和自然驻步交谈的场所。运用数码技术产生的光影交叠，丰富的层次让界面表皮更具深度感。分层次的双曲面天空在LED灯光的映衬下，塑造出一种期待和神秘感。

歌剧院的主色调采用传统剧院的大红色和经典的马蹄形平面。由黑色金属网和红色GRG饰面板围合而成的曲面，加强观众厅的围合感。条状的GRG板在垂直方向，高低起伏，再现建筑造型中“水纹”的主题，并起到声学扩散体的作用。

音乐厅作为一把精心打造的乐器，主色调为黄色，平面是古典的鞋盒式布局。受安徽民间艺术折纸艺术的启发，天面造型采用有利于声学扩散的多折面造型，如同一颗被精心切割出来的宝石。音乐厅侧墙所采用MLS声学扩散体，凹凸划分看似自由、随机，具有现代审美理念。

多功能厅内设8台升降平台，通过升降台与座椅布置相结合的方案，剧场可实现5种主要的组合变换。作为承载着现代视听体验的演出机器，黑灰色的金属网板和深色木格栅的搭配，体现着强烈的实验性、高科技感和视觉冲击力。

Taking about five years the construction of Hefei Grand Theatre that is located in the core area of Hefei new administrative and cultural district was completed in September of 2009. With cost about a hundred millions U.S. dollar, the new grand theatre standing near the Swan Lake, a large piece of man-made water surface, greets the newly built government office building not so far away. With total floor area of 60,000 square meters, the theatre has a 1517 seats opera house, a 977 seats concert hall and a 508 seats multi-functional theater. Other facilities such as rehearsal rooms, lobby, F&B services and exhibition spaces are included but not limited within the structure. The new grand theatre ends the history of the city that was incapable to build such a contemporary performing arts center. It greatly stimulates the city's social, economical and cultural development.

In the original master planning, the grand theatre and an art gallery, with different sizes and characters, are respectively located at the two sides of the central axis of the new district. The architects were aware of and solved the challenging issue that spatial balance must be achieved by deliberately dealing with the sizes, forms and functions of the two different structures. As a result, a stable triangle spatial relation was established, which helps to strengthen the spacious and central feeling of the city core area.

The theatre takes an elliptic form as its thematic configuration in order to eliminate the obvious difference between the front elevation and side elevations, and appears as a characteristic individual. The varied soft curve of the building roof is inspired by the water wave of Swan Lake and looks like a pearl at the waterfront.

Many measures for energy saving and sustainability are applied in the project. For example, the solid metal roof with well insulate materials occupies most of the building envelop, which greatly reduces the air condition load; high performance glass curtain wall ensures sufficient day lighting and saves energy consuming as well; metal louvers are installed in the exterior wall area between two roofs at different heights to help natural ventilation. Furthermore, Water resource heat pump was also introduced in as one of the important sustainable design measures.

The large and high lobby space connecting the three venues hosts three terraces which aresetback one by one vertically. It not only facilitates the circu ation but also makes the space more open and interactive. The varied form of the staircases, the observation elevators and the balconies at the different levels are all helpful to create visual pleasure.

The conventional U-shape was applied into the auditorium space design and Chinese

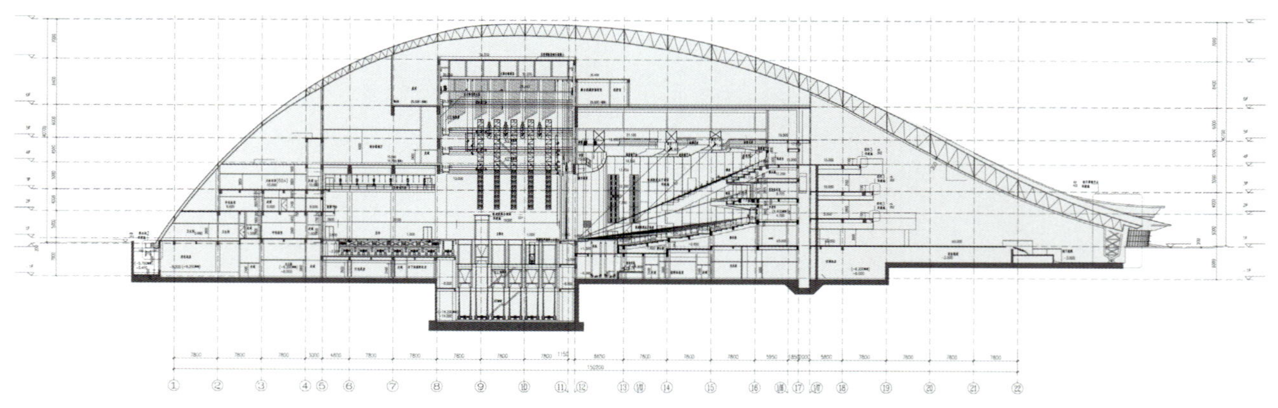

red was painted as the thematic interior color tone. Furnished with the black wire mesh and red adulatory GRG panel, the side wall not only helps the sound diffusion but also strengthens the warm enclosure feeling of the auditorium.

The concert hall looks like a piece of well manufactured musical instrument with a light yellow as the color tone. Classical shoes box shape was adopted as its space form. Inspired by the local paper folding art, the ceiling of the concert hall introduced a folding configuration. It not only provides richer sound vibration but also presents a unique diamond-looking ceiling form.

To ensure both of a proper sound vibration and aesthetical success, the MLS diffusion panels (which is proved as a well performance sound reflection device up to now) were furnished on the wall. With the effort of the architects, the texture of the interior wall appears free, random and music rhythm looking.

Eight pieces of movable mechanical platform are installed as the floor of the functional theater, which can be flexibly adjusted to form various layouts and levels for different performance needs. The theatre just looks like a modern machine for performance, so as to be borrowed as the theme of the interior design. Dark grey is the color tone of the hall. Pure concrete, black metal mesh and dark wood grill are the basic finish elements for the wall so that the space character of experimentalism, high-tech, and strong visual shock could be well emphasized.

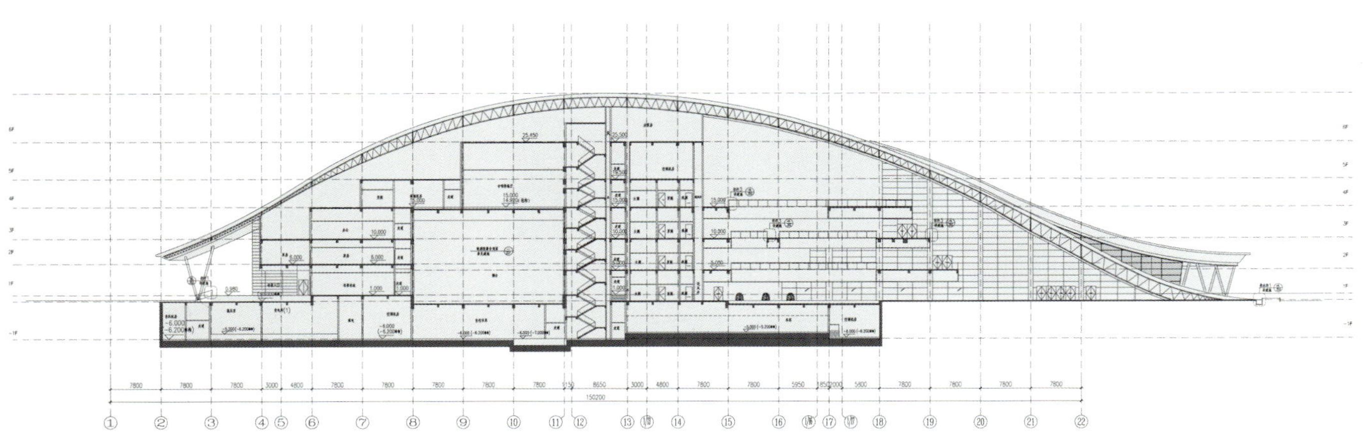

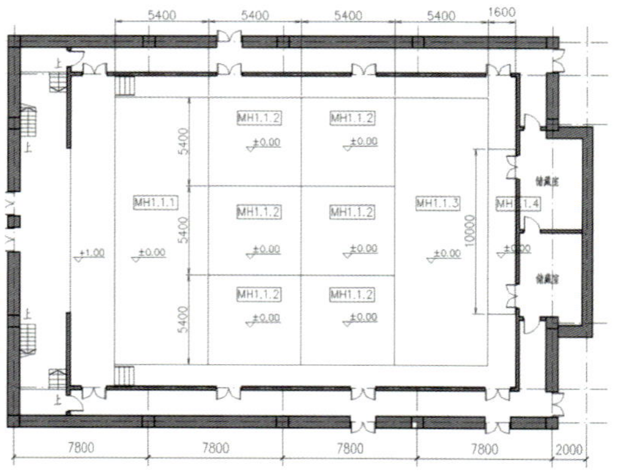
5400
5400
5400
5400
1600
MH1.1.2
MH1.1.2
MH1.1.1
MH1.1.2
MH1.1.2
MH1.1.3
MH1.1.4
MH1.1.2
MH1.1.2
±0.00
+1.00
10000
7800
7800
7800
7800
2000

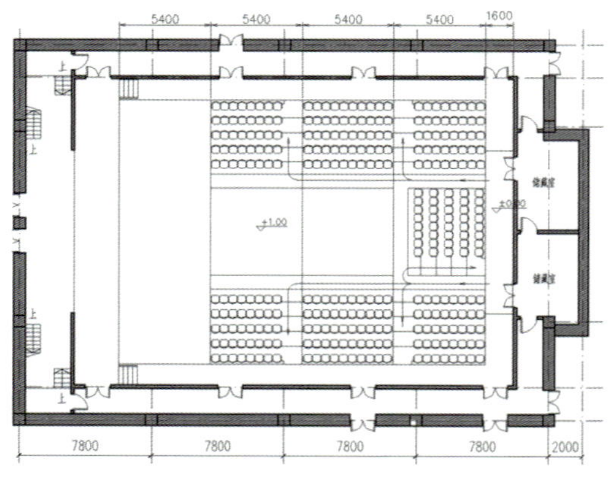
5400
5400
5400
5400
1600
+1.00
±0.00
7800
7800
7800
7800
2000

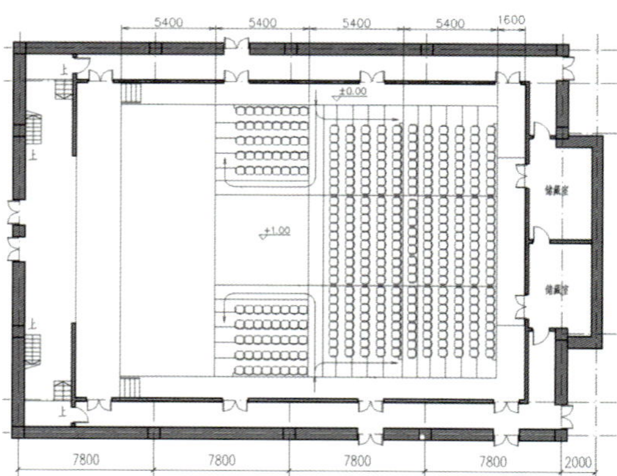
5400
5400
5400
5400
1600
±0.00
+1.00
7800
7800
7800
7800
2000

EXIT

Baishui Stockade Hot Spring Resort Planning and Design

白水寨温泉度假村规划设计

设计单位：美国PURE建筑师事务所
面积：100 830 m²
业主：广州海景集团
时间：2009年12月

Design firm: PURE ARCHITECTURE
Size: 100 830 m²
Client: Guangzhou Haijing Group
Design date: Dec, 2009

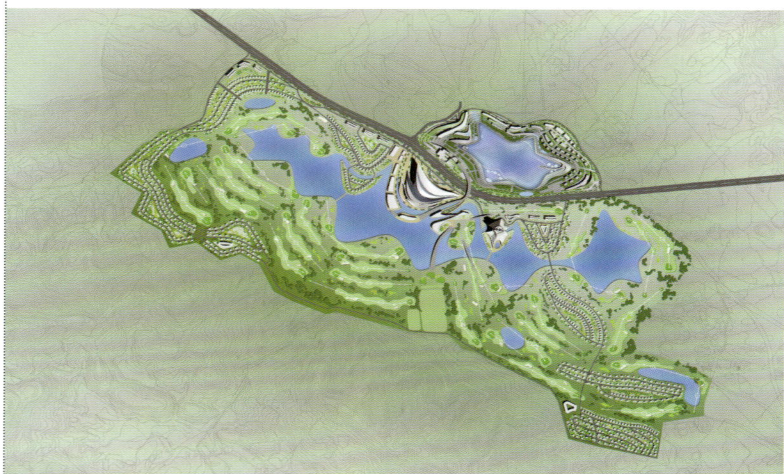

Shi Guoping, RA, LEED AP
施国平 RA, LEED AP

Huang Xiaojiang,BArch, MArch, SBA
黄晓江 BArch, MArch, SBA

PURE

PURE ARCHITECTURE 美国PURE建筑师事务所

公司简介

PURE于2002年创建于美国加利福尼亚州洛杉矶市，2007年在上海创建了中国分部——上海纯粹建筑设计有限公司。PURE是中国将先进计算机技术应用到建筑设计上的领军团队之一。我们在设计中致力于通过激发人在空间中的运动将建筑、景观与城市紧密地结合在一起，来创造一个动态、关联的居住生活环境。

具有东西方结合的教育和职业经历使得PURE一方面关注全球化背景下当代建筑所面临的新挑战，以及日益更新的计算机技术对当代生活的影响；另一方面关注本土文化，研究中国大规模城市化进程中所出现的种种城市与空间问题。我们认真对待每一个项目，积极配合业主实现项目最大价值，同时提高中国环境品质并共同创造面向未来的当代中国建筑。

PURE在旅游休闲、商业娱乐综合体、文化、地标、生态节能和城市更新等项目类型上积累了丰富的经验；服务的客户包括多个国内外政府、地产开发机构和文化产业机构。

施国平，2001年毕业于洛杉矶加利福尼亚大学并获得建筑学硕士学位。在校期间，他从师于在电子建筑设计领域著名的Greg Lynn教授，并被选拔参与Bernard Tschumi教授的工作室。

他曾先后工作于北京的马达思班事务所，洛杉矶的Gensler和Jerde等事务所。2002年，他在洛杉矶领导创办了PURE建筑师事务所，并于2007年在上海成立中国分部。他参与并赢得了多个国际设计竞赛一等奖，包括上海文化公园概念设计竞赛，武汉汉江两岸总体规划设计竞赛，珠海林雨洞艺术社区设计竞赛（2008年建成）等。

他曾分别在多所大学讲座，并在《时代建筑》、《城市建筑》、《南方建筑》、《O2》等杂志发表文章。PURE的建筑作品多次在中美两地展出，包括2004年UCLA校友优秀作品展和2007年UCLA的Uncontested作品展。PURE的艺术装置《公共空间》参加了2007年大声展，艺术装置《动画椅的第二人生》参加了2007年深圳与香港城市与建筑双年展，以及2008年北京建筑艺术双年展。

黄晓江，在深圳大学学习并获得建筑学学士学位，之后在伦敦的AADRL获得建筑学硕士学位。他拥有荷兰建筑师资质认可，在2009年成为美国PURE建筑师事务所合伙人之前，他先后在英国的Building Design Partnership和Hadfield Cawkwell Davidson建筑师事务所工作，在商业建筑、城市综合利用开发项目和总体规划设计上都有丰富的实践经验，同时也获得多个建筑竞赛奖项，其中帮助Building Design Partnership赢得英国伯明翰新伊丽莎白综合医院规划和设计竞赛，入围AJ/Urban Splash举办的Tribeca国际建筑设计竞赛。他的设计作品曾刊登于多本专业杂志，包括Architect’s Journal（英国）和建筑业导报（中国）。他还编写了《互动环境设计与研究》一书，并于2004年由中国建筑工业出版社翻译出版。2006年，他被上海《室内设计师》杂志邀请成为海外编委。

CHANEL
HERMES

Company Profile

PURE was founded in Los Angeles, California, 2002 and in 2007, its China studio was opened in Shanghai. PURE is one of the leading practices in China to apply advanced computer technology in architectural design. It dedicates to creating a dynamic and related living environment and reexamining contemporary architectural design in China which is undergoing a dramatic urbanization in a very short period of time. We fully devote ourselves to every project opportunity, working together with the clients to reach their ultimate goals, to improve the quality of our environment, and to create futuristic Chinese architecture.

Huang Xiaojiang studied architecture and received his Bachelor degree of Architecture in Shenzhen University. He continued his study and received Master degree of Architecture in Architectural Association Design Research Laboratory (AADRL) in London. He is a qualified architect in the Netherlands. Before joining in PURE as a partner in 2009, he had worked for several award winning practices, including Building Design Partnership, Hadfield Cawkwell Davidson in the UK where he gained intensive experience in retail sector, mixed-use development and master planning, and as a team member (BDP) to win Queen Elizabeth Hospital in Birmingham and his design work TriCUBE shortlisted for Architect's Journal/Urban Splash Tribeca international competition.

He is also the main author of Design and Research on Responsive Environment, which has been translated into Chinese and published by China Architectural Industry Publisher in 2004. In 2006, he was invited as a member of the editorial board for Interior Designer magazine in Shanghai.

Shi Guoping graduated from Department of Architecture and Urban Design, University of California in 2001 with a Master's Degree in Architecture. In school, he studied under Professor Greg Lynn and was chosen to participate in Bernard Tschumi's workshop.
He has worked in Beijing at MADA s.p.a.m, and in Los Angeles at Gensler and Jerde architectural offices. He co-founded PURE Design Lab in Los Angeles in 2002, and opened PURE's China office in Shanghai four years later. During his professional career, he has led to win numerous international design competitions, including Shanghai Cultural Park, Wuhan Han Riverfront Master Plan, Zhuhai Forest Creek Art Community (to be finished in 2008), etc.
He has given lectures in Hunan University and Shenzhen University, and written articles for Time Architecture, Urban Architecture, South Architecture, O2, etc. PURE's work has been exhibited internationally, including the 2004 and 2007 UCLA Selected Alumni Exhibition, the 2007 Get It Louder Exhibition, the 2007 Shenzhen and HongKong Architecture and Urbanism Biennale, and the 2008 Beijing Architecture Biennale.

心身、心灵、心智三位一体是人修身养性的最高境界。在繁杂快速的城市生活中，这种生活品质已经缺失。星湖湾，将为顾客重拾这种身心的自我平衡。

首先我们合理利用基地不可复制的自然与建筑景观最大化资源优势，创造一个情景交融的世外桃源。原有的池塘被改造成一个100 000 m^{2}的海星状湖面，沿1 500 m湖岸新规划的浅水区为游客提供了与自然接近的最佳媒介。在六个湾处形成一系列的视觉通廊，让白水寨瀑布、卧佛山等成为项目背景。其次我们通过突出强调产品的差异性最大化项目经济价值，创造一个地标性的度假中心。

完备的度假产品包括艺术中心、五星级酒店、温泉公寓、湖滨别墅、高尚spa中心与运动休闲天地，为多样化的顾客层服务，它们包括：

城市富有阶层的投资置业

城市家庭的假日天堂

企业团体的休闲会议中心

年轻一代的喜庆殿堂

艺术创作者与爱好者的交流天地

The harmony between body, soul and mind, the three essentials of human beings, is the ultimate goal of our life. The harmony, however, has been weakened and disappeared gradually within the stressful urban complex. The Star Bay will provide an inclusive environment for our customers to rebuild the spiritual, mental and physical harmony. First, the combination of the spectacular landscape features forms the surrounding and the proposed elegant architectural elements, creates a romantic, energetic and celebrated Xanadu.

The existing pond is transformed into a 100 000 m^2 starfish like lake – Star Lake, comprising a shallow water area with 1 500 meter long shore. There are six visual corridors to each of the six star bays to allow both Baishuizhai Waterfall and Wofo Mountains being part of landscape for the Star Bay Resort. Secondly, the variations of the proposed services from the design scheme maximize the value of the project financially within the current market. The Star Bay Resort is an ideal and iconic resort with a wow effect, including an Art Centre, A Five-star Hotel, Service Apartments, Lakeside Villas, Spa Centre and an open sports park. The complex is designed to attract all different customers, such as investments from middle class, holiday homes for families, conference center for corporations, wedding venues and honey moon destination for young couples.

Kunshan East Town Urban Planning & Design

昆山东部新城城市规划与设计

设计单位：美国PURE建筑师事务所
内容：城市规划与设计
业主：昆山市经济开发区规划局
面积：880公顷
时间：2009年1月至今

Design firm: Pure Architecture
Program: Urban Planning and Design
Client: Kunshan ETDZ Planning Bureau
Area: 880 Hectors
Design date: Jan., 2009-Current

我们试图将昆山东部新城建设成一个极具“乐活”气质的新江南水城，在上海国际化大都市和苏杭传统江南水乡文化中探索昆山自身的个性特色。“水”“城”“园”融为一体是东部新城的核心规划理念，并建设成昆山的新经济，新引擎，新城市，新中心，创造新江南园林城市的典范：水在城中，城在水滨；园在城里，城在园中。基于东城得天独厚的夏驾河水系和发达的科技产业园区，东城在保持夏驾河的生态品质的同时，将主要城市功能沿河布置，以提升周边土地的整体价值和促进其开发与经营，为现有园区提供完善的城市功能，包括城市核心区地标五星级超高层酒店，生态度假园区，滨水商业园，行政文化园等。东西走向的滨水商业文化水街由夏驾河公园延伸至社区内部，每条街廊都具有独特功能和景观。由公交、水上巴士、BRT、轨道交通等构成的复合交通体系激活整个城市系统，打造出一个快乐、繁华、生态并具有诗意的现代服务型宜居城市。

Kunshan East New Town is a newly developed satellite town for Kunshan City. Our proposal is to establish the new town as a typical New Canal Town with 'LOHAS' sustainable life style. East New Town also looks for a unique identity in terms of economic and urban morphology from separate herself to other cities within the Yangtze River Delta area, such as Shanghai, Hangzhou. On the base of the well developed technology-industry park and the natural feature Xiajiahe River Park within the new town, a 4-tier green park and 8 canal streets compose a continucus urban park system, which reaches to all major functional districts and communities. An integrated public transportation system, including shuttle bus, subway, water bus and BRT, connects the new town to Kunshan city center and other surrounding cities.

中央公园——夏驾河和运动公园

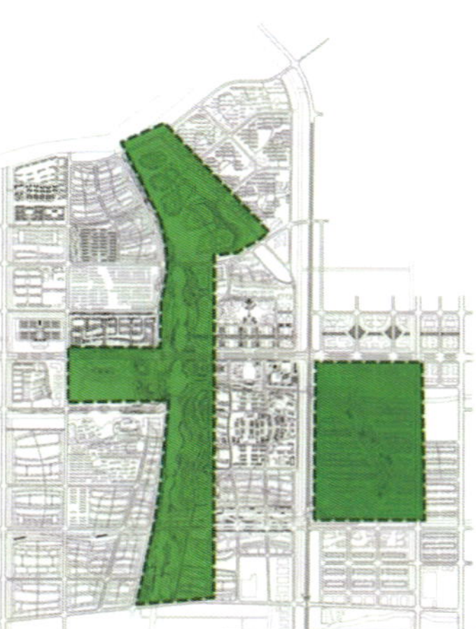

边界公园——滨水商住社区公园

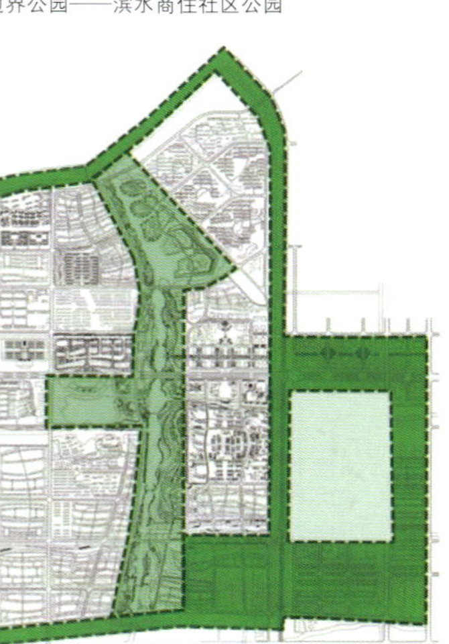

联系公园——滨水商业文化公园

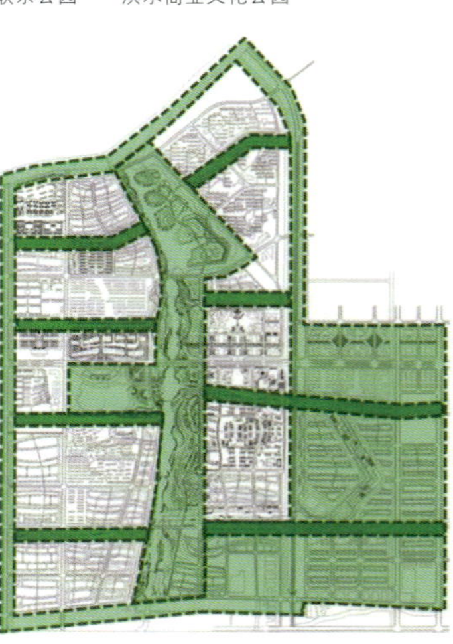

渗透公园——社区公共休闲公园

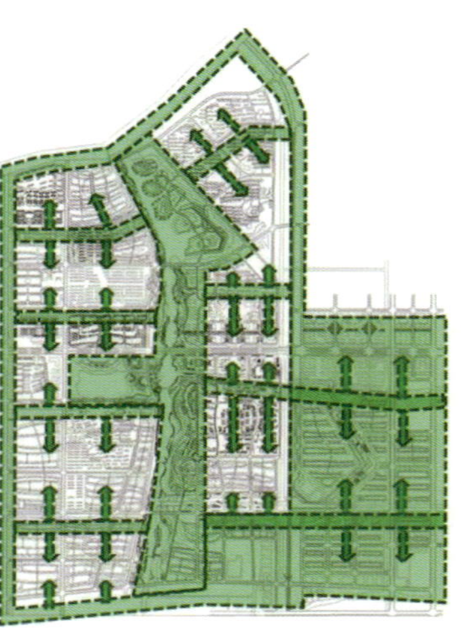

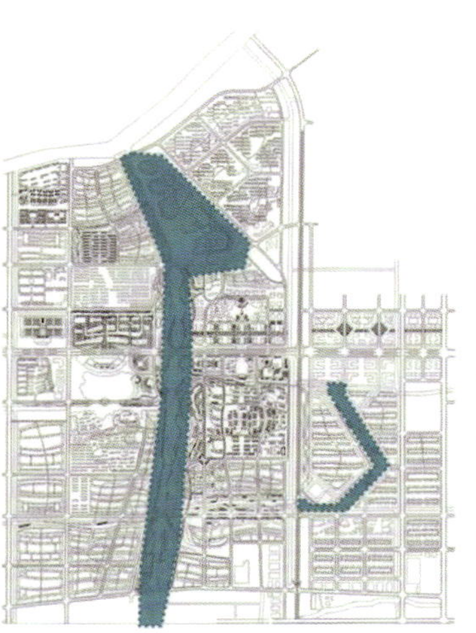

夏驾河主体水系——城市水上公园

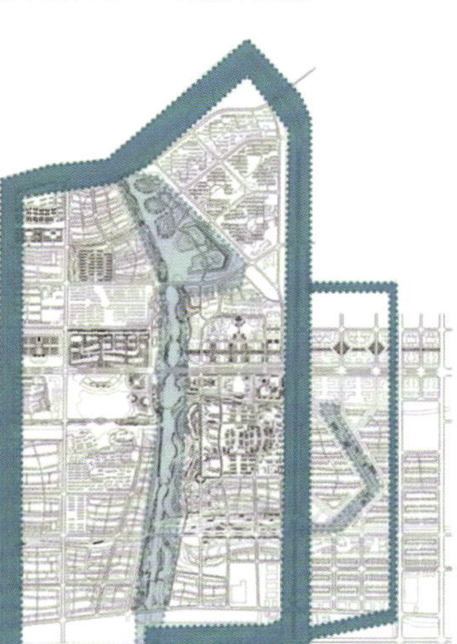

城市边界水系——环城滨水景观带

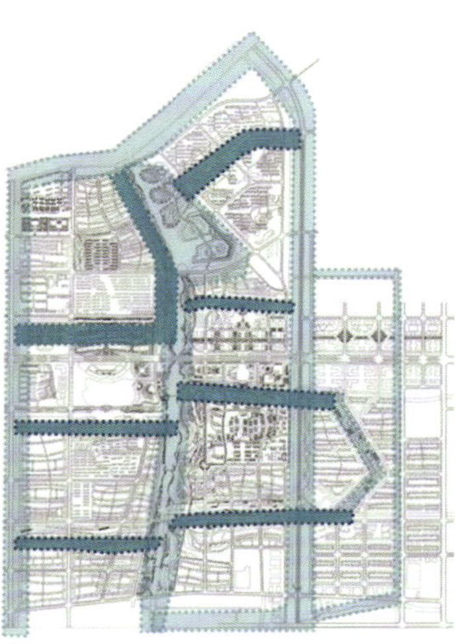

城市水街——风情文化水街

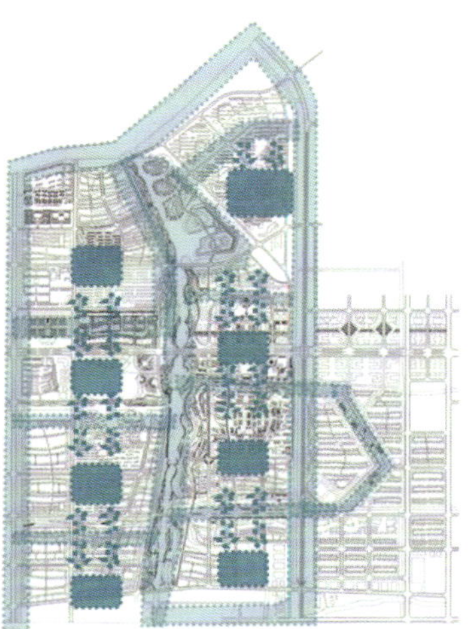

组团水景——社区特色水文化

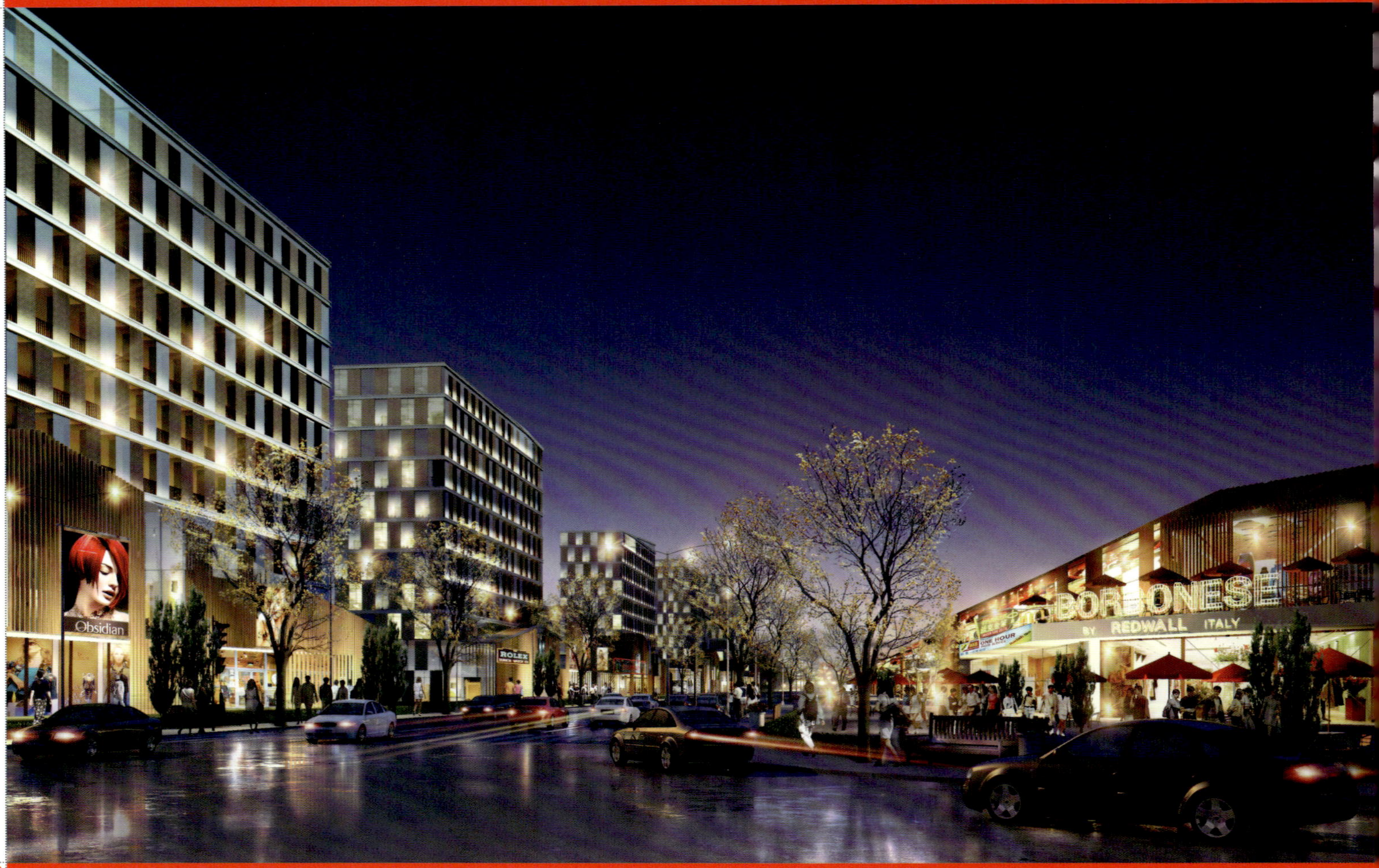
Obsidian
ROLEX
BORBONESE
BY REDWALL ITALY

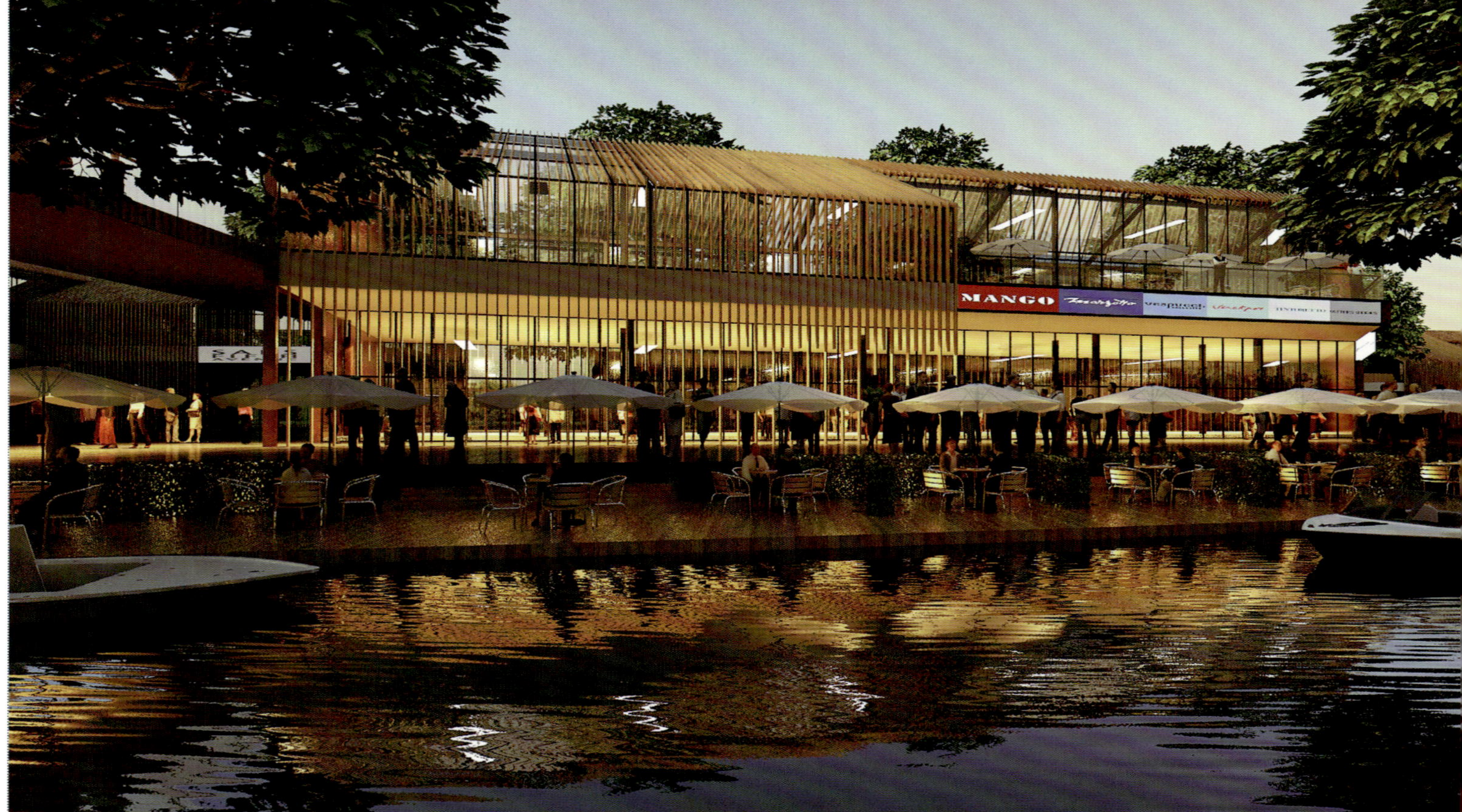

MANGO

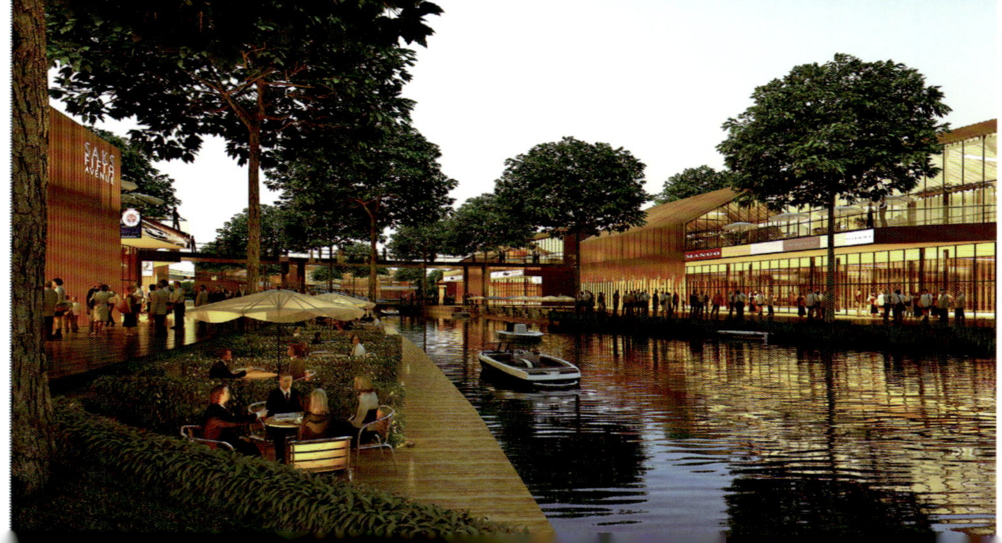

中央开放空间——夏驾河和运动公园

边界开放空间——边界绿地及水系统

水街开放空间——滨水商业娱乐系统

渗透开放空间——社区公共休闲系统

Lihu Lake Observation Tower

无锡蠡湖宝界山观光塔

设计单位：美国PURE建筑师事务所
业主：无锡市政府
面积：2 000 m^2
时间：2008年12月–2009年1月
合作方：中联程泰宁建筑师事务所

Design firm: Pure Architecture
Program: Observation Tower
Clients: Wuxi Municipal Government
Area: 2 000 m^2
Design date: Dec., 2008–Jan., 2009
Collaborator: ACCTN

宝界山位于太湖第一名胜鼋头渚之中，在其顶峰建立的这个观光塔不仅可以观赏太湖壮阔而优美的自然景观，而且其本身应该变成太湖景观的一个新标志物。我们以"太湖石"为设计源泉，建筑体形如太湖石，自然而充满活力；其内部空间的组织方式也依法太湖石，大大小小的孔洞既是交通空间，也是向外观赏景色的取景框，同时还最有效地保证建筑的热工通风效果。洞的密度与大小从下往上逐渐加大，反映出内部功能的变化。建筑提供两组路径，两种完全不同的人文体验。一组慢速的行走路径，步移景异，进入塔楼后通过环形楼梯拾级而上可以从不同的洞看到框景后的不同景色。一组快速的直达路径，经电梯到顶层观景平台，豁然开朗，一览众山小。

此外，停车场和盘山步道都采用有顶的金属网架遮盖方式，上覆盖攀藤植物，提供上山的林荫大道。同时，缝补山体伤疤，使从塔上俯瞰的视野一片葱郁盎然。盘山步道一侧设画廊，塔下一层有小型博物馆，可以陈设太湖风光主题的艺术展，使观景演绎为自然、人文双重景观的体验。

Baojie Moutain has the best view overlooking the gorgeous Taihu Lake. Located on the top of the mountain, this observation tower will not only provide visitors access to those views, but itself becomes a new landmark to be seen from the lake. The form of the tower resembles the porous Taihu Stones, which originates from this area. Those holes are not only where the circulation system penetrates, but also the viewing frames to look outside. The density of the openings rises from the bottom to the top, reflecting the program of the spaces inside. Visitors can reach the viewing deck on the top through two different paths. One circles up along the stairs located on the periphery of the building, where views change following the movement of body. Another one is the direct access through the vertical elevator, providing dramatic viewing experience.

The pathway from the parking lot to the tower is covered with plants growing from the metal mesh structure. It provides shade to the visitors, and more green while they look down from the top. There are some outdoor galleries along the pathway, leading to the museum located on the podium of the main building.

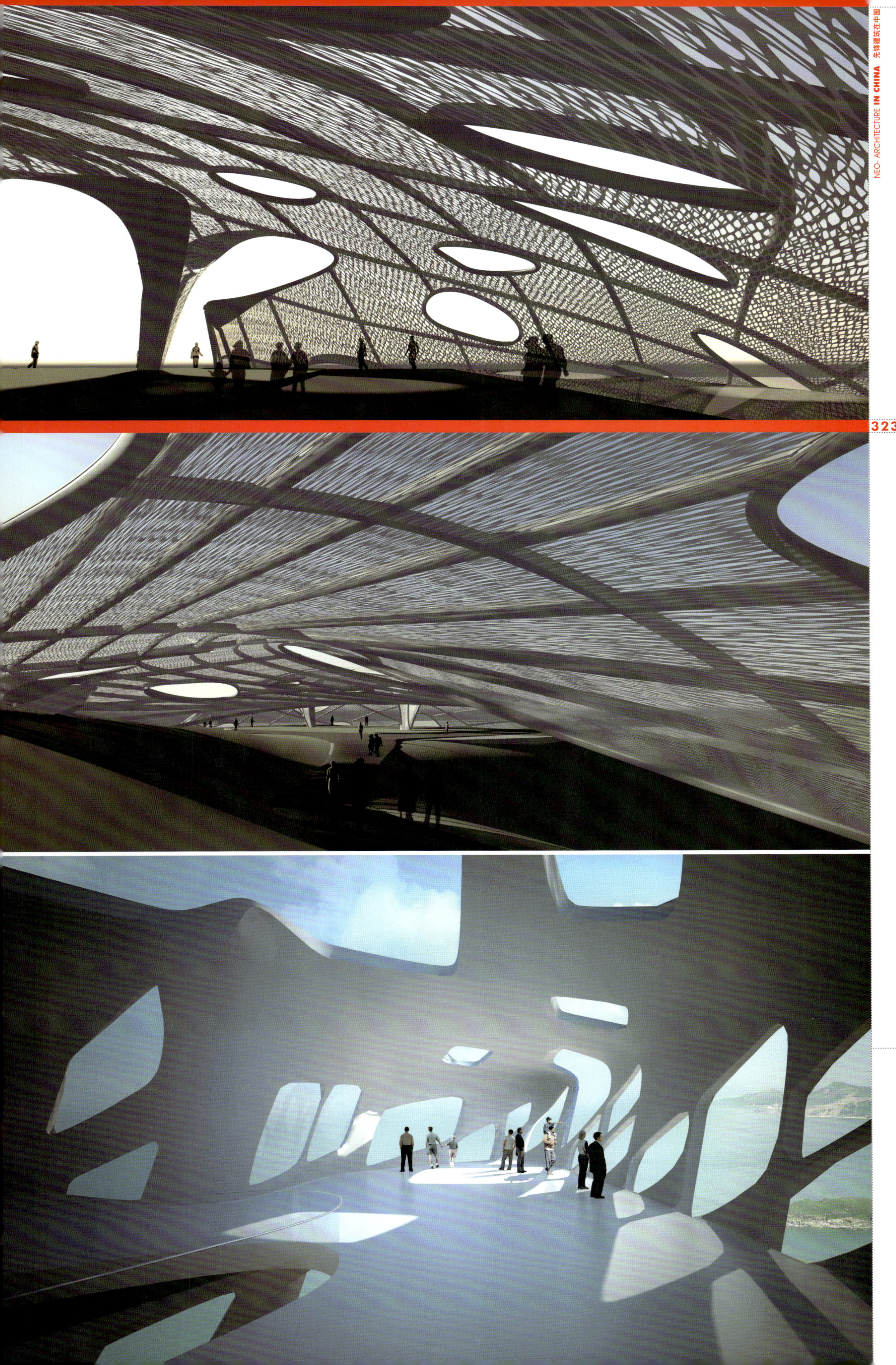

Jiangyin Tourism Bureau Office Building

江阴园林旅游局办公楼设计

设计单位：美国PURE建筑师事务所
时间：2009年1月–2009年2月

Design firm: PURE ARCHITECTURE
Time: Jan., 2009–Feb., 2009

业主是园林旅游局，场地又位于一个城市公园内，我们设想这个办公楼建成之后不仅能够与现有的公园环境融为一体，而且能够成为其中新的景点，体现出业主部门建设与美化城市景观的工作特点。我们把所有的空间分成三个部分，两个独立的办公部门分别设计成两栋板式办公楼，其他的公共部分则都安排在一个覆土式的场地建筑里，它们既独立又联系。平缓的公共部分绿色屋顶可以让公园游人自由地漫步穿行，既保证了公园空间的完整性，又增加公园观景的空间维度。而板式办公楼的外墙则采用印花玻璃幕墙，除了保证办公空间的私密性之外，植物的图案以及它对周围自然环境的映射使建筑成为公园及对面河流所聚焦的新"人造景观"。

This proposed office building for the Jiangyin Park Management and Tourism Bureau is located in a public park along a river. It should become an organic element of the surrounding landscape. The building complex has two rectangular glass boxes facing to the river, with office spaces for two different departments. All other public programs are arranged in a landform base covered with grass. Its gradual slope provides park visitors easy access across the roof of the building without interruption. The skins of the office building are etched with plant textures, not only to provide privacy to the space, but also to create focus points of the new man-made landscape.

The New Mass Art Center of ChongQing

重庆市群众艺术馆新馆

设计单位：重庆市设计院
主创建筑师：钟洛克、胡晓燕、何凌峰、杨洋
设计时间：2009年
基地面积：3 740 m²
建筑面积：21 369 m²
绿化率：10%
容积率：1.2

Design firm: Chongqing Architecture Design Instute Of China
Lead designer: Zhong Luoke, Hu Xiaoyan, He Lingfeng, Yangyang
Design date: 2009
Site area: 3 740 m²
Building area: 21 369 m²
Green percentage: 10%
Volume fraction: 1.2

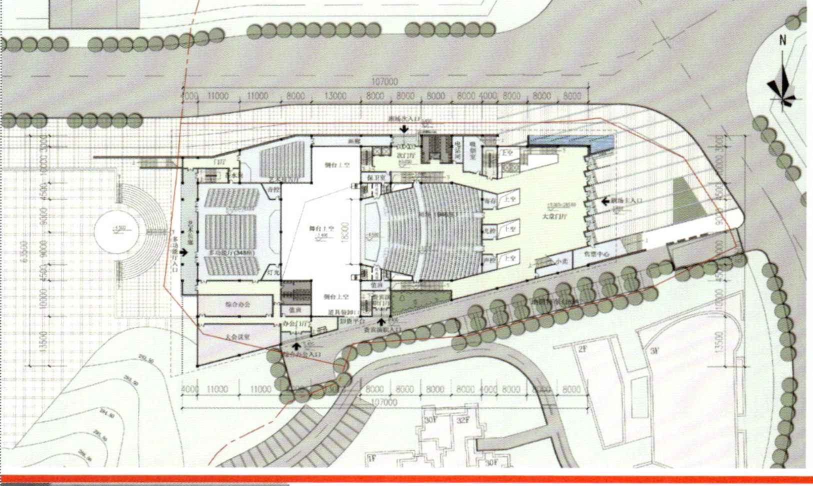

Zhong Luoke
Chongqing Architecture Design Instute Of China/director of A5 studio

钟洛克
重庆市设计院　建筑院副总建筑师/A-5工作室主持人

简历
1993年9月–1997年7月就读青岛理工大学建筑工程学院建筑系
1997年8月–2006年3月重庆市设计院第二建筑分院任副主任建筑师
2006年3月–2007年3月重庆市设计院方案创作所任所长
2007年9月–2009年5月就读重庆大学房地产管理学院房地产MBA
2007年3月–2009年5月重庆市设计院第五建筑分院任院长及建筑院副总建筑师
2009年5月至今重庆市设计院建筑院副总建筑师及A–5工作室任主持人

主要工程设计作品
四川美术学院实验实习楼(已建成并投入使用)
南充市行政办公楼一号楼(已建成并投入使用)
重庆工商大学厚德楼(已建成并投入使用)
重庆市委礼堂改造(已建成并投入使用)
重庆国际信托投资有限公司办公楼(已建成并投入使用)
和记黄浦重庆北部新区项目
重庆红鼎公寓(已建成并投入使用)
重庆市红岛大酒店(五星级酒店)
庆金融商贸广场（超高层双塔）
重庆市上清寺开发广场（超高层双塔）
重庆海棠晓月滨江温泉大酒店（75层）
重庆中华新城(已建成并投入使用)
重庆上海城二期C区(已建成并投入使用)
重庆市人民广场三期及三峡博物馆
重庆海尔.海语江山住宅小区(在建高档社区)
云南省昆明市千益丰住宅小区(在建高档社区)
重庆软件园一期(在建科技园区)
北京渔阳饭店(五星级酒店、建成并投入使用)
重庆市政府办公楼(方案设计中)
重庆天和大厦(80层超高层写字楼及五星级酒店，方案设计中)
重庆市教委办公楼（在建中）
重庆市群众艺术馆新馆（国际投标入围）
重庆银行大厦（国际投标入围）

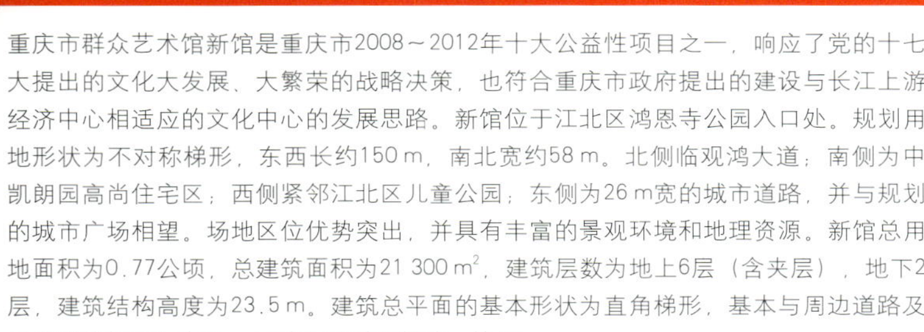

重庆市群众艺术馆新馆是重庆市2008～2012年十大公益性项目之一，响应了党的十七大提出的文化大发展、大繁荣的战略决策，也符合重庆市政府提出的建设与长江上游经济中心相适应的文化中心的发展思路。新馆位于江北区鸿恩寺公园入口处。规划用地形状为不对称梯形，东西长约150 m，南北宽约58 m。北侧临观鸿大道；南侧为中凯朗园高尚住宅区；西侧紧邻江北区儿童公园；东侧为26 m宽的城市道路，并与规划的城市广场相望。场地区位优势突出，并具有丰富的景观环境和地理资源。新馆总用地面积为0.77公顷，总建筑面积为21 300 m^2，建筑层数为地上6层（含夹层），地下2层，建筑结构高度为23.5 m。建筑总平面的基本形状为直角梯形，基本与周边道路及用地形状相平行布置，与城市关系取得统一协调。

新馆方案设计的总体理念：

1 地域特色——巴山夜雨

本方案将建筑形体融入到整个基地环境中，起伏的山体造型象征重庆的“巴山”；建筑立面细部设计则隐喻了重庆的“夜雨”，设计运用通透的大面积玻璃幕墙外贴竖向的磨砂玻璃条模拟朦胧的山中雨景，也体现出夜雨缠绵、山色朦胧的意境。

2 文化传承——戏台旧梦

完整大气且出挑深远的大坡屋面则体现了巴渝传统老戏台建筑的坡屋顶特色，在室内外观演空间上借鉴了传统戏台的造型及空间特色，设计了下沉式广场观演空间和室外屋顶观演空间等。

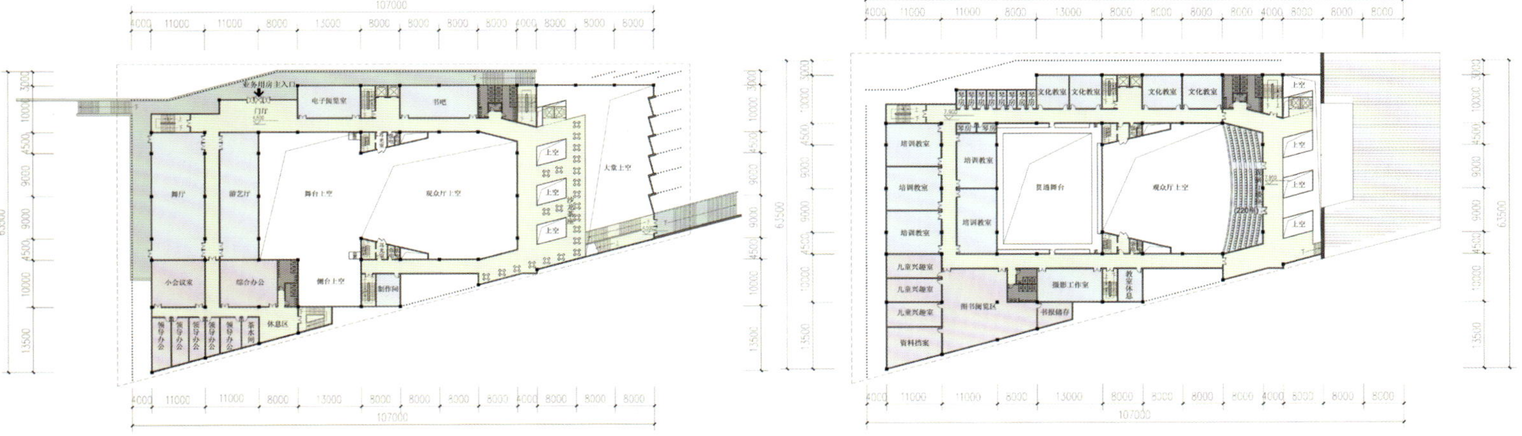

Chief introduction

Studied in the Department of Achitecture in Qingdao University of Science and Technology from 1993 to 1997.

Assistant master architect of the second branch of Chongqing Institution of Building Design from 1997 to 2006.

Superintendent of Creational Bureau Office of Chongqing Institution of Building Design.

Attend MBA School in College of Real Easte Management of Chongqing University from 2007 to 2009.

The dean of the 5th Branch of Chongqing Institution of Building Design and the assistant architect of the institution.

Master of A5 Studio and assistant master architect of Chongqing Architecture Design Instute Of China.

Main projects

Experiment and Practice building of Sichuan Art College (built and in use)

No.1 administrative office building of Nanchong City (built and in use)

Houde Building of Chongqing Industrial and Commercial Universtiy(built and in use)

Auditorium rebuilt of Chongqing Municipal Party Committee (built and in use)

Office building of Chongqing International Trust & Investment Co. Ltd. (built and in use)

project of Hutchison Whampoa Co., Ltd in the new nothern district

Hongding apartment in Chongqing (built and in use)

Hongdao Hotel in Chongqing (5-star hotel)

Chongqing square of Financial and Business (twin towers of super hige-rise building)

Chongqing development square of Shangqingsi (twin towers of super hige-rise building)

Chongqing Haitang Xiaoyue and spring Hotel (75 floors)

Chongqing China new city (built and in use)

C district of the second period of Shanghai city in Chongqing (built and in use)

the third stage of People Square and The Three Gorges Mesume in Chongqing

Haier and Haiyu Residence in Chongqing (top grade residential community under construction)

Kunming Qianyifeng Residence of Yunnan Province (top grade residential community under construction)

the first stage of Chongqing Software Park (science park under construction)

Yuyang Hotel in Beijing (built and in use)

official building of Chongqing Municipal Goverment (in design)

Chongqing Tianhe Masion (office building of super high-rise building for 80 floors, 5-star hotel, in designing)

office building of education bureau of Chongqing (under construction)

The New Mass Art Center of ChongQing (be shortlisted for international bid)

Chongqing Bank Masion (be shortlisted for international bid)

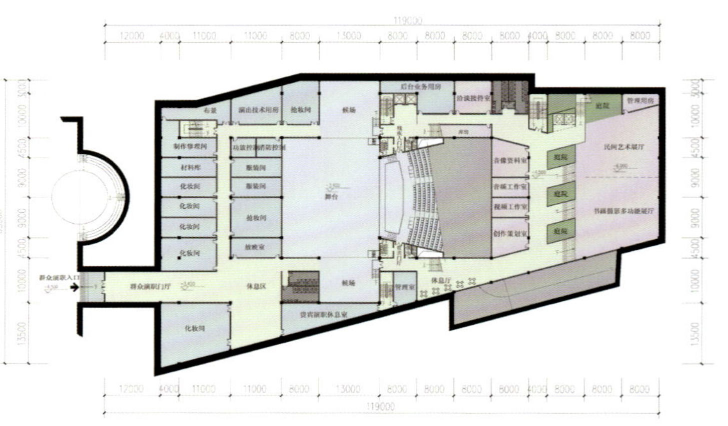

3 历史文脉

——竹

将竹简化成竖向钢柱有规则地排列在建筑的三个主要外立面上，既起到遮阳的作用，又形成统一、简洁的外立面效果和光影斑驳的柱廊空间。

——瓦

建筑的坡屋面上细的条梁是传统建筑屋面瓦的抽象而来，丰富了建筑的第五立面。

——门

在剧场主入口的地方，利用排列整齐的成组的立柱，塑造了川东民居里推开的木板门的意境，吸引人们的进入。

重庆市群众艺术馆新馆将成为设施完备、功能齐全、特色突出、西部领先、全国一流的现代综合性文化艺术活动中心；将成为展现巴渝地区浓厚的地域文化特征和历史文化特色的重要文化窗口；将成为重庆市又一标志性的公共文化建筑。

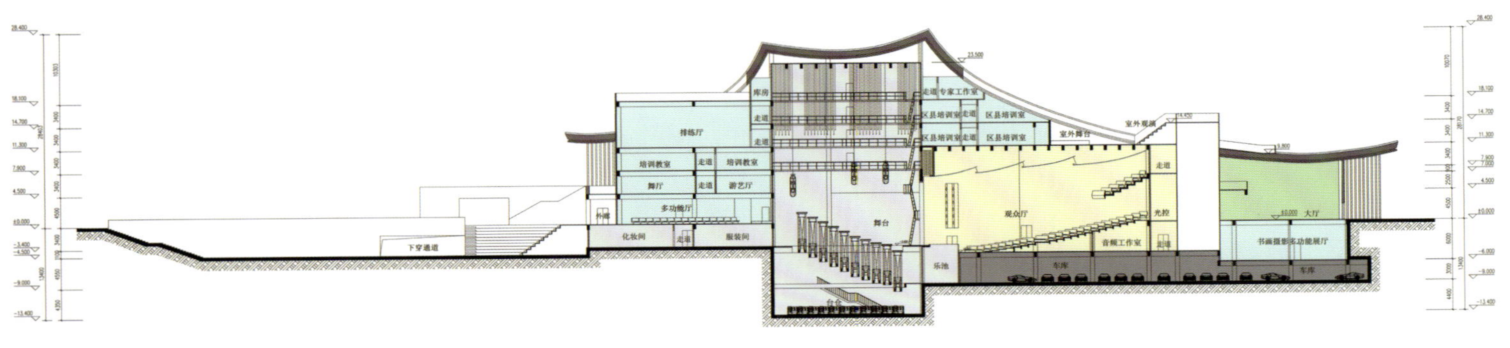

The New Mass Art Center of Chongqing is one of ten commonweal projects in 2008—2012 of the city, echoing the strategy of "culture development and prosperous" proposed in the 17th congress of CPC, corresponding to the development thoughts of "building cultural center suitable for economic center of the upper reaches of Yangtze River."

The new hall is located in the entrance of Hongen Temple in the northern district. The site is a dissymmetry trapezia. The length from east to west is 150 meters, and the width from south to north is 58 m. Guanhong Avenue is on the north of the site and Zhonglang top grade residence on the south. The western part is closed to Children Park and the eastern of the site is urban street of 26m width, towards which is urban square. The location has outstanding advantage and possess abundant landscape and geographical merits. The overall area of the site is 0.77 ha, and the overall building area is 21 300 square meters. 6 floors are over ground and 2 underground. The structural height is 23.5 m. The basic shape of the building is trapezia of right-angle, which is laid out parallel with the road and site shape, having the harmony relation with the city.

Overall concept for the new art center

Local character – "Ba Mountain and Night Rain"

The building form is based on and conformable to the whole site environment in this program. The undulating shapes as mountains symbolize the "Ba Mountain" of Chongqing, while the derailed design of the facade show a metaphor for "Night Rain". A large area of clear glass wall pasted with vertical frosted glass pieces is used to simulate misty raining scenery in mountains, by which a touching and gleaming atmosphere of the mountain and night-rain would be incarnated.

Cultural heritage

– Old dream about the Stage

The large sloping roof with complete structure and far overhang is a kind of traditional character as old stage buildings of Bayu. Descented and outdoor performance spaces cre planned, which has used the experience of traditional stage form and space features.

Historical context

– The Bamboo

Vertical steel columns which imitate the form of bamboo are regularly arranged in the three main facades of the building, not only to shade the sunlight, but also to form a united and pithy facade effect and mottled portico space.

– The Tile

The thin sloping roof beams of building are abstracted from the tradition architecture tile, which enrich the building's fifth facade.

– The Door

In main entrance of theater, some rows of columns are used to express a conception as opened wooden-door in the folk house of East Chuan District, which would encourage people to enter.

The New Mass Art Center of Chongqing will become an integrated modern cultural art center which has complete equipment and prominent function. It would be a special window to Bayu district for its local history and traditional culture display, and a new cultural landmark of Chongqing.

Chongqing Bank Building

重庆银行大厦

设计单位：重庆市设计院
主创建筑师：钟洛克 、王练、胡晓燕、何凌峰、杨洋
设计时间：2009年12月
基地面积：4 463 m^2
建筑面积：110 000 m^2
绿化率：14.7%
容积率：7.97

Design firm: Chongqing Architecture Design Instute Of China
Lead designer: Zhong Luoke, Wang Lian, Hu Xiaoyan, He Lingfeng, Yangyang
Design date: 2009
Site area: 4 463 m^2
Building area: 110 000 m^2
Green percentage: 14.7%
Volume fraction: 7.97

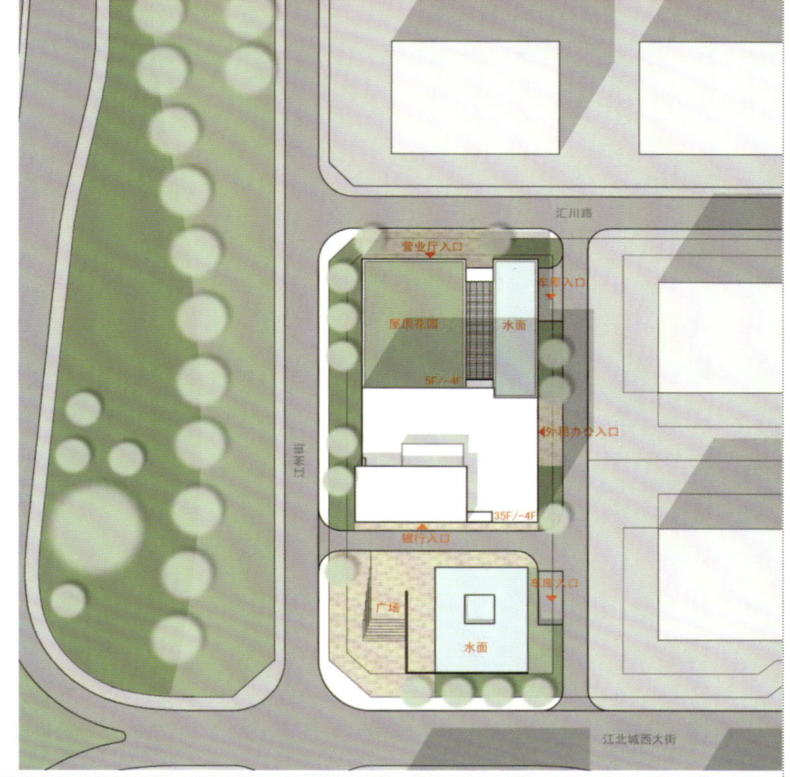

重庆银行大厦位于重庆江北城中央商务区A04—1地块，是重庆银行总部及其职能管理部门的办公大厦。

本项目位于黄花园大桥北桥头，是进入江北城中央商务区的门户地段，项目用地位于江北城西大街路北，汇川路南，江州街东，占地约1公倾，地块呈规整矩形，南北长约140 m，东西宽约70 m。地块内地形为缓坡，东北角地势较高，西南角地势较低，相对高差约6 m。周边城市路网均已完成，交通便利。

总体理念

1. 地域特色——山 河流 峡谷

重庆这一商业港口城市是我国人口最多的城市之一，坐落于云贵高原的边上，由长江上游段与嘉陵江两江汇聚分割而成。由于其富有传奇色彩的山脉，峡谷等地貌，得名“山城”。

这些富有明显地域特征的山脉，河流，峡谷，给本案设计概念提供了丰富的灵感：塔楼体量的错动，悬挑隐喻重庆高低错落的山脉；贯穿数层的竖向空中花园犹如重山中叠落的溪流；横向转折的空中阳台更类似山腰的青松；整个建筑俨然一幅饱含对重庆充满热爱的山水画。

2. 行业特质与文化传承

古币

结合重庆银行大厦的行业特质，我们联想到我国源远流长的古钱币文化。从商代的贝币、战国的刀币、布币，秦代的方孔圆钱，到清末的机制币，在这些数以万种千姿百态的钱币中，我们挑选出“莽币”这一无论从外形设计，还是币面书法艺术都达到了非常完美高度的古币作为设计模本，提炼、抽象为我们的外立面幕墙的单元，用现代的建筑语言，将行业特质与文化传承无缝连接。

聚宝盆

在我国的民俗中，聚宝盆即为镇宅之宝，是财富的象征。“聚宝”即是善于敛财，这往往是与勤俭节约联系在一起的，只有这样才能使财富生生不息。而“水”更是我国儒道思想的精华：“上善”，“水利万物”。设计将此美好祝愿融进入口广场的设计中：一片近1 000 m^2的方形镜面水池，水缓缓流入下沉式庭院中，生生不息，周而复始。

3. 空中花园与城市阳台

设计将两层通高的空中花园植入平面中，意在改善办公内部微环境，丰富空间感受。同时结合城市阳台，屋顶花园的设置，充分利用外部和内部的景观资源。

重庆银行大厦设计大方，庄重；在设计细节上体现着项目的顶级品质和重庆银行的行业特质；室内办公空间舒适，大气；室内外交通便捷。大楼集创意性，标志性，寓意性，前瞻性，经济性于一身，成为构思独特，个性鲜明，内容丰富的行业精品建筑之一。

体量分析

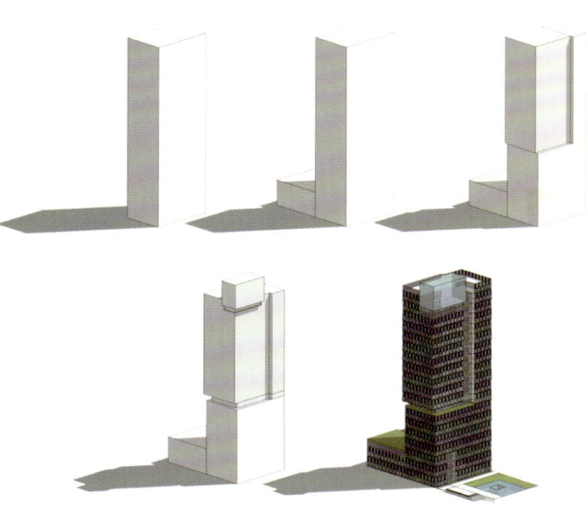

空间分析

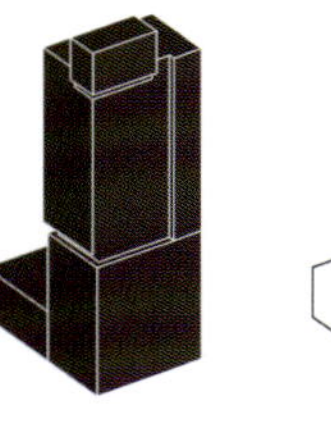

量体叠砌概念

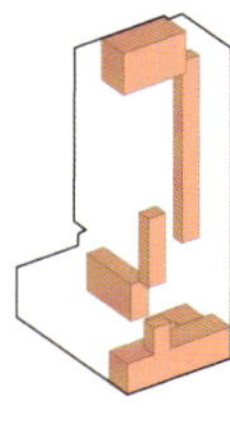

中庭空间概念

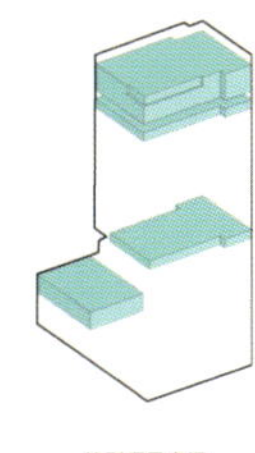

特别项目空间

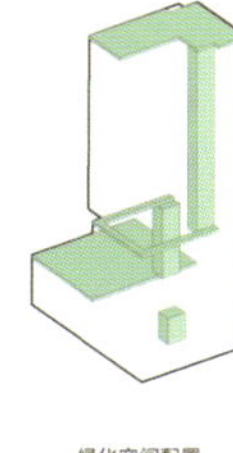

绿化空间配置

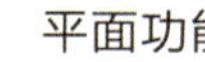

平面功能

地下四层至地下二层主要为设备用房和车库，可停放558辆车。

地下一层平面功能主要为网络机房，员工餐厅及厨房。通过一层大厅北侧的扶梯和和核心筒内电梯，可将人流引入到地下一层。员工餐厅为大空间，三面围合着一个种植翠竹的下沉庭院。入口广场的水面沿着玻璃缓缓流入下沉庭院中，与边庭的绿化景观相映成辉，共同打造生机盎然的地下空间。

一层平面主要功能分为四个部分，一是南侧银行大楼的主入口大厅及展厅；第二部分为东侧外租办公区的门厅，可直接通过大台阶上到二层的带状中庭；第三部分为部分临时停车、卸货区及机房。

二层平面的主要功能为银行营业大厅及商务中心。两部分功能由一个通高四层的带状中庭联系起来，在带状中庭中布置了休闲咖啡茶座，植物及LED显示屏，可作为营业大厅的功能补充，形成互动。

三层平面的主要功能分为营业大厅办公和两个中型会议室。

四，五层平面为两层通高的多功能大会议厅，及中型，小型会议室，部分办公室。6层至15层为外租区办公楼，16至34层为银行自用办公楼，顶层（35层）为空中会所。

重庆银行大厦设计大方、庄重：在设计细节上体现着项目的顶级品质和重庆银行的行业特质；室内办公空间舒适，大气；室内外交通便捷。大楼集创意性、标志性、寓意性、前瞻性、经济性于一身，成为构思独特、个性鲜明、内容丰富的行业精品建筑之一。

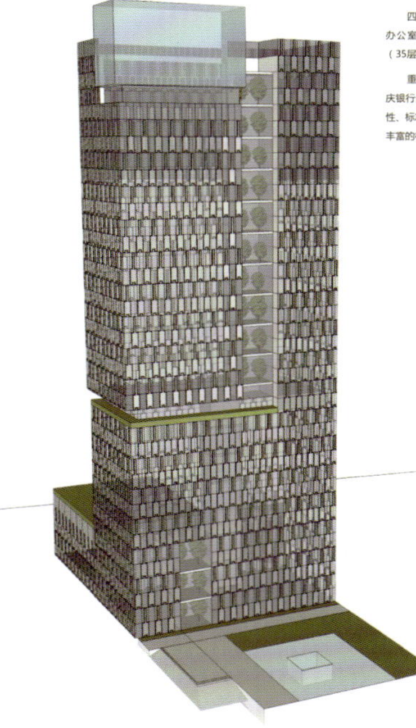

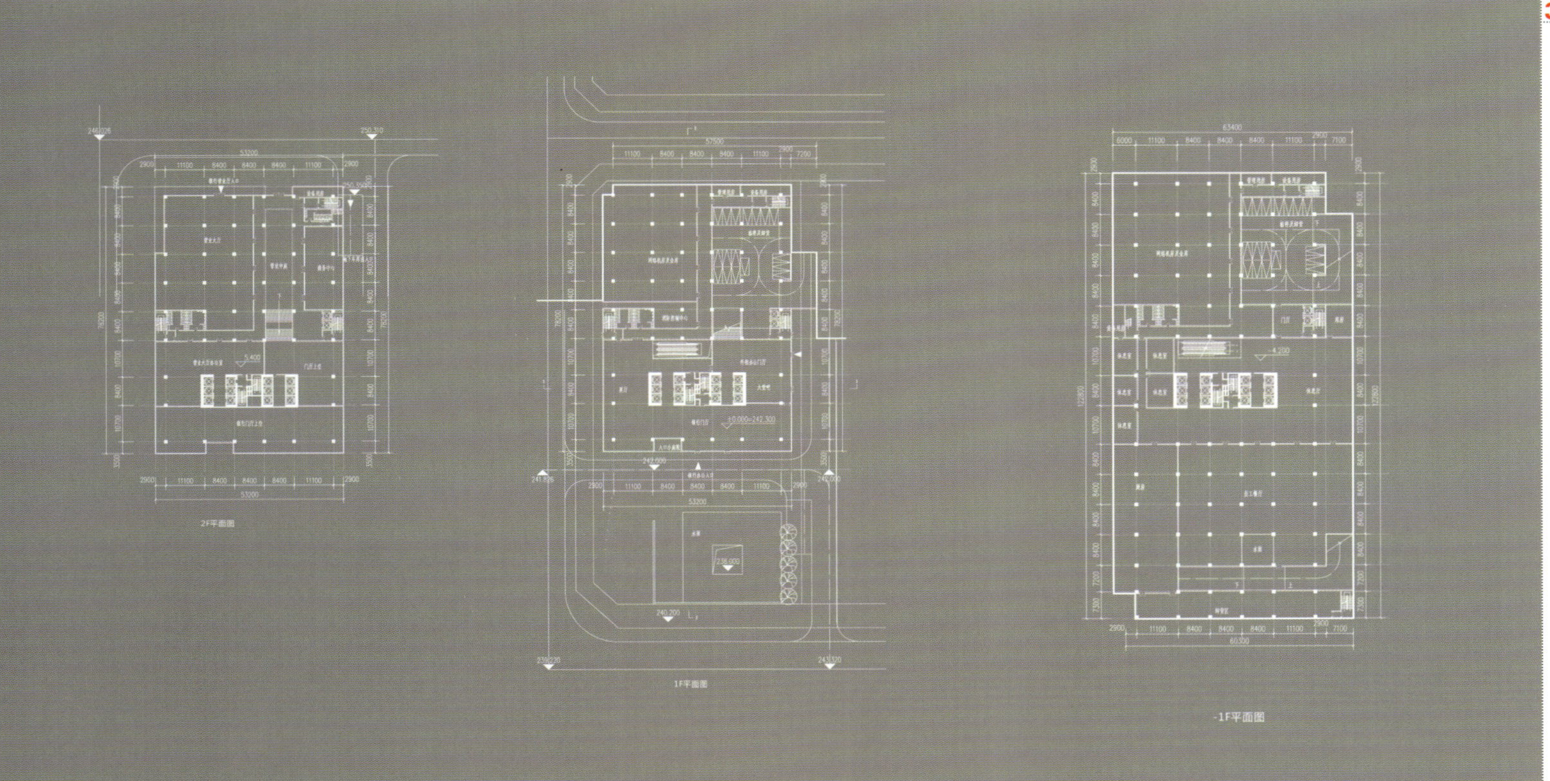

Chongqing Bank Building is located in A04-1 block of central commercial district in the north city of Chongqing. The building is the headquarter of Chongqing Bank and office building for its management affairs.

The project is located in the north side of Yellow Garden Bridge, which is the entrance point where to enter the north central commercial district. The project site is at north side of the west avenue in north city, and south side of Huichuan avenue, which has an area of 1 ha. The site is a rectangular block, with 140 m long from north to south and 700 m width from west to east. The land terrain is gentle, and northeast corner is 6m higher to the southwest corner. The transport network has been completed around project site, which would provide a convenient traffic.

Overall concept

Local character–Mountain, River and Canyon

As a commercial port city, Chongqing is one of the most populous cities in China. It is located in the edge of Yunnan Guizhou Plateau, and formed by the division of the upper reaches of the Yangtze River and Jialing River. The city is famous for its legendary mountains, canyons and other landforms, and is named as "Mountain-city".

These mountains, rivers and canyons with significant geographical features have provided plenty of inspiration for project design, such as the interleaving of the tower mass which has a metaphor for the high-and-low wandering mountains of Chongqing, the vertical hanging garden through several layers which represents the flowing-down streams from a mountain, and the horizontal air terrace which is more like the turning pines at mountainside. By all elements, the whole building expresses a great love to Chongqing, as a Chinese landscape painting.

Industry character and Culture heritage

Ancient coin

Industry character of Chongqing Bank Building supports an association with China's ancient coin culture. There are a great number of shapes and forms in ancient coins, from cowrie coins of Shang Dynasty, knife coins and cloth coins of Warring States, square hole coins of Qin Dynasty, to banknote coins of Qing Dynasty. From all above, we choose "Mang Coins", which have reached a very high degree of ancient coins as a perfect model of the design. The elements have been epurated for the design of the facade wall of building, by which the industry character and culture heritage are connected seamlessly by the modern architecture language.

"Treasure bowl" (Cornucopia)

In China's traditional custom, the treasure bowl is most precious in a family, which is

a symbol of wealth. Furthermore, the only way to collect treasure always connects with thrift. In another side, "water" is the essence of Confucianism and Taoism of China, such as "being good as water" and "water do good for everything". So such good wishes are contained in the design: a nearly 1 000 m square mirror pond, from which the water slowly flows into a sunken courtyard and comes into a circle.

Hanging garden and urban terrace

A two-layer high hanging garden is designed into the building to improve the office micro-environment and enrich the space feelings. At the same time, urban terraces and roof gardens are planned to make a full use of external and internal landscape resources.

Chongqing Bank Building expresses a generous and solemn atmosphere. Its design details display the project's top quality and industry characteristics of Chongqing Bank. It has comfortable and capacious indoor space and a convenient indoor-outdoor transportation. Different elements such as creativity, symbol, emblem, perspective and the nature of economic are centralized in the architecture, which make it become one of the unique and distinctive buildings of construction industry.

Xu Tiantian
DnA Design and Architecture

徐甜甜
DnA Design and Architecture建筑设计事务所

美国哈佛大学城市设计专业 硕士学位

中国清华大学建筑设计专业 学士学位

工作经历

2000－2004年 实践于美国、荷兰等国际性建筑事务所，包括鹿特丹OMA (RemKoolhaas)和波士顿LWA Achitects；

2004年至今 在北京主持DnA Design and Architecture建筑设计事务所

获得奖项

2009 被英国ICON杂志评选为世界20位最具影响力的年轻建筑师

2009 DnA工作室入选由美国城市设计委员会评选的2008建筑事务所

2008 纽约建筑联盟青年建筑师奖

2008 WA中国建筑奖

2008 英国《建筑评论》国际青年建筑师奖

2006 WA中国建筑奖

Xu Tiantian is founding principal of DnA Design and Architecture Beijing Office, an interdisciplinary practice of city planning, urban design and architectural design. Xu received her master degree of Architecture in Urban Design from Harvard Graduate School of Design, and her Bachelor degree of architecture from Tsinghua University in Beijing. Prior to establishing DnA Beijing, she worked at a number of design firms in the United States and the Netherlands, including OMA/ Rem Koolhaas. Xu has taught at the Central Academy of Fine Arts (CAFA) in Beijing, and has been a guest critic to numerous schools including Tsinghua University and Tokyo Chiba Institute of Technology. Xu also participates in Asia 21: Young Leader Forum by Asia Society.

Award

2009 20 Most Influential Designers by Icon Magazine, London
2009 Emerging Architects by Urban Land Institute, Washington DC
2008 Young Architects Award, the Architectural League, NewYork
2008 WA China Architecture Awards, Beijing
2008 AR Award Honorable Mention, London
2006 WA China Architecture Awards, Beijing

Songzhuang Artist Residence

宋庄艺术公社

设计单位：DnA Design and Architecture
设计师：徐甜甜
项目地址：北京市通州区宋庄镇
基地面积：1 400 m²
建筑面积：5 300 m²
楼层：5层
摄影：周若谷

Design firm: DnA Design and Architecture
Designer: Xu Tiantian
Site area: 1 400 m²
Building area: 5 300 m²
Floor: 5
Photographer: Zhou Ruogu

随着中国当代艺术家的激增，艺术家对居住和工作空间的需求也随之扩大。坐落在北京六环以东的宋庄艺术家村就正经历着由于这种增长所带来的变化，20个面向鱼塘的艺术家工作室应运而生。

按照工作室的居住和工作两种主要功能，每一个单元都包含两种不同的尺度与组合：工作部分为6m高的简洁的方盒子，居住部分高3m，有一系列几何形空间容纳起居、厨、厕功能，体量高差决定了每个单元的工作和居住功能或在同层联系或通过楼梯联系。整个建筑立面采用压型钢板，水平活动平面则是当地典型的红砖。

这20个工作室就像叠加在一起的集装箱，不仅和场地原有的工业气息相呼应，而且创造富有张力的外形和独特的建筑空间。体量的虚与实、光与影，创造变化的室外交流空间，为艺术展示提供了更多的可能性。当地艺术节开放工作室时，这片区域可以为参观者带来多样的空间体验，同时成为丰富的创作展览现场.这个带有艺术创作和居住功能的建筑何尝不是位于艺术村的一种另类美术馆?

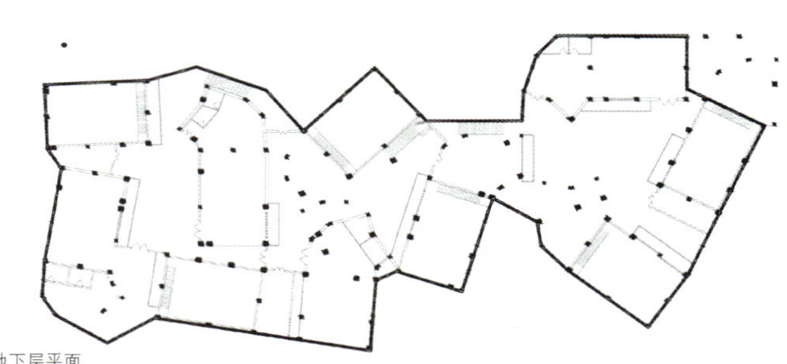
地下层平面

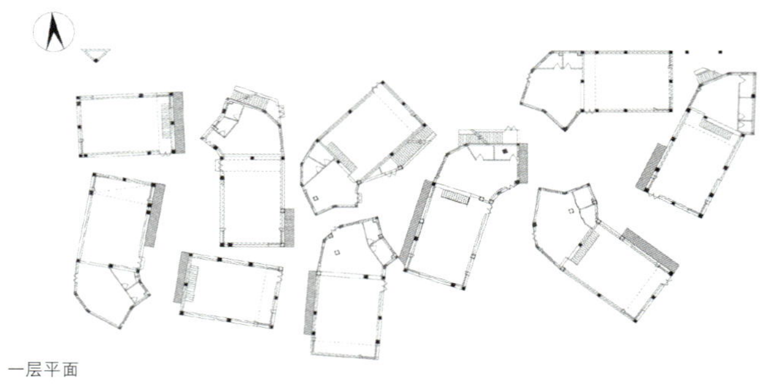
一层平面

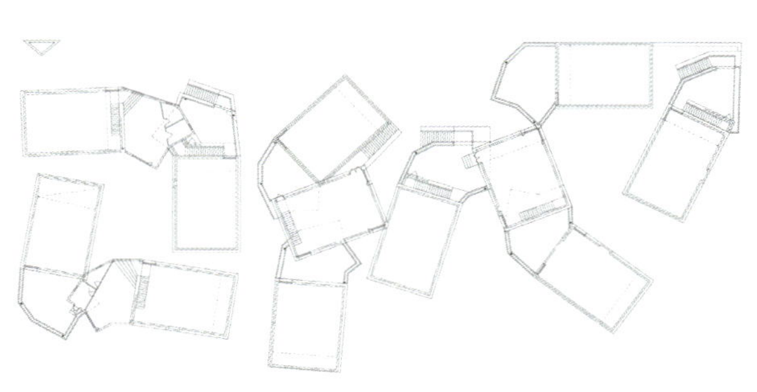
二层平面

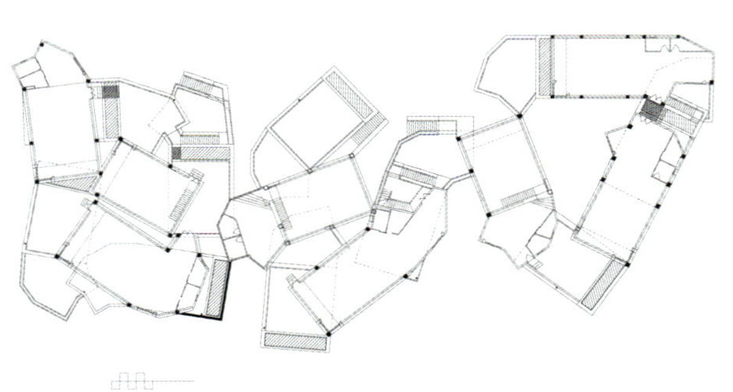
三层平面

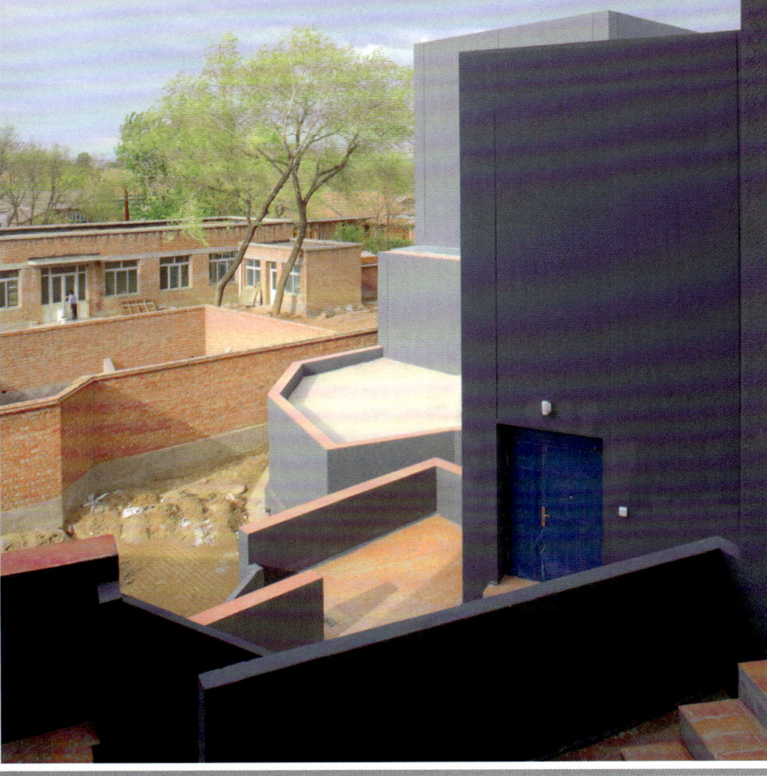

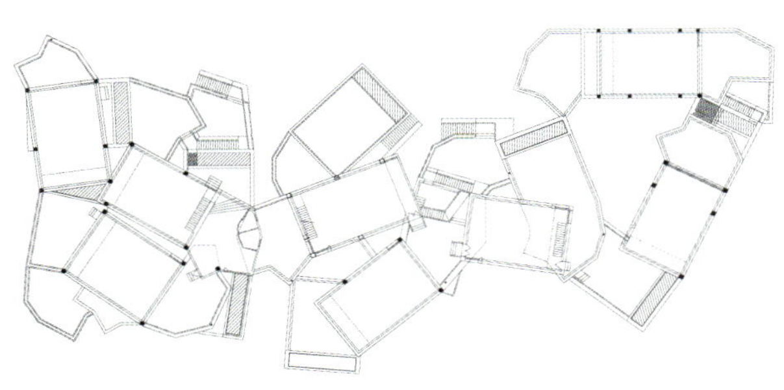

0 5 10m

四层平面

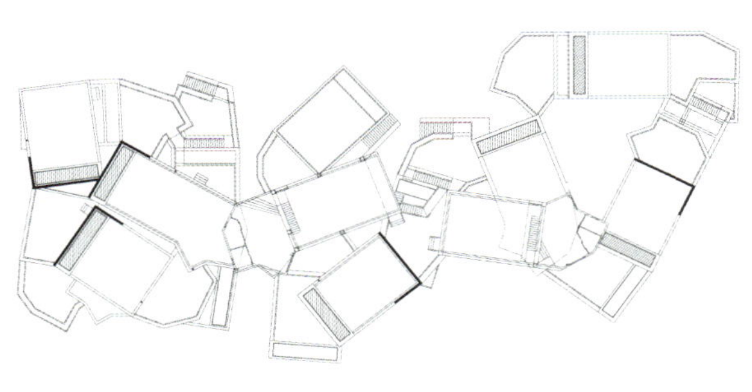

0 5 10m

五层平面

Located right next to east sixth ring road of Beijing city, Songzhuang Artist Village is undergoing a dramatic expansion of artist population and increasing demand of artists' working and living space, a 20-units artist residence facing a fishpond at a former outdoor storage lot is one of the local development targeting such demand.

The programmatic requirement of working and living defines the height and geometry of both volumes: 6 m height for working and 3 m for living; a simple rectangular box for studio and a complex geometry for living indicating bedroom, kitchen and toilet. Living volume is plugged into working volume either on the same level or led by stair to upper level.

These 20 units are regarded as containers stacking up on this former industrial outdoor storage lot, creating an expressive configuration and spatial quality. The interplay of volume and void, light and shadow allows artists and visitors to constantly explore and experiment the outdoor community space, which could be the extension of art production and presentation as well as linking these 20 units as 20 individual showrooms on open studio days.

In other words, this complex becomes an alternative museum for living art creation and exhibitions.

Ordos Art Museum

鄂尔多斯美术馆

设计单位：DnA Design and Architecture Beijing
设计师：徐甜甜、纪尧姆奥布里、陈英男
基地面积：4 200 m^2
建筑面积：2 700 m^2
楼层：2层
摄影：周若谷

Design firm: DnA Design and Architecture
Lead designer: Xu Tiantian, Guillaume Aubry, Chen Yingnan
Site area: 4 200 m^2
Building floor area: 2 700 m^2
Floor: 2
Photographer: Zhou Ruogu

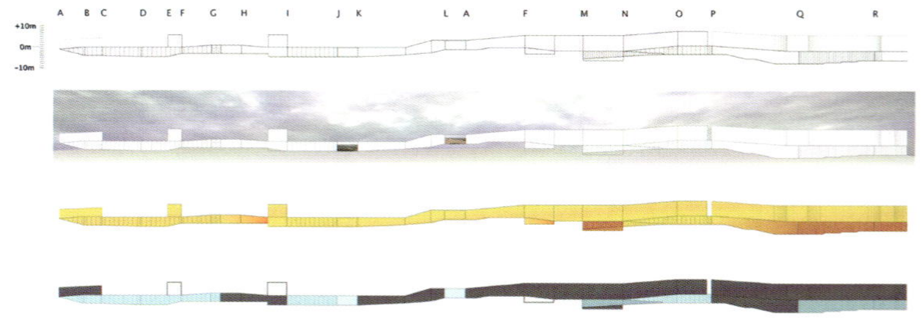

美术馆有两条功能主线：公共展览线路和内部资料线路。
展览的交通以线性展开，水平低矮的入口顺沿沙丘坡地的自然地形扭转，在高处则挑起远望考考什那水库，继而反转，以自身建筑作为结构承载，蜿蜒回落到地面展厅——公共展览流线的结束高潮，或又向下延续开始内部资料流线——作为出口与入口相互对望，整个公共交通呈现一个“8”字形的连续线路。
建筑形体因此在沙丘上蜿蜒延展，与地形相互作用形成半围合的院落或广场。
这个流线空间一路上跌荡起伏，根据高度和周边地势形成大小高宽尺度不同的横截面。沿路结合景观、空间和地势，或以尽端点式玻璃幕远眺水库，或以侧墙连续玻璃引入院落风景，或以顶部开窗围合展览内容。
光线也因此多样化，光影和空间交织出特有的节奏。
在这个节奏里，建筑空间内的艺术情景和外部自然风景交替呈现，参观者的心理空间在艺术情境、建筑尺度和自然风光之间弹性转换。

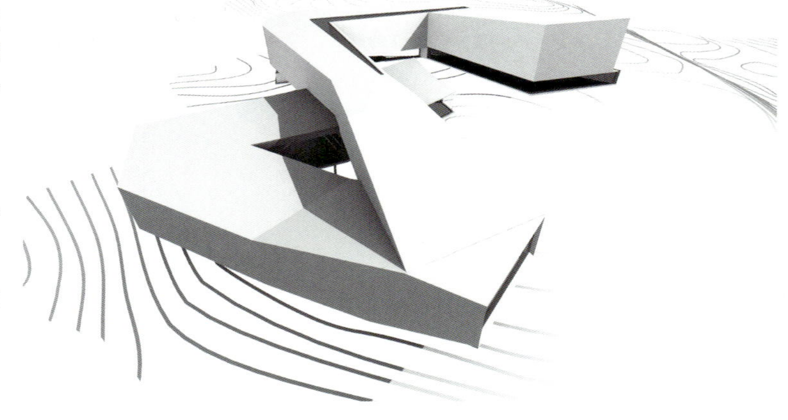

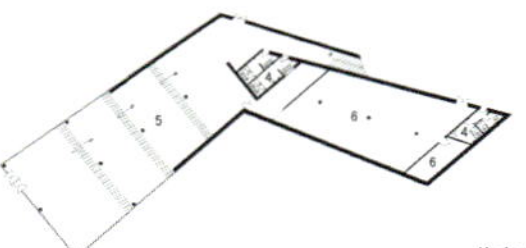

Underground Floor Plan
研究资料层平面
4 厕所/Toilet
5 研究资料/Research&Archive
6 贮藏/Storage

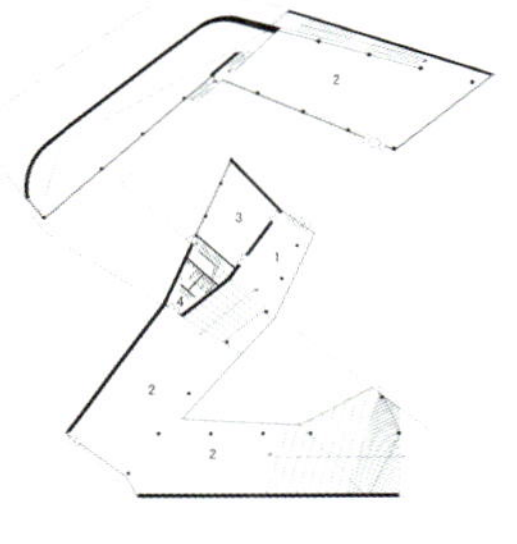

一层展厅平面
1st Floor Plan
1 大厅/Lobby
2 展厅/Gallery
3 办公室/Office
4 厕所/Toilet

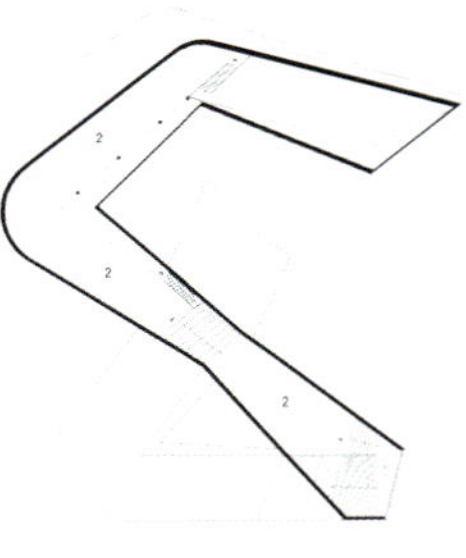

二层展厅平面
2nd Floor Plan
2 展厅/Gallery

Ordos Art Museum is the first building of Ordos' new civic center on a stretch of sand dunes along the lake that is dedicated as a "public corridor" with art and cultural facilities. This 29,000 sq.ft. exhibition and research space is distributed within an undulating form with a central span lifting clear off the ground, suggesting a desert viper winding over the dunes.

The space is conceived as one uninterrupted room with a series of openings absorbing natural light while offering cinematic views of the raw surroundings; the art exhibition mingles with the natural landscape that becomes an integrated experience for views.

Xixi Leisure Center

西溪休闲中心

设计单位：DnA Design and Architecture
设计师：徐甜甜
层数：3层
基地面积：20 000 m²
建筑面积：6 300 m²
项目委托方：杭州西溪国家湿地公园三期工程有限公司
设计时间：2008年1月–2009年7月

Design firm: DnA Design and Architecture
Designer: Xu Tiantian
Floor: 3
Site area: 20 000 m²
Building area: 6 300 m²
Design phase: Jan., 2008–Jul., 2009

西溪休闲中心是坐落在西溪国家湿地公园的12个艺术和文化建筑群的单体建筑之一。这个建筑群是由杭州市政府委托给12名中国建筑师的集群项目。杭州以其悠久的历史、丰富的文化和西湖景观而众所周知，而西溪艺术和文化建筑群则恰恰促进了其文化及旅游业的发展。

休闲中心延续了原有湿地的路径和形态，营造出由地面上的休闲功能空间和下沉的活动池塘组成的连续、开敞的空间形态。在二层，特色水疗室则成为相对独立的空间，就像漂浮在水上的睡莲一样，娱乐空间从它下方经过。

这种荷叶的组织和连接方式使人们从户外的步行道通过中间的各层荷叶到达屋顶上的小池塘，从而最终在屋顶揭开了这片湿地面纱。

在荷叶间的逗留会勾起人们似曾相识的感觉，好像我们祖先千百年前的一个幻想，经过这么多年的紧张心理和生理上的变化，我们，作为人，仍然可以轻如一片鸿毛，敏捷如一条祥龙一样，在这充满微风和熏香的自然环境中逗留！

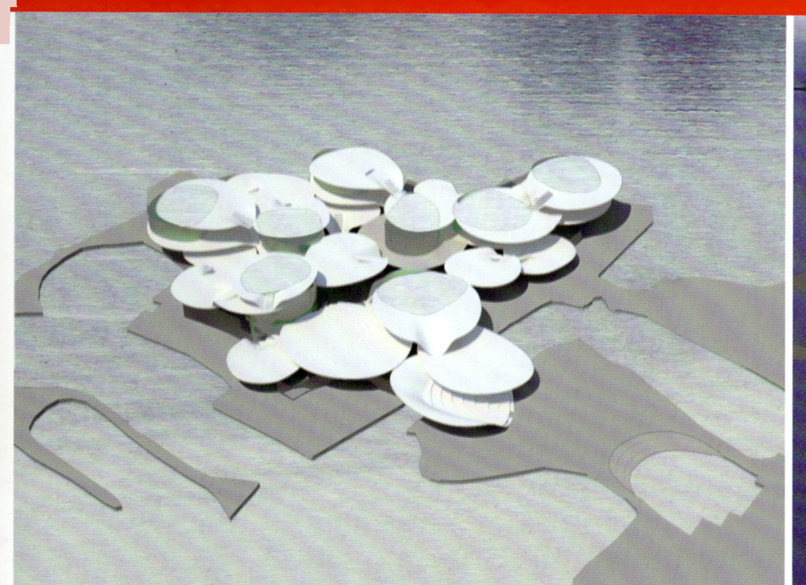

Xixi Leisure Center is one of the 12 buildings located in an art and culture compound in Xixi National Wetland Park, a cluster architecture commissioned to 12 Chinese architects by Hangzhou city government. Hangzhou has been well known for its long history, rich culture and the West Lake landscape. Xixi art and culture compound is part of development to stimulate cultural tourism.

The leisure center will house leisure function as open and continuous circulation on ground level and sunken into activity pools imitating paths and ponds of wetland topography, while on second level, spedicalized SPA rooms become rather individual spaces, like the thumbnail floating in water lily leaves, carried by leisure circulation underneath.

In such an atmosphere, tender and bulk columns are applied like a bamboo forest supporting the volumes and leaves.

The format and organization of leaves lead an outdoor promenade from the paths up to roof terraces discovering small water lily ponds, eventually unveiling the wetland to a panoramic view from above.

A pause on these leaves might evoke a déjà vu, a fantasy traced back thousands of years ago from our ancestors' belief, that after years and years of intense mental and physical training, are we, human beings, able to pause upon water, light as a fur, alert as a dragonfly, meditating the breeze and aroma in our nature?

Shandong Broadcasting & Television Center

山东省广播电视中心

设计单位：中国建筑设计研究院
方案设计：崔愷、李凌、任祖华、吴斌、周旭良
设计主持：崔愷、李凌
建筑：任祖华、谢悦、武志、李惠琴
结构：陈文渊、王文宇、邵筠、张付奎、王超
给排水：宋国清
设备：劳逸民、王加
电气：贾京花
电讯：杨宇飞
总图：王雅萍
室内：张晔、冀勉、李晨晨
基地面积：22 530 m^2
建筑面积：105 980 m^2
摄影：张广源

Design firm: China Architecture Design & Research Group
Director in charge: Cui Kai, Liling
Designer: Cui Kai, Li Ling, Ren Zuhua, Wu Bing, Zhou Xuliang
Site area: 22 530 m^2
Total floor area: 105 980 m^2
Photography: Zhang Guangyuan

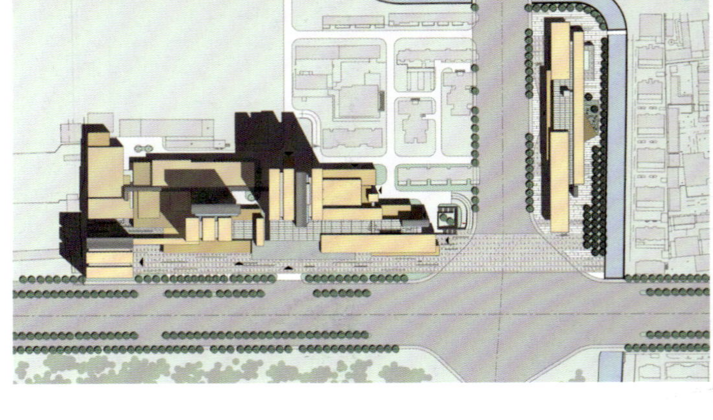

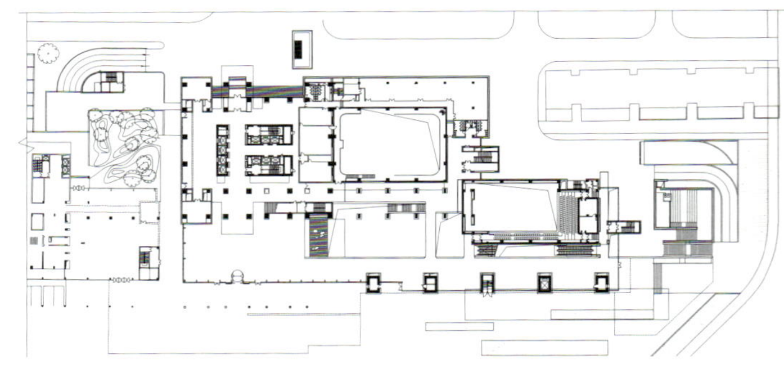

Cui Kai
China Architecture Design & Research Group

崔愷
中国建筑设计研究院

简历：

1957.08.13	生于北京
1984.10	毕业于天津大学建筑系　获硕士学位
1984—1985	建设部建筑设计院　建筑师
1985—1987	深圳华森建筑与工程设计顾问有限公司　建筑师
1987—1989	香港华森建筑与工程设计顾问有限公司　建筑师
1989—1996	建设部建筑设计院　高级建筑师、副总建筑师
1997—2000	建设部建筑设计院　副院长、总建筑师
2000—今	中国建筑设计研究院　副院长、总建筑师
	国家工程设计大师

获奖：

1997	"全国优秀科技工作者"
1998	"国务院特殊津贴专家"
1999	"国家人事部有突出贡献的中青年专家"
1999	"国家百、千、万人工程"人选
2000	"国家设计大师"
2003	"法国文学与艺术骑士勋章"
2007	"梁思成建筑奖"
2007	"亚建协金奖"

兼职：

中国建筑学会副理事长
全国注册建筑师管理委员会副主任
全国高等学校建筑学专业指导委员会委员
国际建筑师协会国际竞赛委员会联席主任

国际建筑师协会副理事
香港建筑师学会会员
北京市人民政府顾问
常熟市人民政府顾问
北京市金融街建筑顾问
东莞松山湖高科技产业园建筑顾问
天津大学兼职教授
南京大学兼职教授
西南交通大学兼职教授
多家专业杂志编委
多家社会媒体顾问

Date of birth:
Aug.13th, 1957, Beijing, P. R. China

Education:
Oct. 1984, Master Degree of Engineering, Department of Architecture, Tianjin University

Employment Record:
1984-1985 Architecture Design Institute: Ministry of Construction, Beijing, Architect
1985-1987 Huasen Architectural & Engineering Design Consultants Ltd., Shenzhen, Architect
1987-1989 Huasen Architectural & Engineering Design Consultants Ltd., Hong Kong, Architect
1989-1996 Architecture Design Institute: Ministry of Construction, Beijing
Senior Architect, Vice Chief Architect
1997-2000 Architecture Design Institute: Ministry of Construction, Beijing
Vice President, Chief Architect
2000-now China Architecture Design & Research Group, Beijing
Vice President, Chief Architect, National Design Master

Personal awards:

1997 National Best Science and Technology Worker
1998 Expert who enjoys special subsidy from the State Council
1999 Excellent Mid-young aged Expert of the Ministry of Personnel
1999 Candidate of "National Hundred, Thousand & Ten Thousand Reserves Project"
2000 National Design Master
2003 French Culture & Art Cavalier Medal
2007 Liang Sicheng Award
2007 ARCASIA 2007 Gold Award

Part-time Jobs:

Deputy Board Member, UIA (International Union of Architects)
Vice President, Architectural Society of China
Vice Director, National Architects' Registration Committee
Co-director of UIA Competitions Commission

Member, National College Education Architecture Professional Tuition Committee
Member, HKIA (the Hong Kong Institute of Architects)
Adviser, Beijing Metropolitan Government
Part-time Professor, Tianjin University
Part-time Professor, Nanjing University
Part-time Professor, Southwest Jiaotong University
Member, Several Professional Magazine Editorial Committees

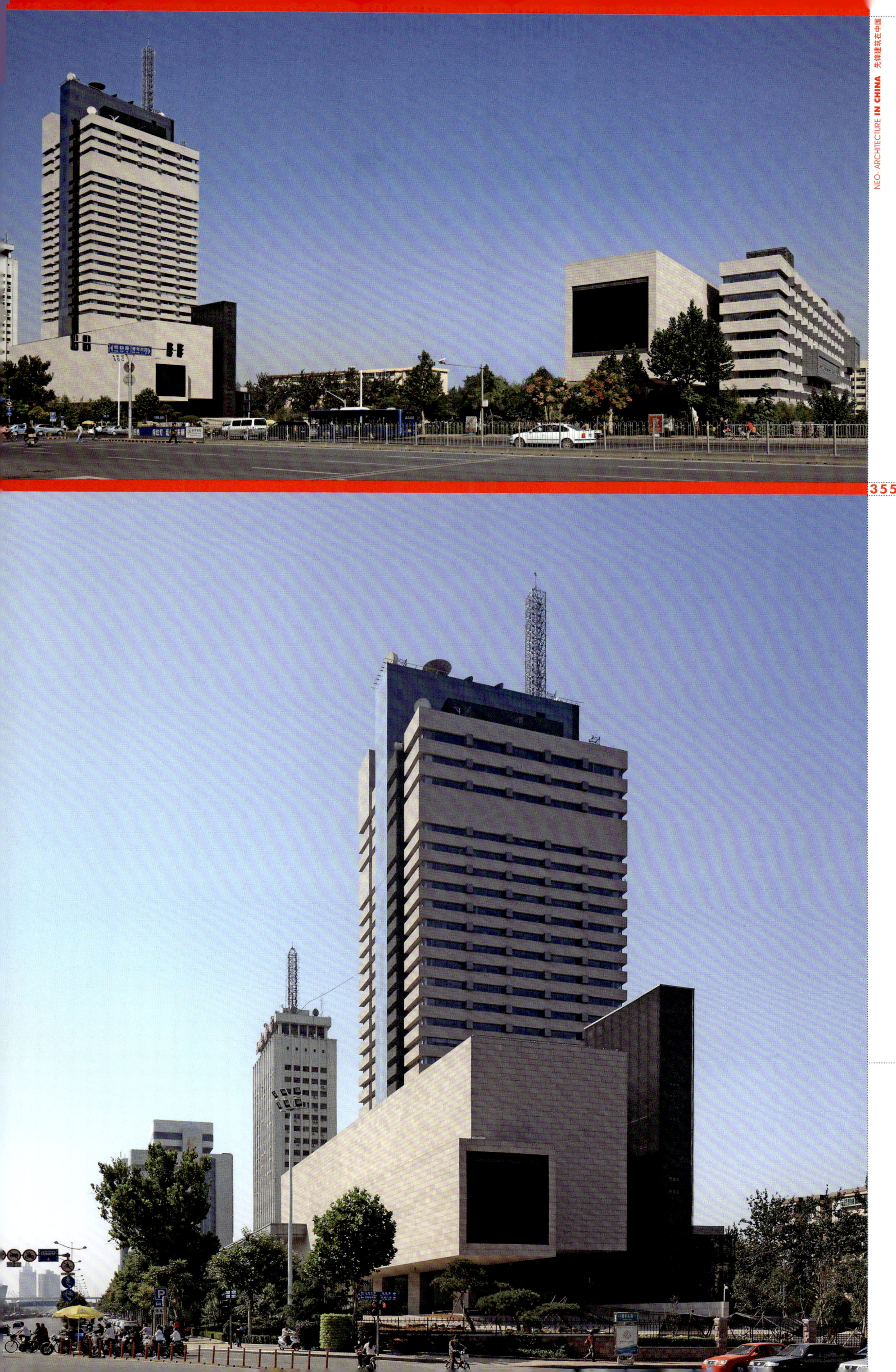

山东省广播电视中心位于济南由千佛山至趵突泉和大明湖的景观轴线上。广电建筑普遍具有非常复杂的功能工艺要求，而作为原有山东省广电中心的扩建项目，且用地跨越主要干道，广电大厦的设计还需要解决与各个建筑互相衔接、统一改建的问题。

建筑群的西侧为新建的广电主楼和改扩建的旧建筑组成的广电中心综合业务楼，东侧为以各类经营活动为主的媒体中心。位于狭长用地上的建筑，通过连串排布的长条实体和玻璃厅虚实相间，空间形态明确而富有震撼力。建筑体量西高东低，在道路交叉口形成夸张的悬挑，使得建筑物无论对于行人，还是周边高层建筑的俯瞰，都保持了恰当的体型。两处建筑通过建筑语言、形态的整体设计，成为文化轴线上重要的节点。新建主楼西侧有主楼、技术裙房和广电宾馆等需要保留的原有建筑，通过对这些建筑原本掩藏的因功能不同而导致的不同层高进行充分暴露，获得了一种丰富而富有趣味的造型因素。

以“巨石”作为隐喻的外部形象，体现了山东的地域性和文化底蕴，同时也以巨型筒体结构支撑、悬浮和主楼层层叠合的形态，以及这一手法在室内设计中的延续，形成建筑强壮、简洁、富有力度的整体氛围。

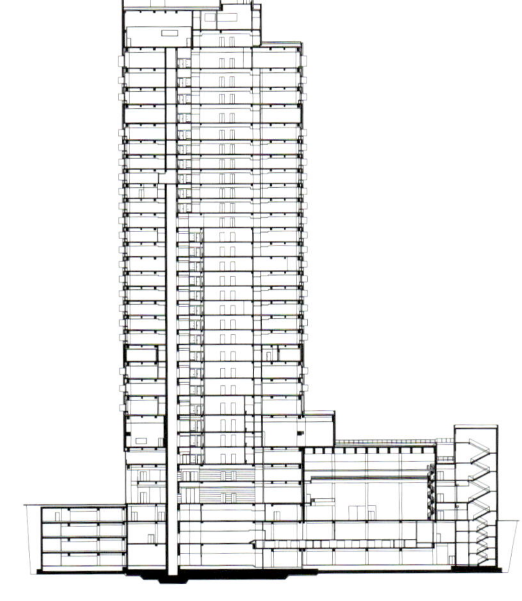

Occupying a spot on the landscape axis of Jinan city, from Qianfo Mountain to Daming Lake, the project was not only designed to accommodate those extra complicate functions, but also resolve all the existing problems of the various structures built in different stages, creating a seamless, state-of-the-art facility.

A busy street splits the site into two parts: on the west site, a new-built tower dominates the comprehensive skirt building containing those intricate, while a new media center for various businesses is situated on the opposite side of the street. On both narrow sites, a series of solid slabs run horizontally and vertically, in contrast with the glass pavilions, defining an intricate and impressive spatial system. The huge tubes are cantilevered extensively to gesture to the road, providing a remarkable image for pedestrians and views from the surrounding high-rise buildings. The expressive architectural language defines the site a pivot on the main axis of the city. Those existing structures are sufficiently exposed to emphasize the different story heights caused by the various functions, which also be treated as some interesting factors of television center.

Granite slates draw on the colors and textures of the mountains natural environments of Shandong. Although not literal, the exterior image of the building was informed by the memory of huge mountains, an indigenous feature of Shandong. Accompanied by the interior design, the huge slabs and the exterior multi-layered composition reinforce the strong, solid and powerful image of the building.

Artist Colony
北京西山艺术工坊

业主方：北京西山产业投资有限公司
设计单位：中国建筑设计研究院
建筑师：崔愷、时红、喻弢、关飞、邓烨、连荔
结构工程师：朱炳寅、王奇
基地面积：12 880 m^2
总建筑面积：24 225 m^2
摄影：张广源

Design firm: China Architecture Design & Research Group
Design team: Cui Kai, Shi Hong, Yu Tao, Guan Fei, Deng Ye, Lian Li
Site area: 12 880 m^2
Building area: 24 225 m^2
Photography: Zhang Guangyuan

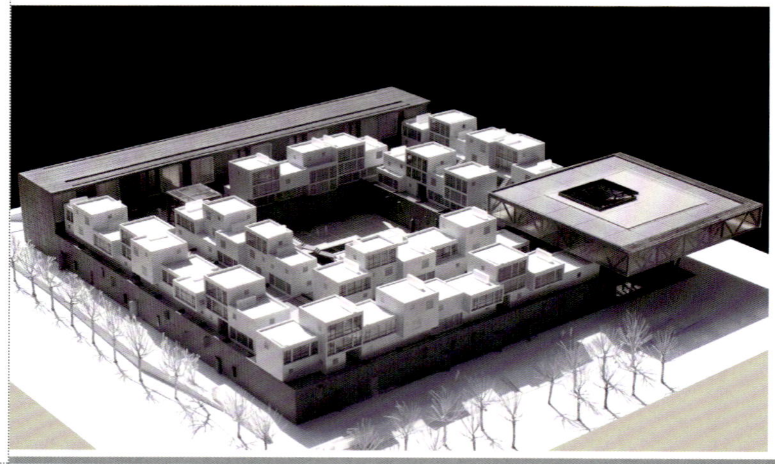

当需要在一个108 m×108 m，限高15 m的方形场地中安排75套艺术家工作室时，我们只能想到一个词——扎堆。有趣的是，这就是中国艺术家的生活状态，艺术家都喜欢扎堆。这是一次带策划色彩的艺术聚落设计，容纳艺术创作和生活的建筑单体通过群体规划的方式布置，相互毗邻，形成街道与大院空间；单体的聚集形成“圈子”，底层是对大众开放的“艺术圈子”；二层屋面上则是属于艺术家自己的内街社区——“生活圈子”。

我们用“漂浮容器”来形容单体中艺术家创作与生活的相互关系：工作就像潜水，一种憋足了劲的创作活动；而生活就像呼吸，一种悠闲的漂浮状态。这种沉浮状态在设计中表现为，工作空间处于底层5.4 m的高大空间，而生活空间则像一个个白盒子悬浮其上，它们可以脱离，也可以进入下层工作空间，形成丰富的若即若离的空间体验。盒子里每层是7 m × 7 m的方正空间，贯穿各层的功能墙的引入使得厨卫和管井等必备元素可独自形成一个功能岛，以强调居住空间的纯粹性和灵活性。

在整个建筑的西北角，艺术展示厅被提升到10 m，让出一个模糊了内外界限的空间，打破封闭的“圈子”，这里不仅是群落的主入口，也将是艺术家与大众互相碰撞和浸染的乐园。

When the architects were asked to deposit 75 suits of artist studios in a 108 m × 108 m site, with a height limitation of 18 m, the only thing they can image is one word – stacking. What is interesting, is that exactly describes the situation of Chinese artist's real life – artists are always gregarious animals. An art village, containing artists' creation and living activities, is formed here. Through the elaborate planning process, street and courtyard are encircled by a mass of modules, the assembly of individuals. On the ground level is the opened "art circle" for public, while the second level is an inner street – "living circle" for artists' themselves.

The concept – "floating container" is employed to represent the interaction of working and living in the same studio unit. For artist, working looks like driving beneath water surface, holding his breath to do his best; while breathing freely well depicts his leisure life in the rest time. Living spaces are several pure white boxes, floating above the 5.4 m high working spaces. Raised up or sunken down, they exhibit various spatial relationship between working and living. With a 7 m×7 m square plan for every floor, each white box is equipped with a functional island including all the necessary service pipes to maximize the flexibility of the living spaces.

On the northwest corner, a huge glass box, the exhibition hall for artists, is elevated to 10 m, interrupting the enclosure of the "circle". Without legible boundaries of outside and inside, the intricate void serves as the main entrance of the art-studio cluster, and emphasizes the nature of this complex, a paradise of communication and infection for artists and public.

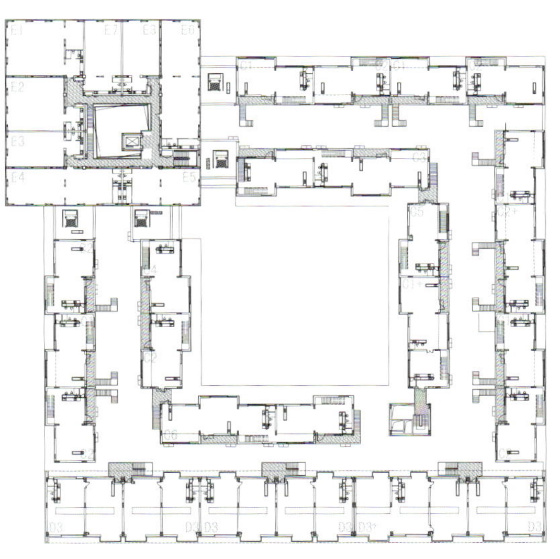

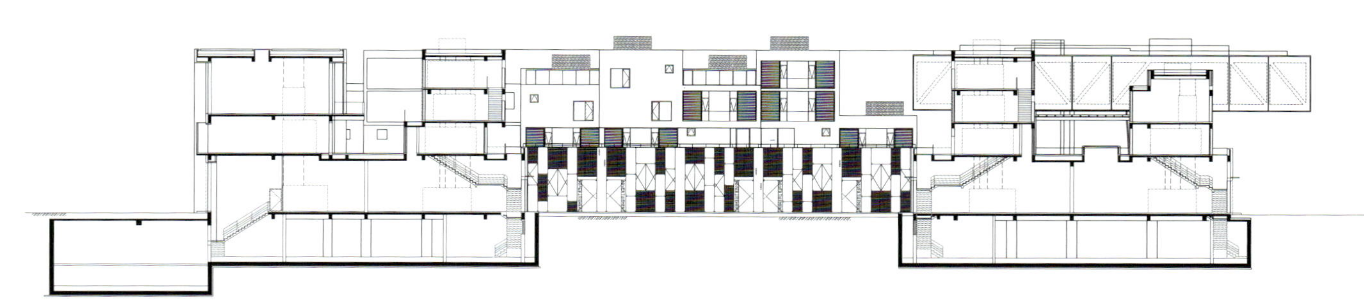

Alibaba Corporate Headquarters, Hangzhou, China

阿里巴巴集团新办公园区

设计单位：HASSELL
完工时间：2009年10月
规模：150 000 m^2

Design firm: HASSELL
Date of construction completion: October, 2009
Gross floor area (sqm): 150 000 sqm

阿里巴巴集团新办公园区位于杭州市内，总面积约150 000 m^2，是中国现代办公空间的典范。整个园区呈现校园式风格，灵活而实用的开放式办公环境。

阿里巴巴是中国电子商务的龙头企业之一，运营着世界上最大的网络贸易市场，为国际和国内贸易提供服务。可容纳约9 000名员工的动态建筑，其设计反映了企业内部联系的多样化和活力。

阿里巴巴集团新办公园区总体规划的原则都是基于理念的连贯性、明确性和社区性作出的——该理念也是对阿里巴巴电子商务至关重要的。这些原则指导了设计的方向，从单一的外部工作站的视角到较大的办公场所的社区性。

通过HASSELL公司建筑师、室内设计师以及景观设计师共同协作开发，园区的设计围绕中心开放空间展开，并且构成了一个建筑物组团，建筑物4至7层的层高各异。

设计中考虑到了建筑形式以及设计的“各个位置间的空间”，因此每个元素都决定了另一个元素。宏伟的中央空间伴随着一系列更加私密的花园，这些花园培养了这个较

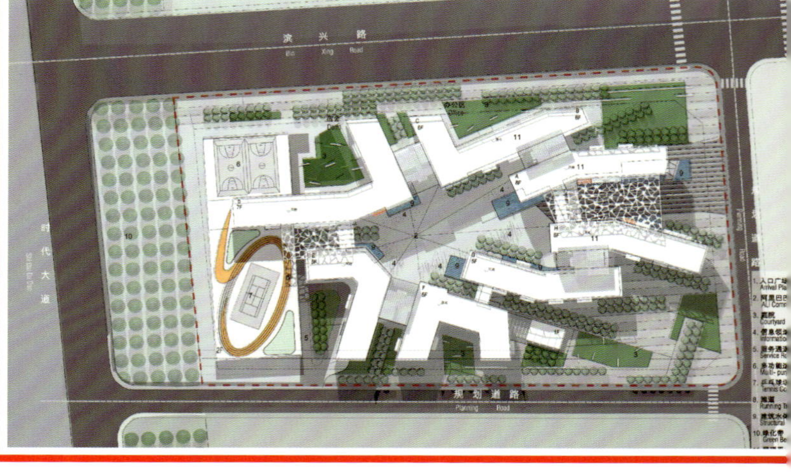

HASSELL

澳大利亚HASSELL

HASSELL成立于1938年，是澳大利亚最具规模的跨学科、多专业设计顾问公司。HASSELL的分支机构遍布澳洲、中国、泰国、越南等国，集团员工近1 000名，设计范围包括：建筑设计、室内设计、景观设计、规划及城市设计。

HASSELL的创新理念、丰富经验和真诚服务多年来始终被客户高度推崇。资深的专业团队，多种文化背景的设计师，通过多专业的荟萃整合，一如既往地为客户的发展注入非凡价值。

HASSELL的创意之旅始终综合考虑项目的整体环境，斟酌细节，锐意创新，亦将可持续发展理念贯穿于设计的每个环节。

HASSELL来到中国已20余年，目前在上海、北京、香港、重庆和深圳都建立了设计事务所，完成的项目遍布国内各主要城市，创建了非凡的业绩。我们对中国各地的历史背景、文化特色有相当的认识，对客户的需求和各类程序也极为熟悉。我们相信，通过和谐的沟通，定能为客户量身定制独特而实用的设计方案。

Established in 1938, HASSELL is one of the largest multidisciplinary design consultancy practice, with offices in and throughout Australia, China, Thailand, Vietnam, etc., and over 1,000 employees. We are structured around the key disciplines of architecture, interior design, landscape architecture, planning and urban design.

HASSELL has been recognized for our creativity, experience and cordial service. As a collaboration of experienced design professionals with global diversity, through the integrated application of these disciplines, HASSELL is able to consistently add significant value to its clients' developments. Our design journey begins with a shared exploration of the overall context of a project. We examine the details, challenge preconceptions and assumptions, and integrate sustainability into every design process.

HASSELL has begun to cultivate China market more than 20 years ago. Up to now, we have established offices in Shanghai, Beijing, Hong Kong, Chongqing and Shenzhen. With completed projects throughout various major cities in China, we have accomplished excellent achievement. We have good understanding about historic background and culture of different places around China, as well as client needs and design process. We believe that harmonious communication will ensure responsive, unique and practical design outcomes.

大合作团体中的个人。人性化的建筑形式以及狭长的楼板在清晰的尺度上创造出一种强烈的地方感，并且建立了贯穿园区的物理衔接。

视觉通透性——能够看见里面或穿过大庭院看到综合体其他部分的内部——同样是达到需要的社区性与连接性感觉的关键。

杭州的环景由花园组成的网络所环绕，遮阳幕表现为中国式样的冰式窗格，这样的窗格设计突出，贯穿城市著名的古典园林。

可持续设计集成特色是为了将对园区环境的影响减到最小，同时最大程度地发挥其对健康的贡献，保持人们的良好状态，并保证其增强周围的社区性。

将灵活多变、开放式的办公场所设计为活力四射且有益健康的环境，鼓励在整个综合体中进行非正式和创新的会议。中心、内外街道、桥、屋顶平台以及战略性目的点都促进了合作的意向。

建筑和楼层板的布局、外立面的设计增大了所有工作站的自然采光以及空气对流。南立面上的水平遮阳篷阻挡正午阳光的照射，减少了对冷气的需求，而竖向的遮阳篷则遮挡了西下的阳光，在对立面上的开放式窗户促进了空气对流。

项目的成功之处在于：

1. 在一个企业园区建立了中国新的国际办公场所标准。
2. 被动性可持续发展以及文化上指导的设计原则赋予了设计成果活力。
3. 设计增强了园区内企业的社区性渴望。
4. 建筑成果始终忠于原有设计目标。

The new Alibaba Headquarters, located in Hangzhou, is a benchmark for the modern workplace in China, comprising 150,000 square metres of flexible open plan office space within a campus style layout.
The masterplan principles for the Headquarters are based on the concepts of connectivity, clarity and community – concepts that are also vital to Alibaba's e-commerce business. These principles guided the design from the perspective of a single workstation outwards to the greater workplace community.
Developed collaboratively by HASSELL architects, interior design and landscape architects, the campus is arranged around a central open space and comprises a cluster of buildings that vary in height from four to seven stories.
The built form and the designed 'spaces between places' are integrated so that each defines the other. The grand central space is accompanied by a series of more intimate gardens that nurture the individual within the larger corporate community. The humanised scale of the built form and the long, narrow floor plates help to create a strong sense of place at a legible scale, and establish physical connection throughout the campus.
Visual permeability – or the ability to see into and across the major courtyards into other parts of the complex – was also key to achieving the desired sense of community and connectivity.
The Hangzhou context has been embraced with garden networks and sunshading screens that represent Chinese ice-pattern window screens which are prominent throughout the city's renowned historical gardens.
The sustainable design incorporates features to minimise the campus' environmental impacts while maximising its contribution to the health and wellbeing of its population and ensuring it enhances the surrounding community.
The flexible, open plan workplace has been designed to be a positive and healthy environment and to encourage informal and creative meetings throughout the complex. Hubs, internal and external streets, bridges, roof terraces and strategically placed destination points contribute to the collaborative intent.
Buildings and floor plates have been arranged and the facade designed to maximise access to natural light and cross ventilation to all workstations. Horizontal sunshades on the south facade cut out mid-afternoon sun reducing the need for cooling and vertical sunshades cut out western sun. Openable windows on opposite facades promote cross ventilation.

The successes of the project are:

1. New International workplace standards established in China within a corporate campus environment
2. Passive sustainability and culturally led design principles informing the design outcome
3. Design aspirations reinforce corporate community aspirations within campus
4. Built outcome remains true to original design aspiration

Beijing Tianzhu International Fanancial and Commercial Centre

北京天竺国际商业金融中心

设计单位：DGBK Architects International
设计时间：2009年
基地面积：25 000 m²
建筑面积：110 000 m²
绿化率：50%
容积率：3
建筑密度：50%

Design firm: Dgbk Architects International
Design date: 2009
Site area: 25 000 m²
Building area: 110 000 m²
Green percentage: 50%
Volume fraction: 3
Building density: 50%

基地位于北京市顺义区天竺镇后沙峪国家展览中心南侧，北临城市主干道裕翔路，东临规划裕东路，西临馨园路，基地南侧为项目一期住宅部分——澳金园别墅区。基地东西长约330 m，南北进深约80 m，呈带状分布于新国展南侧。

该开发项目的定位是支持和服务于国家展览中心及周边的高档居住区。工程等级为III级大型公共建筑，建筑面积约110 000 m²，其中地上750 000 m²，地下350 000 m²，建安造价约4亿元人民币。

定位准确的酒店设计与新国展充分对应折线型的商业，最大化其沿街展开面，多首层的创新商业设计

连续、丰富、交织的商业空间和由此带来的全新购物体验。

强调私密、景观用途灵活的高档空中会所

共同构筑了本项目设计的主要特点，同时将天竺国际商业金融中心成为又一地标性 建筑。

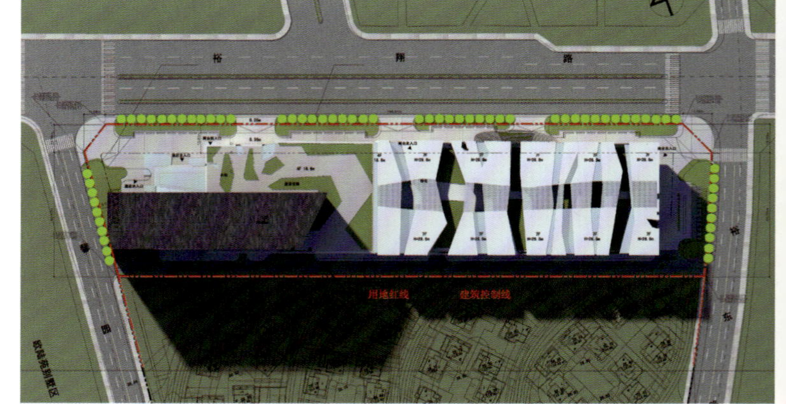

DGBK

design excellence | innovation | collaboration

DGBK ARCHITECTS INTERNATIONAL

发展历程

DGBK1972年成立于加拿大温哥华，目前已在加拿大、美国、中国等国家的多个城市开设分公司，项目遍及美洲、欧洲、澳洲和亚洲的十余个国家。DGBK凭借其高品质的专业设计获得了诸多国际殊荣，取得了业界的高度认可。DGBK在中国的业务始于1994年，并于2007年在上海成立了亚洲区总部，并在北京、首尔等城市设立了分支机构。DGBK始终将卓越设计、创新技术和精诚合作（DESIGN EXCELLENCE、INNOVATION、COLLABORATION） 作为经营宗旨，并通过我们的服务诠释 “设计创造价值”的核心理念！

设计团队

DGBK的国际设计团队为公司在世界各地项目的成功提供了技术上和文化上的专业保障。公司的注册建筑师资质涵盖美国、加拿大、英国、中国等国家，并拥有加拿大皇家建筑师协会、加拿大绿色建筑协会、美国建筑师协会、LEED绿色设计等权威机构的认证。

业务范围

DGBK的业务范围涵盖城市规划、投资策划、大型公共建筑设计、民用建筑设计、室内装饰设计、园林景观设计、建筑节能和智能节能化等领域。

特色专长

DGBK一直把特色专长设计作为发展的重要方向，在城市规划、大型城市综合体、医疗建筑、木结构建筑、绿色设计等领域取得了突出的成就，形成了业务广泛、特色突出的风格。

方案一

Company History

DGBK Architects entered design world in 1972 in Vancouver, Canada, and has steadily grown in size and stature to become one of North America's most highly regarded architectural practices. The firm currently has offices in Canada, USA, China and other countries with over 300 employees. Our work spreads throughout the world, including projects in Canada, USA, China, Korea, Japan, Australia, India, and the South Pacific. The 2003-2004 annual project value was over 1.2 billion US dollars, which ranked us as one of the top Canadian firms.

Since 1994, DGBK has been actively involved in the China market for more than 15 years, and has completed a great number of landmark projects. In order to meet the increasing needs of our Asian clients, DGBK established its Asian headquarter in 2007 in Shanghai, and opened several representative offices in Beijing, Wuxi, and Soul. By 2008, DGBK has accomplished over 100 projects in more than 30 cities in China, Japan, South Korea, and India.

Our success has been a product of our principle of "Design Excellence, Innovation, and Collaboration". DGBK believes in the philosophy of "Design Creates Value" and will consistently address that through our service.

Design Team

DGBK has over 300 associates and professional employees, including over 60 registered architects, and 12 LEED certificated architects from America, Canada and China. Our people come from around the world and bring a truly international background of experience and understanding, both professionally and culturally. This international point-of-view contributes to the success of our work by providing a broader insight and a deeper appreciation for the different influences that apply to the design of the built environment in other parts of the world.

Scope of Service

Our project experience is extremely broad, including master planning, investment and programming, large-scale commercial complex, health care, residential, sports and recreational, educational, conventional, hospitality, transportation, interior, landscape, green design, and building-intelligent systems.

Expertise

We are specialists in sustainable design and innovative technologies such as wood framed buildings, and have lectured and written on those subjects throughout the world. Our work has been internationally recognized through awards from both professional associations and clients.

The history of DGBK's green design started from 1972. In the following years, DGBK consistently applied green design into most of our projects, and won numerous international awards. DGBK is regarded as one of the world's leading green design firms, and is accredited by both USA and Canada LEED associations.

Key Achievement

DGBK has established long-term collaboration with international and local design firms, all levels of governments, developers, and well-known enterprises. DGBK was invited by the Shanghai and Guangzhou city governments as the selected firm representing Canada to develop the master plan for the 2010 Shanghai Expo and 2010 Asian Games.

方案一

方案一

The project is located to the south of Houshayu National Exhibition Center in Tianzhu Town, Shunyi, Beijing, with the urban main road Yuxiang road to the north, the planning Yudong road to the east , Xinyuan road to the west, and the first phase of residential part – Aojinyuan villa area to the south. It is 330 m from the east to the west, and about 80 m from the north to the south, lying like a belt on the south of the new National Exhibition Center.

The developing project orients to supporting and serving the National Exhibition Center and the high level residential districts around. It is a III-level large public building area, of which is about 110 000 m^2 with 75 000 m^2 on the ground and 35 000 m^2 below. Building cost is around 400 million RMB.

The design of the hotel is well oriented, and the commercial space fully corresponds to the new National Exhibition Center with its folding line type, which maximizes the outspread face along the street.

Multi-first-floors' creative commercial design

Continuous, abundant, interlaced commercial space and the whole new shopping experience it brings.

Focusing on privacy, landscape, and flexible-used top grade aerial chamber

Elements above all together construct the main characteristics of the design of the project, meanwhile, making Tianzhu International Financial And Commercial Center another landmark.

方案二

方案二

National Enterprise Museum

中国国家中小型企业博物馆

设计单位：DGBK Architects International
项目规模：13 000 m^2
设计时间：2008年

Design firm: DGBK Architects International
Scale: 13 000 m^2
Design date: 2008

中国国家中小企业博物馆(NEM)旨在展示中国企业在改革开放政策后的几十年中发生的日新月异的变化和取得的巨大成就。博物馆总建筑面积13 000 m^2，位于无锡市市郊，包括展示部分、多媒体中心、行政及会议中心。本方案的基本构思原则在于将建筑向湖岸线方向推移，并将其一部分景观直接伸入湖中，最大限度地体现水景与建筑空间的对话。将建筑与道路间的空间拉大后形成花园和绿化隔离带，创造出独特的入口景观。主体建筑的空间形态充分地与地形和地势呼应，追求建筑与环境的共生和融合。通过屋顶坡道和绿化，人们可直接从室外广场自然过渡到建筑的屋顶，在由自然环境到建筑这一过程中，我们始终强调建筑的人文景观环境与自然景观条件的自然交互，从而使得建筑成为环境的一部分，构筑了一幅浪漫大气的自然景观与人文景观交相辉映的书画长卷。

The objective of National Enterprise Museum (NEM) is to show the significant development of Chinese Enterprises over the past decades since the reform and opening-up policy. This 13 000 sqm facility is located at the suburb of Wuxi, and includes exhibition, multi-media centre, administration and a conference centre. The main concept of the design is to make the museum a public gathering place that can attract people. The green sloped roof and central openings effectively connect the museum with the beautiful natural context.

Taizhou OCT Golf Club-House

泰州华侨城高尔夫会所

设计单位：DGBK Architects International
项目位置：江苏省泰州市
项目规模：5 000 m²
设计/竣工时间：2008年—2009年

Design firm: DGBK Architects International
Location: Taizhou, Jiangsu
Scale: 5 000 m²
Completion: Designed in 2008
Construction in 2009

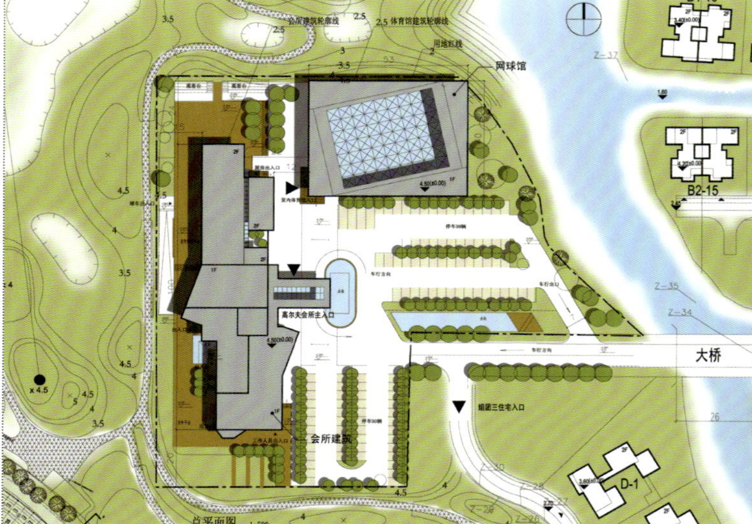

本案位于泰州溱湖风景区西端，建筑面积5 000 m²。项目面临的挑战之一是需要在局促的场地中满足一个流线复杂的两个建筑单体。项目拥有极佳的地理条件：地处整个高尔夫球场的中部，享有坡地、草场与树林的绚丽景致。设计结合场地环境，合理布置垂直与水平的交通流线，强调功能及空间节奏的变化，以期通过现代、别致的空间与材质组合创造出具有独特人文气息的休闲空间。

在建筑形态和建筑表皮的设计上，本方案通过对中国传统建筑的研究，提炼出具有很强中式特色的元素，通过变化将这些元素以现代感的建筑手法加以运用。本方案运用的中式元素包含坡屋顶、中式窗格、白墙和木结构。在本方案中，坡屋顶的变形打破了常规坡屋顶的对称性，结合功能，进行了大面积小角度倾斜的处理，局部运用了屋顶落地，亦顶亦墙的方式，屋面选用了金属材质，使整个建筑更具有变化性和现代感。本方案在白墙的处理上使用了比较现代感的不规则开窗，局部毛石表皮的处理，打破了一体通白墙面的单调性。本方案对传统窗格纹理进行单纯的几何提炼，变化出的表皮结构运用到门窗，遮阳板室内装饰上，从细节上突出中式的特点，材质同样以金属为主。在大厅、餐厅等大空间加入了木结构的支撑，木结构对于这种挑高的大空间有很好的装饰效果，同时能给整个室内环境带来更多的暖色彩及亲和力。本方案的设计理念是打造成为一个具有中式韵味同时具有现代感视觉冲击的会所建筑。

Located in the west Qinhu lake scenic resort, this project has an area of 5,000 square meters for the construction. One of the most Challenging aspect is that the desigers have to create two complicated sole architecture body in such a small area. This project is in the middle of the golf course which enjoys spectacular views, including sloping lands, lawns and forests. We have carefully considered the relationship between the site and surrounding environment, the requirements of horizontal and vertical traffic, so that all the needs could be met and a well organized design could be provided. Besides, some modern materials have been applied, in order to create a unique recreation centre with a literary image.

Wuxi Cultural and Sports Centre

无锡文化体育中心

设计单位：DGBK Architects International
基地面积：70 000 m²
建筑面积：17 700 m²

Design firm: DGBK Architects International
Site area: 70 000 m²
Building area: 17 700 m²

文化体育中心综合体项目包括一个1200座席的剧院、一个图书馆、一个3 500座席的体育馆、一个室内游泳池和一个供市民使用的文化中心。

This complex includes a 1200-seat theater, a library, a 3500-seat sports centre, an indoor swimming pool, and a cultural centre.

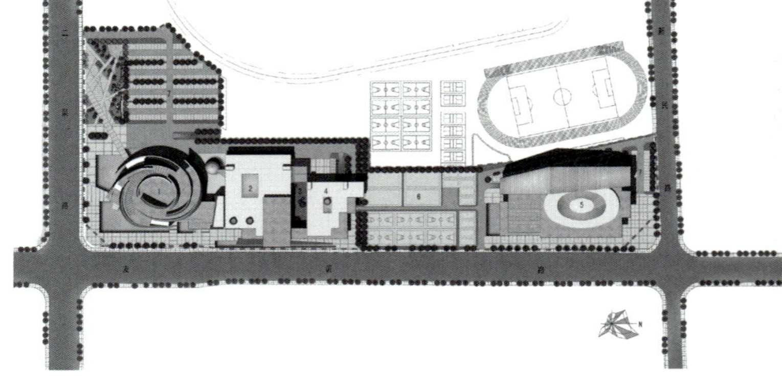

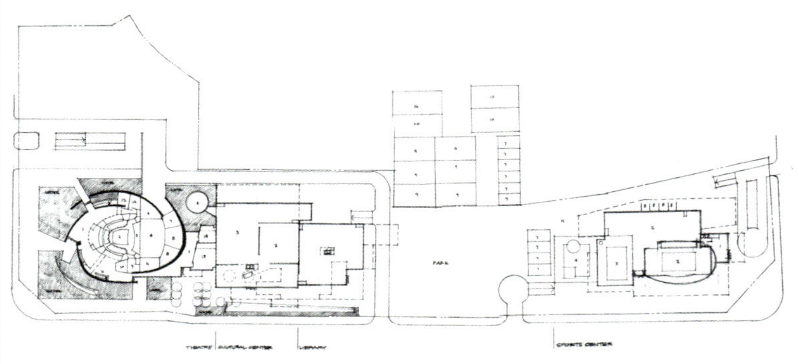

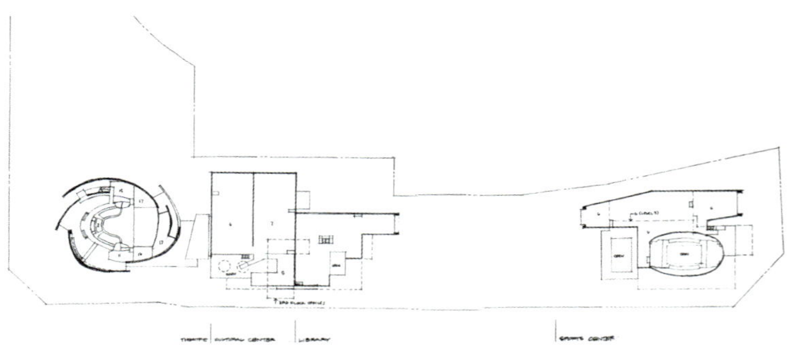

Yinhui Group Skyscraper
银辉集团大厦

设计单位：DGBK Architects International
建筑面积：150 000 m²
高度：280 m
投资：35亿人民币

此280 m超高层建筑是无锡市核心商业区的改造和扩建工程二期的核心部分。该项目建成后将成为无锡市的第一高楼，并进入世界最高的100个摩天楼之列。这个项目包括高端购物中心、写字楼和五星级酒店。购物中心从地下2层到地上4层，并在地下部分与周边商业体和城市地铁连接。办公部分从5层到45层，酒店占据顶部楼层。

绿色设计与可持续发展是该项目的重要设计内容。建筑形体充分考虑采光和风力影响。垂直鼓风涡轮机在建筑角落发电。其他电能通过光伏玻璃产生。雨水和中水的回收利用系统在本项目中投入，热能也可从垃圾中提取。

Design firm: dgbk Architects International
Building area: 150 000 m²
Height: 280 m
Budget: 3.5 billion RMB

This project is core part of the second phase of the city commercial area redevelopment. This 270m skyscraper will be the city's highest building and ranked as noe of the top 100 in the world. This complex includes a shopping centre occuping from the ground to the 4th floor, office building from 5th floor to the 45th floor, and the rest for a 5-star hotel.

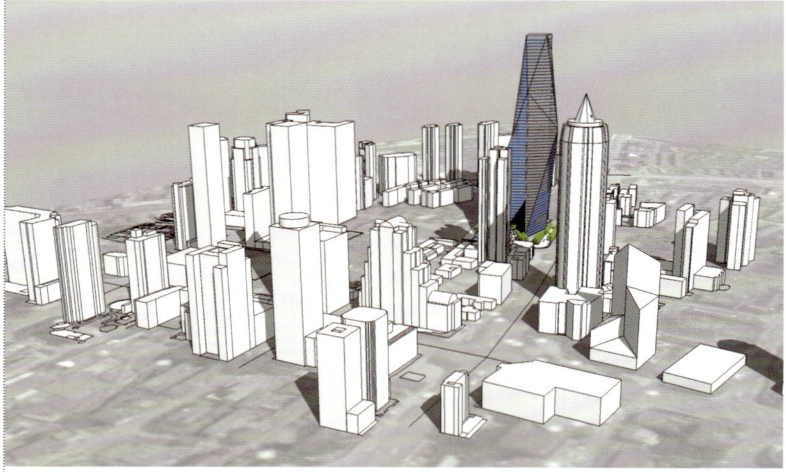

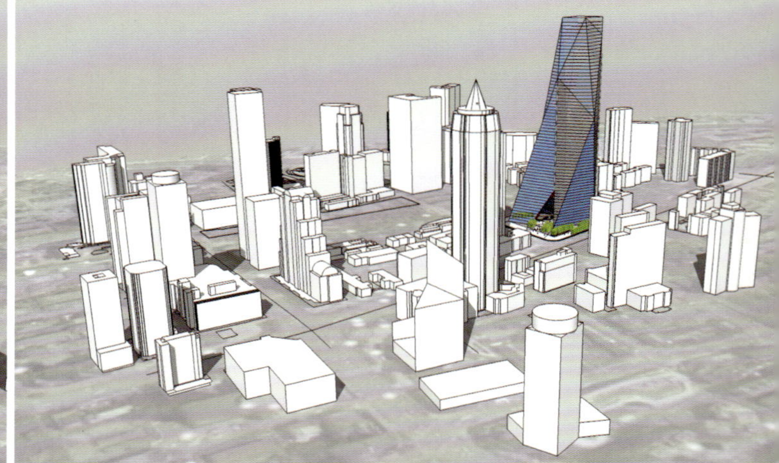

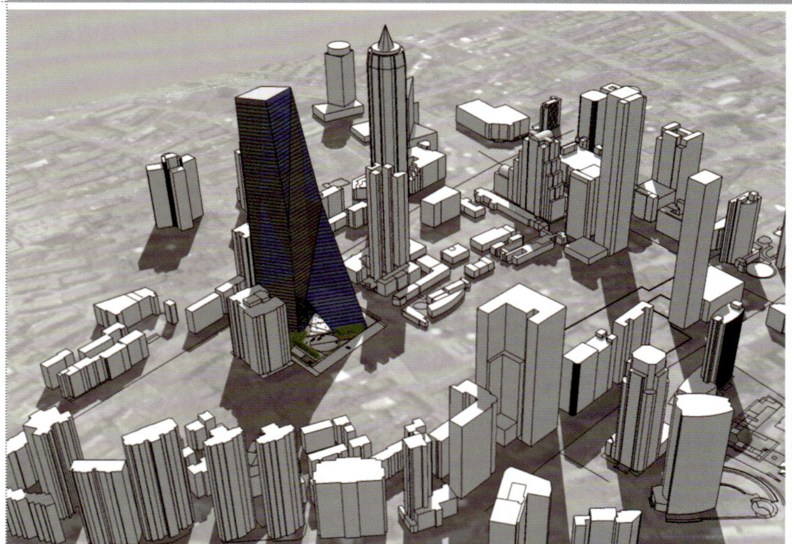

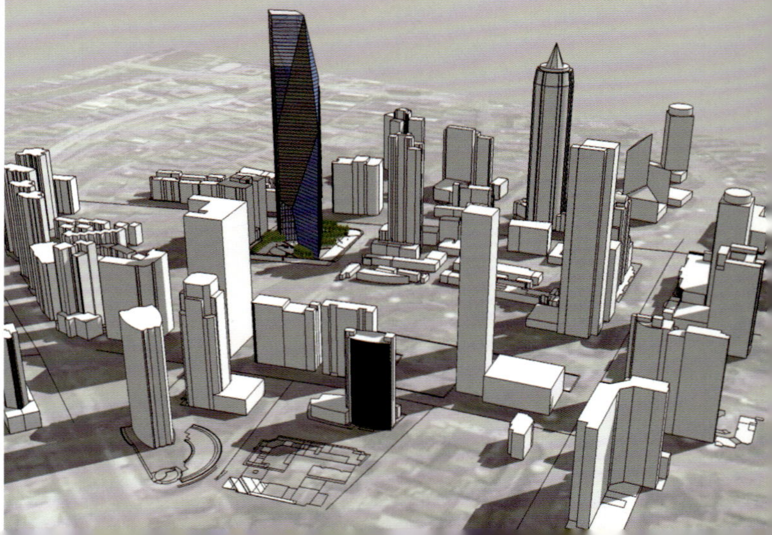

Oct Group Qin Lake Hotel

华侨城泰州溱湖酒店

设计单位：DGBK Architects International
项目位置：江苏省泰州市
基地面积：39 070 m²
建筑面积：49 600 m²

Design firm: Dgbk Architects International
Location: Taizhou, Jiangsu
Site area: 39 070 m²
Building area: 49 600 m²

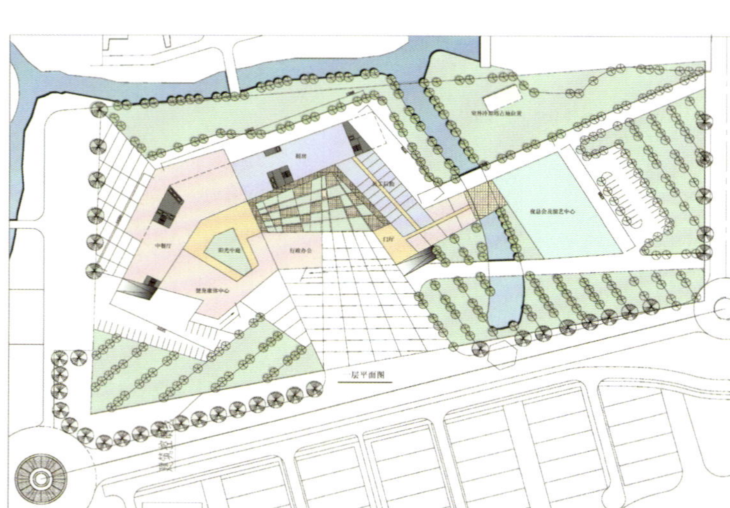

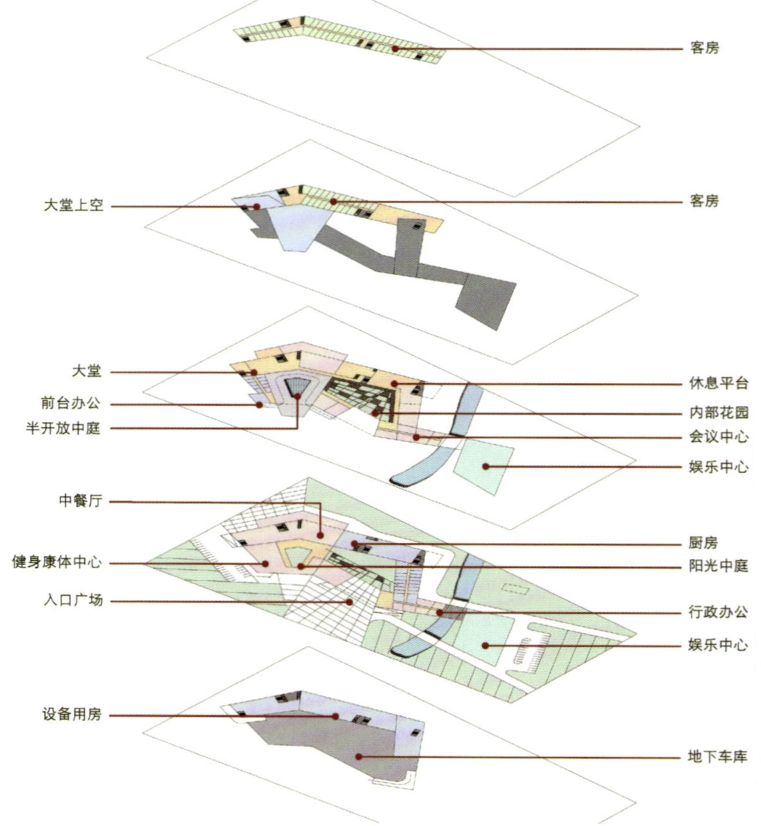

该酒店位于著名的国家级旅游度假区——江苏溱湖湿地风景区内。设计标准为五星级，定位为苏中地区最高档的会务型度假酒店，主体建筑六层，局部七层，包括酒店客房、会议中心、娱乐中心及各类餐饮设施等。

该项目强调通过现代手法诠释中式建筑与场所精神。设计突破传统中式建筑的常见手法，通过对传统中式园林、塔楼、台地、院落等的现代演绎，形成富于创造性和标识性的建筑空间。裙房对中式传统坡屋顶建筑形式加以转换，以现代不规则形态加以体现。景观设计借鉴中式园林借景、框景、步移景异等手法，充分打造度假型酒店的宜人氛围。酒店主体外墙内侧为中空LOW-E玻璃幕墙，外侧表皮通过对中式传统建筑窗格的提取、变形、演化，以百叶形成了既具节能功效，又变化丰富的外表皮结构。外侧表皮通过开启与闭合、百叶透光率的差异，营造出建筑外立面永恒变化的效果。

This hotel is located in the famous Qin lake national resort and the development goal is to make this project one of the best design hotels in the Yangtze Delta Region. The main part of this hotel is 6-storey, and includes different standard suites, conference centre, entertainment centre, restaurants and other leisure functions.

The feature of this project is the contemporary interpretation of the traditional Chinese architecture. The design integrates the spirit of Chinese traditional garden, courtyard space, sloped roof and typical materials with modern architecture features. The double-skin façade is inspired by the Chinese traditional window grid, and the angular form of the building is a modern transform of the Chinese typical sloped roof.

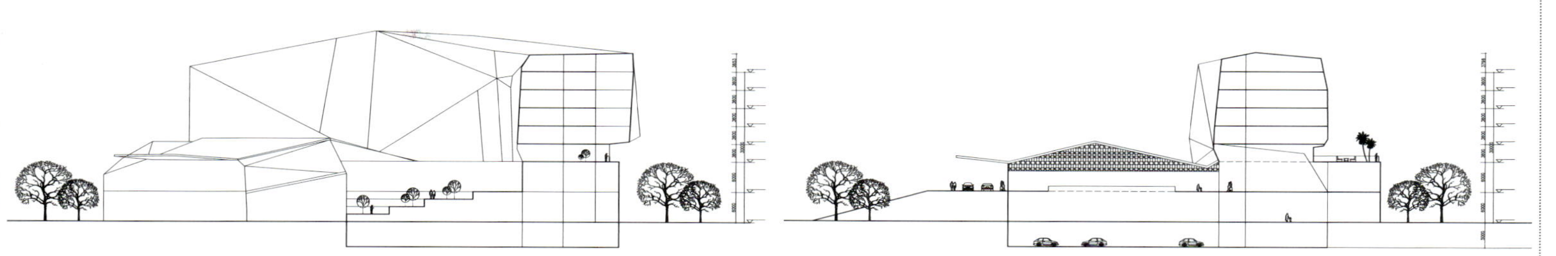

Chengdu 10-3 Block Conceptual Design

成都10–3地块设计竞赛概念方案

设计单位：明创建筑设计咨询（上海）有限公司
设计时间：2009年6月–2010年2月
用地面积：16 437.7 m²
建筑面积：273 490.6 m²
容积率：12
建筑密度：49.5%

Design firm: Ming Lai Architects Inc.
Lead designer: 2009.6–2010.2
Site area: 16 437.7 m²
Building area: 273 490.6 m²

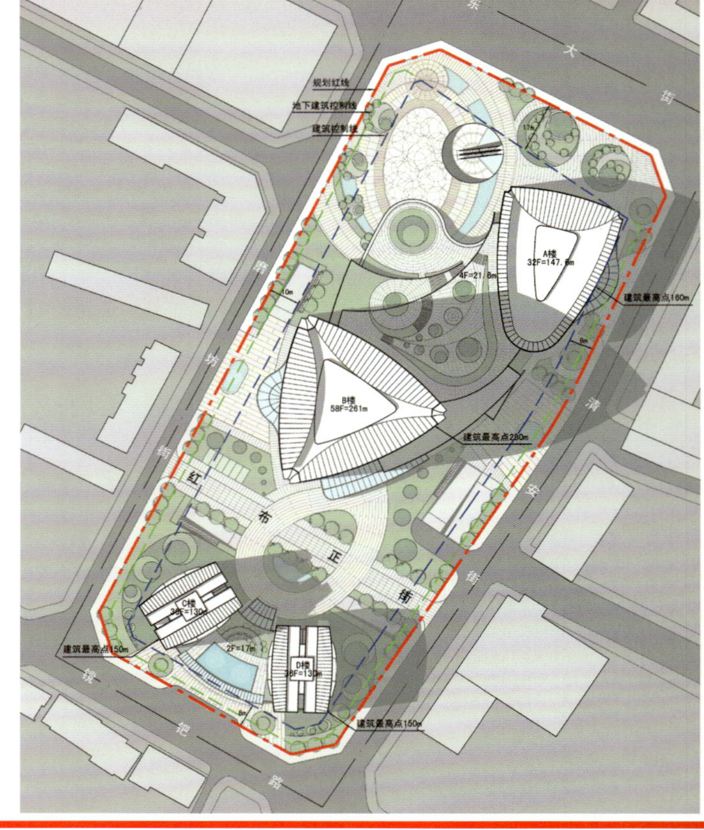

Lai Mingzhi
Ming Lai Architects Inc

赖明志
美国伊利诺州注册建筑师
美国建筑师协会会员
美国明创建筑设计咨询有限公司主持建筑师

赖明志于1997年获得美国伊利诺州理工学院硕士学位，1996年获芝加哥建筑师协会奖。过去十二年来在美国GP建筑设计公司以资深建筑师及专案总监的角色参与过许多国内外项目的设计规划工作。2008年成立美国明创建筑设计咨询有限公司——Ming Lai Architects Inc.（MLAI）。赖明志在国内主导及参与过的项目超过十个，地点涵盖上海、北京、苏州、成都、南京及天津等地。项目包括上海钻石大厦、苏州建屋大厦、成都明宇金融广场、南京国际广场、苏州凯悦酒店、苏州港华研发大楼、惠州凯悦酒店及天津万豪酒店等。多年来建筑理念的实践，除了对办公、酒店及综合体等的设计及需求上，有深层的了解之外，其专业能力与丰富经验也广受业界及客户的肯定。MLAI公司的设计服务范围包括大型综合开发项目、办公大楼、星级旅馆、服务公寓、集团总部等。赖明志本身独特的设计风格承袭现代建筑大师密斯凡德罗的建筑理念，以合理性及经济性为前提，尊重并融合当地的文化特性及社会传统，运用新科技及永续建筑的概念，创造简洁、优雅的建筑作品。

Lai Mingzi obtained his master degree from Illinois Institute of technology in 1997. He is one of the 3 recipients for the Architect Club of Chicago Award in 1996. Ming Lai Architects Inc. (MLAI) was established in 2008. This fledging architectural company is headed by Ming C. Lai, who brings with him a distinguished international portfolio. Prior to founding Ming Lai Architects Inc., he spent 12 years with GP, an established American architecture company as senior architect and project leader, playing a pivotal role as the designer and project manager for many large international projects. In China, Ming Lai has led and involved in more than ten projects in Shanghai, Beijing, Suzhou, Chengdu, Nanjing, Tianjin and many other cities. His projects include the Shanghai Lujiazui Diamond Tower, Suzhou Genway Tower, Chengdu Mingyu Financial Plaza, Nanjing International Center, Suzhou Hyatt Regency Hotel, Suzhou Ganghua research Tower, Huizhou Grand Hyatt Hotel and Tianjin Marriott Hotel, to name just a few. His profound understanding of the design and needs of offices, hotels and mix-use development is based on his years of a combination of theory and practice. Thus, he wins approval of his clients about his professional capacities and rich experiences. MLAI provides service to large-scale mix-use development projects, office buildings, star hotels, service apartments, corporation headquarters and many more. Its distinctive style hints of the design philosophy of master architect Mies Van der Rohe. To the premise of rationality and economics, it is able to incorporate local culture and traditions with the use of technological advances and ideas of sustainable construction to create simple, but elegant architecture.

整体立面意象上，灵感来自于中国传统的容器——瓷瓶。280 m的主塔楼高度结合瓷瓶的文化意涵及其优美的线条，宜于在西侧喜年广场及本地区大量的方正建筑群中脱颖而出。

本项目将商业、办公、酒店、住宅等功能结合成一个综合体，由4层的地下商场及停车库，4层的商业裙房及4栋分别为150 m到280 m的超高层体量所组成。其中，A栋为高度160 m面向东大街的纯办公楼，B栋为高度280 m，结合酒店及办公的地标性建筑。两栋住宅楼分别为150 m高、面对锴钯街的建筑，以涉外舒居型精装城市豪宅的户型为主。

塔楼平面造型以三角形为主，在面积相同的情况下，三角形的周长比方形更长，各楼层的景观面更大，且三面皆可成为主立面，无论从城市的任一方位皆呈现地标形象。同时在不影响各层功能的原则下，配合瓷瓶的曲线将三角形的尖端向内切角，160m塔楼为上下外突中间内斜，主楼为上下内斜中间外突，两栋塔楼立面形成对比，外观的曲面，具有戏剧性和动感的造型。酒店位于主塔楼顶部，办公电梯核心筒向内缩减，房间位置向核心筒后退，不仅减少面积浪费，同时利用此优势，将此部分外立面设计成一个内凹如镜子般、朝向东大街的弧面，强化地标性的同时，给城市空间造成富有冲击力的视觉震撼。

The overall design idea comes from the traditional Chinese vessel – the porcelain vase. The main tower block stands at 280 meters encompassing the cultural significance and outlines of a beautiful porcelain vase. It easily stands out among the surrounding buildings.

The project comprises of retail, offices, hotel and residential as a whole development. With 4-story basement for car parking facilities, 4 floors of retail spaces and 4 tower blocks ranging from 150 to 280 meters. Tower A with a height of 160 meters facing Dong Da Jie East Avenue purely function as an office building, Tower B with a height of 280 meters is landmark building with hotels and offices as its main functions. The two 150 meters high residential facing Dang Ba street serves as a luxurious condominium within the city.

The main plan of the tower is triangular in shape. Under the same situation when compare to a square, area wise, the length of the triangle is longer, every level of the view is wider and all three sides act as the main facade from any point within the city thus enhancing the image of a landmark building. Keeping in mind the curvature of a porcelain vase, without affecting the nature of the programs within, the 160 meters building tower curves inwards in the middle while the top and bottom extends outwards, meanwhile the main 280 meters building tower bulges out in the middle and curves inwards at the top and bottom thus creating a dialogue between the buildings, a dramatic and dynamic design. Hotel rooms are situated at the top of the building, office elevator core are reduced to allow for the hotel rooms and not wasting any unwanted areas. Using this as an advantage on the facade design, this part of the facade is concave inwards like a mirror facing the main street Dong Da Jie East Avenue thus enhancing the landmark image as well as providing a visual richness within the urban fabric.

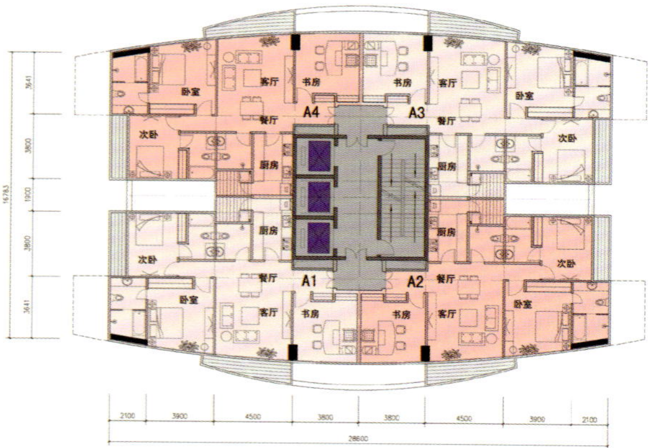
A1
A2
A3
A4
卧室
客厅
书房
餐厅
次卧
厨房

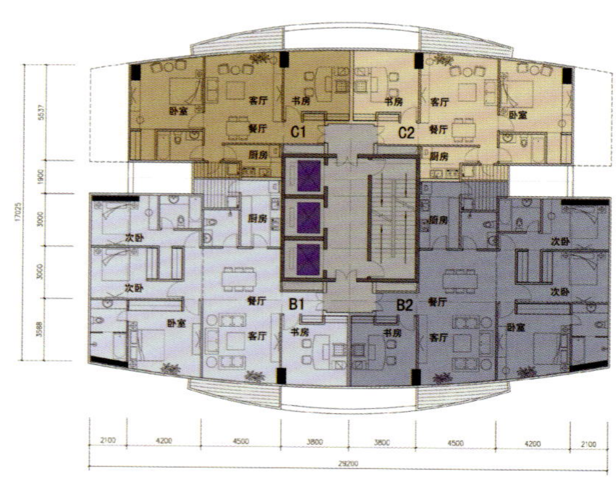
B1
B2
C1
C2
卧室
客厅
书房
餐厅
次卧
厨房

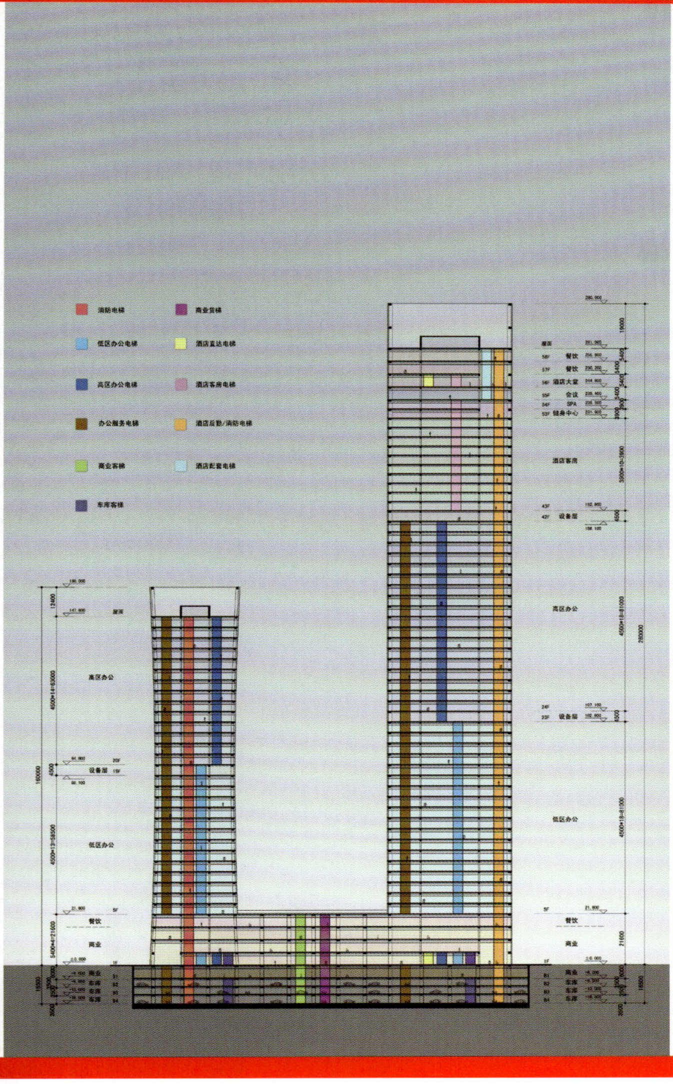

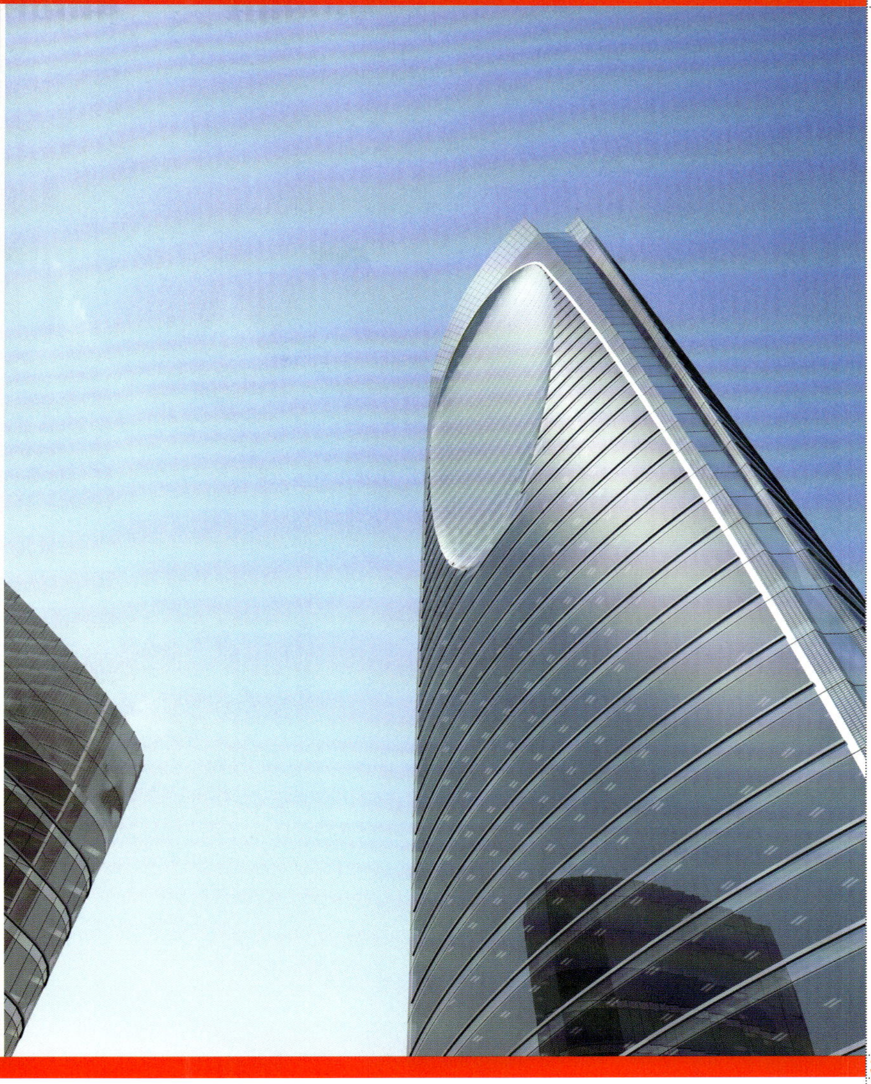

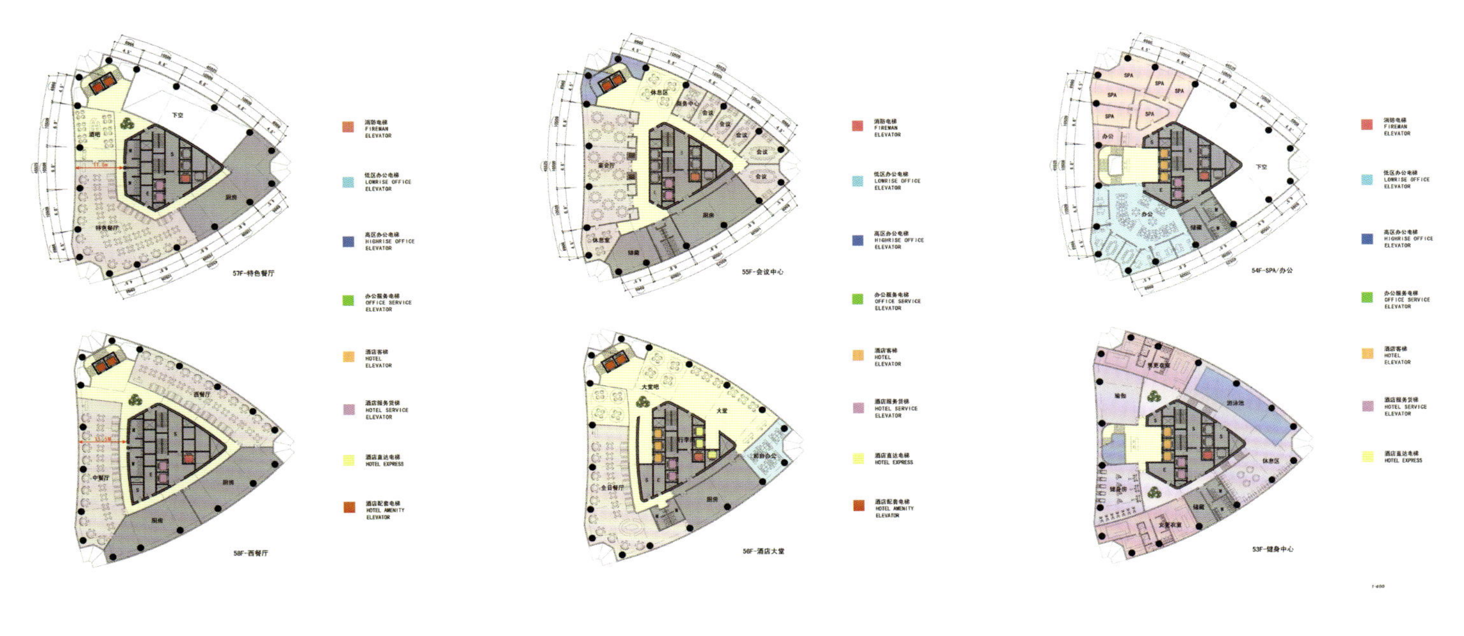

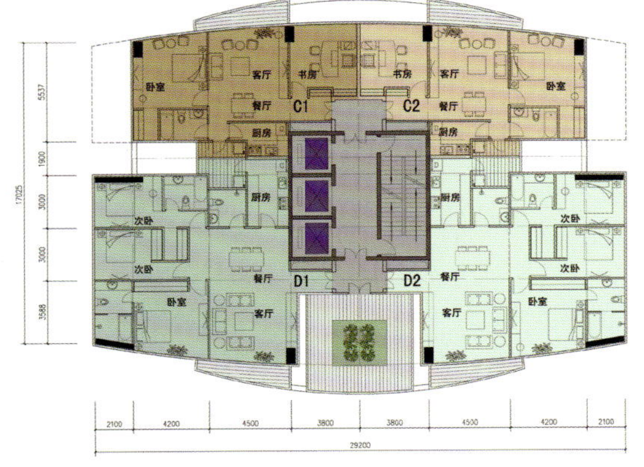

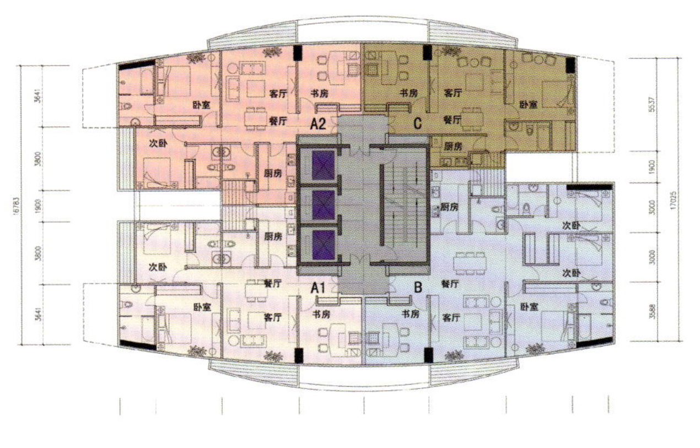

Suzhou Ganghua Gas Company Tower

苏州港华燃气研发大楼

设计单位：明创建筑设计咨询（上海）有限公司
设计时间：2009年7月–2010年6月
用地面积：12 386.6 m^2
建筑面积：74 970.7 m^2
容积率：4.37
地上层数：23层

Design firm: Ming Lai Architects Inc.
Lead designer: 2009.7～2010.6
Site area: 12 386.6 m^2
Building area: 74 970.7 m^2

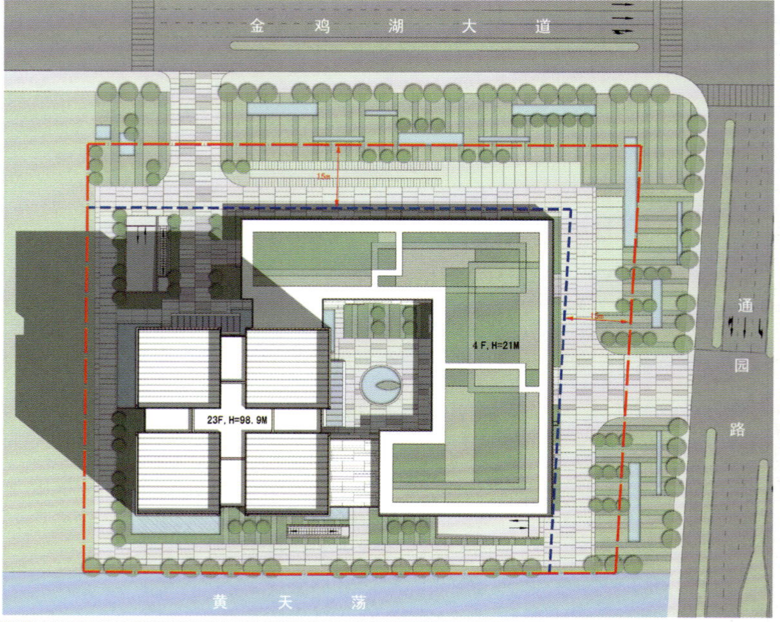

本项目将办公、会议、展厅及餐饮等功能分别结合在这个标志性体量当中。建筑高度为99 m，共23层。体量上由2层地下室，4层裙房及19层办公塔楼所组成。塔楼位于基地西南角，平面设计方正，四个转角向外延伸，暗喻中国古代铜鼎的造型。自各个方向仰视，塔楼外观皆相同，与公司文化内涵结合，凸显港华忠诚，正直，公平，公正的企业理念。裙房体量配合塔楼的造型呈矩形，主立面沿东南北三方向配置，空间及沿街立面最大化，满足功能上的需求。建筑意象的灵感来源于港华燃气公司的"亲商便民，以客为尊"的企业宗旨。塔楼立面造型上将"以人为本"的精神融入其中，利用"人"字形将体量设计成一个人行走般的体态暗示。建筑立面运用简洁的外墙分割，流畅的垂直、水平金属线条与玻璃的融合，没有其他过多的装饰造型，体现现代建筑的风貌。外墙材料以低辐射镀膜中空玻璃（Low-E玻璃）为主，落地玻璃由办公室内向外眺望，园区景观一览无遗。

This landmark building stands at 99 meters tall with 2 floors of basements, 4 floors of podium and 19 floors of office spaces. It consists of offices, meeting rooms, showrooms and restaurants. The tower is located on the south-west corner of the site. Plan is in the form of an equilateral square with four corners extending outwards just like the ancient Chinese relic, the bronze tripod or cauldron. Looking up from all directions, the appearance of the tower are the same, which reflects the cultural connotation of the company, highlighting the company ideals in loyalty, integrity, fairness and justice. In relation to the tower form, the podium is in a rectangular shape maximizing the main facade along the street with regards to the functional needs. Architectural design inspiration comes from the company's motto of "pro-business convenience, customer oriented" slogan.

Tower elevation design incorporated the spirit of "people first", using the Chinese character "human", it suggests a person in a walking pose. Modern facade design using a fusion of metal and glass in vertical and horizontal simple division enhances the simplicity in modern architectural design. Full height glass curtain-walls using Low-E coated insulating glass provides an unobstructed view from the internal spaces out into the park and surrounding landscape.

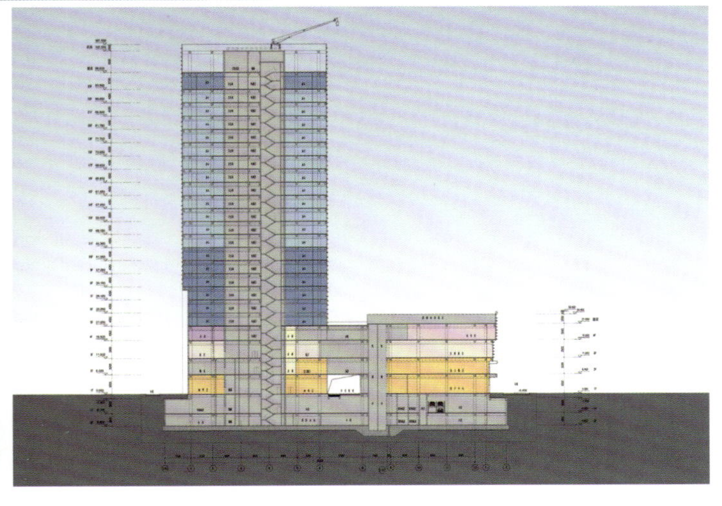

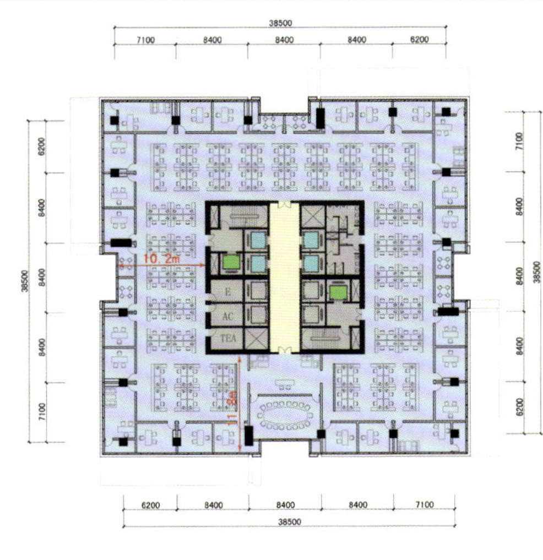
38500
7100 8400 8400 8400 6200
6200 8400 8400 8400 7100
38500

Suzhou Industrial Park No.425 Site

苏州工业园区425号地块设计竞赛概念方案

设计单位：明创建筑设计咨询（上海）有限公司
设计时间：2010年3月–2010年4月
用地面积：9 613 m²
建筑面积：38 863 m²
容积率：3.1

Design firm: Ming Lai Architects Inc.
Lead designer: 2010.3–2010.4
site area: 9 613 m²
Building area: 38 863 m²

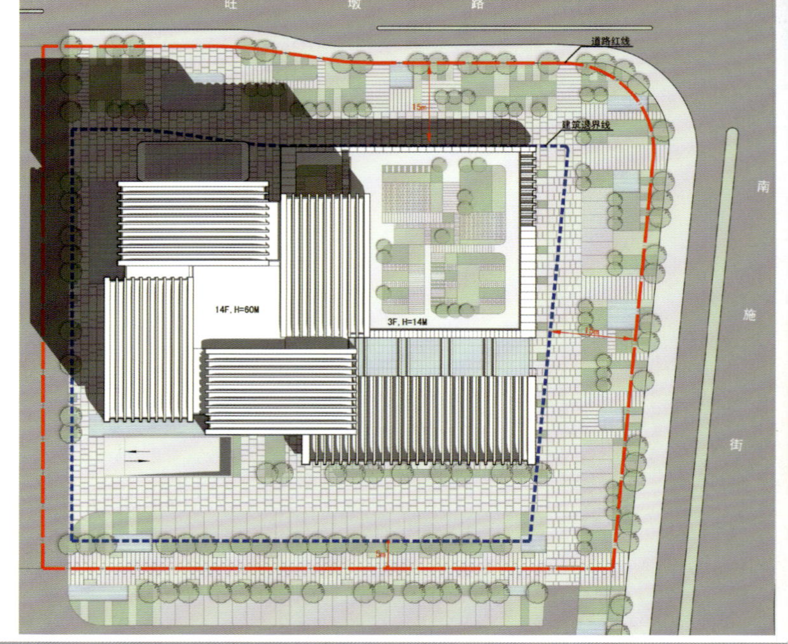

建筑总高度为60m，共14层。体量上由1层地下室、3层的多功能裙房及11层办公所组成。建筑体量上，由于建筑限高60m，在满足容积的情形下，整体建筑将呈现较矮胖的比例关系。为避免笨重呆板，同时要呈现挺拔的建筑形象，在塔楼平面上将四个转角向外延伸，略呈风车造型。外形上如同四个矩形互相咬合，减小立面的面宽。同时裙房体量在二层以上悬挑3.5m，除提供首层行人遮风避雨的功能外，视觉上亦垂直压缩其裙房高度，使整体建筑横竖之间的比例关系大为改善。外墙以中空玻璃为主体，四个错位的角落运用不锈钢框架勾勒出独特的建筑语汇，简洁的立面分割、流畅的垂直金属线条与玻璃的融合，没有其他过多的装饰造型，呈现现代办公建筑的挺拔形象。

This 60-meters high is with a total of 14 floors comprises of 1 basement, 3 floors of podium and 11 floors of office spaces. In order to comply with the plot ratio requirement and a height limit of 60 meters, the proportion of the building would become short and fat. To avoid a clumsy massive and rigid form, four corners of the tower block are extended outwards in a form of a windmill. Four rectangular volumes interlock each other to reduce the width of the facade. The podium on the 2nd floor is cantilevered 3.5 meters above ground providing pedestrians with shelter from the sun and rain. It also helps to reduce the massiveness of the podium visually and improve the overall proportion of the building. facade uses glass curtain-wall system with vacuum glass, four corners of the building uses stainless steel framework to portray the uniqueness of the architectural language. Modern facade design using a fusion of metal and glass in vertical and horizontal simple division enhances the simplicity in modern architectural office design.

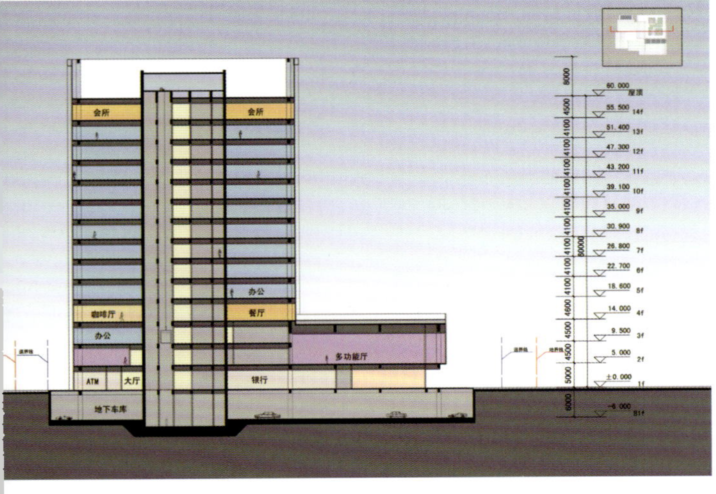
会所
会所
办公
咖啡厅
餐厅
办公
多功能厅
ATM
大厅
银行
地下车库
60.000
屋面
55.500
51.400
47.300
43.200
39.100
35.000
30.900
26.800
22.700
18.600
14.000
9.500
5.000
±0.000
-6.000

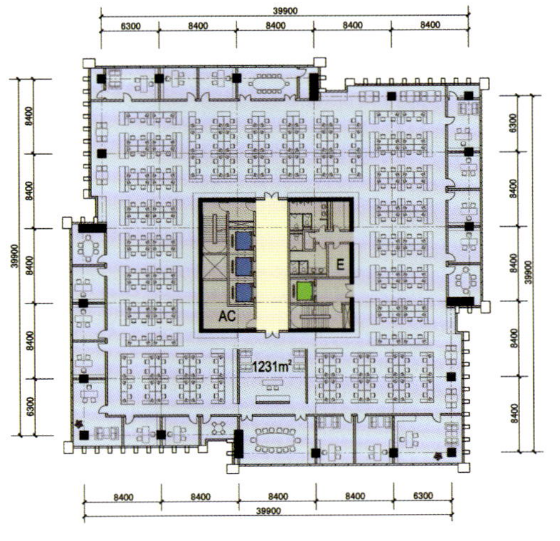
39900
6300
8400
8400
8400
8400
1231m²
AC
E
8400
8400
8400
8400
6300
39900

Church of Suan-Lien Elderly Center, Taipei

台北三芝双连社会福利园区礼拜堂

设计单位：潘冀联合建筑师事务所
设计团队：潘冀、黄种财、谢伟士、陈伯桢、吴晓云、李翩
基地面积：33 100 m²
建筑面积：1 264 m²
建筑层数：地下1层、地上2层
摄影：陈弘暐、陈逸文、谢伟士、潘冀联合建筑师事务所

Design firm: J. J. Pan & Partners, Architects & Planners
Design team: Joshua Jih Pan, Chung Tsai Huang, Wei-shi Hsien, Steven B. J. Chen, Hsiao Yuan Wu, Pen Lee
Site area: 33 100 m^2
Building area: 1 264 m^2
Photographer: David Chen, Yi-Wen Chen, Wei-Shih Hsieh, J. J. Pan & Partners, Architects & Planners

Joshua Jih Pan
J. J. Pan & Partners, Architects & Planners

潘冀
潘冀联合建筑师事务所

1942年生于天津。

1963年毕业于台湾成功大学建筑系后赴美国莱斯（Rice）大学建筑系进修专业学士课程，并于1967年取得纽约哥伦比亚大学建筑及都市设计硕士学位。在60年代末，处于纽约的Philip Johnson与Davis、Brody等建筑事务所工作。9年后返台，塑造成了设计、建筑实务与社会使命兼容的修正性现代主义者人格。

1976年加入宗迈建筑师事务所成为合伙人。

1981年成立潘冀建筑师事务所。2000年改为潘冀联合建筑师事务所。近30年来以贯彻设计品质、充分掌握建筑技术，对台湾建筑提出解答，尤以具备训练良好的监造人员驻地监造、负责到底的专业态度深获业主肯定。作品既具现代主义的利落，又有后现代的亲切人性尺度。诚信严谨、笃实精确的风格，成为中国台湾第一个获美国建筑师协会（AIA）院士（Fellow）资格的建筑师，至今完成500余件建筑作品，广获国内外建筑刊物之刊载并赢得三十余项设计奖项。

1996年获选为台湾杰出建筑师，2003年荣膺台湾建筑学会会士。

Joshua Jih Pan was born in Tianjin. After his graduation from the Cheng Kong University in Taiwan, he went to America and continued his architectural training at Rice University to obtain Bachelor degree of Architecture. In 1967, he received Master degree of architecture and urban design from Columbia University in New York. In the late 1960s, with nine years working experience at firms such as Philip Johnson and Davis Brody Associates in New York, he was fully equipped in design and practice with social mission. In 1976, he joined Fei & Cheng Associates as a partner. He established his own practice in 1981 as J.J. Pan & Partners, Architects and Planners. Over nearly 30 years, he has consistently maintained a high design quality and has upgraded Taiwan's architectural standard. His professional performance is most evident when observed from the well trained staff he puts on site to oversee his projects. His designs contain the terseness of modernism, but also take into account the humanity of post-modernism. With his thoughtful, sympathetic and reliable design and delivery, Pan has become the first architect from Taiwan, China to be elected to the American Institute of Architects. He has won more than 30 design awards and has completed over 500 projects, many of which has been widely published by journals home and abroad.

礼拜堂的构想从基督教常用之符号「鱼」作为表明信仰的象征。配合曲折的河沟及地界，以两条弧线勾勒出鱼形平面，钢架沿着弧线撑起二张曲面，形成完整之型抗结构，以230吨的精简用钢量，创造长40×宽26×高18公尺之空间。

引「帐幕/幔子」为礼拜堂外观姿态。左右弧形外墙采平接烤漆铝板，前后采光大窗以玻璃帷幕组构，外露柱脚则反映「帐篷坚固的橛子」稳固地卯定在大地。室内侧将"米"字钢架直接露出，形成结构蓬架，钢构间之三角空间设计特殊之内倾板片，让室内侧墙提供不同之声波反射角，使反射音可均匀扩散，并运用悬吊的三角形弯曲反射板，提供讲台之声响向远方传递，以兼顾诗歌吟唱与讲道研习的演说需求。观众席分两楼层，提供550个座位，地面层前排提供轮椅为长者使用，侧边开敞走道可衔接大厅与失智专区。

家具造型构想源自内墙的分割形状，考虑长者的行动及生理障碍，与宗教礼仪及节日而设计，为长老教会量身打造。

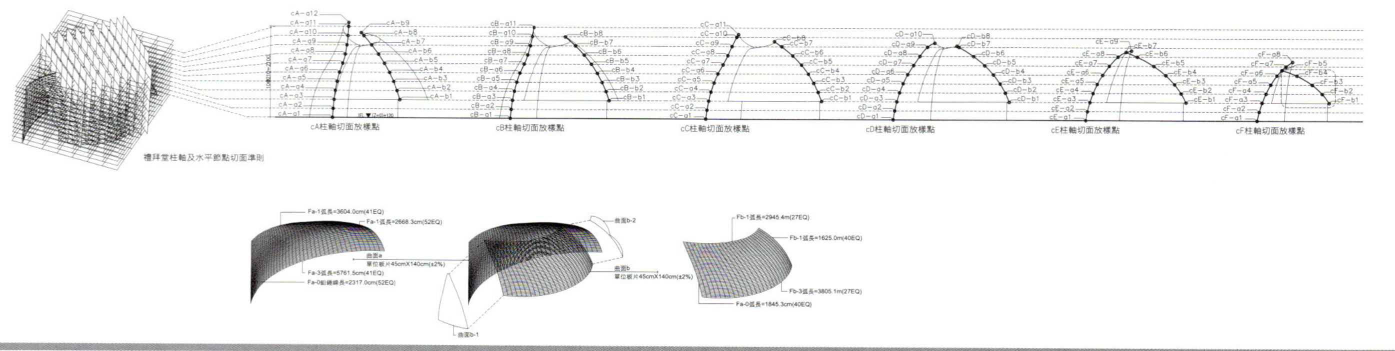

The symbol of "fish" for the Christian faith inspired the design concept of the church building. The shape of the building is drawn along the winding ditch and land boundary with two curving lines forming a fish figure. The steel frame rises up along the two curved planes, forming a complete arched structure. A minimal quantity of 230 tons of steel created a space of 40m/L×26m/W×18m/H in dimension.

The exterior form of the church takes on the imagery of "tent". The arching exterior claddings are butt jointed kynar finished aluminum panels, with large glass curtain walls at both ends to admit light. The revealing pedestals firmly stationed on the ground reflecting the "fixed pegs of a tent." The asterisk-shaped steel truss in the interior is exposed to form a structural frame, with an inward tilting panel placed inside the triangular space formed by the steel members to provide different reflecting angles. The resonance is thus evenly diffused, and a suspending triangular reflection panel is used to facilitate the transmission of voice on the podium to distant corners, fulfilling the requirements of lyrical chorus and speaking. The mezzanine seating area provides 550 seats, and the front rolls at the ground level accommodate the elderly on wheel-chair, while the side passageway connects the lobby and the Dementia Care Zone.

The furniture is designed with the concept deriving from the sectioning pattern of the interior walls, taking the kinetic and physical constraints of the elderly into consideration. The entire design based on religious ceremony and rituals is tailor-made for the Presbyterian Church in Taiwan China.

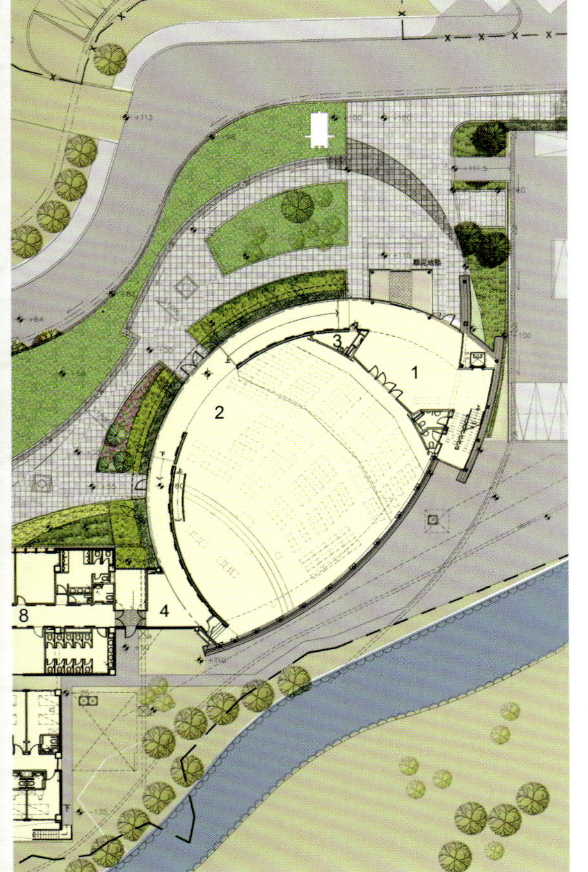

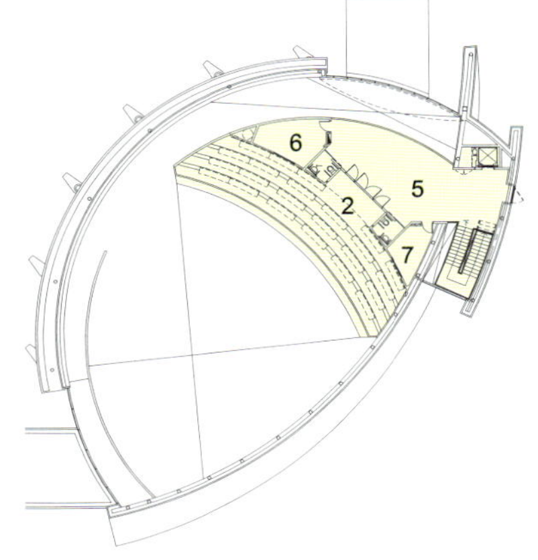

1 floor

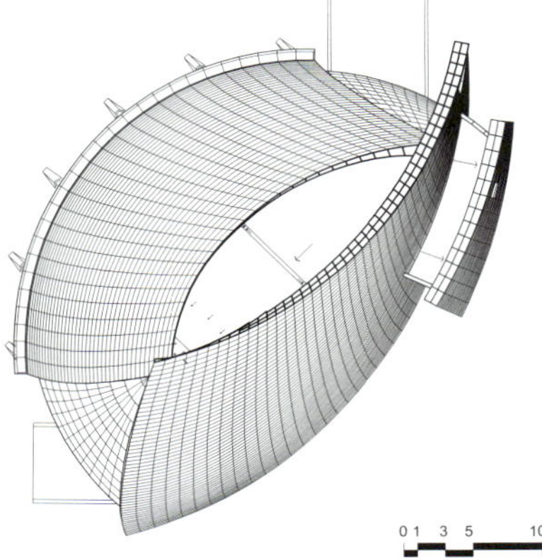

2 floor

0 1 3 5 10m

1. Hall
2. Audience seats
3. Acoustic control roc
4. Passage
5. Foyer
6. Control room
7. Nusery
8. Caring building

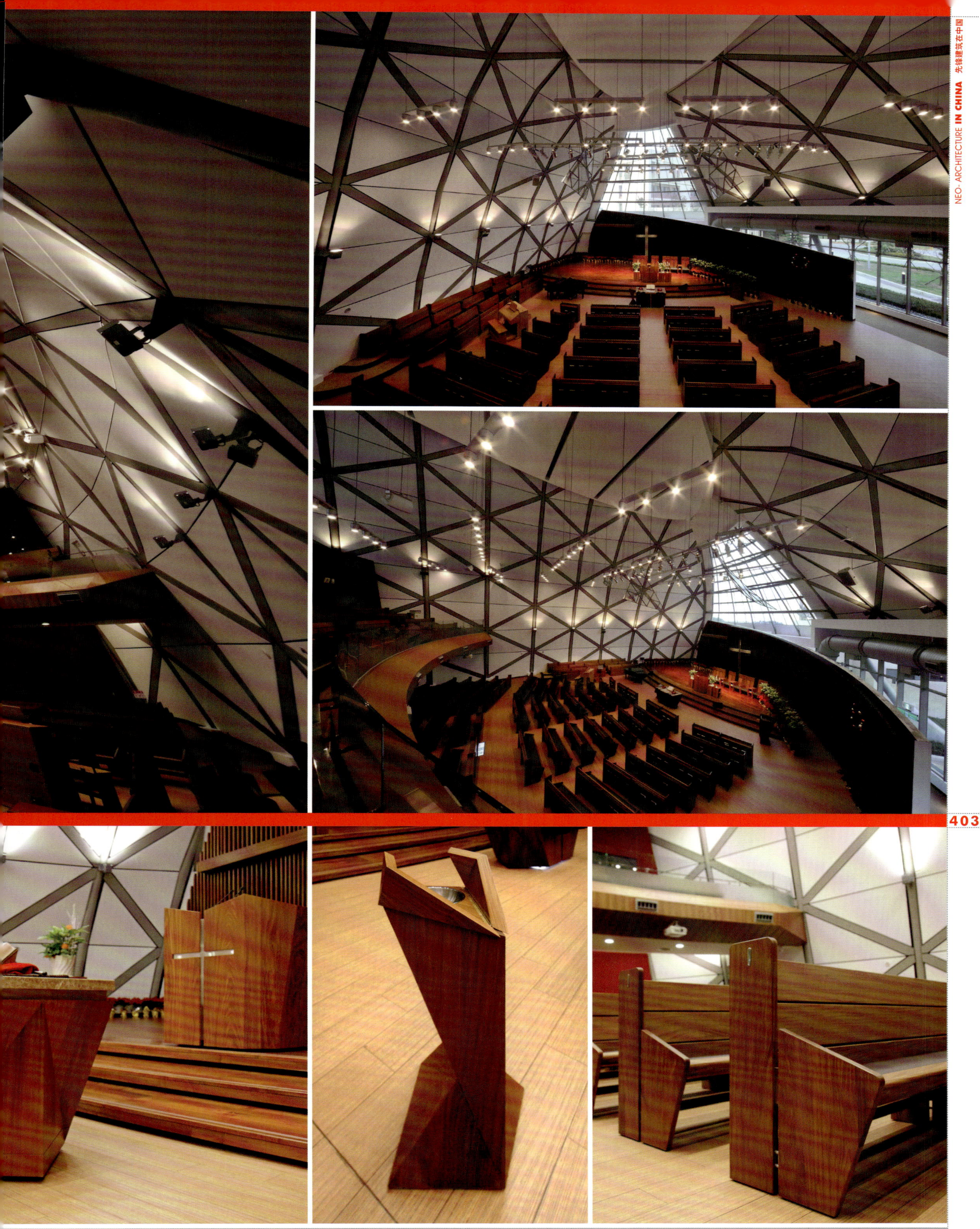

Pegatron R&D Center, Shanghai
和硕联合科技上海园区研发运筹楼

设计单位：群裕设计咨询（上海）有限公司、潘冀联合建筑师事务所
设计团队：潘冀、贺马丁、侯秉宜、吴柏德、林志翰（Pega Casa）、李政宜
基地面积：24 159 m²
建筑面积：41 867 m²
建筑层数：地上6层
摄影：王正强、潘冀联合建筑师事务所

Design firm: Horizon Design Co., Ltd. (Shanghai)
J. J. Pan & Partners, Architects & Planners
Design team: Joshua Jih Pan, Martin Hagel, Pin I Hou, Peter Wu, Zhi Han Lin, (Pega Casa) , Zheng Yi Li
Site area: 24 159 m²
Building area: 41 867 m²
Photographer: John Wang/ J. J. Pan & Partners

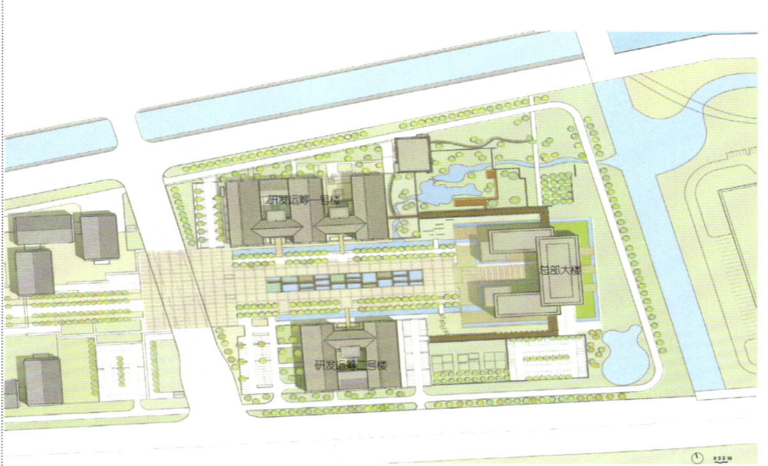

本研发大楼是七幢研发建筑群中第一幢完工的建筑，其位置在基地主轴线与研发楼群中央水景二轴线的交界处。建筑量体分为3栋6层楼长条形建筑，包括研发办公楼、高级干部宿舍与公用设备辅房三部分。建筑群的配置采用合院院落的空间架构，组织所有的主要建筑与外部辅助空间。

外形处理上，运用江南徽派建筑白墙灰瓦的极简风格与当地传统材料，创造兼具现代美感与地域特色的建筑。徽派建筑内院与主堂合用的空间手法，亦在本设计中予以强调，特别是室内、外空间与材料的延续性、内院水景、户外公用水渠及农耕趣味是本案景观设计的主题，与建筑共同营造出江南人文气息的高科技研发环境。

The R&D Building of this project is the first to be finished in the group of seven R&D Buildings, located in the interface between the main axis of the site and the axis of the central waterscape of the R&D Building group. The building mass consists of three 6-floor long-shaped buildings, including the R&D Building, the top executive dormitory and public facility ancillary room. Configuration of the building cluster adopts the spatial structure of multiple section compound, organizing all the main structure and the external auxiliary spaces.

The formal design features the white wall and gray tile of the minimalist Hui architectural style southern to the Yangtze River along with local materials to create the aesthetically modern building with regional flavor. Incorporation of the inner court and the main lobby of Hui style architecture is a prominent characteristic of this design, particularly the continuity of materials for the indoor and outdoor structures. The themes of landscape design in this project include the inner court waterscape, the outdoor public trenches, and the farming interest. The diversity of themes working together with the building creates a high-tech R&D environment.

西向立面图

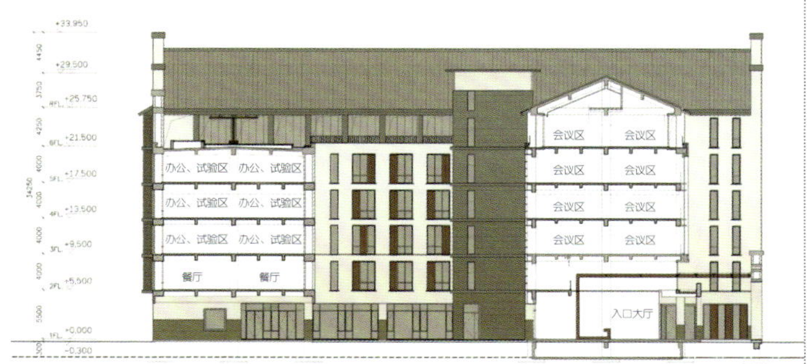

办公楼剖面图

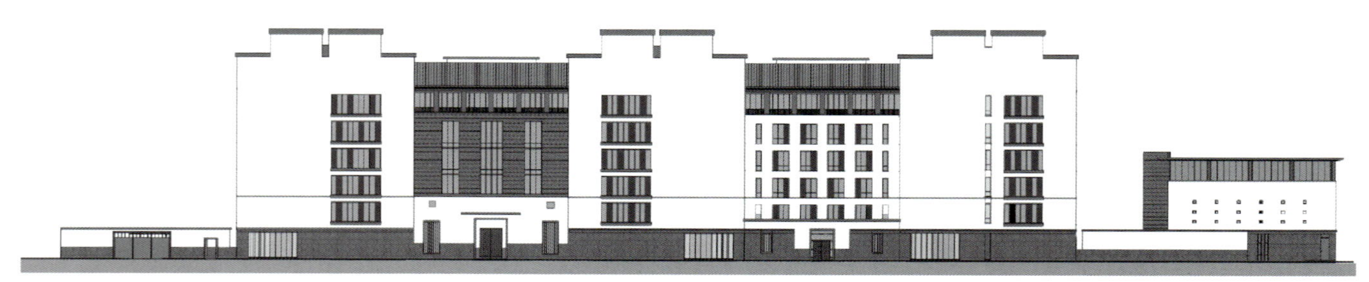

南向立面图

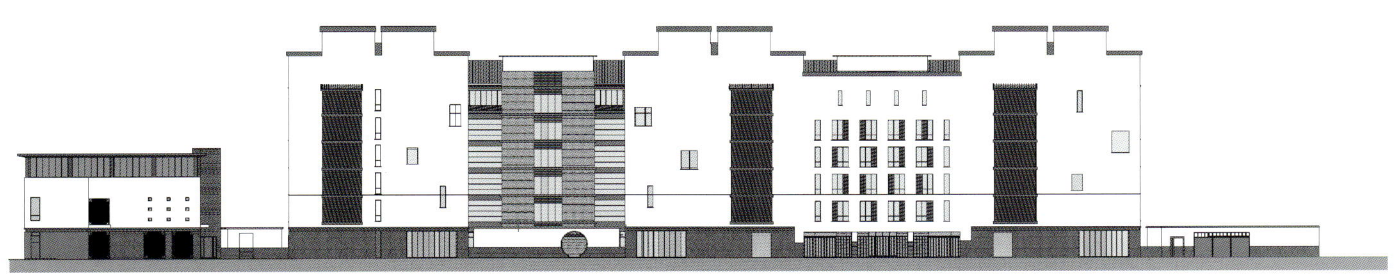

北向立面图

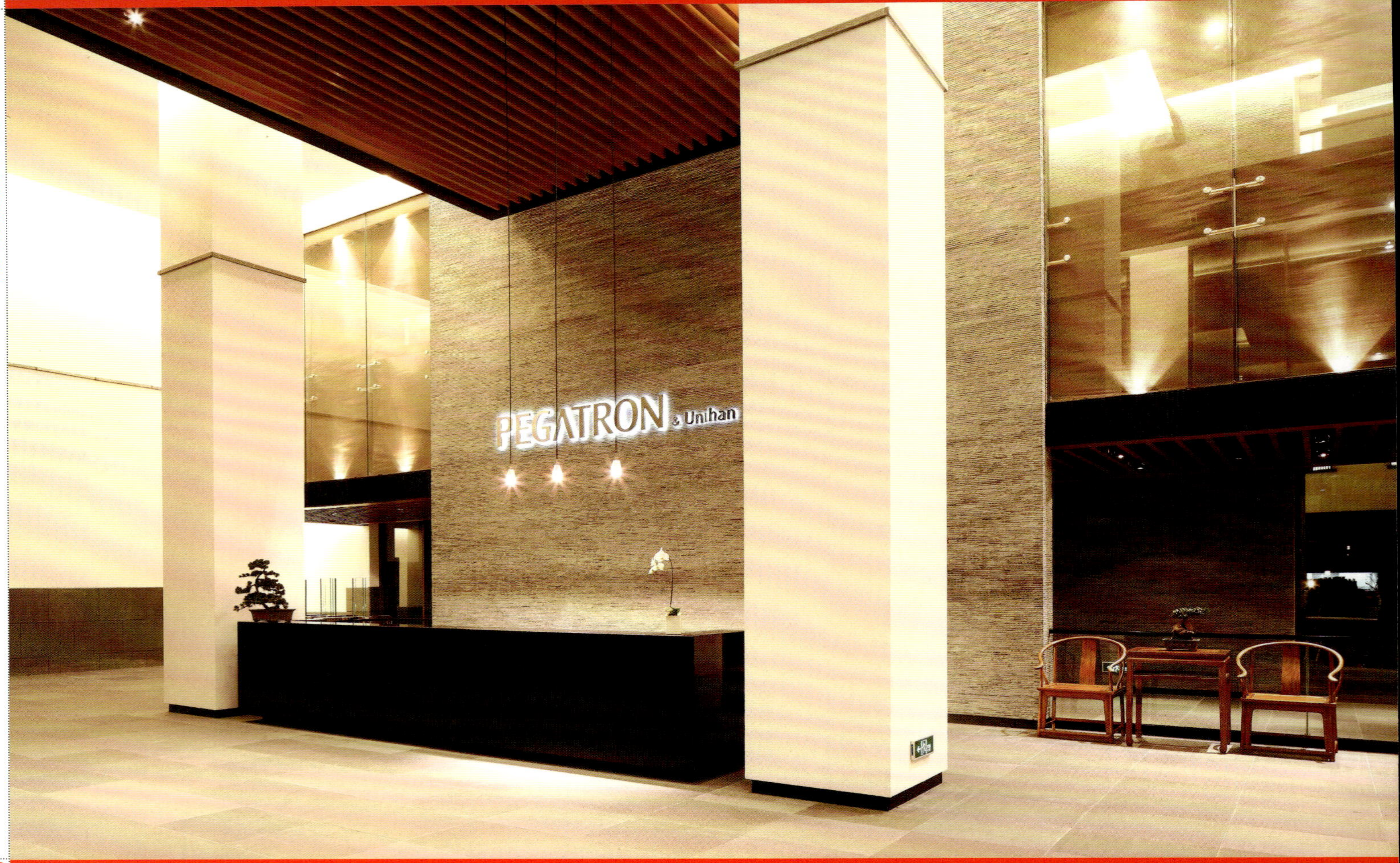
PEGATRON & Unihan

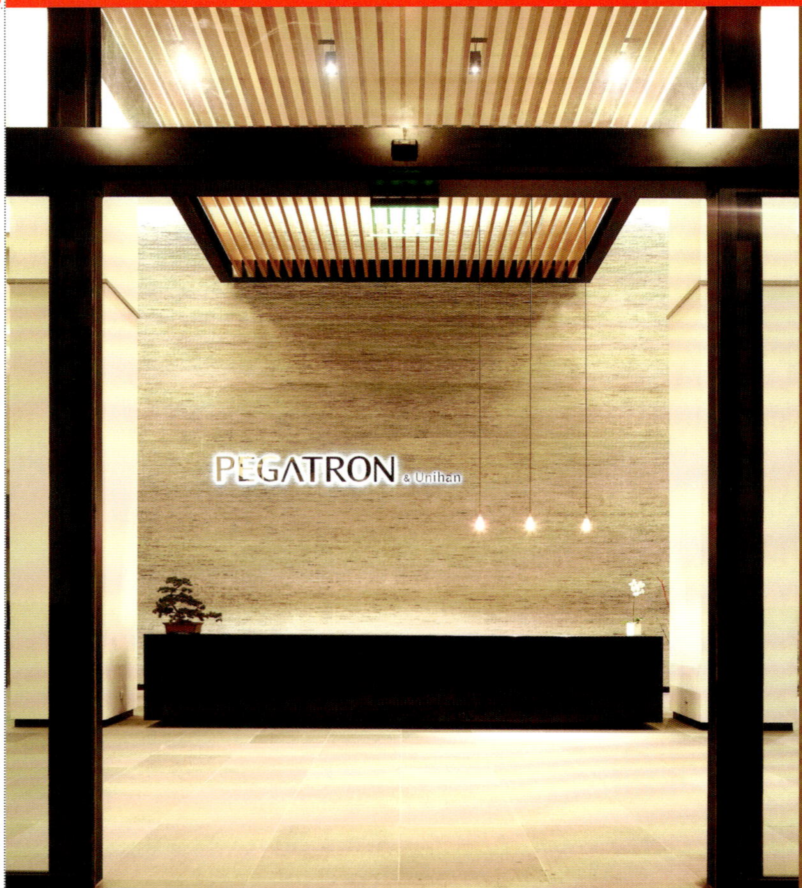
PEGATRON & Unihan

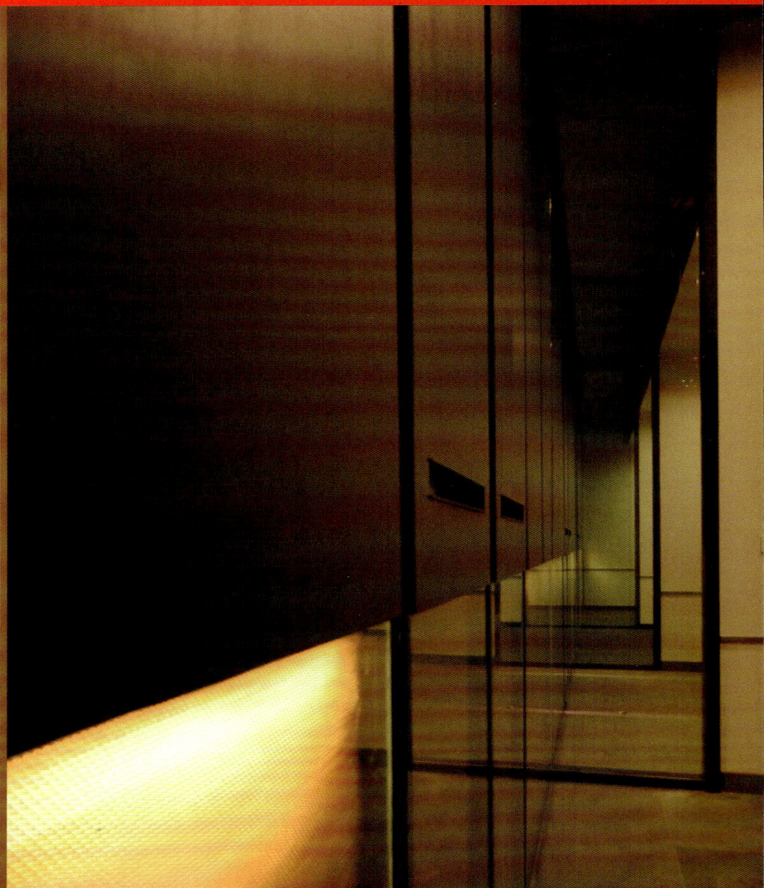

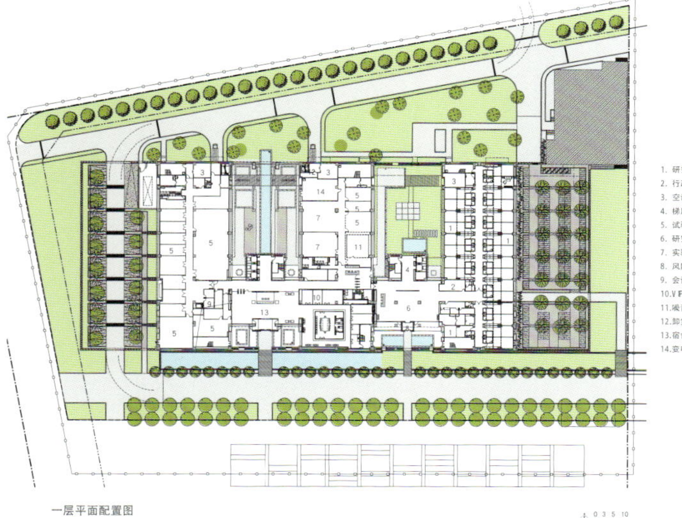

1. 研究室
2. 行政管理
3. 空调机房
4. 梯厅
5. 试验室
6. 研究区大堂
7. 实验区
8. 风除室
9. 会议室
10. VIP会议室
11. 噪音试验室
12. 卸货区
13. 宿舍区入口大堂
14. 变电室

一层平面配置图

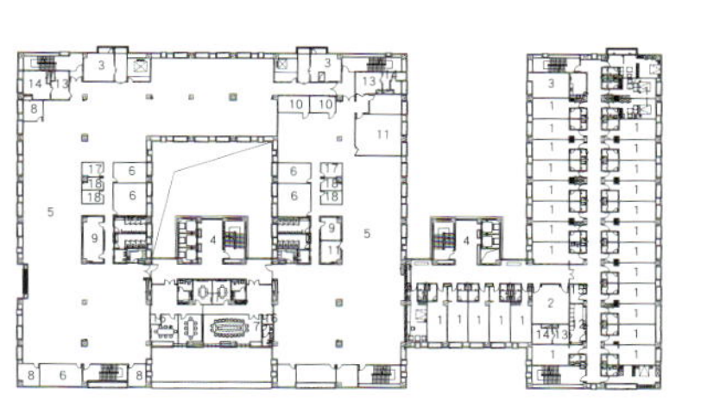

1. 研究室
2. 交谊室
3. 空调机房
4. 梯厅
5. 办公.试验区
6. 会议室
7. VIP会议室
8. 主管会议室
9. 休息区
10. 机房
11. MIS机房
12. 洗衣房
13. 弱电间
14. 强电间
15. 储藏室
16. 吸烟室
17. 实验室
18. 讨论室

三~五层平面配置图

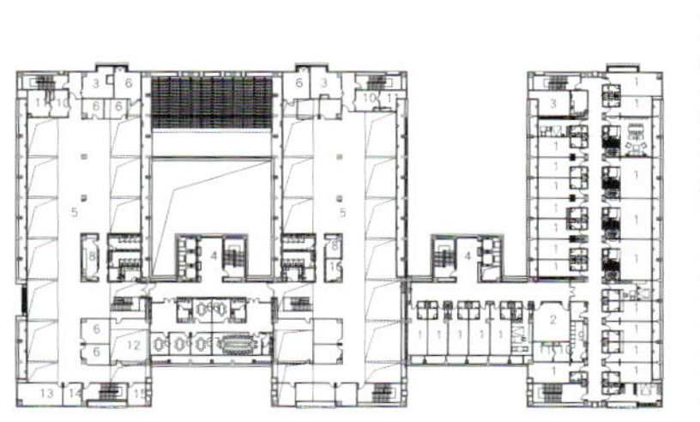

1. 研究室
2. 交谊室
3. 空调机房
4. 梯厅
5. 办公.试验区
6. 会议室
7. VIP会议室
8. 休息区
9. 洗衣房
10. 弱电间
11. 强电间
12. 训练教室
13. ID摄影棚
14. 手工模型室
15. 讨论室
16. MIS机房
17. 储藏室

六层平面配置图

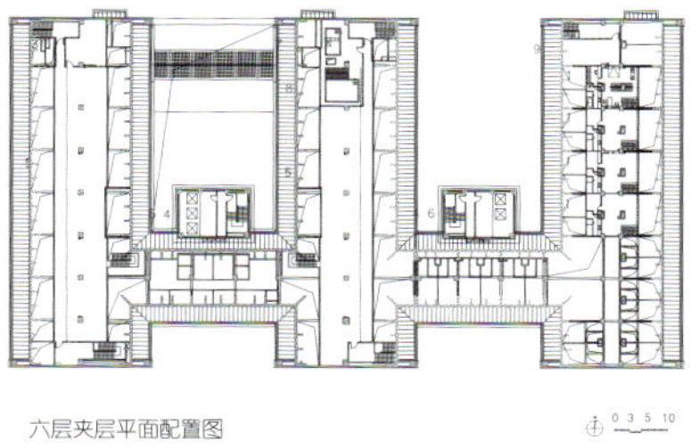

1. 研究室
2. 交谊室
3. 机房
4. 梯厅
5. 办公区
6. 电梯机房
7. 消防水箱
8. 生活水箱
9. 排烟机房

六层夹层平面配置图

Thousand Leaves Courtyard, Xuzhou

徐州千叶院概念设计

设计单位：德默营造建筑事务所
项目团队：陈旭东、Matej Dobis、徐鑫、Paulo de Araujo、沙少磊
方案设计时间：2009年11月—2010年4月
建筑面积：1 000 m²
层数：三层
结构：钢结构
造价：200 000元

Design firm: DAtrans Architecture Office
Designer team: Chen Xudong, Matej Dobis, Xu Xin, Paulo de Araujo, Sha Shaolei
Design date: 2009.11–2010.4
Building area: 1 000 m²

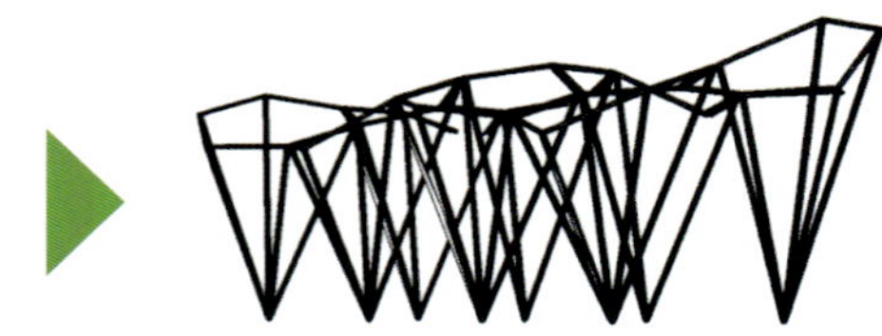

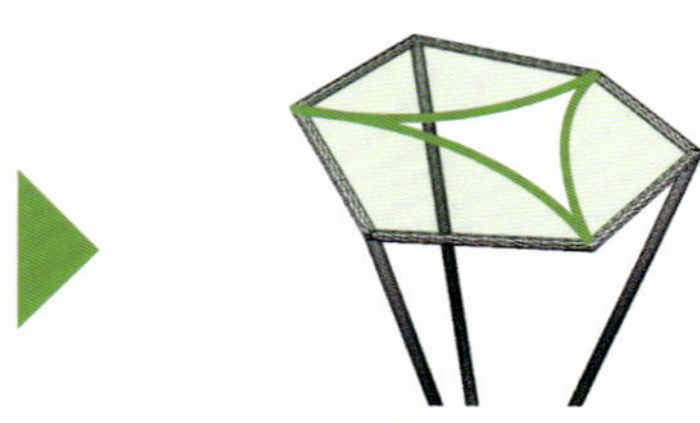

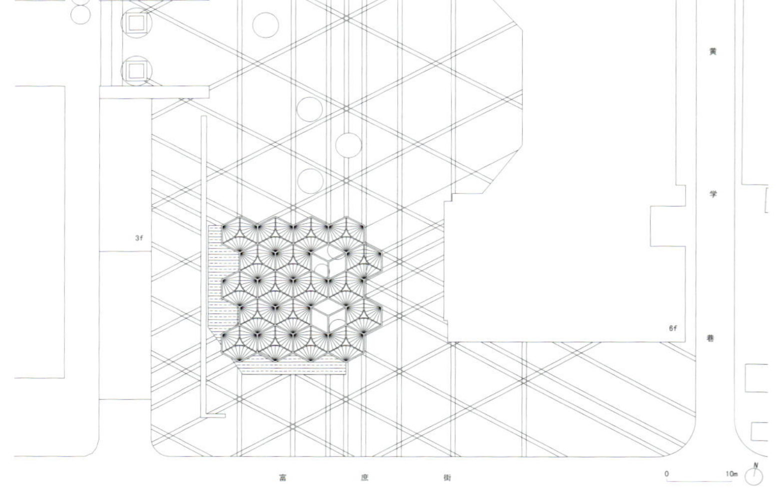

DA 德默营造 trans

DAtrans Architecture Office

德默营造建筑事务所

德默营造是2001年成立于德国柏林的国际化都市建筑艺术设计研究机构，于2004年在上海组建德默营造建筑事务所，以积极的态度和专题概念，介入当代中国城市更新改造，以多学科、跨领域、国际化的操作，实务与学术研究互动的工作方法，参与到中国的建筑和设计实践中，并尝试在材料和技术实验基础上，探索新建筑美学的可能性。

现有城市设计师、建筑师、景观设计师、平面设计师和艺术及经济管理专家组成的多专业复合型团队，同国际多家设计咨询、技术支持和研究机构形成长期稳定的交流与合作网络。

德默营造重要的设计项目有：Art Deco凹凸家具库、杭州滨江双塔、M50/莫干山50号总体规划及建筑改造、开封火车站前城市设计、与艺术家艾未未合作的杭州西湖江南会、广东美术馆人文图书馆以及瑞典斯德哥尔摩公共图书馆竞赛等。同时，获得多项建筑竞赛的奖项。

德默营造的项目已被《纽约时报》、美国《建筑实录》、意大利《Domus》、德国《建筑世界》和《时代建筑》等国内外知名大众和专业媒体报道和收录，并出版有研究和作品集《二手摩登：M50/莫干山50号的城市营造》。

德默营造也活跃在如伦敦中国发电站艺术展、深圳建筑双年展等国内外重要专业和艺术展览文化活动中。因其具有代表性的、对当代城市建筑的思考和结合中国文化气质的独特实践，受到荷兰国家建筑研究所、比利时布鲁塞尔建筑中心的邀请，参加当代中国建筑展，引起了广泛的关注和讨论。

DAtrans, founded in Berlin, an international metropolis, in 2001, is an organization of architecture design, and set up its office in Shanghai, 2004. DAtrans positively participates in the rebuilding of China's cities with its internationalized operations and plays a role in the practice of Chinese architecture and design by working practically and academically as well. Meanwhile, Datrans is trying to explore the possibilities of new architecture art through constant experiments of materials and techniques.

Current work team is composed of staff from different fields, including city designers, architects, landscape designers, graphic designers and experts on art, economy and management. It has established exchanging and cooperative network with many international organizations of design consulting, technique support and research.

The important projects of DAtrans are: Art Deco Furniture Gallery, Twin-tower Hangzhou, M50 Urbanreno Shanghai, city design in front of the railway station Kaifeng, Jianghanhui Hangzhou (cooperated with artist Ai Weiwei), Public Library in Guangdong Museum of Art and an international competition of City Library Extension in Stockholm, Sweden. And DAtrans won some architectural competitions.

DAtrans's projects were reported and collected by some well-known and professional magazines such as New York Times, Architectural (U.S.A), Domus (Italy), Ctopos (Germany). Besides, DAtrans has its own research and work collection Second Hand Modernity: the urban renovation of M50.

DAtrans also goes around some professional exhibitions of art and culture both at home and abroad. It has drawn more attention and discussion since it was invited by National Architecture Institute Netherlands and Architectural Center Brussels, Belgium because of its thinking on modern city architecture and unique practice of integrating Chinese culture.

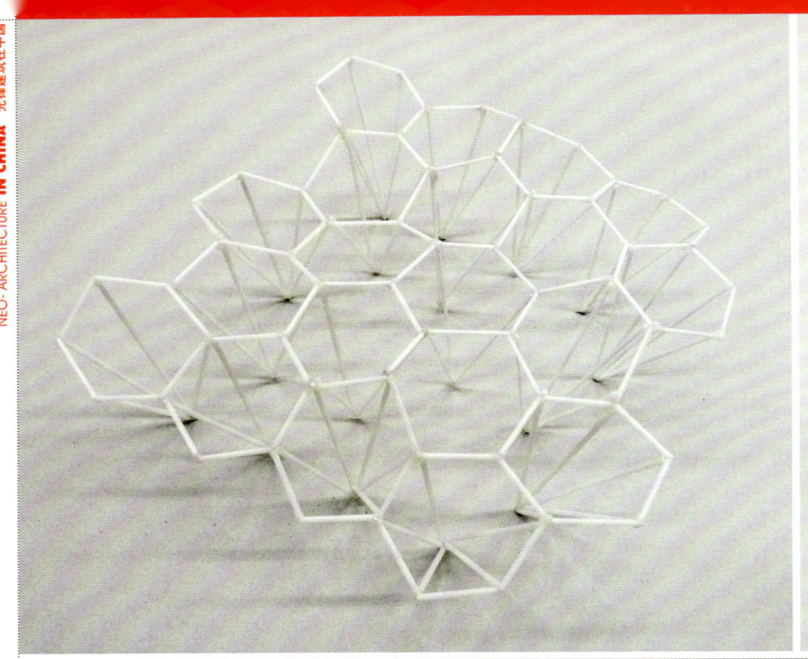

项目简介
项目基地位于徐州市鼓楼区彭城一号时尚休闲商业广场，地处市中心核心商圈。“彭城一号”作为城建重点工程项目和最重要的城市十大商圈之一，业主希望我们能在商业广场沿富庶街的入口区域设计一个标志性建筑，并兼备展示中心的功能以吸引和服务大多数人。

设计概念
设计从自然中提取灵感，以徐州市树银杏树作为形式的母体——外露颀长的圆形钢柱和动态起伏的曲形屋面犹如一片在微风吹拂下缓缓摇曳的银杏树林，室外耀眼的阳光透过银杏叶状的半透膜投下的斑驳光影更给人们一种林中漫步的氛围。

设计手法
建筑的主入口位于屋顶东部建筑最高点其下覆盖的半室外区域——作为一个完全敞开的公共空间以开放友好的姿态迎接着由南端富庶街进入广场的主要人流；镂空的两片六边形屋顶下栽种了几株银杏树，配合建筑边缘一片水景，让整个空间与自然交融。
建筑采用钢结构作为主体框架结构，用通透的玻璃幕墙围合立面，并在顶面覆盖一层半透膜，整个建筑轻盈柔和。功能上，我们在建筑的一层，设置了一个小型的咖啡厅以及一间自助银行为广场上的人们提供便利舒适的服务；建筑二层为一个完整的室内展厅，可根据需要举办各类公关活动，如展览、开幕式、推广会或商务派对等；三层为一个小型的观景平台，亦可作为景观咖啡或冷餐会的场地。在晚上，通过灯光的变化，建筑呈现出银色和黄色两种色调。

设计过程
设计过程中，我们将若干个外接直径为6 m的正六边形按蜂窝状排列，形成了建筑的基本平面。然后利用计算机造型软件设计出一个如波浪般起伏的三维曲面，并通过将基本平面投影至该曲面，从而最终得到了富有韵律感的顶面主梁结构。
每个六边形主梁作为一个模数单元被弧形的次梁划分为三片“银杏叶”；由一根细长的钢柱连接每片“银杏叶”恰似依托住树叶的叶柄，“叶柄”斜撑至地面与剩余的两根钢柱交汇于六边形投影的中心点。连续相交的斜柱与主梁形成一个个三角形框架，为结构的稳定性提供了保障。
我们利用这个模型单元将自然界创造的银杏树叶以建筑的语言诠释，通过增加模数单元实现建筑的自由生长，借助建筑流动的形体和柔软的轮廓，带给人们关于自然的联想，希望通过简单的几何结构的衍生及组合，创造出非几何的脱胎于自然的有机体。

二层平面

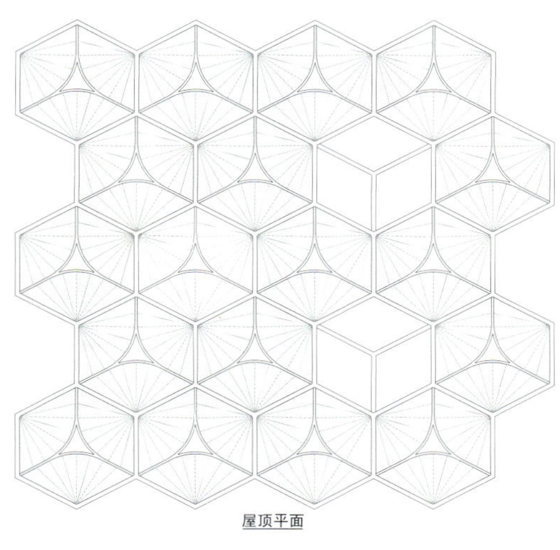

屋顶平面

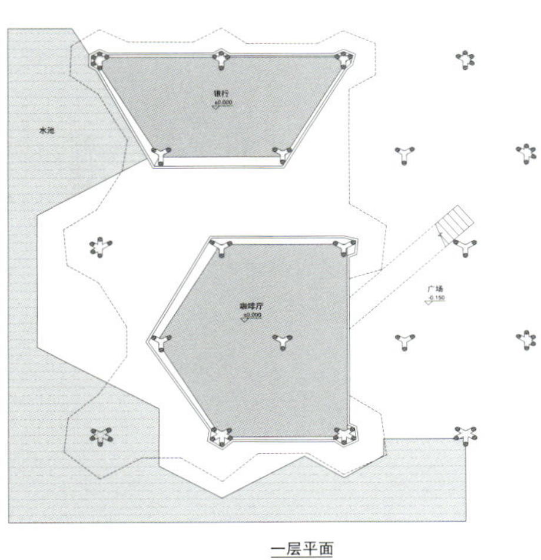

一层平面

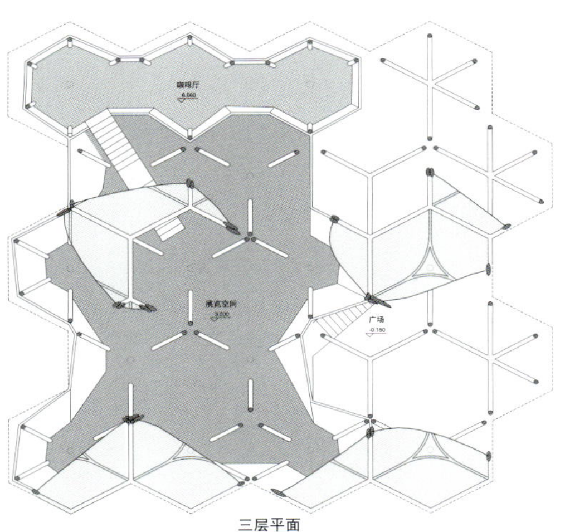

三层平面

Project Introduction

This project is located at the fashion and leisure square downtown in the Gulou District, Xuzhou. "Pengcheng NO.1", as the key project of city construction and one of the ten important commercial circles, our clients hoped that we could construct a landmark at the entrance in the Fushu Street of this commercial square to function like a showing center so as to serve and attract most people.

Design Concept

The design was inspired by the nature, borrowing shape of the ginkgo, city tree of Xuzhou. Curved roof with a long round steel pillar is like a gingko leaf swaying in the breeze. Dazzling sunshine outside throws patchy shadow on the ground through semi-transparent membrane of leaf-shape, creating a forest-like environment for wandering.

Design Techniques

The east of the roof is the highest part of the building, under which is the main entrance, a semi-open area welcoming people from Fushu Street. Under two pieces of hexagon-shaped roof are growing several gingko trees, and around the edge of building flows water. The space each piece is integrating with nature.

The building looks gentle and soft, constructed in a steel structure, wrapped up in glass walls and covered with a semi-transparent roof. As to function, we spare an area for coffee and ATM on the first floor for people at the square to enjoy all the comfort and convenience; on the second floor is an inside hall which could be used for all kinds of public activities such as exhibitions, opening ceremonies, promoting meetings and business parties; on the third floor is a platform for sight-seeing, or for coffee and buffet. In the evening, the building takes on yellow and silver colors alternatively due to the changing of light.

Design Process

During the design process, we faveolately arranged several regular hexagons whose outer diameter is 6 m to form the basic plane of the building. And via design software we had a three dimensional waving thing onto which we projected the basic plane to finally get the girder structure which is full of rhythm.

Every beam of hexagons, as one model unit, is divided into three "gingko leaves" by curved secondary beam; and there is a long thin steel pillar stringing up those "gingko leaves" which are like being supported by footstalks, and the "footstalks" go slantingly to meet the other two steel pillars at the center of hexagon's projection on the ground. Continuous cuts between slanting pillar and beams have formed triangle frames which guarantee the stability of the structure.

We illustrate gingko leaves born in the nature by the use of model units, and by adding them the building could grow freely. The flowing body and gentle outline of the building bring about associations with nature. It is hoped that the simple geometrical derivation and combination will create a non-geometrical organism which is born from nature though.

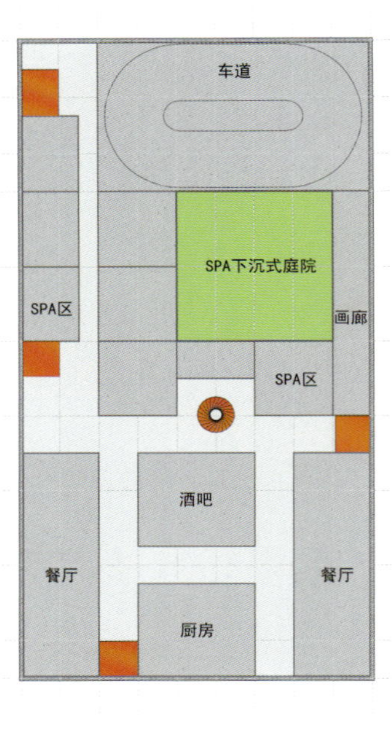

地下一层平面

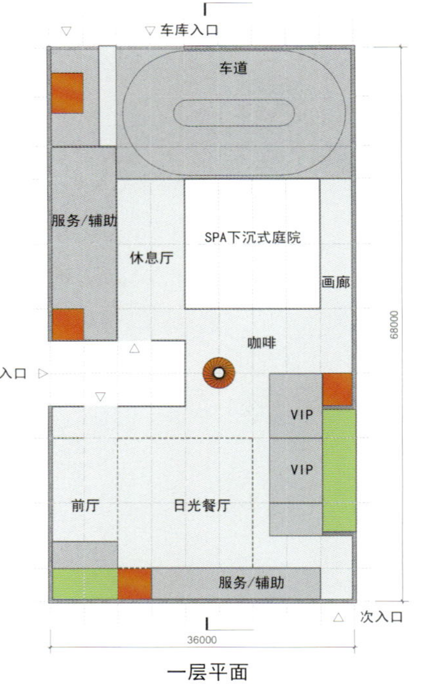

一层平面

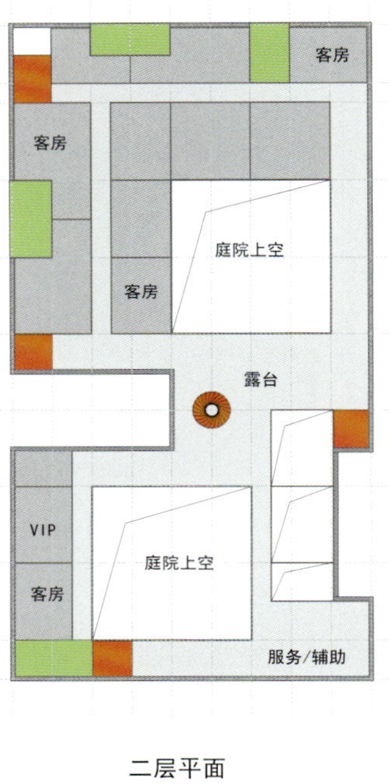

二层平面

功能使用区　绿地庭院
交通流线区　公共活动

Tiandi Courtyard, Beijing
北京天地合院

设计单位：德默营造建筑事务所
设计小组：陈旭东、严梦菲、陈杨
基地面积：2 000 m²
建筑面积：6 900 m²
结构：钢结构
主要材料：锌板、印刷玻璃和木材等

Design firm: DAtrans Architecture Office
Designer team: Chen Xudong, Yan Mengfei, Chen Yang
Site area: 2 000 m²
Building area: 6 900 m²

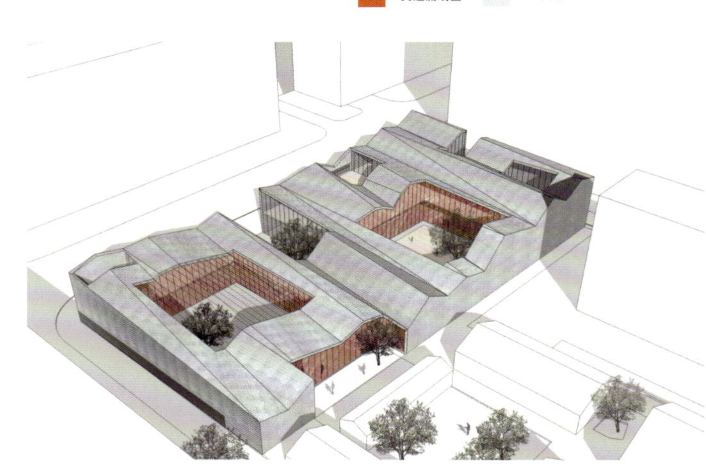

1. 基地　2 体量　3. 褶皱　4 虚空

概念形成

项目基地边长40 m × 80 m，位于北京金宝街，在精品百货金宝汇南侧与其隔街相对，东临文化保护建筑沈从文故居。

基于对中国传统居住建筑四合院的研究，本次设计行为本身就是一次对于现代建筑如何汲取传统四合院空间特征的探索过程。四合院的布局与空间特征体现了传统中国向外保守封闭、向内开放共享、长幼有序的大家庭生活形态。这些空间的特征正是一家身处闹市功能复合的精品酒店所需要的——对外保有私密性，内存共享交流空间，分区明确。

由于基地长宽特点和酒店的功能划分需要，我们以一个两进四合院布局为参照，把建筑南北向分为两个空间性质不同的区域——南为“客厅”，空间开放气氛热闹，用作餐厅、酒吧；北为“居室”，空间私密气氛安静闲适，用作酒店卧房、spa会所。南北各有一内院，一动一静，是南北两区空间性格的集中体现。布局上建筑体量尽可能满铺整个基地，以此在保证一定建筑面积的前提下尽量压低建筑高度以接近传统四合院适宜居住的建筑尺度，并能够预留出一定面积的室外内庭院。

由于由一整座建筑代替了传统四合院的小尺度建筑群，除了高度控制，我们对建筑屋顶采用了褶皱的处理手法，以削弱连续的长立面带来的体量感。褶皱屋脊也在一定的模数前提下采取不同高度，造成高低错落的生动感。屋顶西北高东南低，除了功能上的需要，也是对东侧文物建筑沈从文故居的致敬。北部屋顶局部开小口作酒店卧房的独立私密庭院，是旧时大家闺秀的待遇，体现精品之质。

建筑外部材料以灰色锌版和红色丝网印玻璃为主，丝网印图案取当代艺术家丁乙的极简主义作品[十示]。将时尚的材料和当代艺术精神与传统北京四合院灰与红的色彩作了融合。

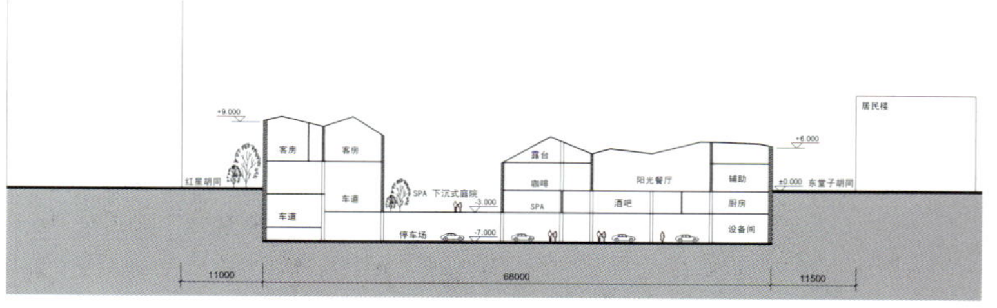

剖面图

The size for the base of the project is 40 m x 80 m. It locates at Jinbao Street, Beijing. Crossing the street, the Jinbaohui Department Store is in the north of the project; the east of the project is the former residence of Shen Congwen, which is a cultural protective construction.

Based on the research of the traditional Chinese residence construction, courtyard, the design is in fact a process of probing into possible approaches to absorb the features of traditional Chinese courtyard in a modern construction. The arrangement and void natures show the lifestyle traditional Chinese extended family: conservative to the outside while outgoing and sharing with the family, and a strict order exists among the family members. Such a void feature is exactly what a public house deep in the crowded city requires: privacy to the outside world, sharing space in the construction, clearly partitioned zones.

Considering the shape of the base and the function division requirement, we take a two-yard courtyard for reference and divide the construction into two parts of different void natures: parlor in the south, the space of which open and the atmosphere hilarious, is used for dining room and bars; habitable room in the north with privacy and quietness is used for bedrooms and spa. Each of the parts has a yard. The vigor in the north and the stillness in the south, exhibit the nature of the different voids. As for the arrangement, the volume of the construction is desired to cover the whole base, so as to lower the altitude to approach the normal height of traditional residential courtyard and save certain space for the inner yard without sacrificing the construction area.

Since a single building is to take place of a mini-sized architectural complex of traditional courtyard, besides the control of the height, we apply drape technique to the roof to diminish a possible feeling of enormous dimension arising from continuous long facade. Also, the different heights of the plicate ridge at the base of a certain modulus create aliveness. The north-west of the roof is higher than the south-east, which shows respect to the cultural relic architectural complex, i.e. former residence of Shen Congwen, besides meeting the functional requirement. The small open in the northern roof for the bedrooms is a special treatment which only the daughters of grand families can receive, and shows the fine status of the architecture.

The main exterior materials of the project are grey zinc plates and glass with red silk net. The silk net takes the idea of minimalism in the work of Ding Yi (Shishi), and combines the modern materials and modern art spirits with colors of grey and red of traditional Beijing courtyards.

Urban Renovation of M50

M50艺术园区建筑改造

设计单位：德默营造建筑事务所
施工设计：上海现代设计集团（一期）、德默营造（二期）
设计团队：陈旭东、Max Mueller、鲍伟、杨光、陈启春、左欢、蒋迪、Bojra Trujillo、严梦菲、Lucy Schofield、陈婉云、陈杨、闻一峰、Heloise Le Carrer
造价：1 700万
基地面积：29 600 m^2
建筑面积：11 048 m^2
主要材料：仿旧面砖、玻璃、金属幕墙和粉刷等
结构顾问：马骥
艺术指导：丁乙
指示系统设计：复旦视觉艺术学院
建筑遗产保护顾问：阮仪三、上海名城文化研究中心
摄影：张宗眉、德默营造

Design firm: DAtrans Architecture Office
Design team: Chen Xudong, Max Mueller, Bao Yang, Yang Guang, Chen Qichun, Zuo huan, Jiang Di, Bojra Trujillo, Yan Mengfei, Lucy Schofield, Chen Wanyun, Chen Yang, Wen Yifeng, Heloise Le Carrer
Site area: 29 600 m^2
Total floor area: 11 048 m^2

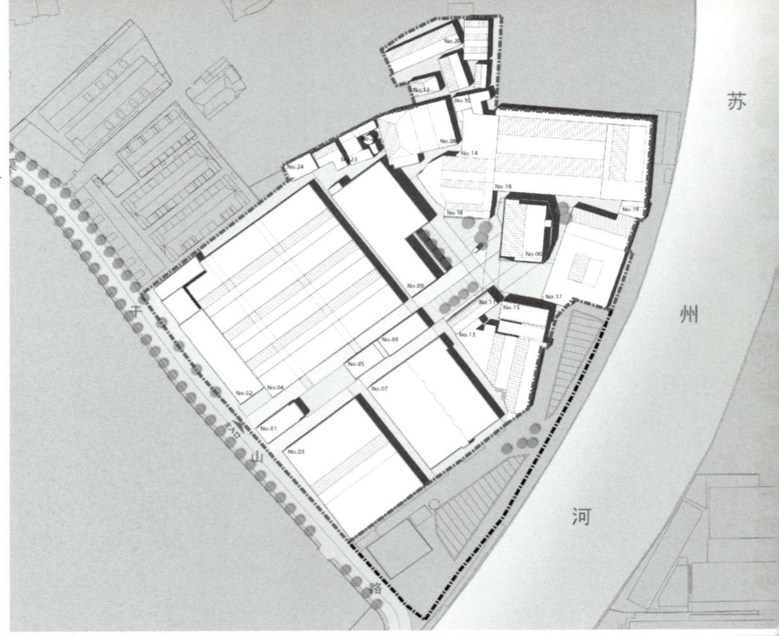

有着70年显赫历史的莫干山路50号是20世纪30年代上海民族工业的发源地之一，同样的苏州河沿岸的厂房，在20世纪90年代末由于众多有影响的艺术家和文化机构的进驻，使其成为上海城市生活和当代文化的重要地标。2005年4月被上海市经委挂牌为上海创意产业聚集区之一，命名为M50创意园。同时，M50被美国《时代周刊》列为全球“推荐参观之地”，其影响力直逼纽约苏荷区和法国塞纳河。

德默营造为莫干山路50号设计了整体改造方案，包括合理功能布局、环境整治，并确定了改造的总指导方针，即确保其在转型和改造的整个过程中保护这一园区原有的特点和完整性，并且使整个改造过程具有可持续性。2005年完成了园区入口广场和信息中心的建筑改造方案设计。在随后的时间中，陆续完成了凹凸家具库、东八书仓和爱普生影艺坊等改造项目。2009年开始二期改造的设计和施工。

No.50, Mogan shan Rd is one of the cradles of the national industry in Shanghai in 1930s with an eminent history of 70 years; the workshop along Suzhou River has also become important landmark of the urban life and culture of Shanghai, since many influential artists and cultural institutions moved in the late 1990s. In April 2005, it was approved by Shanghai Municipal Economic Commission as one of the gathering zones of Shanghai creative industry, and named M50. At the same time, M50 is listed as the global "Recommended Place to Visit" by Time. The influence of M50 rivals SOHO area in New York and Seine in France.

"Demo Tectonic" designed the overall reconstruction plan, which includes reasonable functional arrangement and environmental renovation, and sets the general guiding disciplines of the reconstruction, i.e. to keep the original features and integrity in the process of transformation and reconstruction, and to guarantee the whole process continuable. The design for the reconstruction of the Entering Square and the Information Center was finished in 2005. In the succedent time, the reconstruction of the Concavo-convex Furniture Storehouse, East Eight Book Depository and Epson Studio Gallery were completed. The design and construction of the 2nd phase of the reconstruction began in 2009.

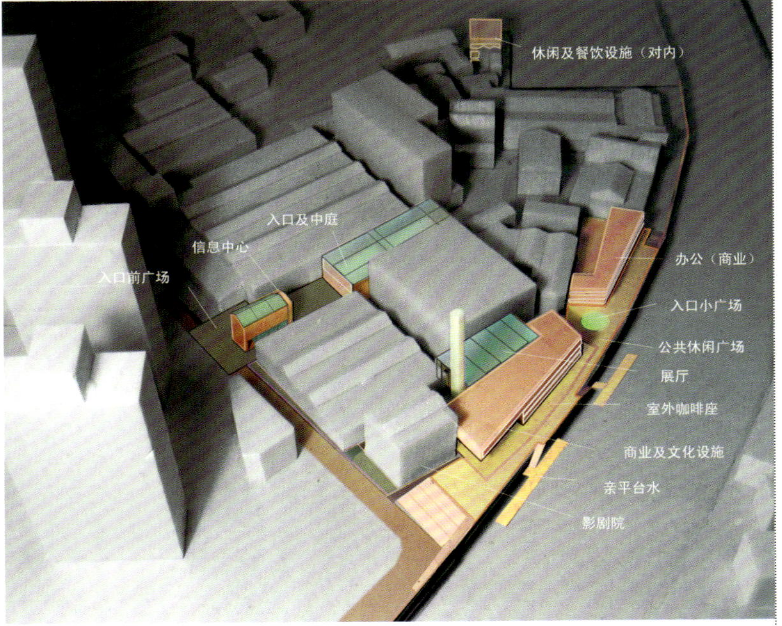
休闲及餐饮设施（对内）
入口及中庭
信息中心
入口前广场
办公（商业）
入口小广场
公共休闲广场
展厅
室外咖啡座
商业及文化设施
亲平台水
影剧院

Hongqiao Linkong Plot 10-3 & Plot 11-3 Design

虹桥临空10–3与11–3地块方案设计

设计单位：摩德工程咨询（上海）有限公司
合作单位：JMWB Architekten
设计时间：2010年
项目类型：国际竞赛

Design firm: MOD Engineering Consulting (Shanghai) Co., Ltd.
Cooperation firm: JMWB Architekten
Design Date: 2010

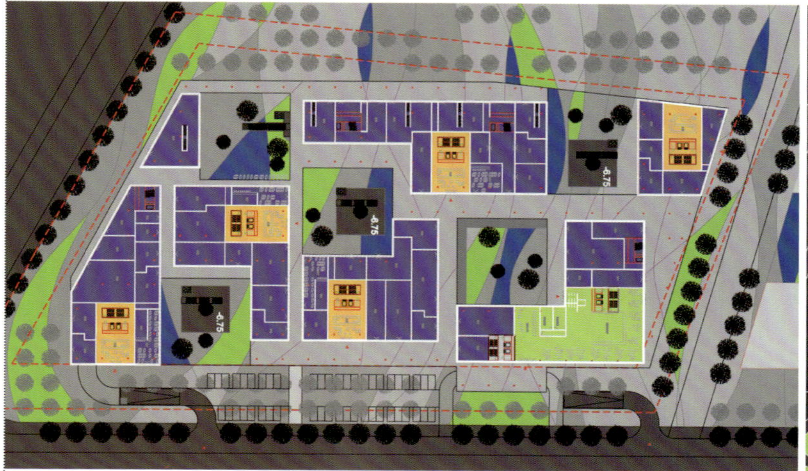

MOD

德中建筑·摩德

MOD Engineering Consulting Co., Ltd.

摩德工程咨询（上海）有限公司

摩德工程咨询（上海）有限公司是一家外商独资（德国）设计咨询专业公司，其设计咨询的范围包括城市规划、建筑设计、景观园林等。

公司的宗旨是“以先进理念吸引业主，以优秀作品打造品牌”。

公司的设计团队来自德中两国，通过德国在城市及建筑设计上的先进理念与中国市场实际情况相结合，为业主提供优质的服务。

摩德公司的创始人及法人代表为德国注册建筑师、德中建筑协会主席陈冰先生。

MOD Engineering Consulting (Shanghai) Co., Ltd. is a wholly foreign owned (Germany) professional design consulting company, the design consulting scope of which covers urban planning, architecture and landscape etc.

The tenet of the company is "To attract customer with advanced ideas; to promote the brand by find works".

The design team of the company is mainly from Germany and China. Excellent services are provided to the customers as a result of the combination of the advanced architecture design idea from Germany and the actual situation in Chinese market.

The founder and legal representative of MOD is Mr. Chen Bing, who is a Certified Architect of Germany and the Chairman of Germany-China Architecture Association.

SALON & ACADEMY
Häagen-Dazs
Panasonic
SIEMENS
ARMANI
collezioni
UNITED COLORS OF BENETTON

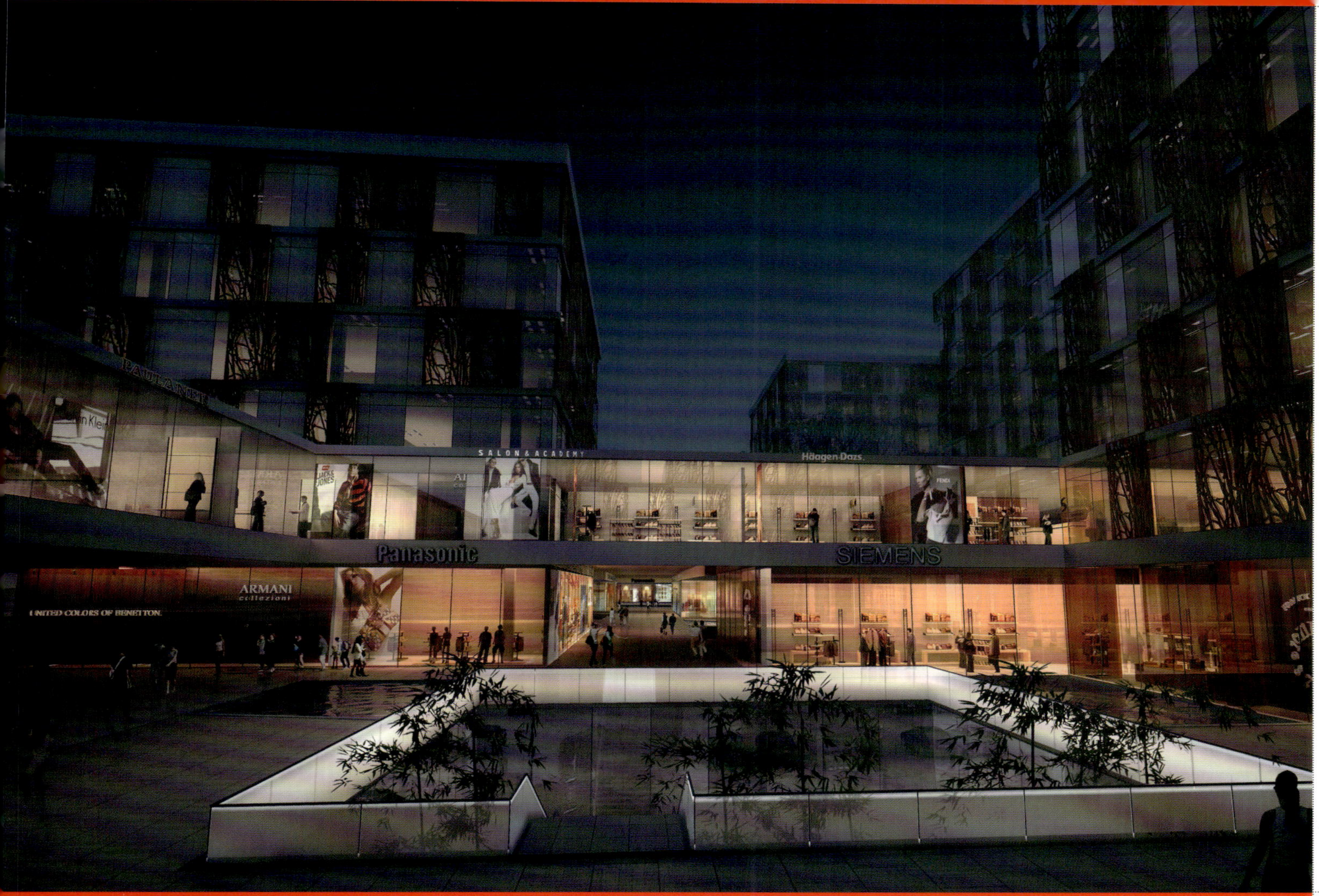

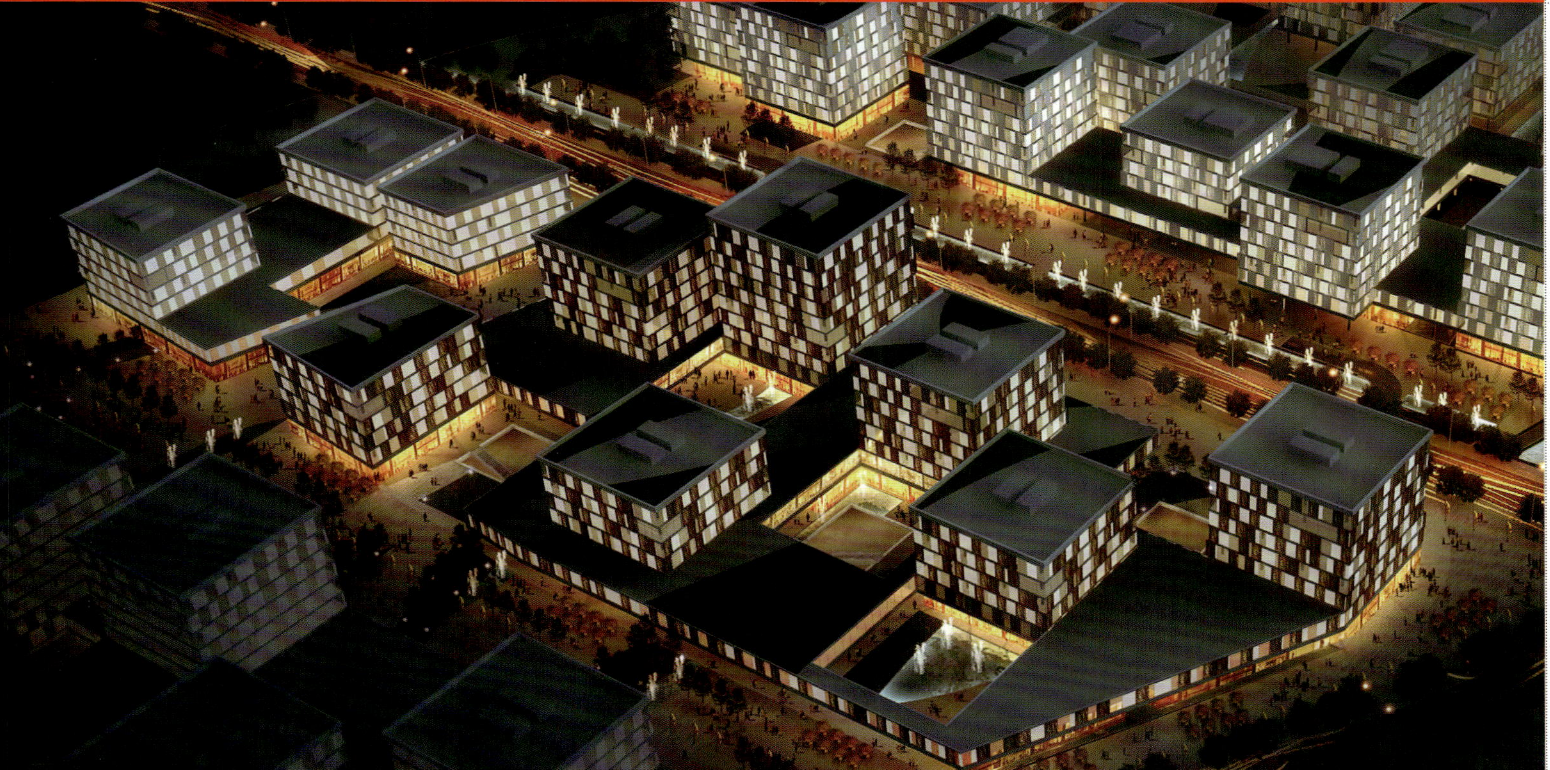

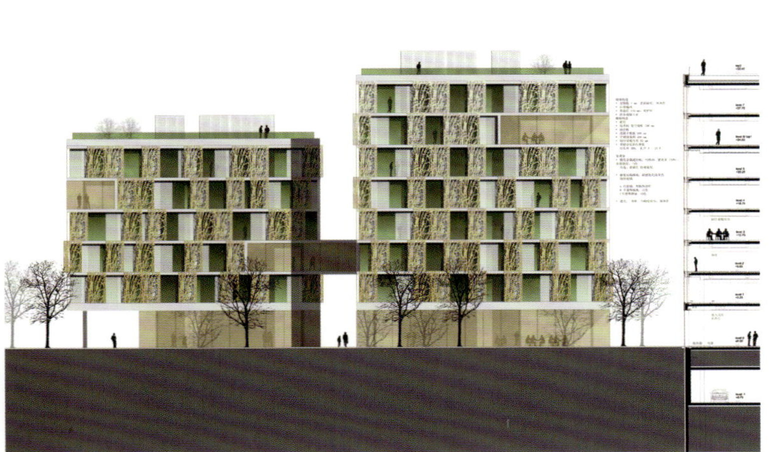

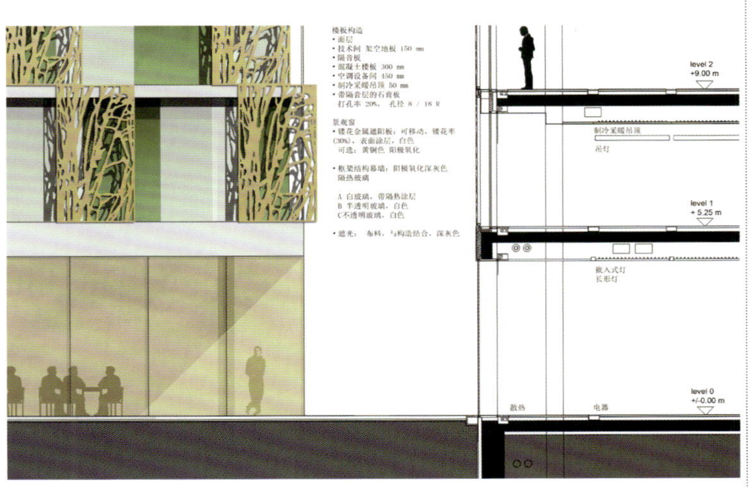

楼板构造
• 面层
• 技术间 架空地板 150 mm
• 隔音板
• 混凝土楼板 300 mm
• 空调设备间 450 mm
• 制冷采暖吊顶 50 mm
• 带隔音层的石膏板
打孔率 20%， 孔径 8 / 18 R
景观窗
• 镂花金属遮阳板：可移动，镂花率(30%)，表面涂层，白色
可选：黄铜色 阳极氧化
• 框架结构幕墙：阳极氧化深灰色
隔热玻璃
A 白玻璃，带隔热涂层
B 半透明玻璃，白色
C不透明玻璃，白色
• 遮光： 布料，与构造结合，深灰色
level 2
+9.00 m
制冷采暖吊顶
吊灯
level 1
+ 5.25 m
嵌入式灯
长形灯
level 0
+/-0.00 m
散热
电器

本设计方案肌理从周边多样的城市环境中突显出来，整体化结构中布置的内庭空间提供各单元的交通连接以及各功能区的自然采光。五个不同主题的内庭形成引人入胜的空间序列，将步行者引入安宁的内庭空间中去。

The texture of this design outstands from the various city environment surrounded. The cortile space in a uniformed structure provides traffic connection between different units and natural light to each function area. Five cortiles with different themes form charming space series, which attract pedestrian to the tranquil cortile space.

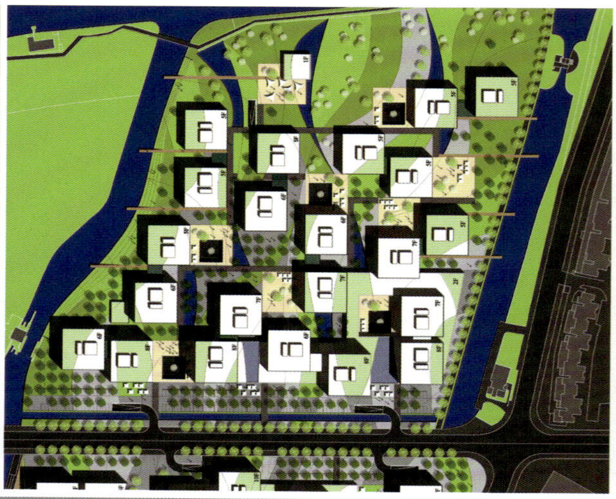

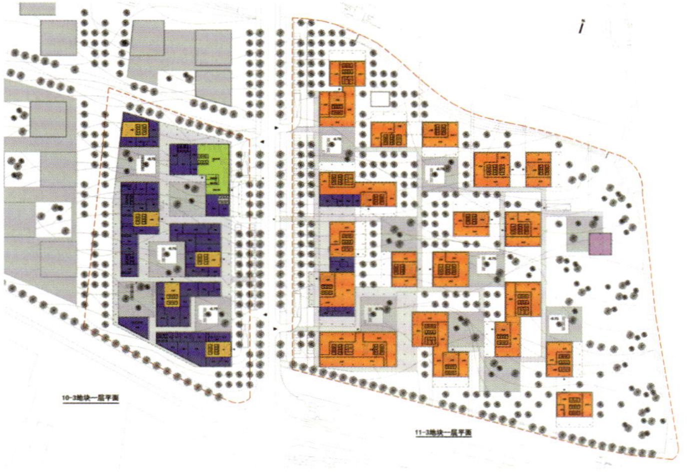
10-3地块一层平面
11-3地块一层平面

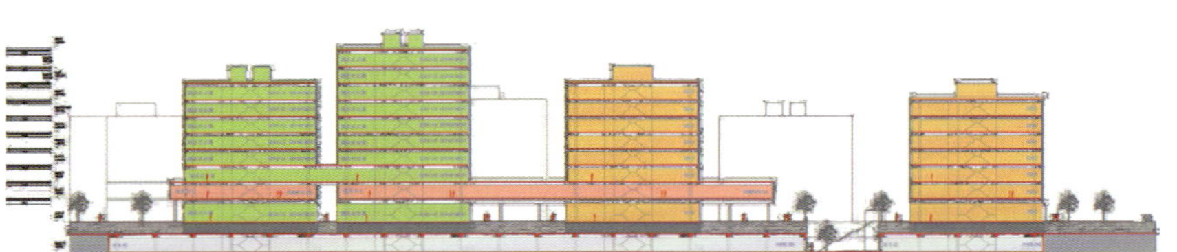

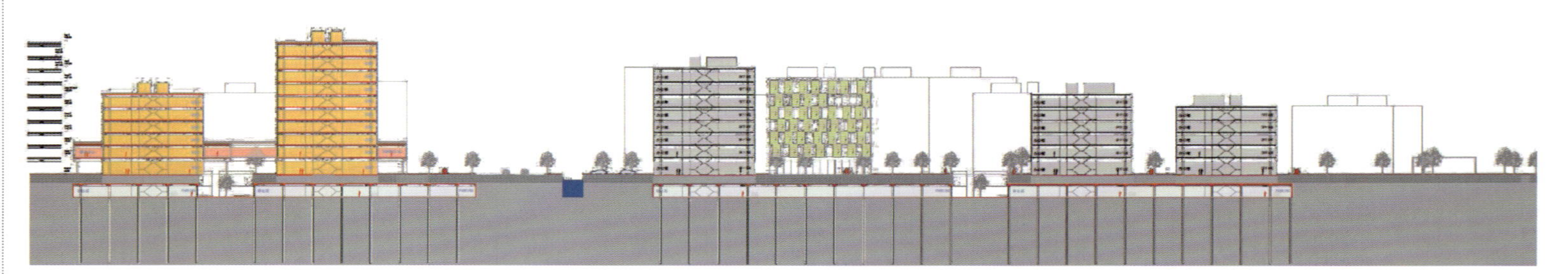

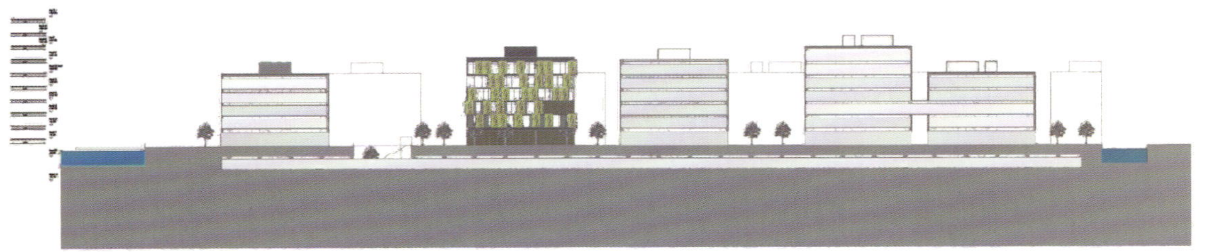

Longmen Club, Mianyang

绵阳龙门酒店会所

设计单位：翰时国际建筑设计公司
建筑面积：7 104 m²

Design firm: A&S International Design
Total floor area: 7 104 m²

A&S 翰时国际建筑设计 INTERNATIONAL DESIGN

翰时（A&S）国际建筑设计咨询有限公司是由国内外建筑师共同创立的建筑设计公司。公司创立于美国亚特兰大，2002年在中国北京正式注册。公司的目标是把国际上先进的建筑设计与规划理念和技术介绍到中国，并按照国际标准，为业主提供高质量的设计服务，为新世纪中国城市与建筑的发展做出贡献。翰时（A&S）国际可在建筑设计、城市设计、室内设计、景观设计等各领域，为业主提供全方位的服务。

翰时（A&S）国际采用国际化的理念，专业化的设计，地域化的服务，强调对客户的理解与尊重。翰时国际的敬业精神、专业知识、实践经验、市场活力已经成为有建设任务的业主们强有力的帮手和顾问。翰时（A&S）国际的设计人员有着近二十年的世界各地的现代化建筑设计经历，对城市社区规划及各类型的建筑/工程设计，如公共建筑、居住建筑、医疗/实验室建筑等，有着丰富的经验与广泛的专业知识，并注重结合中国国情将绿色生态、环保措施等高新技术及全新的观念，融入到设计当中。自公司创立以来，由翰时（A&S）国际参与的城市社区规划设计及各类型的建筑/工程设计项目遍及中国许多地区，如城市社区规划类有中国国家疾病预防控制中心（总体规划）、胶州老城区商业中心改造、成都龙潭总部基地等项目；居住建筑类有北京康成花园别墅、北京五栋大楼、北京洋房、北京新天地、孔雀城三期、京都高尔夫别墅等项目；公共建筑类有绵阳电业局城区供电局、安徽国际护理学院、浙江新和成总部、大连兴昌办公楼、优山美地美术馆、北京格拉斯小镇、蓝光IBP总部等项目。

自2003年起，翰时（A&S）国际凭借着先进的设计方法及过硬的专业技术，应邀参加了国内多个项目的国际竞赛活动并中标。荣获2004年度CIHAF中国建筑二十大品牌影响力设计公司、CIHAF2005中国房地产二十大品牌影响力规划建筑景观设计院、中国商务建筑设计机构10强、中国地标建筑卓越设计机构20强等多个奖项，其设计作品也屡次获奖。中国的建筑建设正处于向现代化高速发展的阶段，国际水准的专业现代化建筑规划与设计对建筑事业成功地走向现代化发展之路具有极其重要的意义。我们致力于将建筑的功能及其人文文化内涵融合为有机整体，创造出与众不同、符合国际潮流与标准的现代化建筑。

A&S International Design Co., Ltd. is a professional architectural design consulting firm, which was established in Atlanta, USA and registered in Beijing, China in 2002. The goal of this company is to bring advanced international planning and design theories and technologies into China, and provide high-quality services for clients. A&S is positioned to provide integrated services in architectural design, urban planning, interior design, landscape design and etc.

With international ideas, professional design and local service, A&S emphasizes the understanding and respect to clients, which have already become good consultant for clients with construction tasks.

The principal architects in A&S have almost 20-year experience in design practice around the world. They are rich experienced in all kinds of urban planning and architectural design, including residential property and public facility, healthcare/lab facility etc. Furthermore, based on unique Chinese culture and environment, A&S always has been dedicated to incorporating high-tech building techniques and brand-new concepts like ecology and environmental protection in their designs.

Since its establishment, A&S has participated in most areas of China in urban planning and different kinds of design projects. The urban planning projects include China national disease prevention and control center (Master Planning), Jiaozhou residential facility planning, Chengdu Longtan headquarter planning and etc. The residential property projects mainly are Beijing Kangcheng Villa, Beijing Five Buildings, Beijing Xintiandi, Jingdu Golf Villa and etc. The public projects include Mianyang Electric Power Supply Bureau, Anhui International Nursing College, Zhejiang Xinhecheng Corporate Headquarters, Dalian Xingchang Office building, Youshanmeidi Art Museum, Languang headquarters and other projects.

中西合璧——特点：融合中式建筑的心理认同感和西式建筑的厚重，可回避纯中式或纯西式风格的缺点，长短互补。

西式——优点：厚重、尊贵、价值感强；缺点：异国情调也带来文化上的不认同，难与整个区域尤其是商业水乡小镇风格协调。

中式——优点：历史、文脉、本土感强；缺点：建筑语言份量轻，易留下简陋落后印象。

建筑——材料：石砌结构的厚重感、年代感、神秘感；空间：庭院围合、空间层次感表达中国房子的味道；

装饰：朴素的美感，加以少量历史上沉淀下来的符号语言。

环境——园林式酒店的自然风格

焦点空间：简练神秘

休闲空间：舒适亲切

边缘空间：自然幽雅

Chamber of Longmen Hotel in Mianyang

The characteristic of combination of Chinese and Western style combines the psychology of identifying with Chinese architecture and the massiness of western architecture. This method avoids the shortcoming of pure Chinese and pure western architectural style to reach the optimal effect.

Western style–Advantages: massiness, respectful and valuable;

Shortcoming: exoticism takes the strange feeling to the culture, which is hard to besuitable for the style of the whole area, especially the small business water town.

Chinese style–Advantages: historical, context and localization;

Shortcomings: the architectural language is felt light, and easy to leave the impression of simple and dropping behind.

Building–Material: the massiness of the stone building with agelong and mysterious feelings ;

Space: enclosure of the yard, the feeling of the spacial abundant grades shows the tastes of Chinese architecture;

Decoration: plain aesthetic feeling, added by the signal language deposited from the history.

Environment–natural style of the garden hotel

Focus space: simple and mysterious

Leisure space: comfortable and kind

Edged space: natural and elegant

RIHAN.CC 新书推介

最新出版

《A–Z II》

《A–Z III VOL.1》

《A–Z III VOL.2》

《A–Z III VOL.3》

《A–Z III VOL.4》

《A–Z III VOL.5》

《柏涛建筑设计作品1998–2009》

《概念建筑 VOL.1》

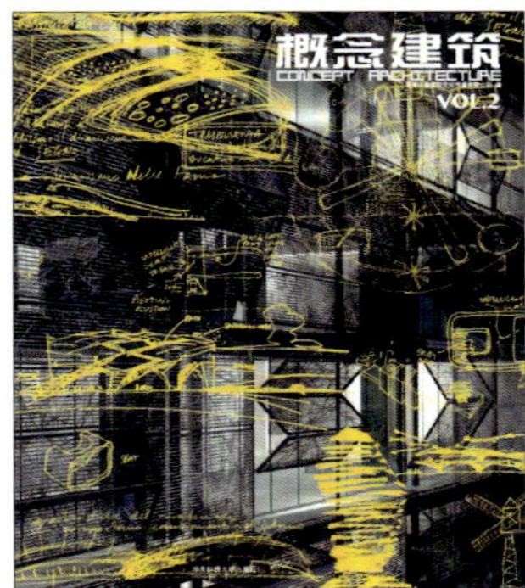

《概念建筑 VOL.2》

《梦幻建筑》

《表现X档案 010.2》

Invitation for Contribution for New Style Properties

日瀚公司《新風樓盤》征稿函

全國首家推出樓盤類圖書
專業的制作團隊
豐富的出版經驗
廣闊的發行渠道

經典的延續需要您的鼎立支持
《新風樓盤》期待您的傾情參與

2002年，我司在全國率先推出了《深圳特色樓盤》系列叢書，展示當時最具特色的樓盤，廣受好評。《新風樓盤》是我司今年重點推出的圖書，將收録國內外優秀房地産開發公司及設計公司的近期力作，記録當代"人居新概念"，讓經典案例一"頁"成名，長效宣傳，經久流傳。

真誠回饋

免費推廣：積極推廣房地産開發公司和設計公司的項目及品牌

圖書贈送：圖書出版后，我公司贈有其作品的書一本作爲紀念

投稿方式

1. 上海市楊浦區赤峰路59弄3號401室編輯部，郵編：200092
2. 日瀚公司唯一指定QQ：415688162
3. 投稿信箱：rhtg@rihan.cc

聯系方式

咨詢電話：021-5976323/65977780/65976141

傳　　真：021-65977143

網　　址：http://www.rihan.cc/

图书在版编目（C I P）数据

先锋建筑在中国 / 香港日瀚国际文化传播有限公司 编著.
—武汉 ：华中科技大学出版社，2010.9
ISBN 978-7-5609-6481-2

I.①先… II.①香… III. ①建筑设计—作品集—世界—现代 IV.①TU206

中国版本图书馆CIP数据核字（2010）第152499号

先锋建筑在中国　　香港日瀚国际文化传播有限公司　编著

出版/发行：华中科技大学出版社
地　　址：武汉市珞喻路1037号（邮编：430074）
出 版 人：阮海洪
责任编辑：张　蕊
责任监印：马　琳
翻译顾问：范　飞
印　　刷：利丰雅高印刷（深圳）有限公司
开　　本：889mm×1422mm　1/16
印　　张：27
字　　数：346千字
版　　次：2010年9月第1版
印　　次：2010年9月第1次印刷
书　　号：ISBN 978-7-5609-6481-2/TU・917
定　　价：378.00元（USD 95.00）

销售电话：010-64155566（兼传真），022-60266199（兼传真）
邮购电话：010-64155588-8825
网　　址：www.hustpas.com